Embroidering the Scarlet A

Embroidering the Scarlet A

UNWED MOTHERS AND ILLEGITIMATE CHILDREN IN AMERICAN FICTION AND FILM

Janet Mason Ellerby

University of Michigan Press
Ann Arbor

Published in the United States of America by
the University of Michigan Press
Manufactured in the United States of America
⊗ Printed on acid-free paper

2018   2017   2016   2015   4   3   2   1

A CIP catalog record for this book is available from the British Library.

ISBN 978–0-472–07263-7 (hardcover)
ISBN 978–0-472–05263-9 (paper)
ISBN 978–0-472–12105–2 (e-book)

For Michaela, Drew, Emma, Isla, Mason, Sean and Elijah

. . . to speak of treasure

On the breast of her gown, in fine red cloth surrounded with an elaborate embroidery and fantastic flourishes of gold thread, appeared the letter "A." It was so artistically done, and with so much fertility and gorgeous luxuriance of fancy, that it had all the effect of a last and fitting decoration to the apparel which she wore; and which was of a splendor in accordance with the taste of the age, but greatly beyond what was allowed by the sumptuary regulations of the colony.

NATHANIEL HAWTHORNE, *THE SCARLET LETTER*

Creative practice . . . can be the long and difficult remaking of an inherited . . . consciousness . . . a struggle at the roots of the mind—not casting off an ideology . . . but confronting a hegemony in the fibres of the self.

RAYMOND WILLIAMS, *MARXISM AND LITERATURE*

Contents

Acknowledgments

Thanks are due to the University of North Carolina Wilmington for granting me the uninterrupted time to write this book.

Special thanks to Bill and Alma Ward for lending us their home near Grandfather Mountain and providing me with an inspiring vantage point from which to begin and to Kevin Donovan for building me my own inspirational lookout, where Grandfather still stands sentinel.

For her steadfast encouragement, resourcefulness, and insight: LeAnn Fields at the University of Michigan Press. For their thoughtful attention to detail and reliable enthusiasm: Alexa Ducsay and Marcia LaBrenz. For their ongoing willingness to read early drafts and reassure me that I really do have something genuine and worthy to say, Clyde Comstock and Chris Gould.

For reading and responding to my first attempts to articulate the themes of this book, for publishing their first iteration in *Adoption & Culture*, and for encouraging me to build on them and write this book: Marianne Novy and Emily Hipchen.

Particular thanks go to the members of Concerned United Birthparents for inviting me into their family and encouraging me to tell not only my own story but theirs as well. Special thanks to Sarah Burns and Mary Ann Cohen for permitting me to use their words and reflections on reunion and loss; to Stephanie Anderson for eloquently speaking about her experience as a birthmother in an open adoption; and to Patricia Salazar for telling her story of determined achievement. And to those students and friends who courageously shared their stories of unwed motherhood but requested that their names be changed. Your stories are valued and important, and your need for anonymity, absolutely understandable. Sadly, the shame of unwed motherhood lives on, but your words will help change that.

Thanks also go to Christine Bertoni and Irene Axelrod at the Peabody

Essex Museum in Salem, Massachusetts, for making it possible for me to include Mary Hallock Foote's illustration of Hester Prynne and Pearl from the 1878 edition of *The Scarlet Letter*. This compelling image inspired me as I wrote and I am grateful to be able to include it here.

Special thanks go to my children, Merideth Fiorucci, Todd De Puy, Helen Setzer, and Kezia De Puy, for once again letting me tell our story and the loving constancy they offer me day-to-day, month-to-month, year-to-year. In memory, thanks goes to my devoted parents, Tom and Helen Ellerby, for not only accepting my decision to tell the truth but also for lovingly accepting all the repercussions of doing so; to my sister, Anne Ellerby Andreasen, who unfailingly practiced unconditional love; and to the sister of my heart, Betsy Ervin. And, "here's to the gang": Ray Andreasen; Rob, Sean, and Elijah Setzer; Michael, Michaela, Drew, Emma, and Mason Fiorucci; Isla De Puy; Mark, Samantha, and Jake Andrew; Martha, Bob, Matt, and Andy Logue; Bob Stull and Louise Kim; Jenny, Andy, Hannah, and Jens Mortensen; Katie and John Andrew; Pam Clifford and Molly Frye; Christine, Hunter and Luke Warwick; and Mary Ellen and Bob Allen.

Much gratitude goes to the extraordinary women who have never wavered in their steadfast friendship and support: Karen Courington, Karen Comstock, Chris Comstock, Betsy Humphrey, Moira MacDonald, Julie Chappell, Barbara Waxman, Katherine Montwieler, Lu Ellen Huntley, Sheri Malman, and Denya Diego. To friends and colleagues who have given their advice, encouragement, and time: Mark Boren, Don Bushman, Michelle Scatton-Tessier, and Katie Peel.

And once again, I most want to thank John Patrick Clifford, who never steps away, who has patiently listened to every word, argued every point, encouraged every paragraph, stood by during every crisis of confidence and computer tragedy, who can always make me laugh, who gives capaciously, who makes me feel abidingly loved in this world.

Introduction

In an age when adolescent transgression against society's mores hardly turns heads, when the rebel is a cinematic hero, and when losing one's virginity as a teenager is no longer cause for panic, it seems paradoxical that a tale of Puritan punishment set in 1650 and written in 1850 remains such a ubiquitous cultural icon. Yet students across America are religiously assigned *The Scarlet Letter* in eleventh grade, typically the year for American literature in high school curricula. Nathaniel Hawthorne's classic novel about a young woman in seventeenth-century Massachusetts who commits a "crime" against Puritan moral law has been a curricular requirement for generations. But perhaps the novel's popularity is not illogical. Perhaps there is good reason why such a seemingly anachronistic plot is still assigned to teenagers.

Hester Prynne, the sympathetically portrayed heroine whose elderly husband has long been missing, bears a child out of wedlock but refuses to name the father. She endures years of public humiliation in a society that forces her to wear a scarlet letter *A* on her dress to mark her adultery. Exiled to the outskirts of town to raise her daughter Pearl and make her living, Hester wears the *A* faithfully, even after Pearl's father, the Reverend Dimmesdale, publically confesses his sin and dies in Hester's arms. Although Hester leaves Boston with her daughter, once Pearl is married and living in Europe, she returns and resumes wearing the scarlet *A*, embroidered into a gleaming work of art that transforms it into a symbol of resilience, autonomy, and solace.

Readers of *The Scarlet Letter* have long been tempted to make connections between Hawthorne's family history and his most famous novel. Some argue that it is a "belated act of repentance" for the "sins of an ancestor," John Hathorne, an unrepentant prosecutor in the Salem witch trials of 1692 who

"saw it his duty to discover any who had joined the devil's band and to extract a confession" (Turner 64). But Hester is not tried for witchcraft. Her
crime is sexual, not satanic. Nonetheless, like the alleged witches of Salem,
she runs afoul of a rigid, puritanical, male-dominated society that metes
out a harsh and isolating punishment. A condemned and ostracized "fallen"
woman pitted against puritanical prejudice and hypocrisy, she serves as the
novel's moral compass, and her survival is impressive, even heroic.

Just as Hester's act of adultery outraged *her* society, publication of the
novel in 1850 outraged puritanical readers offended by the very notion of a
novel about an adulterer. Nonetheless, the novel was an instant best seller,
selling out the original run of 2,500 copies in only ten days so that a second
edition was immediately ordered.[1] Most of Hawthorne's contemporary critics praised the book, though reviewers like Arthur Cleveland Coxe, who believed stories should be of "moral benefit," found Hester "debauched" in mind
even more than body and wondered whether "the French era" had "actually
begun in our literature" (qtd. by Murfin 268). Others, however, praised the
novel for exposing the inhumanity of Puritanism. But, of course, the reviews
did not stop in the middle of the nineteenth century. Critics have continually reevaluated the book. Some, like Henry James in 1879, have argued that
the novel's allure emanates from its ethical content. James maintains that it
is "full of the moral presence of the race" (qtd. by Murfin 276). Others, like
D. H. Lawrence in 1923, have found its attraction in its sensuality, though
for Lawrence, the novel did not go far enough in its approval of the life of
the flesh. Rather, he sees it as an "American reworking of the myth of the
Fall of Man," a "devilish" parable that warbles: *"Be Good! Be good! . . . Be good,
and never sin! Be sure your sins will find you out"* (123). Since that first edition
in 1850, *The Scarlet Letter* has never been out of print and remains one of
the best-selling classic novels on the market with editions available from
publishers such as Dover, Norton, Signet, Penguin, Oxford, and Simon &
Brown, to name a few, and study guides available from Cliff Notes, Spark
Notes, Max Notes, Barron's Book Notes, and more.

The abundance of study guides for the novel is testimony to its enduring
popularity in high school curricula, popularity backed up by a 1993 study
performed for the National Council of Teachers of English. Researcher Arthur Applebee found that *The Scarlet Letter* was being assigned by 52% of
all public schools (in other words, in almost all college-prep classes), and by
85% of all Catholic and independent schools. But this popularity was nothing new. In his earlier 1963 study, Applebee had found that *The Scarlet Letter*

was second only to *Huckleberry Finn* on the list of required secondary school reading. By comparing his two studies, Applebee draws a rather disturbing conclusion for those of us who would like to see the literary canon expand and diversify. He observes, "Rather than being diluted in recent years, the role of the literary canon seems to have been strengthened" (69). In my own public school district, the novel is regularly assigned to all college-bound students, and in my own informal survey of the students recently enrolled in my three college literature classes, 80% of them report having at least being assigned *The Scarlet Letter* in their junior year of high school.

But whether high school students are reading the novel or not, the titular symbol, the scarlet letter, has woven itself into the fabric of American culture. A quick Internet search of references to *The Scarlet Letter* in popular culture turns up a lengthy list that ranges from derivative literary texts to public awareness campaigns. For example, as a gesture of solidarity with Hester's transgressive attitude, popular female rockers are drawn to the scarlet letter. In her 2007 song "Past in Present," Feist sings "The scarlet letter isn't black," and in her 2008 song "Love Story," teen idol Taylor Swift sings, "I was a scarlet letter." The pervasiveness of the letter as metaphor extends to other media as well. For example, there are the twelve film versions of the novel, the first produced in 1908, the latest in 2010; six opera versions; four plays; and on television, adaptations of the novel range from a 1979 PBS miniseries, *The Scarlet Letter*, to a 2010 episode of *The Mentalist* titled "Scarlet Letter." Perhaps the strangest appropriation of the letter comes by way of evolutionary biologist Richard Dawkins, who uses the "scarlet A" as the logo for his Out Campaign for free thought and atheism. When you join the campaign, you can purchase scarlet letter T-shirts, lapel pins, buttons, and stickers ("*The Scarlet Letter* in popular culture"). Clearly the "scarlet A" is endemic, and although it can mean many things to many people, the interpretation always revolves around the basic idea that a young woman is unfairly punished for breaking the rules of a rigid society.

How to account for the durable canonicity of this nineteenth-century romance and the scope of its evocative symbol? What keeps the story of a woman sentenced to wear a scarlet letter so pertinent to twenty-first-century imaginations? Generations of readers, having struggled through Hawthorne's alien nineteenth-century prose style as well as his less-than-compelling introduction, "The Custom-House," have persisted, stepping through "The Prison-Door" and into the New Colony. Why? Whether it is the novel's didactic moralism, its representation of constraints that seem fundamental to civilization, or its portrayal of desires that are deep-seated in the human psyche, *The Scarlet Letter* continues to be assigned to impressionable adolescents. Rather than finding it dated and irrelevant, most young readers regard this tale of shame and redemption as germane to the incompatible moral suppression and sexual desire they must confront as they move into young adulthood and independence. Some hear the message, *"Be good! Be good!"* and insist that Hester is bound for hell. Yet others see her rebellious autonomy as a model for their own future of defiant self-determination.

Almost fifty years ago, as a junior in high school, I read *The Scarlet Letter* with an intensity that surely would have impressed any English teacher, though it might have worried an adolescent psychologist, had I had one. As a sixteen-year-old I was shipped off from my home in Southern California to live with my aunt in Pepper Pike, Ohio, when my parents found out that I was three months pregnant. With my aunt's help and a punishing girdle I was able to keep my pregnancy a secret while I attended Orange High School from September to December, but by the time the New Year came round, my secret could no longer be concealed. I was sent further into exile, to the city of Akron some thirty miles south, to the Florence Crittenton Home, an institution for unwed mothers that was housed in a Victorian mansion right out of Charles Dickens. On the frigid first day of January 1965, I arrived with a small suitcase packed with a few maternity smocks and a copy of *The Scarlet Letter*, ironically the novel I would have been reading had I returned to Orange High School after the Christmas holidays. Faced with my own lonely confinement far from my parents and my hometown, I tore through the novel with an uncommon ardency, and immediately identified with the somber and demure young woman on the novel's cover and with the large, fiery red *A* emblazoned on her breast. Hester became my hero, and as the months passed, I tried to emulate her courage in the face of imprisonment and the birth of her illegitimate child. At sixteen, I too wanted to be beautiful and bold, but Hawthorne had created a heroine I could not even pretend to be, at least not then.

Obviously Hester and I came out of vastly different historical moments and ideological environments. Set in 1650, Hester's story takes place three centuries before my unplanned pregnancy. In Hester's New England, the punishment for female adulterers and unwed mothers was extreme. They were pilloried, imprisoned, banished, and by law, required "to wear a two-inch-high capital *A*, colored to stand out against the background of the wearer's clothes" (Murfin 12).[2] Today it might be a different story, but in 1965, a pregnant and unmarried girl needed to be secreted away. Second-wave feminism was dawning in the United States, but it would be nine years before *Roe v. Wade* would make abortion legal. Although social protest movements including feminism were gaining momentum, I was too young and insulated to realize that I, too, could question authority, and my naïveté allowed me to surrender my baby at birth to an obligatory closed adoption. My parents demanded secrecy about her birth, and I would assiduously obey their edict.

Although women today have greater cultural and political power, unmarried women who have sex are still not free from social opprobrium, and their right to choose an abortion is by no means forever guaranteed. and. Even so, the increasing number of women who choose motherhood outside of marriage face many fewer social penalties. Nevertheless, dependent, unwed teen mothers are still pressured to surrender their babies to adoption, and although most American adoptions are now either open (i.e., the adoptee grows up knowing at least one of her birthparents) or mediated, that shift has not led to an opening of all adoption records. In the majority of states, they remain firmly closed. The disgrace of having an out-or-wedlock pregnancy has diminished, but the moral values the scarlet *A* symbolized are still with us, and with me. I have never been able to fully conquer the shame that un-wed motherhood ignited in me. In 1965, I saw Hester as an enviable model; I still do. But decades of painful experience have taught me a sobering lesson: Hester is more a misleading fantasy than a realistic role model. As a grown woman facing life's challenges, I can sometimes muster her dignity and audacity, but in 1965 such self-reliance was unthinkable; there was no way I could follow the fictional but resolute example she had set.

As a woman who grew up to become a literary scholar, I know that I've not been alone in investing the scarlet *A* with almost supernatural powers of authority. Contemporary critic Hugo McPherson maintains it is a "'talisman' or token of our common nature" (190); Joanne Feit Diehl argues it is a fetishistic object that represents our ongoing conflict between desire and repression. But, more than a single object, Diehl argues, the letter becomes an embroidered pattern of substitutive identifications (241), a "matrix of energies" (237). That matrix is already generating meaning when the narrator of "The Custom-House" stumbles upon the faded *A* two centuries after it adorned

Hester's breast. He realizes immediately that the "rag of scarlet cloth" holds "deep meaning . . . which . . . stream[s] forth from the mystic symbol" (Hawthorne 43). When he places it on his own breast, the narrator experiences a sensation "not of red cloth, but red-hot iron" (43). For him, the A is not just a relic of the past; instead, it is as relevant as it is to me.

Hester must wear the A as a kind of accusatory brand, A for Adulteress, but she reinterprets the symbol by embroidering it extravagantly and later by suggesting other meanings for it such as Angel and Ability. The symbol ultimately escapes the boundaries of the novel, and wide-ranging meanings accrue. Although it has been re-embroidered so lavishly that we may have difficulty discerning the echoes of incriminating sexuality that its wearer once bore, its original link to forbidden desire has never been entirely erased.

Hawthorne himself set in motion the ambiguity of the monogram. Condemned as defiled, contaminated, and carnal, Hester is first imprisoned, then pilloried, then banished to the outskirts of early Boston. Forced to wear the A as punishment, she does so with unshakeable dignity in the face of ongoing ridicule. She lives in seclusion, sumptuously dressing her illegitimate child, Pearl, as the letter itself: "the scarlet letter endowed with life!" (Hawthorne 90). The critic Shari Benstock argues that while Hester's body "is both an agent of human reproduction and a field of representation," Pearl "*is* the scarlet letter in human form" (289). For Pearl the A stands for Adored, though Hester's unflagging adoration of Pearl is occasionally tempered by the child's effervescent devilishness. After all, when Hester dresses Pearl as the A, she is reminding her fellow citizens of Pearl's illegitimacy, hence ensuring for Pearl the same social isolation she endures. Hester herself insists that Pearl inhabit the badge of illegitimacy. Some of the leading citizens of Boston regard Pearl as an "infant of pestilence" (90); others as "demon offspring" sent "through the agency of [her] mother's sin to promote some foul and wicked purpose" (88); still others as "some such half-fledged angel of judgment,—whose mission [is] to punish the sins of the rising generation" (91). Barbara Garlitz proclaims Pearl "the most enigmatic child in literature" (689). Her illegitimacy makes her vulnerable to paternalistic colonial law, which could separate her from her mother, and her precocious unpredictability adds to that vulnerability. No one is comfortable with indeterminacy.

Because Hester willingly shoulders her "heap of shame" (74), her punishment is not rigorous enough for the "leading inhabitants" of Boston, who cherish a "more rigid order of principles in religion and government" (89). Pronouncing her irrevocably "fallen, amid the pitfalls of this world" (96), they judge her unfit as a mother, incapable of providing a moral education for Pearl. When Hester learns that the magistrates want to take custody of Pearl and transfer her "to wiser better guardianship" (89), she rushes to the governor's mansion to defend her maternal qualifications. The threat infuses her with dazzling resistance. For the first time, she sheds her despondent acceptance of her punishment and passionately protests the law that has condemned her. Her argument is an early example of an emotional female discourse in that it is "backed by the sympathies of nature" and personal experience rather than male logic and reason. She acknowledges that she has fallen from a Christian path, but she maintains that her disgrace has made her a better teacher. "Laying her finger on the red token," she exclaims, "The badge hath taught me,—it daily teaches me,—it is teaching me at this moment,—lessons whereof my child may be the wiser and better" (96). In her recent book, *Adopting America*, Carol J. Singley identifies the spirited debate between Hester and the magistrates as "arguably the most famous custody case in American literature" (70). Hawthorne uses this contest to complicate the *A*'s original signification (adulteress) and purpose (humiliation), recasting it as a superior moral instructor over Puritan orthodoxy.

As the scene unfolds, Pearl is unwilling to restrain her elfin defiance and perversely refuses when asked to recite her catechisms for the skeptical magistrates. When they ask her who made her, she insists that rather than having been made by God, she was "plucked by her mother off the wild roses, that grew by the prison-door" (97). When Hester hears this wildly unorthodox response, she realizes she is going lose her appeal. Passionately, she turns to divinity to defend her maternal prerogative, insisting not once but twice, "God gave me the child!" Standing up to her tormenters, she swears that she will not be parted from Pearl—her "sole treasure to keep her heart alive" (98). The "venerable pastor" John Wilson tries to reason with her, claiming, "My poor woman . . . the child shall be well cared for!—far better than thou canst do it" (98). Panicked, her voice rising almost to a shriek, Hester cries, "I will not lose the child!" Unsurprisingly, neither Hester's ardent defense nor her uncharacteristic boldness changes the elders' minds. Desperately she turns to the Reverend Dimmesdale, Pearl's secret father, who has stood mute throughout the debate. "Speak thou for me," she begs. "Thou knowest what is in my heart, and what are a mother's rights, and how much the stronger they are, when that mother has but her child and the scarlet letter!" (98).

In fact, Hester is justified in claiming her rights as Pearl's mother. Singley points out that "English law granted fathers custody of legitimate children, but it assumed that illegitimate children outside the patriarchal household were not subject to statutes or entitled to their protections. Women were encouraged to raise their children as single mothers so long as they remained under control of the state" (71). However, in this exchange, Hester has no respected or authoritative status from which to speak, and we sense that no matter how eloquently she presents her claim, she will be unable to argue for her rights persuasively, especially given the punitive judges she faces. With defeat looming, she knows whom to turn to, and when Dimmesdale comes to her defense, the magistrates readily reconsider, even though Dimmesdale's argument fundamentally reiterates Hester's. He maintains that "God gave [Hester] the child, and gave her too, an instinctive knowledge of its nature and requirements ... which no other moral being can possess" (98). "Is there not," he asks, "a quality of awful sacredness ... between this mother and this child?" (98). Pearl, he argues, will "remind her, at every moment, of her fall—but yet ... teach her ... that, if she bring the child to heaven, the child also will bring its parent hither!" Without hesitation, the magistrates find Dimmesdale's argument of "weighty import" and resolve to allow Hester to keep Pearl, the only stipulation being that Dimmesdale supervise her catechism. Unknowingly they endow Pearl's birthfather with paternal authority. Most importantly, both Hester and Dimmesdale cite the letter's capacity to teach as cement for the mother/child bond. Their argument mollifies the magistrates, who want the letter to serve as a means of punishing Hester and Pearl. Ironically, Hester has manipulated the letter's import to serve her purposes. Singley astutely observes: "Committed to raising her child, Hester transforms her badge of shame into one of power historically denied mothers" (73). Although the letter remains an isolating, unremitting marker, it also now ensures her rights to Pearl, her only source of affection.

However, ideology's unrelenting influence is difficult to fully evade, especially for Reverend Dimmesdale, who having once violated society's norms by fathering Pearl, cannot bring himself to confess his paternity publicly. Instead, he resumes his life according to the rigid dictates of Puritan morality. But Dimmesdale suffers more from his hypocritical secrecy than Hester does from her public humiliation. In his recent essay "The Moral Instinct," Steven Pinker draws some conclusions that can help explain Dimmesdale's agonizing duplicity. Almost universally, Pinker observes, people value "loyalty to a group ... and conformity to its norms. They believe that it is right to defer to legitimate authorities and to respect people with high status. And they exalt purity, cleanliness and sanctity while loathing defilement, contamination and carnality" (36). Hidden in the heart of Boston's puritanical authority, one that Hawthorne describes as "despotic in its temper" (131), Dimmesdale can neither renege on his loyalty to that group—one that has granted him privilege and security—nor forget his "defilement" and "carnality." When he finally ascends the scaffold with Hester and Pearl and "bears on his own breast . . . his own red stigma," the spectators are astounded by the scarlet letter, which all but his "friends" see imprinted in his flesh. Hawthorne will not verify the origins of Dimmesdale's *A*. Some contend it is the result of Chillingworth's necromancy; others, "the ever active tooth of remorse . . . manifesting Heaven's dreadful judgment by the visible presence of the letter"; and others, the result of Dimmesdale's own "course of penance," one that has compelled him to "[inflict] a hideous torture on himself" (195, 197) and makes him one of literature's first "cutters."

At the same time, Hester's husband, Chillingworth, also keeps Dimmesdale's paternity a secret, though only to avoid the belittling label of "cuckold." He sadistically exacts his revenge on Dimmesdale by slowly, mercilessly driving him mad. And although his calculated dissembling, like Dimmesdale's, is ostensibly self-serving, the resulting secrecy is lethal for both men.

Marginalized by her community, Hester feels little solidarity with it. Her banishment allows her to resist the impulse to conform: she is "little accustomed, in her long seclusion from society to measure her ideas of right and wrong by any standard external to herself" (130). She develops, instead, a moral instinct that goes far beyond the stringent code that punishes her. Rather than turn bitterly misanthropic, like Chillingworth, Hester becomes "a well-spring of human tenderness" (131). Furthermore, wearing the *A* also gives her a "freedom of speculation" (133); "The world's law [is] no law for her mind" (133). Exile allows her to adopt a more instinctive, socially unconstructed moral code, and "allows us to embrace her as the rebel progenitor of 'our' community" (Doyle 262).[3]

Hester cannot save Dimmesdale or Chillingworth. Dimmesdale surrenders his physical and psychological health to corrosive guilt. And the morally desiccated Chillingworth, in the throes of a psychopathological mind-set, shrivels and dies once Dimmesdale, the object of his pathology, is removed. Since Dimmesdale's and Chillingworth's deaths release Hester from their thrall and from Boston, she and Pearl can disappear across the sea to a life free from the humiliating *A*. Hester's decision to return years later, wearing the *A*, though not even the "sternest magistrate of that iron period would have imposed it" (200), is perplexing and continues to serve as grist for critical analysis and fictional reconsideration.[4] Regardless, she is still propelled by her quest to redefine the letter, for she continues to embroider its meaning. In the years that follow, the *A* is so thoroughly overlaid by her artistry that it becomes something to be "looked upon" by the community "with awe, yet with reverence too" (200). Hester herself becomes a kind of antipuritanical guru sought out by confused, desperate women suffering from the wounds of "sinful passion" (201). To them she prophesies that a "new truth [will] be revealed, in order to establish the whole relation between man and woman on a surer ground of mutual happiness" (201). From his 1850 vantage point, Hawthorne not only interrogates the assumption that Hester has broken a moral law by committing adultery but also exposes the merciless rigidity of the "venerable" moralists of Boston in 1650. By the novel's conclusion, Hester's identity has been irrefutably ennobled by her resilient resistance to dogma. The regal *A* on her tombstone symbolizes much, but perhaps most importantly, it stands for her courageous and necessary struggle to overcome absolutist morality.

My scholarly fascination with Hester and Pearl and more generally with the unwed mother plot in American literature and film comes out of my own embroidered experiences with unwed pregnancy, enduring shame, and irrevocable regret. Critic Diane P. Freedman refers to such a highly personal connection as "that psychically unrestful juncture . . . of the personal and the theoretical" where borders of self and genre collide (21). Since the conventional, impersonal models of academic criticism will not serve this unrestful collision, I have followed the example of innovative critics like Freedman, Jane Tompkins, and Elaine Showalter by practicing an autobiographical, sometimes even confessional criticism to more authentically ground my scholarly observations in my uniquely female experience. And so I am drawn back to those three long winter months at Florence Crittenton and the traumatic birth of my daughter.

Like so many middle-class girls in the 1960s who abruptly left high school and "went away," I felt enormous guilt for my pregnancy and then ingenuously agreed to all the adult machinations that were put into play to keep my pregnancy and my daughter a secret. Because I was made to think that I had no choice, I surrendered her for adoption. Although I was told by my well-meaning parents and even the social worker that then my ordeal would be over—that after giving birth, I would easily take up my life where I had left off—I found their promises painfully empty. Instead, I returned home, emotionally shattered, with a psychological scar that became an integral strand in the fabric of my selfhood. Like Hester, I learned that once branded with the *A*, I could not remove it. For decades I worked assiduously to keep my secret. I was incapable of talking about it, and yet it smoldered in my psyche, continuously unsettling me, affecting pivotal decisions, damaging intimate relationships, and sometimes shaking the very foundations of the unsteady self I was trying to construct. Nonetheless, carrying my shame and trying to sublimate the energy that emanated from it was not entirely wasted effort. I grew up first to be an enthusiastic and then a skilled reader and eventually a literary scholar. But even so, the day finally came when I realized that if I was ever going to lead an honest and psychologically healthy life, I could no longer hide this most secret, most integral part of myself. I would have to learn, as Hester once did, how to expose my shame, how to wear the *A* exposed and if I could, embroider its effect.

After many halting and painful attempts, I finally told the secret of my unwed motherhood and my illegitimate daughter in my first book, *Intimate Reading*. Bringing my uncommon perspective to literary analysis, that book discusses how reading contemporary women's memoirs autobiographically gave me the courage I needed to reveal my own story. The memoirs I read are by brave women who kept shame-laden secrets only to find that in order to live healthfully, they had to live openly. Writing *Intimate Reading* did much to ameliorate, if not erase, the shame I carried. And, remarkably, it led to finding and being reunited with my lost daughter. I then wrote a memoir, *Following the Tambourine Man*, chronicling my journey since sixteen.

Although it is no longer a cloaked part of my psychological identity, my past continues to haunt me. I do not wear it with equanimity. Even though I now know that my tale is far from unique and that it includes loving reconnections, I still find myself cringing and blushing whenever I retell the story. Exposure does not mitigate the internal burden of shame. If anything, that burden is more clearly permanent. I accept that and pragmatically find surcease and value where I can, knowing that it kindles my compassion and motivates my teaching. My marginalization has given me a hypersensitive lens, acutely and uncomfortably attuned to coercion, domination, hypocrisy, prudery, cruelty, and more. It prods me to support vulnerable women and girls; it permeates this book. And so, I take up the scarlet letter again as a pivotal trope, a uniquely American legacy, the public humiliation of sexually transgressive women. By tracing the numerous literary reiterations of Hester up on the pillory and by interrogating the letter's cultural and social ramifications, I hope, like Hester, to re-embroider it with imagination and creativity rather than shame and humiliation.

Although I am not a professional historian, I do appreciate that all discourse is situated in time and place. Knowing this and therefore respecting each text's particular historicity, I cautiously draw intertextual connections between them. Taken chronologically, they repeat, supplant, sublimate, and transform what Peter Brooks calls a "master narrative," or more specifically, the seduction plot and its aftermath for female characters. According to Harold Bloom's theory of misreading, each new narrative reiterates its literary precursors and historical precedents as it attempts an imaginatively unique swerve from them.[5] As the moral values that inform our culture evolve and the social penalties for unwed motherhood and illegitimacy diminish, the narratives that reflect these cultural shifts change accordingly as their authors make their revisionary swerves. But their narratives do not simply mirror societal mores. These stories are shaped by culture, and in turn, culture is then shaped by them. As literary vehicles of ideology, they do important cultural work as they affirm, subvert, reinforce, or challenge the prevailing moral standards that affect the lives of unwed mothers and their children.

It is important to remind ourselves that a symbol like the scarlet *A* is never totalizing. Although I feel as if I know the *A* all too well, I've never felt there is a definitive, monolithic meaning in either *The Scarlet Letter* or in the texts that follow and anticipate it. Although Hawthorne's *A* is powerful, it is generative rather than definitive. As it transcends history, its moral ramifications are reasserted and revised in narrative after narrative. The letter refuses to conform to a time-worn truth or a dependable, established definition. Instead it produces an imaginative field of embroidered connotations that have been creatively reworked by generations of writers whose female characters have endured versions of its implications.[6] Because of my own experience with the letter, I know its undeniable reach in American culture. I have granted it extensive authority, felt its caustic consequences, and, sometimes, even been able to capture the capricious defiance it can ignite. Thus with hard-earned knowledge of the shame it signifies, I follow the symbol through generations of American fiction. Although the actual letter will fall away, I see its ongoing influence as the ripples of its initial weight move out through different narratives. Sometimes, even the literal *A* itself resurfaces. As it transforms and proliferates, it remains dangerously potent. Its significance in defining unwed mothers cannot be underestimated, for it is not yet safely relegated to history or confined to the realm of fiction. As a symbol, its meanings and influences are ever with us.

The *A*'s endurance in American literature seems extraordinary, but it comes from a long tradition of narratives about remarkable though often tragic women who refuse to be constrained by prescribed cultural expectations. The patriarchal ecclesiastical and civil governance of colonial Boston first imposed the scarlet letter on Hester Prynne, but authors have used women's bodies for literary and mythological narratives for millennia, including tales of abduction, rape, seduction, illicit pregnancy, and illegitimate birth. These narratives have been usually told as cautionary tales that warn, intimidate, and shock girls. I often wish I had paid closer attention and read them more carefully so as to better resist if not subvert the master narrative of the fallen woman. But instead, my own story of adolescent passion, secret pregnancy, punishment, and surrender adheres to a well-worn design. I am unwittingly a member of a pantheon of unwed mothers whose stories are told and retold, again and again.

Even so, there are variations. To win my readers' sympathy, I could have told my own seduction story so as to become a powerless victim of male sexual aggression. There are plenty of tragic narrative models at hand from that perspective. Or to secure my readers' disapprobation, I could paint myself as a wantonly flagrant, heedless girl who deserves her punishment. There too I have many poignant exemplars to draw upon. That I should have suppressed my own sexual desires goes without saying; female self-control is a putative assumption in the fallen woman's master narrative. In 1965, my girlfriends and I knew we had to be the umpires when it came to heavy petting. We whispered about letting a boy get to first base, second base, third base, and, heaven forbid, home plate. I know this analogy sounds dated, but when I asked my college students about it, they knew exactly what I was talking about. The analogy of a woman's body to a baseball diamond still holds as does the double bind I found myself in at sixteen: I was encouraged by my authoritarian father to be agreeably submissive and by my adventurous peers to be sexually enticing, but at the same time, I was expected by both my parents and my peers to be steely against all serious efforts at sexual follow through.

The responsibility imposed on me at sixteen to be more sexually disciplined than my boyfriend is still obligatory for young women in heteronormative America. In pop culture, in literature, and in life, when heavy petting shifts to sex (whether due to mutual desire or male coercion), the assumption remains that it's girls who are at fault because they either let down their guard or give in to their "unnatural" passions. My mother accused me of the latter, though in her vernacular it was called having "hot pants." Exasperatingly vulnerable to male desire, females are held to blame for all moral lapses and punished for opening the door to their own ruin. The sexual double standard was and is relentlessly imposed: men like my baby's father are excused and maybe even admired for sexual immoderation, since they can't help themselves, while sexually active, unmarried women are still promptly branded with the contemporary moniker for fallen women—"sluts," à la Rush Limbaugh and his ilk.

In the not-too-distant past, young women who got pregnant out of wedlock were not only labeled fallen, they were anathema. Although that has changed a good deal, the labels "unwed mother" and "teen mother" can still cause shudders. Then and now, they have been represented in literature and in culture as out of control or, more tellingly, uncontrollable. Here's a indicative anecdote: In my hometown, county commissioners recently voted to turn down a $9,000 grant from Planned Parenthood that would provide IUDs for unmarried mothers who came to public health services for birth control. Their rationalization was the same as Limbaugh's: they felt that taxpayers should not pay for women who, in their words, had already made poor judgments to engage in even more sexual activity. Although fallen women may no longer face death or exile, cultural condemnation has abated little.

As a professor of English and women's studies, I make my living by reading and discussing Western literature. I repeatedly find depictions of sexually attractive female characters in the novels I teach and write about, but I also find that if those characters are to remain sympathetic in the master narrative that I describe here, they cannot be sexually assertive. In this controlling scenario, they are either "pure" or "ruined," "angelic" or "monstrous."

Western culture abounds with stories of seduction for which the victim is blamed, beginning with Persephone, who is seized by Hades and taken to the underworld. Forced against her will to eat the red seeds of the pomegranate, Persephone serves as the archetypal scarlet woman—the innocent, sympathetic, ravished beauty who must leave the sphere of her mother every year and return to captivity as Hades's consort. The seeds of the pomegranate prove fertile. Indeed, literary history provides us with a lineage of Persephones, Callistos, and Philomenas; abducted, raped, or seduced, they are marked with red in one symbolic manifestation after another. As the novel as a genre develops in the eighteenth century, fallen women become fundamental to the genre's foundations, and we see again and again that artless innocence like Persephone's makes women defenseless against the trickery of lurking debauchers. "Innocence," observes feminist critic Patricia Spacks, "is a broad avenue to corruption," and when heroines, no matter how blameless, fall prey to seducers, they are not allowed "even ambiguously happy fates" (30). Although virginity may no longer hold the cultural cachet it once did and unwed mothers and their babies are no longer social pariahs, they have still not lost their centrality as subject matter for narrative.

As a part of this lineage, I have found myself the object of narrative fascination. Whether I am speaking to a gathering of academics or our local Red Hat society, audiences almost never want to hear about my scholarly work as a feminist critic or my commitment to adoption reform. Instead they want to hear the myriad contextual details and heartbreaking consequences of that long ago night on a scratchy avocado-colored couch when I surrendered my virginity and conceived my daughter. Stories like mine continue to captivate readers as well as film and TV audiences who consume chronicles of passion, capitulation, and calamity. I assume this appeal is not just prurient or vindictive; nonetheless, fictional unwed mothers must pay for their sexual acquiescence more often than not, as have I with my own recurring emotional winters that send me back to a Hades of depression and regret.

Persephone's symbolic pomegranate seed has flourished throughout Western culture, gestating and transmogrifying as scarlet women one by one have taken it up and tasted its consequences. Characters such as Queen Guinevere, the Wife of Bath, Moll Flanders, Clarissa Harlowe, and Tess d'Urberville populate the European literary canon, along with one of the most tragic of all, Tolstoy's Anna Karenina. As we will see in the first chapter of this book, the American literary tradition begins with the stories of fallen women, including one authored by one of our most revered founding fathers, Benjamin Franklin. His resourceful heroine, Polly Baker, will be followed by colonial America's adaptation of the tragic "master narrative" in which seduced women give birth out of wedlock and promptly meet their demise. But when I began this project, it was with Hester and the *A* that was pinned to her breast.

In Hawthorne's novel, no matter how assiduously Hester embroiders the letter and tries to free it from the "literalism of [her] Puritan ancestors," it continues to deliver an emphatic moral message (Budick 172), a message that reverberates even as I write. According to Benstock, "the female body is both an agent of human reproduction and a field of representation, emblematized" (289). More importantly to my purposes, the pregnant woman's body exposes the "relation between . . . biological representation and symbolic representations"; it "serves as the space where social . . . and cultural values are inscribed" (289). Given current social and cultural values, we may want to argue that the body of the pregnant unwed mother signifies liberation from puritanical morality, but it simultaneously carries warnings of the complicated consequences of such liberation.

Hawthorne's novel kept me company during my exile at Florence Crittenton and Hester gave me a model of courage, capability, and dignity. But there was no way I could follow her example. I simply did not have the critical skills that would have allowed me to interrogate class and age biases, prejudices that judged me as unworthy. I accepted without question the mainstream values that write off teenage mothers as unfit. and the cultural given that relinquishing a child to adoption is almost always considered morally good. I was acclimatized to a society that automatically approves of adoption as morally upright: a birthmother's unselfish answer to unplanned pregnancy.[7] And as we learn in the biblical account of the "Judgment of Solomon," mothers will sacrifice almost everything to save their children. When King Solomon calls for the splitting in two of a baby claimed by two mothers, he identifies the "true" mother when she declares she will sacrifice all claim to her child in order to keep it from being killed (1 Kings 3:16—28). In 1965 multiple voices in American culture told me outright that I should make such a sacrifice, for I would do my baby real harm by keeping her. I was told I lacked the requirements of age and financial security that were required to be a good mother. Compliantly I surrendered my claim to my child rather than harm her, rejecting my right to motherhood with no idea of the emotionally wrenching twists my forfeiture would take.

What advice could Hester, now an archetype ingrained on our collective imagination, have offered me in 1965? Sadly, she could provide me little more than an example of the salubrious nature of hard work and a model of stoicism and courage in the face of tragedy. Unequipped to take an oppositional stance, I could not follow her ultimate example and declaim, "I will not lose [my] child!" (98) when asked to surrender my daughter. Ironically, after returning home with my own secret A, I was expected to take the route of the tortured Dimmesdale, denying my child and keeping my secret at all costs because the truth would surely be my undoing. But like Dimmesdale, my secret *A* was seared on my conscience, if not imprinted on my flesh. Significant traces of the puritanical ideology of New England 1650 were very much alive in middle-class California 1965, where appearances reigned supreme. My family, I believed, had to be protected from my ignominious fall, and my daughter, I was told, needed to be protected from the disgrace of illegitimacy.

Although my own physical exile in Ohio was temporary, my sense of psychological difference from others and the corresponding emotional distancing it encouraged kept me an outsider for years. Like Hester, I was a loner, but unlike Hester, who implausibly manages to sustain herself and Pearl by needlework, I was still a girl without any means to survive free of the material ties of my parents' affluence. As the exhilarating tenor of the sixties heightened, I found a way to respect my otherness by casting myself as a rebel, and I loved to think of myself in rebellious terms. I marched; I protested; I can even remember weaving flowers through my hair at a sit-in outside the administration building at the University of Oregon. The times "they were a-changin'," and the new zeitgeist gave me the chance to question middle-of-the-road moral authority in a role that was empowering—up to a point. Whenever my rebel status clashed too conspicuously with my mainstream parents, I found myself reluctantly acquiescing to their authority. My parents were hell-bent on getting me back to "normal," and I was still umbilically attached to their milieu and unable to cut the cord. As a role model, Hester remained an unachievable ideal.

I have come to respect the emblematic *A*'s resilience. It may no longer be literally sewn to our clothing, but its implications continue to latch on to women and children in fiction, film, and life with a tenacity that still surprises. And Hester? I believe she can be a pragmatic model for unwed mothers, that she can be realistically emulated, but for me, she remains ambiguous: alluring but inevitably remote. I still try to imitate her courage and proudly own up to my unwed motherhood and all its complicated repercussions, yet ultimately, shame and embarrassment will out. Nonetheless, it is this irremediable discomfort that, I believe, has motivated me to trace the evolution of Hester's "sisters." In the literary derivatives that follow *The Scarlet Letter*, unwed mothers continue to struggle against moral establishments that permit men (not as venal but not entirely unlike Dimmesdale and Chillingworth) to dodge paternal responsibility. Some, like Hester, will have to solve the dilemma of their pregnancies on their own; others will turn to extended family members (many of whom will be punitive) for protection. Although the transgressions that complicate their journeys will be recast, they are not entirely different. Like Hester in Puritan England, future unwed mothers will be labeled unsuitable mothers and ruined women,

The urge to emulate Hester as a rebel has continued, although the significance of her *A* has undergone what at first seems a surprising alteration. In her essay "Hawthorne's Pearl: Woman-Child of the Future," Cindy Daniels notes that women "willingly don [the] metaphorical *A* upon their own breast" (235). And, in fact, one of my undergraduate students, Laura, who had just returned from a trip to Hawthorne's House of Seven Gables, came to class not long ago proudly wearing a T-shirt emblazoned with a large, red, gothic *A*, which she had purchased for just $15 at the adjacent Museum Store. Laura's *A* goes well beyond Hester's early punishing letter and the more ennobling late-in-life *A* that designated her as a saintly, moral guru. It is more aligned with the rebellious performance that I tried to stage as a sixties flower child and that Swift tries to suggest in her lyrics, "I was a scarlet letter." As we talked about Laura's *A* in class that day, we discovered that it serves a jaunty, irreverent purpose. Students saw this contemporary version as a symbol not only of young women's general rebelliousness but also of sexual autonomy and the end of social censure for sex outside of marriage. The shame it once carried seems to have vanished, at least for these college women. Nonetheless, even in its latest cheeky renditions, this sexually liberating *A* is not risk-free. We might sport it on a T-shirt for a few days, but that's far different from facing the life-altering costs of out-of-wedlock, unplanned pregnancy that it was originally used to designate.

In the chapters that follow, it is worthwhile to note that we will not find another literal scarlet *A* pinned to a woman's breast until the symbol resurfaces in the 2010 film, *Easy A*, a comedy that appropriates the *A* with a contemporary twist. At first glance, this rehabilitated *A* seems to celebrate female sexual autonomy. We might even assume it has finally lost its demeaning function, but the celebration is short lived and the narrative ultimately provides an instructive example of the enduring aura of disgrace that even a glitzy Hollywood makeover and the perky, impish actress Emma Stone cannot expunge from the archetypal *A*.

Wishing for the kind of public respect and social emancipation that Hester gained from wearing the scarlet letter in colonial Boston, Olive Penderghast (Emma Stone), a high school student in Ojai, California, takes Hester's example to heart. Olive is the beautiful, irascible outsider whom I could only have dreamed of being in high school. Scholarly but hardly a wallflower, she chooses to remain on the margins of a vapid, ruthless clique-culture. Unlike her classmates, Olive actually takes the time to read *The Scarlet Letter* for her English class, after which she decides to narrate her contemporary version of Hester Prynne. By way of her webcam, Olive quickly exercises her well-versed, witty ingenuity. Mimicking Mark Twain, she begins by declaring, "The rumors of my promiscuity have been greatly exaggerated."

Olive has instigated her own "fall" by fabricating a tale of lost virginity so that her best friend, Rhiannon, will stop pestering her. Despite popular culture's innumerable representations of teenagers who eagerly play fast and loose, casual sex is still beyond the pale for girls in Olive's small town. When the news of her sexual initiation goes viral, Olive is labeled "super slut," the first of many negative monikers she will bear. The gossip becomes even more scurrilous when Olive decides to put her notoriety to good use. She pretends to have sex with her gay friend Brandon, the target of homophobic, bullying peers, and then with several other persecuted nerds who enlist her "bad" reputation to bolster theirs.

The double standard is still firmly in place at Ojai North High School. The boys whom Olive "helps" earn instant manly credibility, while Olive becomes a social pariah for "throwing her cat at everybody." Her peers call her "tramp," "bimbo," "sex monkey," "floozy," "dirty skank," "trollop," "Jezebel," "harlot," and "whore." But their name campaign doesn't get Olive down. *Easy A* is a comedy with no tragic birthmother in sight. In fact, Olive's mother confesses that she has been hoping Olive does get "knocked up" so she that can have a second shot at raising kids. Nor is there an evil Chillingworth haunting Ojai. As film critic Stephen Holden notes, the "designated villains (a circle of pious Jesus freaks . . .) exhibit the daffy comic exuberance of the teenagers in *Glee*." It also helps that Olive is "indefatigably self-assured, clever, [and] attractive" ("Being Naughty")—not the qualities that most self-conscious, overly sensitive adolescent girls possess. Rather than deny the rumors or retreat in shame, Olive defiantly decides to channel Hester Prynne by emblazoning a red *A* on her new, revealing black corset and boldly wearing it to school. The girls are aghast; the boys, enchanted. The *A* may still be sewn with threads of illicit adultery, but for Olive, *A* is for *A*wesome; it announces allure, audacity, and erotic promise.

The crisis is engineered when Olive agrees to carry out Hester's martyrdom by taking the fall for the school guidance counselor, who has given one of her students chlamydia, until the price of such sacrifice is just too great, even for chirpy, ingenious Olive. It's one thing to be accused of prostituting herself, another to be accused of spreading a venereal disease. Olive confesses to her webcam, "A lot of people hate me now; I kind of hate me too." She sheds her A and extricates herself from the kerfuffle by telling the truth: she's still a virgin. "You know," she adds, "it was just like Hester in *The Scarlet Letter* except that's the one thing the movies don't tell you. How shitty it feels to be an outcast." With her Prince Charming waiting beneath her window on his riding lawnmower to sweep her away, she proudly proclaims she may keep her virginity until her wedding night. The end.

Easy A is a sweet, pleasing movie, partly because the scarlet letter is ultimately so inconsequential. The hypocritical Jesus freaks are exposed; the real adulterer is revealed; Olive's reputation is restored with little harm done; and she is justly rewarded for her zesty generosity. More importantly, the A has been re-embroidered, but not finally redeemed. Olive has accented it with sexy fun and erotic allure, but finally, she must be freed from its still-punishing burden. She appropriates the A to make a point, but when its symbolic implications become too grave, she can easily, unlike Hester, remove the A in order to realize cinematic "true love." Donning it has been an adventure, but now she's back on track, undamaged and intact, ready for conventional, heterosexual, monogamous life. As Holden notes, "For all its hip posturing, [*Easy A*] is fundamentally and safely puritanical" ("Being Naughty"). Even today, if the good girl is going to "get the guy," she must be able to offer him if not virginity, at least some form of purity along with the assurance that she will never merit the scarlet letter.

Which brings me back to my own story, one shared by tens of thousands of girls who like me surrendered their children for adoption in the decades before *Roe v. Wade*. When I was sent from my home in Southern California to Ohio, of course I did not have to don an actual scarlet letter, but my story is much more like Hester's than Olive's. When the tight girdle would no longer hide my pregnancy, my body became like little Pearl's, the A in material form. But rather than "adored," my body stood for the "anathema," and propriety insisted I be sequestered, like Hester, for the duration of my pregnancy. We at Florence Crittenton felt like social outcasts, singular in our exile. A socially sanctioned system deprived us of any authority over our bodies, our futures, and the future of the babies we carried. We were, in fact, part of an era that's come to be referred to as the "baby scoop." We supplied the adoption industry with healthy white babies for infertile couples. Between 1945 and 1973, one and a half million babies were relinquished for adoption (Fessler 8). Our bodies were both instruments of reproduction and symbolic fields. We may have worn no literal *A*, but plenty of demeaning labels attached themselves to our psyches: "bad girl," "nympho," "unwed mother," "used goods," "ruined," "bitch," "whore." And unlike the insults Olive managed to shake off so effortlessly, these labels weren't funny. Even worse, our babies would be labeled "illegitimate" or "bastard." We wanted to escape, and we were erroneously told that the psychologically condemning labels we bore would be immediately erased just as soon as we delivered. Our humiliation would become someone else's blessing.

But cultures change. Today, girls are seldom secreted away in maternity "homes." Nonetheless, as we look at contemporary versions of teenage unwed mothers, we will see they still carry a stigma not unlike my stubborn *A*. Our culture has not yet put aside what Adam Pertman, the director of the Donaldson Adoption Institute, identifies as "the lingering cultural stereotype of birth mothers as uncaring or ignorant young teens who choose adoption to crassly jettison a nettlesome problem" (10). In his influential book *Adoption Nation*, Pertman calls this stereotype "unmitigated and corrosive nonsense" (10). Unfortunately, mainstream culture has yet to recognize it as such. Adoption professionals have learned that the vast majority of birthmothers do not "forget and get on with their lives" (Pertman 12). Although adoption is built on someone's heartbreak and loss, there are obviously those who still want to believe and get us to believe that a woman can relinquish her child and then put the experience aside and pretend she didn't part with a piece of herself (Pertman 18). That's not only magical thinking, it is dangerous thinking.

Back in 1965, I was administered a spinal block, so I did not feel my daughter being born, but I immediately heard her crying. She was not placed on my stomach, like most newborns are, but when I asked, I was allowed to look at her for about a minute, but not to touch her rosy, glistening cheek or her wet, dark hair. I could see that the umbilical cord had been cut; its small, yellow-gray stump extending from her navel was all that was left of our lives' physical connection. Her tiny perfect hands were furiously grasping at the shockingly cold air around her. She wouldn't stop crying, but I knew that I could soothe her, if they would just let me hold her. I begged the nurse: "Please, please, just let me have her. Please give her to me. Please." The nurse shook her head firmly: "No, I'm sorry; I can't." I was lucky to have had the chance to see my daughter. It was common practice back then to remove the baby immediately from the delivery room so that the young mother would never even know her child's gender. This was supposed to make it easier to forget. But such forgetting is not possible.

My daughter's birth established an unexpectedly immediate and powerful connection that was supposed to be effortlessly severed. There's a story here that dominant culture still represses, even though Hester Prynne knew it well and proclaimed it eloquently. It's the story of the years and years that followed my daughter's birth when I would fall into bleak days, weeks, and months of depression as I recalled losing her with deep, permanent regret. Her tiny image still abides with me. It has clarified rather than faded over the years, and though I have met and come to know the lovely, accomplished woman that my fully grown daughter has become, my wailing baby girl remains crystalline in my memory. I cherish her endurance and forever grieve her loss.

My daughter's birth was an irreparable tear in the fabric of my adolescence, a rent that became the most meaningful and consequential event of my life. Although my pain, guilt, and regret seared into my conscience at a specific historical moment and in a different psychological environment, I know what Hester knew but what so many others don't seem to grasp: denial is a flawed strategy. No matter how hard I try not to feel and not to recall, the day I lost my baby still haunts me. I encounter the memory over and over again: the delivery room, the precise sounds of my baby's cries, my sobs, the image of my daughter, so vulnerable, so perfect.

The potent and oppressive scarlet letter has not been vanquished, neither in my psyche nor in contemporary culture. It is only more deeply entwined under multiple layers of cultural embroidery. Olive Penderghast easily slips out of its weave and my student, Laura, temporarily enjoys the notoriety it grants, but for an unwed mother, it's not that easy. The A lives on, threaded into our history. At one point in *The Scarlet Letter*, Hester tries to throw away the A, insisting "The past is gone!" (159), but it is Pearl, the embodied A, who insists that it be returned to her mother's breast. Hester is "unable to 'erase' or transcend the scarlet letter," and goes with it to her grave (Tomc 489). Nonetheless, her example of tenacious and rightful maternity lives on, and we would do well to remember the words she utters when the elders try to take Pearl away: "She is my happiness! . . . Ye shall not take her!" We would do well to remember Hester, who knew that losing her child would be more punishment than she could ever bear.

The other night, my protective niece was annoyed to find her nine-year-old daughter, Madison, watching a rerun of the popular TV show *Glee* at my house. She took particular umbrage that Madison had been exposed to the story line about Quinn, a teenager who gets pregnant, gives her baby up for adoption, and then lies about it. When I defensively reminded my niece that Quinn's story is my story, she half-heartedly apologized, but the damage was done. Absurdly overly sensitive, I dashed upstairs distraught. Hester, my unattainable ideal, had eluded me once again. It seems impossible to live up to her example of dignity and forbearance; instead I'm vanquished by one tactless assumption: little girls need to be protected from the likes of me.

Irrational? Absolutely. Unavoidable? Apparently not. Embarrassed, humbled, and sorry, I realize that even after years of reading, researching, and writing about the stigma of unwed motherhood, and after decades of living with the shame of my own version of the ever-present *A*, it continues to destabilize me. As I pondered my sorry state, my entire project began to crumble. How misled I had been to think that Hester could be a practical model for living and breathing birthmothers! Hawthorne created a highly idealized, romantic heroine capable of slaying a formidable dragon and remaking it into a beautifully embroidered emblem of courage. But Hester is not real, and most unwed mothers, whether fictional or real, are pursued for a lifetime by a fire-breathing dragon called shame. It may seem as if the scarlet *A* that Hawthorne appropriated has gone into hibernation, or it's been replaced by different markers, or that its ugly heart has been covered over by decades of creative embroidery, but the shame it produces has not been extinguished or assuaged. And so I remain, defined by it, compelled by it, pressed to follow the narratives it generates.

CHAPTER PRÉCIS

The book that follows is organized both chronologically and topically. Although I continue to respect the scarlet letter as a powerful symbol that haunts American storytelling, the *A* itself disappears after decorating Hester's tombstone, not to resurface until it flares up on Olive's corset in *Easy A*. Nonetheless, the symbolic import of the color red will pervade most of the texts I address, and more importantly, the shame it generates does not disappear. Thus, I follow the shame not only to offer a cultural history of the enduring yet evolving figure of the fallen woman but also to consider my own connection to fictional unwed mothers and the moral (or immoral) lessons they encounter.

Chapter 1, "The Unwed Mothers of the Early American Novel," examines Benjamin Franklin's bawdy "Polly Baker," followed by the first three novels published in newly independent America, *The Power of Sympathy*, *The Coquette*, and *Charlotte Temple*. Each tells a tragic seduction narrative with a pedagogical purpose: to defeat licentiousness and advance female virtue. As such, the heroines who fall from propriety in these novels are indelibly marked as ruined. Some are deemed so "polluted" by extramarital sex that they must die shortly after childbirth, and their babies are inexorably marked by their illegitimacy.

Chapter 2, "Theodore Dreiser's All-Giving Angel: *Jennie Gerhardt*," discusses Dreiser's *Jennie Gerhardt*, a novel that had to be cut by at least 16,000 words because its protagonists, Jennie and Lester, were not properly punished for their sexual liaison, and because the manuscript contained references to birth control—a taboo subject in 1911. The novel serves as an important interrogation of the fallen woman, and is a bitter critique of patriarchy, class privilege, and the social elite. Jenny serves as a reiteration of the nineteenth-century "angel of the house," the self-effacing, all-giving archetype. Unlike Hester, she does not evolve into a self-directed heroine and never revises the conviction that she does not deserve happiness.

Chapter 3, "Edith Wharton's Female Enforcers" discusses Wharton's novella *The Old Maid* and short story "Roman Fever," narratives in which shrewd, unforgiving women driven by patriarchal convention enforce the rules of old New York's privileged class. In each narrative, a mother lives a double life, carefully guarding the passionate sexual transgression that led to the birth of her illegitimate daughter. As a way to demonstrate the intense cultural bias against unwed mothers, Wharton uses revealing tropes such as blood in *The Old Maid* and red yarn in "Roman Fever" to re-embroider the scarlet inheritance borne by fallen women. In the novella, Wharton exposes the cruel extent to which socialite Delia Ralston will go under the guise of morality to keep her cousin Charlotte and Charlotte's illegitimate child from infecting the Ralston clan. The birthmother is ostracized by social appearances and moral rigidity, forcing her to capitulate to Delia's machinations. In "Roman Fever," we again find two women dueling for control, but in this story the one who knits with scarlet yarn finds a way to put scandal to good purpose.

Chapter 4, "The Scarlet Women of William Faulkner's *The Sound and the Fury*," explores the symbolic threads that Faulkner weaves in order to embroider the story of Caddy, his most beloved fallen women, and the illegitimate daughter she abandons. Caddy emerges as a powerful female-subject-in-process that each of the novel's narrators fails to master. Her illicit sexuality is inherited by her illegitimate daughter, giving us an opportunity to witness the lifestyles of two "scarlet" women or, I would maintain, "modern" women in a new historical context.

Chapter 5, "The Unwed Mother Triumphant: Celie and Alice Walker's *The Color Purple*," analyzes the tragic but ultimately triumphant story of Celie and explores how racism has influenced assumptions about fallen women and illegitimacy in America. The Jezebel, the image of the sexually denigrated black woman, can leave some black women and girls vulnerable to socially tolerated male violence in appalling ways. Celie's pregnancies define her as fallen and worthless. Her stigmatization makes her vulnerable to social condemnation and to those who can and do exploit her. Her identity is constructed around the inherently critical and isolating label of "ruined." Only with the emotional, educational, and economic resources that Shug extends to Celie is she able to refashion her mantel of shame and construct an empowered, creative autonomy.

Chapter 6, "Illegitimacy and Sexual Violence," begins with a discussion of "One Holy Night," by Sandra Cisneros, a short story that demonstrates the dangerous reach of patriarchal entitlement, a reach that crosses borders, a reach that labels girls as either pure or ruined. The story goes beyond unwed pregnancy to demonstrate the lethal vulnerability girls face when their bodies become the prey of dangerous men. Building on this theme, Dorothy Allison's novel *Bastard out of Carolina* provides an unflinching representation of the dangers that come with adolescent sexuality, teenage motherhood, and the vulnerability of illegitimate children as young mothers try to create families that will meld and prosper. This 1950s version of unwed motherhood is onerous for Anney Boatwright, and just as Hester's shaming *A* is passed onto Pearl, Anney's shame is passed on to her illegitimate daughter, Bone. Like Pearl, Bone becomes an embodiment of her mother's illicit sexuality and she is designated a bastard by the state of South Carolina. Unlike Pearl, who seems to emerge from illegitimacy unscathed, Bone cannot elude the damning implications of the label she inherits.

Chapter 7, "Birthmothers in Exile" considers Louise Erdrich's *Love Medicine* and Reynolds Price's *Kate Vaiden* in an effort to see how the stigma of unwed motherhood and illegitimacy are compounded by guilt. Both novels give us birthmothers who abandon their infant sons. In *Love Medicine*, June Morrissey and her son Lipsha provide us especially vital and poignant portraits of the heartbreaking dimensions of unwed parenthood on the North Dakota Ojibwe reservation. In *Kate Vaiden*, Kate gives us a touching and often humorous account of the lasting ways an unwed mother atones for her decision to leave her child behind. Both June and Kate leave their sons with a capable extended family, but the guilt they carry for their decisions is relentless and isolating. They both lead lonely lives far from home and face untimely deaths.

In chapter 8, "Fathering Illegitimacy," short stories by Sherman Alexie, "Junior Polatkin's Wild West Show," and T. C. Boyle, "The Love of My Life," and Anita Shreve's novel *Light on Snow* represent very different responses to the challenge of becoming a birthfather. Junior Polatkin, a smart Coeur d'Alene Indian who wants to do the right thing, would like nothing more than to be a committed and responsible father for his son, but unmerited racial stereotypes keep him from realizing that aspiration. Boyle fictionalizes the story of Brian Peterson, a real-life birthfather who murdered his infant daughter by throwing her in dumpster minutes after her birth. Fascinated and perplexed by the tragedy, Boyle writes "The Love of My Life" in hopes that a fictional rendition of the scandal would help explain how a bright, well-loved, and well-off young man could do such a thing. His story is as galvanizing as the actual event itself, but as vindication, it cannot succeed. In Shreve's novel an unwed mother is represented as a social "problem" whose youth and lack of resources leave her and her newborn infant vulnerable to an iniquitous birthfather.

Contemporary fiction brings new renditions of the resiliency of an unwed mothers shame as it moves from century to century, culture to culture, and across generations. In chapter 9, "The Legacy of Secrets," Amy Tan's *The Bone Setter's Daughter* and Anna Quindlen's *Blessings* give me the opportunity to discuss the social demonization of unwed mothers in Chinese, Chinese American, and American cultures. In Tan's novel, the stigma of unwed motherhood is passed from an old-world Chinese grandmother to her immigrant daughter and on to her unknowing and thoroughly Americanized first-generation granddaughter in insidiously damaging ways. The bestselling novel *Blessings* demonstrates that the popularity of narratives based on fallen women has not diminished. Given our more forgiving, less shame-laden attitudes toward unwed mothers and their babies, we might assume that the punishments leveled at the Chinese grandmother in *The Bone Setter* would be abated in *Blessings*, but Quindlen presents a contemporary narrative that is no less vilifying.

In chapter 10, "Birthmothers in the Adoption Triangle," I examine Caroline Leavitt's novel *Girls in Trouble* and Tim Kirkman's film *Loggerheads*. Although a few of the previous narratives discussed have represented birthmothers who surrendered their babies to familial adoptions, Kirkman's and Leavitt's narratives focus specifically on post-1960s adoptions, when agencies began to regulate anonymous, closed adoptions, like the one to which I regretfully acquiesced. Birthmothers were promised confidentiality and, in so doing, agreed to sever all ties with the children they surrendered. The adoption triangle—adopted child, adoptive parents, birthmother—materialized, the very foundation of which is secrecy. Leavitt and Kirkman provide portraits of birthmothers who, like me, are haunted not only by regret and sorrow but also by serious psychological consequences. Their difficulties lead back to the children they surrendered, children they grieve for with an intensity that cannot be quelled years and years after giving birth. The narratives represent the complications for all parties in the adoption triangle when birthmothers attempt to reenter their surrendered children's lives.

In chapter 11, "Comedy and the Unwed Mother," I examine a few of the many films to examine unwed motherhood and illegitimacy (a term that has fortunately lost its punitive implications) that appeared from 2007 to 2009. The films *Knocked Up*, *Then She Found Me*, and *Juno* are meant to be comedies, and even given my bruised sensitivity to all things concerning unwed mothers, I found myself laughing through these films even as I cringed. Given the greater latitude toward sexual content in film, it is no wonder that filmmakers have turned to the unplanned pregnancy narrative for raw material. The archetypal fallen woman is still very much with us, and now that she is no longer abhorrent, she can be the butt of the joke as well as a vehicle for social criticism.

My last chapter, "Bearing Sorrow," I work with Ann Patchett's *Run*, Lorrie Moore's *A Gate at the Stairs*, and Rodrigo Garcia's *A Mother and Child*, three narratives that uncover birthmothers' painful situations that are often suppressed when we tell stories about adoption. In the two novels, Patchett's *Run* and Moore's *A Gate at the Stairs*, the comedy of a preceding chapter gives way to serious representations of despairing and disparaged women coping with unplanned pregnancy and the ethical repercussions for adoptive parents and their adopted children when the past will not stay buried. Rodrigo Garcia's *Mother and Child* tells the stories of a teenage unwed mother, Karen, and her illegitimate daughter as they struggle with the legacy of shame, isolation, and regret that has been relentlessly passed on. I end here not only because the film serves my chronological objectives, but also because Karen's story best captures my own enduring efforts to live with sorrow, and, I suspect, the efforts of most birthmothers.

In my conclusion I try to make sense of the narrative trajectory I have followed by offering several visions of possibility by way of the heroic stories of several young women coping with unwed motherhood today. Their life experiences demonstrate that the narrative structures that consign unwed mothers and their illegitimate children to castigation, exile, and death can be contested; they can be transformed. I then turn to the poignant stories given me by birthmothers who, like me, surrendered their babies and have suffered from their loss for years. All have been joyfully reunited with their adult children only to find that their sorrow refuses to lift, their regret refuses to dissipate. In writing about loss, Judith Herman helps explain why:

> We are, as it were, marked for life, and that mark is insuperable, irrecoverable. It becomes the condition by which life is risked, by which the questions of whether one can move, and with whom, and in what way are framed and incited by the irreversibility of loss itself. (472)

We are marked for life by our losses. I have learned I cannot remove the mark. It is the irrevocable a priori of my life, my own well-embroidered crimson accompaniment, my scarlet A. Like Hester, I no longer even want to be free of it. Instead I continue to embroider it with the strong threads of remembrance and respect.

As an intimate reader informed by reader response and feminist theories, I know that the literary experience can and does affect the living one. Books do cultural work. Whether their portrayals of illegitimacy and adoption in American fiction are fairy tales or realistic representations is consequential. The experience of protagonists such as Hester Prynne, Jennie Gerhardt, Charlotte Lovell, Caddy Compson, Annie Boatwright, and Juno MacGuff can intimately affect the experience of twenty-first-century unwed mothers and their children. Although in contemporary American literature and culture it would seem that the damning power of Hester's scarlet letter has been vanquished, this book will demonstrate that we cannot celebrate uncritically—not yet. Unwed mothers wear no brand and they have more autonomy than their literary foremothers to make their own choices. Nonetheless, contemporary bias remains. They are still bound by their maternity, and their choices are limited ones at best.

As I peruse my index, I find I have depended on well over a hundred experts to help me write this book, but it must be noted that, again, it was one particular book that set me on my course. In *Reading Adoption*, Marianne Novy remarks that too often, "literature about adoption exalts the adoptive mother and degrades the birth mother" (30). It is Novy's hope that when "[adoptive parents], adoptees, and birth parents understand something of the way literature has fantasized about them, they may be able to break the hold of some of those fantasies" (28). It is my hope that *Embroidering the Scarlet A* will contribute to this process, that unwed mothers, illegitimate children, and those who read and write about them may be able to break the threads that have bound them to tired plots and worn-out stereotypes. With hopeful anticipation, I look forward to new, fresh, and empowering narratives.

CHAPTER I

The Unwed Mothers of the Early American Novel

While I was at Florence Crittenton, I attended high school with about six other girls in the basement of the old Victorian mansion where we lived. My subjects were Language Arts, Earth Sciences, American History, and French, and because there was no mathematics teacher available that winter, there was no math instruction, a small mercy for me. Our teachers were kind, encouraging retired women. I wouldn't profit again from such a low student/teacher ratio until Ph.D. seminars twenty years later. Since I was the only girl studying French, I even had the benefit of a one-on-one tutorial with Madame Lapaire, a tall woman in her seventies who always dressed in black and seemed to me like a reincarnation of Miss Clavel from my childhood *Madeline* books. Miss Clavel is the intimidating but ultimately benevolent nurse who is always trying to keep Madeline out of trouble. I was in way too much trouble for even Miss Clavel's abilities, but Madame Lapaire did throw me a lifeline. First, just from seeing her for an hour a day, five days a week, for three months, my French got much better. I finally mastered the subjunctive mood, something I had failed to do in second-year French, but at Florence Crittenton, the subjunctive became a relevant verb form for me since it is used to express actions and ideas that are uncertain, like emotion, doubt, fear and trembling. Sometimes I felt like I was living in the subjunctive that winter.

In French II, I had been utterly baffled by the first novel I was assigned in French, *L'Etranger*, so I was happy that Madame had no wish to repeat that encounter. Instead we read *Un coeur simple* and *Candide* together. I read out loud as she corrected my pronunciation and then patiently listened to my translation. Maybe rereading *L'Etranger* would have been more relevant, since I was soon to face my own existential crisis, but bearing in mind that I was just sixteen, it's no wonder I appreciated Flaubert's selfless Félicité and Candide's advice *pour cultivar mon jardin*, to cultivate my garden, much more than Camus's creepy murderer. And Madame's tutelage took me well beyond third-year French. When she was first getting to know me, she asked: "Qu'aimez-vouis faire mieux?" What do you like to do best? "Je voudrais vous lire." I love to read. "Qu'est-ce que vous aimez lire?" What do you like to read? "Long romans." Long novels. With that, Madame took it upon herself not only to read French with me but to supplement my Language Arts class as well. Don't get me wrong; I loved working diligently through the grammar workbooks we were given in that class, and I was an ace at building intricate sentence diagrams. But Language Arts at Florence Crittenton was really a grammar class, not a literature class, and having consumed *The Scarlet Letter* the first week I arrived, I was hungry for more fiction. Madame fed me novels (in English) from her own bookshelves.

In her memoir *French Lessons*, Alice Kaplan tells about studying French as a teenager. The word for the kind of work she did is *bosser*, which, Kaplan explains, "comes from a word meaning 'hunched' and means hunkering down to work, bending down over some precious matter" (56). Kaplan "found her ability to concentrate" at a Swiss boarding school with Monsieur Frichot. I found mine at Florence Crittenton with Madame Lapaire. I averaged a novel a week that winter, moving eclectically from *The Scarlet Letter* to *Gone with the Wind*, to *A Tale of Two Cities*, to *Marjorie Morningstar*, and finally to Thomas Hardy, everything by Hardy.

I was at the perfect age and in the perfect circumstances to find Hardy's heartrending melodramas utterly enthralling. I identified intimately with Eustacia Vye of *The Return of the Native*. With exquisite misery I wept for Fanny Robin of *Far from the Madding Crowd*. But it was Tess d'Urberville who seemed to epitomize my experience, so much so that I named by baby Sorrow, just as Tess had done. I carefully copied word-for-word one passage from Madame's novel, a passage about Tess's solitary nighttime walks as her pregnancy becomes more and more obvious. Like me, Tess was hidden away during the last months of her pregnancy; she would only emerge after dark to walk alone in the woods. Filled with guilt, Tess sees the rain and wind as God's just punishment for her weakness, but Hardy offers a corrective, and the passage gave me another way of thinking about my own pregnancy. I still have that piece of well-worn, lined notebook paper covered with my faded teenage script. It reads:

> But this encompassment of her own characterization, based on shred of convention, peopled by phantoms and voices antipathetic to her, was a sorry and mistaken creation of Tess's fancy—a cloud of moral hobgoblins by which she was terrified without reason. It was they that were out of harmony with the actual world, not she. Walking among the sleeping birds in the hedges, watching the skipping rabbits on a moonlit warren, or standing under a pheasant-laden bough, she looked upon herself as a figure of Guilt intruding into the haunts of Innocence. But all the while she was making a distinction where there was no difference. Feeling herself in antagonism she was quite in accord. She had been made to break an accepted social law, but no law known to the environment in which she fancied herself such an anomaly. (91)

Once again, it was a novel that furnished me with a different moral compass, a way of looking at my "crime" in a more forgiving way. If I was to believe Thomas Hardy, I had broken a social law but not a law of nature.

Although I may have mastered the subjunctive verb form that winter, I didn't yet have the critical discourse to articulate my uncertainties. Madame Lapaire's interest and generosity gave me my first glimpse at the arbitrary nature of social conventions, something difficult to grasp at sixteen, when moral givens went without question and my skepticism was years away. Since then, I have come to see that human constructions—laws, religions, customs, and ideology—have probably always tried to control the reproduction of our species, and one of the most sacred of those constructs was the one that I had unlawfully bypassed—marriage. Anthropology had already confirmed what I was only beginning to suspect in 1965. Writing in 1930, social anthropologist Bronislaw Malinowski concluded that the object of any society "was to prevent the birth of children whose paternity was not absolutely clear" (qtd. in Abrahamson 5). In "Parenthood, the Basis of Social Structure," he established his influential proposition, "The Principle of Legitimacy":

> The most important moral and legal rule concerning the physiological state of kinship is that no child should be brought into this world without a man—and one man at that—assuming the role of sociological fa-

ther, that is guardian and protector, the male link between the child and the rest of the community. I think that this generalization amounts to a universal sociological law, and as such I have called it . . . The Principle of Legitimacy. (qtd. in Laslett, Oosterveen, and Smith 5)

Malinowski's "principle" was never seriously questioned until the 1980s; rather, it stood as a normative rule, one that ethnologists, sociologists, and anthropologists expected to find obeyed in every society, country, and culture.

Now that I have the knowledge and the discourse I lacked at sixteen, I can appreciate just how tightly reproduction and parenthood have been universally bound to marriage and paternity and how hopelessly out of place I was in this schemata. But I was not only inappropriate; by reading anthropologist and structuralist Claude Lévi-Strauss, I learned I was also irrelevant. In the 1940s, Lévi-Strauss described marriage as a social contract between men, not men and women. His theories concerning patrilineal kinship groups demonstrate that they are sustained by the exchange of women to maintain a system that binds *men* together. But I had not been a part of any socially sanctioned exchange; there was no ritual in which a member of the clergy or a representative of the state would ask my father, "Who gives this woman to be married to this man?" There was nothing to bind my father to the father of my baby: no wedding, no promises, not even an acknowledgment of paternity. According to the "moral hobgoblins" of my time, my baby and I were outside the system: extraneous, incomplete, and illegitimate. We had to be concealed, just like Tess and Sorrow.

But that's not all. Historically chastity has been women's most marketable commodity in this exchange system, and I had also lost my most precious feminine attribute, my virginity. At Florence Crittenton, we were acutely aware that this was a huge drawback when it came to the "marriage market." We were more concerned about our lost virginity than our pregnancies, for a while that is, and it's testimony to my naiveté that I eagerly believed an older girl when she told me that if I didn't have sex for seven years, my hymen would grow back and I would be "marriage material" once more. Given the authority of such sexist values, it is no surprise that in literature the preoccupation with women's chastity has always been intense. Even today, as we saw from *Easy A*, women are defined as virgin, wife, and mother, or "slut," "ho," and "skank."[1] That I had willingly had sex with my boyfriend had earned me my mother's "hot pants" attribution and decades more of my own erotic anxieties based on some shady sense of abnormality.

I can see now that "hot pants" is a fairly natural physical attribute given a demeaning label, as are "illegitimate" and "bastard." In her book *Illegitimacy: An Examination of Bastardy*, Jenny Teichman points out that illegitimacy is "not like featherlessness or fecundity. Rather, it is a status, like kingship or slavery or bankruptcy" (10). The illegitimate/legitimate distinction is situated at the crossroads of powerful social institutions that have adhered rigidly to Roman, Christian, English, and American common law, all of which rule that "the only children born legitimate are those who are born in wedlock" (28). Of course, kings and legislatures have legitimized and delegitimized children throughout history, most famously Elizabeth I, who was first illegitimate at birth under English canon law, then legitimized by Henry VII in 1534, later delegitimized in 1536, and finally legitimized in both 1543 and again when she came to the throne in 1559 in an "Act of Recognition," which stated that she was "rightly, lineally and lawfully descended and come of the blood royal of this realm of England" (35). But until the late nineteenth century, for the majority of the English and American public that lived under the auspices of common law, a bastard child was *filius nullius* (no one's child)—no one was obliged in law to care for him or her (60).

In England, until the middle 1600s, about 80% of all recognized out-of-wedlock births resulted in formal charges being brought against the unwed mother who was then incarcerated (Abrahamson 69), as was Hester in her English-ruled American colony of 1650. Nonetheless, laws were also made that enabled a mother or a parish to sue the alleged father of an illegitimate child for a contribution toward its maintenance. These laws were difficult to enforce and, more often than not, the illegitimate infant's total dependence was on its mother at a time when women were economically dependent, property-less, and confined by customs and laws to work for which they received minimal wages or payment in kind (68–69).

The issue of illegitimate birth was of great popular interest in colonial America, especially with the publication of a fictional story (though told as if it were true) in 1747. "The Speech of Polly Baker" was published first in one of London's leading newspapers, the *General Advertiser*, and later in the *Boston Weekly Post-Boy*, the *New York Gazette*, and the *Annapolis Maryland Gazette*. Polly, the heroine of the narrative, has not been sent to jail, but she has been fined and publicly punished four times previously for having children without being married. After the birth of her fifth illegitimate child, Polly states her case to British magistrates, and her speech is "something different in the chronicles of ruined women" (Hall 15). Rather than brimming with shame and regret, Polly argues persuasively that she should not be punished again; instead, the man who fathered her children should be either forced to marry her or fined for fornication. Polly's story has an implausible, even fantastical happy ending; her speech is so persuasive that it not only convinces the court to dispense with her punishment but also moves one of the judges to marry her the next day (Hall 25). Thirty years later, Benjamin Franklin confessed that he had made up the tale of Polly Baker, allegedly "to draw attention to the unfairness of the law which punished mothers, but not fathers, for having children out of wedlock" (Boese). Franklin had good reason to concoct this fable. He had an illegitimate son, William Franklin, whom he acknowledged and supported, and scholars have compiled significant evidence to verify his authorship.

I had never heard of Polly Baker or her speech until I started reading for this project, but I wish I had. She's one of the very few bold, persuasive, and winning unwed mothers I've found. Rather than giving plucky speeches, most unwed mothers suffer the worst possible shame, and it is not their shame alone. Their disgrace spreads, of course, to their illegitimate babies and even to their immediate kin, who, like my parents, expel them from the family to a distant town or even a foreign country. The Pollies and Hesters are few and far between, but their accomplishments, if not quite believable, are satisfying when it comes to indulging my hunger for heroic unwed mothers. Unfortunately Franklin was extraordinary in creating Polly. For his compatriots, there's only tragedy to tell.

Given the popularity of Polly's speech and the importance, as she observes, of adding "to the Number of the King's Subjects, in a new Country that really wants People" (qtd. in Hall 161), it is no surprise that ruined women provide the dramatic intrigue for the first novels published in newly independent America. The fallen woman narrative will not only pervade the American literary tradition, it inaugurates it with William Hill Brown's anonymously published *The Power of Sympathy* (1789), Hannah Webster Foster's *The Coquette* (1797), and "the most reprinted of all American books" (Fiedler 83), *Charlotte Temple*, written by Susann Rowson and published first in England (1791) and then in America (1794). None of these novels, however, contain a clever and resourceful Polly Baker. Their heroines are, more predictably, women who are emotionally and physically devastated by their seducers. Condemning Puritan ideology is applied with rigor, and punishment is the only narrative option. Nina Baym maintains that these first novels are "demoralized literature" in that they "present an unqualified picture of woman as man's inevitable dupe and prey" (*Woman's Fiction* 51), and as we will see, even though these fallen women are demoralizingly tragic, they are not without a certain captivating, popular appeal.

At the close of the eighteenth century, the novel as a genre was under suspicion as proper reading material for young ladies who were learning to read in greater numbers. Their education was becoming more and more imperative, for they "were perceived as being the instructors of the nation's children" (Mulford xvii). Based on my own avid reading at sixteen and the enthusiastic way that I took my beloved heroines to heart, traditional educators were probably right to fear that reading frivolous novels for entertainment could do young women harm by appealing to their inexperienced imaginations. In her *Vindication of the Rights of Women* (1792), Mary Wollstonecraft wisely acknowledges the immense power of fiction over the developing character and warns that for "the fanciful female character, so prettily drawn by poets and novelists . . . virtue becomes a relative idea" (283–84). In her own novel, *Mary: A Fiction* (1788), Wollstonecraft denounces Mary's mother Eliza for her self-indulgent failure as a mother, a failure exacerbated by obsession with novels:

> [Eliza] was chaste . . . but then, to make amends for this seeming self-denial, she read all the sentimental novels, dwelt on the love-scenes, and, had she thought while she read, her mind would have been contaminated; as she accompanied the lovers to the lonely arbors, and would walk with them by the clear light of the moon. (7–8)

Eliza may not have literally fallen, but her reading passions are almost as corrupting as actual licentiousness. Patricia Spacks argues that romantic novels are "themselves direct effusions of fantasy" (Spacks 39), specifically female fantasies of sexual, passionate ardor that are repressed by the superego—a superego that is strictly imposed on culturally refined young women. Yet because such novels are so appealing to the unconscious, and can nurture as yet unrealized sexual fantasies, there was a fear that such novels could "act on the inexperienced imagination as a literal intoxicant" (Baym *Woman's Fiction* 52). Perhaps there still is, especially given the cultural misgivings concerning the massive popularity among teenagers of Stephanie Meyer's *Twilight* series. In 2008, Meyer had to defend the fiercely erotic intensity of the Edward/Bella/Jacob triangle by maintaining that her series actually encourages premarital abstinence.

I do not want to join the chorus of old-school traditionalists who argue that reading romantic novels is "bad" for young readers and that moralistic novels would be "better." Their one-to-one correlations are overly simplified and highly problematic. Yet my own sexual initiation bears out some of this line of reasoning: a romantic narrative did seem to encourage my adolescent passions. The novel I just finished reading days before I agreed to have sex with my boyfriend was *Wuthering Heights*. Many things conspired to affect my behavior: popular culture, emotional neediness, and especially hormones. And it is worth noting that as a reader, I failed to consider that nothing works out well for Heathcliff and Catherine Earnshaw. But I skimmed that part of the novel: I wanted the passion, the yearning, the obsession. I wanted to say "I am Heathcliff!"

In 1847 *Wuthering Heights* was censured for its violence, brutality, and "coarseness," and Charlotte Brontë had to defend her sister Emily's novel as a Christian allegory ("Emily Bronte: Publication of *Wuthering Heights*"). It's no wonder that fifty years prior, in 1790, novelists were obliged to defend their novels as educational tools of reason and judgment. In so doing, they echo Sir Philip Sidney's long-held dictum from 1579: the purpose of poesy is to teach and delight, specifically, to teach virtue (*Apology for Poetry*). Along with reading *Wuthering Heights*, perhaps I should have also been reading *The Power of Sympathy*, or *The Coquette* and *Charlotte Temple*. Colonial novelists were obligated to teach gullible female readers like me to abstain categorically from all coquetry, or the consequences would be dire indeed. Brown, Foster, and Rowson had to demonstrate that although their narratives dealt with unrestrained passions, their purpose was to expose degenerate souls, defeat licentiousness, conquer ignorance, enable readers' judgment, and advance virtue.

THE POWER OF SYMPATHY

In *The Power of Sympathy*, William Hill Brown immediately establishes his didactic and moralistic purpose on his dedication page: "to the young ladies of United Columbia These Volumes Intended to represent the Specious Causes, and to Expose the fatal Consequences, of seduction; To inspire the Female Mind With a Principle of Self Complacency, and to Promote the Economy of Human Life" (Brown 5). Early in the novel, the Reverend Holmes points out, "Most of the Novels . . . with which our female libraries are overrun, are built on a foundation not placed on strict morality." Such novels, the Reverend insists, fail to expose vice and recommend virtue, and are "unfit to form the minds of women, of friends, or of wives" (Brown 21). In fact, the impeccable Mrs. Holmes observes: "Many fine girls have been ruined by reading Novels" (25). Given all these serious reservations concerning the genre, Brown underscores the benefits of his epistolary novel by reiterating in his preface: "Of the Letters before us, it is necessary to remark, . . . the dangerous Consequences of seduction are exposed, and the Advantages of female education set forth and recommended" (7).

As a footnote to one of Mrs. Holmes's early letters, Brown recounts *The Massachusetts Centinel's* (1788) story of a certain Miss Whitman, the real-life woman on whom Foster's *The Coquette* would be based. She was a "great reader of novels and romances and having imbibed her ideas of *the characters of men*, from those fallacious sources, became vain and coquetish" (23). If women like Miss Whitman are going to read novels, which I can testify they do and will continue to do, then Brown must provide them with a novel that will instruct them by using "characters of 'good' virtue and probity" to comment upon the "characters whose bodies and sexual relations could be considered in a promiscuous light" (Mulford xix). In so doing, Brown attempts to represent the pleasures of fantasy while presumably keeping his virtuous and sensible characters firmly in control of the narrative.

Brown's novel proceeds to tell disastrous tales of not just one unfortunate seduction but three: Ophelia Shepherd is seduced by her brother-in-law, Mr. Martin; Fidelia is seduced by the scoundrel Williams; and Maria Fawcett is seduced by the Honourable Mr. J. Harrington.[2] The results of these downfalls are tragic indeed. Each woman is held accountable for bringing about her ruin and each pays dearly for having done so.

Brown's rendition of Ophelia Shepherd's undoing is indicative of what will be American culture's ongoing, unappeasable appetite for salacious stories of fallen women and their plights. Her tragedy is Brown's retelling of an actual scandal involving a prominent Boston family whom Brown so thinly disguises that "apparently everyone in Boston knew on what the episode . . . was based. The members of this family . . . attempted to suppress the book by buying and destroying all copies within reach" (Benson 190), but stories like Ophelia's will not be suppressed. Brown's fictional Ophelia allows herself to be lulled by her brother-in-law Martin's "flattery and dissimulation" into a "dream of insensibility." Ophelia's sins are Persephone's sins: her narcissism and credulity lead her to eat the pomegranate seed (39). After giving birth to Martin's son (and nephew), she wants nothing more than to live a retiring, domestic life, hoping that the "the sincerity of her repentance" might restore "the peace and harmony of the family" (39). But as we have seen, unwed mothers and their illegitimate babies are outsiders; they cannot be peacefully reintegrated into the conventional family. The enraged, implacable patriarch, Ophelia's father, insists that she publically name her seducer, no matter the dishonorable results, but when the day comes for the confrontation, Ophelia's distress gives way to horror and she drinks poison rather than face her father and her seducer in public. As she dies, her last words are a plea for anonymity: "let my crime be forgotten with my name" (40) though, of course, that is the last thing she can hope for. Even though her story is not at all original, it is much too salacious to be squelched; its repetition is inevitable. The lesson drawn at this rendition's conclusion places the onus for the tragedy neither on Martin nor on Ophelia's father but squarely on Ophelia, who "had no friend to enlighten her understanding," and whose "miserable life" had become so "insupportable, there was no oblation but in death" (41). Brown serves as the reader's teacher/friend, driving home propriety's warning: "a prudent pilot will shun those rocks upon which others have been dashed to pieces" (42). The unambiguous morality is hammered in, but not sufficiently for Brown's pedantic purposes.

The next subplot in the novel involves Fidelia, who is happily betrothed to Henry, her childhood friend, but when "the gay Williams" arrives and "is assiduous in his attentions to her," she is distracted and "her little heart is lifted up" (51). Again, we hear echoes of Persephone as Fidelia falls for the seducer's narcissistic trap. Williams lures her to a carriage and carries her off. She is soon rescued by some young men from the village, but not before Henry, "urged forward by the torments of disappointed love," plunges into the river and drowns. When Fidelia learns of Henry's fate, she goes mad. Months later Mr. Worthy, another unfaultable correspondent of the novel, finds Fidelia wandering the fields, now a "poor maniack [sic]," singing a melancholy song in which she blames herself for "hearing the stranger's tender tale" (49) and falling prey to "the baleful art of the seducer" (52).

The third victim is Maria Fawcett, a young woman "arrayed in all the delightful charms of vivacity, modesty and sprightliness" who is "deluded by the promises and flattery" of the married Mr. Harrington, who seduces her and, in so doing, "subscribes her name to the catalogue of infamy" (68). Maria does not commit suicide, but she does "welcome death as the angel of peace" (73) and obligingly expires after giving birth to her illegitimate daughter:

"such is the consequences of seduction . . . the picture . . . of a ruined female" (69). Still, we are told, Maria's death washes out her guilt forever, because, of course, Maria was guilty: "When a woman, by her imprudence, exposes herself, she is accessory; for though her heart may be pure, her conduct is a tacit invitation to the Seducer" (73).

Although the nefarious seducers are consistently condemned throughout the novel, its didactic purpose is first and foremost directed explicitly to young women like the ones Hannah Webster Foster describes in her commentary *The Boarding School: or, Lessons of a Preceptress to Her Pupils* (1798), girls whose imaginations might allow dangerous "romantic pictures of love, beauty, and magnificence . . . [to] lead to impure desires . . . [and] pervert the judgment, mislead the affections, and blind the understanding" (qtd. in Baym *American Women Writers* 22). Ophelia, Fidelia, and Maria must pay with either their lives or their sanity for letting "the blush of modesty" wear off and their hearts "grow torpid" and sink to depravity (Brown 73). Readers are told again and again that women who allow their "desire to be admired" to come first will fall into "meanness . . . Ruin and contempt," "the invariable concomitants" of female "immorality" (74). As an exiled unwed mother at Florence Crittenton, I never thought of myself exactly in Brown's terms. I didn't grow torpid or mean, though I certainly felt ruined and contemptible. But the novels Madame Lapaire loaned me while I was there let me temporarily escape from hard realities, and my voraciousness for novels has never abated. Ironically this passion for the genre eventually evolved into a career choice. Florence Crittenton was a strange boarding school, but the isolation and uninterrupted time I was given to read allowed me to draw my own "romantic pictures of love, beauty, and magnificence." The romantic choices I had made months before, although not perverse, had certainly been injudicious, and my affections had been misled. Of course, I can't really blame that on Emily Brontë, and I'm not sure it would have done any good, but I do wish I had been given William Hill Brown to read as well for at least a modicum of balance.

Ophelia's illegitimate son is never accounted for, but Maria's illegitimate daughter, Harriot, must pay dearly for her mother's seduction. She is raised by Rev. Holmes only to fall passionately in love with Mr. Harrington's son, not knowing he is her brother. Their elopement is halted when the truth is revealed, but Harriot is so horrified by the unnatural passions she felt for her brother that she dies and Mr. Harrington's son commits suicide. The novel ends with one more warning, the inscription he had written for their monument before putting a bullet in his brain:

Stranger! Contemplate well before you part,
And take this serious counsel to thy heart:
Does some fair female of unspotted fame,
Salute thee, smiling, with a father's name,
Bid her detest the fell Seducer's wiles,
Who smiles to win—and murders as he smiles. (103)

My response to Brown's conclusion is a rueful sigh. His stories were meant as cautionary tales so women would not stray. I want to believe that we do not need such "lessons" anymore, that they only serve as cultural artifacts to show how gravely women were punished for breaches of conventional morality. But my frame of mind is more ambivalent. Even as I dismiss Brown's "lessons" as dated and excessive, I keep thinking of the line from the old Peter, Paul, and Mary song that repeatedly asks, "When will they ever learn?" It would be nice to claim that there are no more castigating lessons to learn, that women no longer have to fear the dangers of sexual adventurousness, that they no longer risk becoming the victims of moralistic ideology, but I remain in the subjunctive mood: such claims are not yet ensured.

THE COQUETTE

In the first edition of *The Coquette: Or, the History of Eliza Wharton; A Novel; Founded on Fact*, the author, Hannah Webster Foster, remains anonymous, identified only as a lady of Massachusetts. But her insecurity at being identified must have been assuaged when her novel became extraordinarily popular, with more than thirty editions published by the mid-nineteenth century. Foster does not go to the extreme efforts Brown does to justify the melodrama of her novel, but her purpose is equally didactic. From her protagonist Eliza Wharton's second letter on, we are warned again and again of the dangers incurred when young, effusively cheerful and socially ambitious women earn the label "coquette." Although this novel and *Charlotte Temple* were dismissed by male critics as "melodramas of beset womanhood" (qtd. in Baym "Melodramas" 9), their ongoing contemporary appeal has to do with their heroines' plights that still resonate with young women today. *The Coquette* is always a favorite with my female students. Flirtatious and fun-loving, Eliza is like them, and they readily identify with her quest for social independence.

Described by one suitor, Mr. Boyer, as "naturally of a gay disposition" (111) and by another as "gay, volatile, apparently thoughtless of everything but present enjoyment" (117), Eliza cannot account for her "bewitching charms" that keep pestering admirers close at hand (112). Her friends, Lucy, Mrs. Richman, and Julia, warn her repeatedly that her lighthearted flirtatiousness may put her in danger, that although the path she is taking may appear to be "strowed [sic] with flowers, when contemplated by [her] lively imagination," it is "after all, a slippery, thorny [one]" (113). Indeed her eventual seducer, Major Sanford, identifies her early on as a coquette and, because she is such, he feels entirely justified to "avenge [his] sex, by retaliating the mischiefs, she meditates against [men]" (118).

Although her ultimate purpose will be to warn against coquetry, Foster is more fictionally sophisticated than Brown and creates a move complex protagonist in Eliza than Brown can manage in Ophelia, Fidelia, or Maria. Like my women's studies students, Eliza wants to exercise her free will and explore the adventures that her popularity seems to promise before agreeing to the predictable domesticity of marriage and motherhood. She postpones accepting Mr. Boyer's proposal of marriage, knowing full well that she does not yet have the prudence to be a minister's wife. She admits readily that the charms of youth and freedom beckon her, not the confinement marriage necessarily would demand (126). Naively, Eliza claims she just wants friendships with her suitors, a claim that more than two hundred year later makes me shake my head with misgiving. How many times have I asked a straight male friend in my life, "Can't we just be friends?" Chummy but asexual "friendships" with straight men have been difficult for me to negotiate and have rarely lasted. Not unexpectedly, they don't work well for Eliza in colonial America either.

Eliza insists that "after a while (when [she has] sowed all [her] wild oats)," she intends "to make a tolerable [wife]" (158), but as Smith-Rosenberg notes at this point in history—the aftermath of the American Revolution—such "liberty or 'freedom' for women" is inconceivable (173). "Certain inalienable rights" such as "life liberty and the pursuit of happiness" were not extended to American women. Eliza is faced with the tenacious either/or options for women: angel or monster, subservient helpmate or coquette, virtuous or fallen, virgin or whore. She insists on asserting her right to control her own body, but in doing so, she risks proving Alexander Pope's postulation correct: "Every woman is, at heart, a rake" (qtd. in Foster 146). She is not licentious but her unrestrained exuberance makes her highly vulnerable to Major Sanford's machinations. Though today my students applaud her for speaking her mind and claiming "a space for certain freedoms of actions," in her cultural milieu, her nonconformity guarantees social self-destruction (Mulford xivi).

Sure enough, when Mr. Boyer discovers Eliza alone with Sanford, he accuses her of many things, including levity, extravagance, vanity, indiscretion, and "rendering him the dupe of coquetting artifice" (179). He abruptly withdraws his marriage proposal. To her credit, Eliza regrets leading Mr. Boyer on while she dallied with Sanford, and when Sanford departs without having proposed to her, she realizes she has been played for a fool, gives up "her quest to fuse independence and pleasure" (Smith-Rosenberg 177), and becomes a lonely, depressed recluse. Foster suggests that Eliza's depression is brought on not by her disappointment over the failed love affair with Major Sanford but because she realizes that as a woman, she cannot have autonomy and pleasure if she also wants respectability. When Sanford returns unhappily married to a rich woman, Eliza falls further into depression, so much so that Julia describes Eliza's mind as "not perfectly right" (Foster 202). Perhaps as a result, she gives in to Sanford's sexual insistence. Although Foster gives us no particulars of Eliza's seduction, we understand it is without pleasure or passion. The coquette has become "the ruined, lost Eliza" and expects a child.

Smith-Rosenberg maintains that Sanford's seduction is actually secondary. Eliza has first "fallen victim . . . to the authoritative male discourse of her age" (177), and this is certainly correct. Eliza cannot find herself in the discourse of the patrilineal exchange system. Once she succumbs to Sanford and becomes an unwed mother, she is evicted from the system. She must don the damning label of "fallen" and finds herself so "polluted" and such a "reproach and disgrace" that she goes into hiding. With "not a single wish to live," her only hope is that she be able to carry her illegitimate child "with [her] to a state of eternal rest" (Foster 223). She and her baby die among strangers.

The consequences of Eliza's bid for even temporary autonomy and pleasure are dire indeed. Although we might read her attempt with sympathy and even argue that she manages to set an example of how one might subvert the ideal of "virtuous womanhood," her defeat is so absolute that the merit of rebellion is hardly the lesson we take from the novel. Rather, Foster makes clear that Eliza's sexual fall is of her own doing. Since she played the temptress, she must pay. Even her seducer blames her for playing what we would term "hard to get" and "leading him on." He justifies his actions using military jargon:

> I should have given over the pursuit long ago, but for the hopes of success I entertained from her parleying with me, and in reliance upon her own strength, endeavoring to combat, and counteract my designs . . . If a lady will consent to enter the lists against the antagonist of her honor, she may be sure of losing the prize. (217)

Eliza's effort to make her own way may be tolerable, but pausing to dally recklessly with the man she finds most attractive marks her as sexual bait in a trap of her own making. When she's caught, she's found guilty for assuming she could control her body and her fate. Flirtatious "parleying" with a powerful man is dangerous, then and now. I am always dismayed when my students shake their heads knowingly as we discuss *The Coquette*'s conclusion. They understand Foster's lesson all too well: even in their world, the sexy tease can easily become the sexual victim who "asked for it."

If Eliza represents the fallen woman, her correspondents, Julia and Lucy, serve as virtuous womanly paragons and conclude the novel with moralistic platitudes. Their final letters to one another erase any lingering subversive implications by listing the bitter costs young women will pay if they encourage the attentions of a "rake." Lucy, ever dutiful and sensibly married in the course of the novel, sums up its didactic purpose by issuing a final warning against coquetry: "I wish it engraved upon every heart, that virtue alone, independent of the trappings of wealth, the parade of equipage, and the adulation of gallantry, can secure lasting felicity. From the melancholy story of Eliza Wharton, let the American fair learn to reject with disdain every insinuation derogatory to their true dignity and honor" (241). Lucy underscores one of the cornerstones of courtship: it remains a woman's task not only to control herself (and deny her desires) but also to control the irascible rake, who will persist in her undoing. And although Lucy may call it "virtue," it's virginity she's alluding to. In Hannah Webster Foster's world, virginity is the crucial ingredient to a woman's honor; it is the collateral in the marriage market, the only guarantee to female safekeeping in the patrilineal paradigm, and yet, it is always under siege!

CHARLOTTE TEMPLE

The other wildly popular seduction novel of the time was *Charlotte Temple*, the story of an English schoolgirl, Charlotte, who is seduced by Lieutenant Montraville, brought to America, and abandoned. Leslie Fiedler hated the novel, declaring it "an unwitting travesty of *Clarissa Harlow*" without subtlety, passion, style, or distinction. "What was mythic literature has become subliterate myth," asserts Fiedler (97). Rowson herself confessed that her talent was small. But, as Ann Douglas observes, "a book's popularity is itself a kind of criticism, complex evidence that the best-seller in question expressed the hopes and fears of people who found them nowhere else so forcibly put" (ix). Like Brown and Foster, Rowson touches a highly sensitive nerve in the psyches of young women, appealing to the anxious ambivalence they must have had about seduction. Female readers seemed to dread seduction and desire it, hate lasciviousness and love it, yearn for self-sufficiency and long to be overpowered. And they still do! As I write, the number 1, number 2, and number 3 best sellers on the *New York Times* "Best Sellers" list are the erotic novels by the pseudonymous E. L. James about female submission and male dominance: *Fifty Shades of Grey*, *Fifty Shades Darker*, and *Fifty Shades Free* (May 27, 2012). Most reviewers hate these novels as much as Leslie Fiedler hated *Charlotte Temple*. Their comments range from "poorly written," to "insipid," "juvenile," and "vacuous." Other reviewers find the novels' eye-popping popularity scandalous; but most readers find them completely addicting. No wonder! The novels fit right into the virgin/lecher tradition that got widespread publishing started in America. Susan Rowson knew her female audience well and wrote a novel that would appeal to women's sexual fantasies and their fears. And just as thousands of *Twilight* fans now make the trek to tiny Forks, Washington, to see where Bella and her vampire lover got their start, thousands of Rowson's readers made the pilgrimage to Trinity Churchyard in New York to visit the grave of Charlotte Stanley who, with Rowson's tacit encouragement, was believed to be the real-life prototype for the fictional Charlotte Temple (Douglas xvi).

Rowson's fictional Charlotte, like the archetype, the innocent Persephone, leads a sheltered early life, protected by doting parents. Her sin, if there is one, is naïveté, especially in trusting her worldly teacher, Mademoiselle La Rue, and Mademoiselle's "friends," Lieutenants Montraville and Belcour. Once this threesome lures her away from her parents' protection, she is unable to defend herself against seduction. Socially powerless, she can neither break through the silence and isolation that Montraville and Belcour impose on her, nor even begin to outwit their trickery. Like so many fictional unwed mothers, she falls helplessly into a fatal melancholia and dies shortly after giving birth to her illegitimate daughter, Lucy.

What are we to learn from the feeble, pathetic Charlotte Temple, especially given that Charlotte herself learns nothing? Rather than bildungsromans, in which we would witness the coming-of-age and moral growth of our protagonists, *The Power of Sympathy*, *The Coquette*, and *Charlotte Temple* have nothing to do with their protagonists' moral education. But they have everything to do with the readers'. The novels are meant as warnings. Readers are given notice: when women's bodies get out of control, everything goes wrong; they are infected, so much so that early death is a given. In Rowson's novel, Charlotte's "body usurps the text" and "becomes a metaphor of desire as *symptom*, as a sign of illness" (xxxv). Charlotte's desire/illness is so poisonous that she is allowed no recovery from her fatal melancholia/pregnancy/childbirth. There is no coming-of-age; there is only death.

Charlotte's daughter, Lucy, on the other hand, remains compliantly and conscientiously under the protective umbrella of her adopted family, and is not condemned to death, though she does have to pay for her mother's sins and her own illegitimacy in the novel *Lucy Temple*, published under the titles *Charlotte's Daughter* or *The Three Orphans* (1828). The menace of incest takes over the plot, as it does for Harriot in *The Power of Sympathy*, and Lucy, like Harriot, is prevented in the nick of time from marrying her half brother. Again, like Harriot, Lucy is so devastated by the disclosure that she suffers a near fatal illness. Unlike Harriot, she recovers, but she must still pay. Rather than marry, she is sentenced to a life of chastity in a little seminary where she can minister "to the minds and hearts of . . . young persons" (Rowson 241). Rowson is unable to rewrite the seduction narrative. True to form, she must punish her fallen, unwed mother with death and her illegitimate daughter by relegating her to a nunnery.

Rachel Brownstein observes, "Reading *Clarissa* is like being trapped in a nightmare of trying to escape and knowing the exits will be sealed up before you get to them" (41). *The Power of Sympathy*, *The Coquette*, and *Charlotte Temple* seal the exits as well. Everything that happens feels like a replay. Imprudent unmarried women are served up for our own edification. They flirt; they're seduced; they cross "an absolute line between virtuous and nonvirtuous sexual conduct in women" (Spacks 27). Once their virginity is gone, marriage, the opportunity to participate in orderly sexual life, motherhood, and community, is forbidden. There's nothing left to do but die!

These novels are so heavy-handed it's hard to imagine why they once were considered dangerous for impressionable young women. After all, at the end of the day, they verify only what's permissible. Nonetheless, they also make their readers more familiar with the illicit. Smith-Rosenberg locates their danger in their ability to call "forth [their] readers' repressed desires, permitting those desires to be vicariously enjoyed [as well as] . . . vicariously punished" (167). If so, the novels "most fully represent the conflicts and contradictions" women faced at the end of the eighteenth century in America. American males were espousing the rhetoric of individualism and self-determination, but American women were still under the rigid restraints of domesticity. As Cathy N. Davidson maintains, "*The Coquette* and other eighteenth century sentimental novels are ultimately about silence, subservience, and stasis (the accepted attributes of woman as traditionally defined) in contradistinction to conflicting impulses toward self-expression, independence, and action" (xix). Neither Brown, nor Foster, nor Rowson can imagine a life beyond the social parameters of female powerlessness.

In 1798, Foster reminded her students how lucky they were to live in a country "where the female mind [was] unshackled by the restraints of tyrannical custom" (qtd. in Baym *American Women Writers* 29). But there are few examples of such unshackling in either her novel, Brown's, or Foster's. In those novels, obedient women who follow convention are rewarded with "good reputations" (191) that allow them to move up the orderly ranks of propriety from one sexual designation to another: from virgin, to wife, to mother. Their bodies and their minds remain chained to "tyrannical custom." Polly Baker gives us a brief glance at the possibility of an unwed mother's potential, but her story is ultimately a pipe dream. The women who deviate from this progression of propriety are ruthlessly punished for their sexual downfalls, as are their babies for their illegitimacy.

Students are always glad to move on after finishing these novels; when they write about them, their analyses are laced with gratitude that unwed motherhood is no longer nearly a death sentence. Provided with the cultural background and sexual norms for Hester's story, they look forward to *The Scarlet Letter*, to meeting Hester and witnessing her ability to endure punishment and banishment with dignity. It took me a long time to see that Hester may be just as much an unrealistic fantasy as Polly Baker, but it's hard to give up on our romantic heroines, whether they play to our fantasies of submission and domination or our dreams of agency and autonomy.

CHAPTER 2

Theodore Dreiser's All-Giving Angel
Jennie Gerhardt

My growing congregation of fallen women from *The Power of Sympathy*, *The Coquette*, *Charlotte Temple*, and *The Scarlet Letter* increases dramatically when Hardy creates in 1891 Tess Durbeyfield. Even though I recognized myself in Tess while I was at Florence Crittenton, I did not want to emulate her as I did Hester. Like Ophelia, Fidelia, Maria, and Eliza, Tess is unable to achieve the autonomy that Hester acquires in *The Scarlet Letter*. Instead, she pays a staggering price for being raped by her employer and professed cousin, Alec d'Urberville. Tess's illegitimate child, Sorrow, dies in infancy, and her husband, Angel Clare, deserts her when she confesses her past to him. Angel leaves her destitute, desperate, and once again vulnerable to Alec's unremitting lasciviousness. In the end, even as she is put to death for murdering Alec, she remains Hardy's faultless maiden, crushed by the greed and pride of others but as blameless as the ravished Persephone, as worthy as the saintly Hester. As Hester's literary descendant, she embellishes the mythology of the scarlet woman by detailing its cruel injustices.

Our next fallen angel, Jennie Gerhardt, adds more realistic depth to our archetype of the ruined maid. A colleague gave me a copy of the novel *Jennie Gerhardt* years ago, long before I had started the process of telling my own story of seduction, pregnancy, childbirth, and loss. I was still deep in my own closet of unhealthy dissembling, and I can still recall the way I cringed when I perused the back of the paperback. Just the brief blurb about Jennie's misfortunes hit too many painful psychological buttons. "Why would my friend give me this book?" I wondered. "Does she suspect? Did she catch a glimpse of the scarlet *A* that I've been so scrupulously hiding?" In fact, she knew nothing of my past. I hadn't revealed a thing. She had received a free copy of the novel in the mail and since she already had one, had passed it on to me because I regularly taught an American literature survey. But I was far from ready for Jennie's story and shoved the novel to the back of my book-shelf. Twenty years passed, and I eventually found the emotional safety net I needed to relinquish my secret: I began to live openly and write honestly and as a result, I was reunited with my daughter. More than ever, I was invested in the cultural, historical, and literary chronicles of unwed mothers. Moved by my doomed heroines of the eighteenth and nineteenth centuries, I pulled *Jennie Gerhardt* from the back of the shelf and committed myself to reading it by including it on a syllabus I was creating for a senior seminar called Fallen Women in American Fiction. The novel I had dreaded opening turned out to be a favorite for many of my students and for me as well.

Published in 1911, twenty years after *Tess of the d'Urbervilles* and sixty years after *The Scarlet Letter*, one can easily see, as critic Carol Schwartz affirms, that Theodore Dreiser had been "clearly impressed by Hardy's han-dling of his heroine [Tess]" (20). In Jennie, he creates a flawless maiden who, like Tess, is an innocent, which again, like Tess, makes her easy sexual prey for a powerful man whose rank and wealth allow him to operate with im-punity. In this chapter, I want to talk about Jennie's seduction and the way that her lifelong punishment repeats and supplements the cultural mythol-ogy of the fallen woman and the burdens she bears. When writing about Hester's red insignia, Charles Feidelson argues that her scarlet *A* "opens" an imaginative reality that transcends time and place. It is no longer tied to the material reality of Salem, Massachusetts, 1650 (9). Taking Feidelson at his word, one could argue that Dreiser "opens" the imaginative reality of the *A* on late Victorian Midwestern America, tying it this time to the material reality of Columbus, Ohio, 1880. Of course, Jennie has no actual *A* to bear; Hester and her embroidered badge are long gone. But Jennie is marked by her unwed pregnancy and must bear its ongoing burdens. The scarlet *A* is out of sight, but its onus plays its part in the ongoing literary chronicle of the ruined woman. Jennie's transgressions and her virtues become part of this scarlet legacy as it threads one generation to the next.

H. L. Mencken was perhaps the first to draw a comparison between *Jen-nie Gerhardt* and *The Scarlet Letter* in his review in the *Smart Set*: *Jennie Gerhardt* is "the best American novel I have ever read . . . Am I forgetting *The Scarlet Letter*, *The Rise of Silas Lapham* etc., etc? . . . No: I have all these good and bad books in mind. I have read them and survived them . . . And yet in the face of them . . . it seems to me at this moment that *Jennie Gerhardt* stands apart from all of them, and a bit above them" (qtd. in Totten 37). But getting the novel into print had been no easy task. Frederick Duneka, the general manager at Harper and Brothers, agreed to publish it only after he expurgated 16,000 words and completely rewrote much of what remained (West "Introduction" xv). In so doing, the male protagonist's "fate becomes the dominant motif," and Duneka "all but erases Jennie's subjectivity" (Lingeman 14, Ross 39). Duneka was gratified by Mencken's review and relieved when *Outlook* editor Hamilton Wright Mabie declared Dreiser's "picture of 'Jennie' . . . very winning. One has no sense of moral dirt." Duneka was afraid that even after his extensive revisions, Harper's would be accused of publishing a "sex novel" (qtd. in Totten 39). James L. W. West, who in 1992 edited the edition of the unexpurgated novel that I use for my discussion, observes that the 1911 edition was a text "that was socialized and domesticated by cultural forces of its time," but the restored edition is a "blunt, carefully documented piece of social analysis" ("Composition" 442). Annemarie Koning Whaley agrees, describing the 1992 edition as a probing critique of "the ethical failings of American business . . . [and] the greed and inhumanity of men who . . . willingly sacrifice their own family members for material success and power" (25). Valerie Ross very nearly echoes William Hill Brown's justifications for *The Power of Sympathy* when she praises the 1992 edition for its pedagogical value: the restored *Jennie Gerhardt* "instruct[s] readers about a particular social prohibition—premarital sex for women—and the consequences attendant on its violation" (29).

I doubt Dreiser's novel will discourage premarital sex, but it is a powerful indictment of American capitalism. More importantly, it also interrogates sentimental[1] representations of fallen woman and offers a bitter critique of patriarchal entitlement and class privilege. By using West's 1992 edition with the "original sexual frankness of the narrative reinstated" (West "Introduction" xvii), I want to embrace Duneka's greatest fear and read *Jennie Gerhardt* as a "sex novel" and as a more realistic rendition of the ordeal of unwed motherhood than Hawthorne's romantic fairy tale.

The novel's realism may have come about because the material for it came from Dreiser's own life. His sister Mame was seduced as a teenager by an older man and gave birth at home to a stillborn infant. Later she set up housekeeping with a well-to-do business executive, Austin Brennan, in Rochester, New York. Though Mame and Brennan claimed to be married, "Brennan's family was scandalized and never accepted Mame, causing a permanent breach between Brennan and his brothers and sisters" (West "Introduction" vii). Dreiser's novel, originally called "The Transgressor," taps directly into this background. It opens in Columbus, Ohio, in 1880, where Jennie is one of the legions that Dreiser knew well from his own grim childhood in Indiana. She is just eighteen, wide-eyed, timid, and ashamed of her abject poverty, and "it is with [Jennie] that Dreiser's deepest sympathies lie" (Elias 4). With her father ill and out of work, it's up to Jennie and her mother to stave off the hunger, cold, and unforgiving debts confronting the large family. When they find work as domestics in an imposing hotel adjacent to the state capital, they meet Senator Brander, a distinguished, middle-aged bachelor and Jennie's first seducer.

In the manuscript he submitted to Harper's before Duneka's ruthless editing, Dreiser follows Hawthorne's example and casts his heroine as a saint-like, "natural, romantic … pagan Nature sprite" (Lingeman 10).[2] Uneducated and unskilled, Jennie is younger and much less capable than Hester, but like Hester, she is "barren of the art of the coquette" (Dreiser 33). This soon-to-be fallen angel is not only morally chaste, she is representative of what Dreiser sees as a purer mode of being. For Jennie and those like her who are unspoiled by worldly materialism, "Life … is a true wonderland, a thing of infinity beauty, which could they but wander into it, wonderingly, would be heaven enough. Opening their eyes, they see a conformable and perfect world" (16). However, to "the world of the material … of the actual … of flesh," Jennie's purity is a tantalizing lure: "The hands of the actual are forever reaching toward such as these—forever seizing greedily upon them. It is of such that the bondservants are made" (16). Dreiser knew "the odds [were] stacked against Jennie" from observing the lives of his own sisters and their friends who when working as domestics servants were often "subject to mistreatment, rudeness, and sexual harassment" (West "Introduction" viii) or even more horribly, as in Tess's case, to rape.

Clearly, for both Hawthorne and Dreiser, there should be no hint of debauchery in their heroines. Their reading publics may have been eager for tales of seduction, but only the seduction of noble beauties like Hester or "delightful," "gentle" "day-dreamer[s]" like Jennie, vulnerable, but "beyond … the common herd" (72). Although Dreiser himself loved "the people," he also sometimes considered them "potato minds" (qtd. in Lydon 98), so it was crucial to him that Jennie be penniless yet charming and clean, uneducated yet innately fine minded. When Jennie desperately and guilelessly turns to

Senator Brander to get her brother released from jail (he is guilty of nothing more than taking surplus coal to warm the family's freezing home), Brander exclaims, "You angel! You sister of mercy!" (73) as he seduces her. Jennie is so inexperienced that she does not fully comprehend the physical consequences of intercourse and has no "clear sense of what happened" (74). Befitting Dreiser's naturalistic belief in the inexorable cruelty of fate, it is only after Brander dies of heart failure six weeks later that Jennie realizes she is pregnant.

That her condition is the result of one bewildered moment of submission to a commanding social superior who takes advantage of her confusion is clear; Dreiser does not question Jennie's morality. In fact, for Dreiser, as it was for Hardy, her pregnancy is "a part of her womanhood, a fact of nature to be accepted, even praised" (Elias 4). But for Jennie's parents, the pregnancy immediately marks her as "ruined." Her religion-bound father brands her a "street-walker" and banishes her from the house. Like many "ruined" women, she is more sinned against than sinner. She emerges into the night, "lamblike" with no "realization of her own ability and self-reliance" (95). She is pushed out into a new life, but not one where she, like Hester, can seize the initiative of self-determination. Hester, my American proto-feminist, is equipped with education and skill. She can lead a life both of exile and of service and still support herself and her child; she has the resolve to insist that Pearl is hers alone to raise; she can seize the opportunity to defy Chillingworth and persuade Dimmesdale (at least momentarily) to flee Boston with her. And she can return of her own accord to Boston and take up the A again after she seeing Pearl married into European nobility. But Jennie is ill-equipped to exercise much control over her life; she does little more than drift, buffeted by the needs and demands of others. Dreiser follows her "as if he were watching twigs and leaves float by in a stream" (Lydon 100). To compare Jennie to an inanimate object like a twig may be hyperbolic, but given her bewildered state where men can use her body at their pleasure, the metaphor is compelling.

Banished from home, "She [is] outside now" (88), cast out by those Dreiser describes as strutting, indifferent, selfish little men and made to feel "that degradation was her portion, and sin the foundation ... of her state" (93). Of course, it is not just "little men" but a much more implacable, sinister patriarchal ideology that marginalizes her. The code that insists on ostracism for the unwed mother is imposed, and although Jennie is not jailed or pilloried, her punishment is not entirely unlike Hester's: "Jennie [is] left alone" (94), but not before she is "a marked example of the result of evil-doing," "a mark for the wit and a butt for scorn of men" (94). Even so, Jennie's "naturally sunny disposition" (104) will not be dampened and she maintains her attitude that "life at worst or best [is] beautiful" (95).

In the late nineteenth century, surrendering children for adoption was rare, but Jennie may have lost her baby. Historian Ellen Herman notes, "In 1910 there were well over one thousand orphanages in the United States . . . some [housing] more than one thousand inmates" made up of foundlings (abandoned children), orphans, and illegitimate children (23). Jennie's baby is saved from this fate when Jennie's father reluctantly relents and lets her come home. When her baby is born, "there awaken[s] in Jennie a tremendous yearning toward it." She resolves, "This [is] *her* child . . . and it need[s] her care" (97). As the baby becomes a much-loved member of the family, even Jennie's rigid father is eventually won over by the "little outcast," and the shade of "lingering disgust that had possessed him . . . disappear[s]" (117). With his baptismal blessing, the stigma of illegitimacy lifts from the child, now named Vesta.

Like Jennie, my sunny disposition wasn't completely tamped out by my year away from home. When I returned for my senior year to San Marino High School, the words the editors chose to define me in the yearbook were from the opening song of musical *Oklahoma!*

> *Oh what a beautiful morning!*
> *Oh what a beautiful day!*

Like Jennie, I still found beauty in my life, and I tried to be happy for my parents. But I had a secret fantasy, a counterlife that I would play out: What if my father had let me come home with my baby? I would imagine my days from morning to night, feeding my baby, bathing her, playing with her, studying dutifully to graduate from high school and move on to college, but also being a good mother, conscientious, loving, and competent. In my daydream, my family, especially my father, would love my daughter, much as Jennie's father adores Vesta. She would light up all our lives, our darling girl. We were, of course, too genteel for such an outcome. There was too much respectability; too much social mania for appearances, so Jennie's chance to keep her baby could never have been mine. My fantasy was an ingenuous girl's daydream, a schmaltzy, unworkable exaltation of teenage motherhood that could never have been made real under the upright imperatives of San

Marino. Jennie does get to come home, but her homecoming and Vesta's birth are no sentimental idyll. Her family is so poor that she has to go back to work as a maid in short order.

Although there is still no coquetry about her, the men she encounters at her place of work are unaccountably attracted to Jennie; she is "like a honeypot to flies," which makes her wonder if she is, in fact, "innately bad and wrong" (120). But her only crime is an uncontrived, sensual beauty. Lester Kane, the son of a powerful Cincinnati businessman, sees her as he probably sees all domestic servants—sexually available. Sure that "she [can] be quickly reached," he proceeds to do so by obstinately insisting that she belongs not to herself but to him. Although she is genuinely afraid of him, she also feels a "terrific, inviting, urging," thus becoming our first heroine to actually feel sexual desire, which up to this point has been the exclusive province of men. Dreiser suggests that Lester's and Jennie's natures are temperamentally suited for one another: Lester is a "strong, intellectual bear of a man" and Jennie, "a quiet sympathetic, non-resisting . . . rare flower" (124); he is "an essentially animal man . . . strong, hairy, axiomatic" and she, "soft and retreating" (126–8). Though they may seem like opposites, in the asymmetry of patriarchal pairing, they make a perfect fit: he is powerful, she is weak; he is unappeasable, she is deferential.

Dreiser is quite aware of the Victorian double standard ensconced in America in 1880, when this part of the novel is set (and not entirely erased today). He knows the "social or, rather, unsocial code" that allows men to "sin if [they] so wish, taking [their] choice of feminine beauty," and he knows that when men marry, "the errors of the past do not matter" (129) but if women are to marry, they matter greatly. He carefully delineates the moral and economic contradictions imposed by American socioeconomic hierarchy and buttressed by patriarchy. Taking full advantage of the decadent latitude that wealth permits, the Kanes acquire "as much money and power as they can get, regardless of the health and welfare of others" (Whaley 36), while the Gerhardts, who "don't want much" (373), are the hostages of poverty that is intensified by unforgiving moralistic strictures. Lester sees himself as an entitled conqueror; Jennie sees herself as a ruined failure. Though she pleads to be left alone, "her gentle no, no, no's" (136) only make Lester even more determined to have her. ("No" means "yes" in the language of male seduction.) "Why go on fighting?" (153), she asks herself. She might have been able to escape Lester had her family been economically secure, but their destitution pushes her to become Lester's mistress. He agrees to support the family, but only if Jennie agrees to live with him. Although she wants to work (133) and even enjoys it, Jennie's value as a wage-earning woman is utterly insufficient; "she has only herself to sell" (Hapke 16).

Crippled by shame, Jennie cannot bring herself to tell Lester about Vesta, though she knows now that she must raise the issue of pregnancy, that "any such relationship with him mean[s] motherhood for her again" (158). Dreiser takes a risk by having Lester promise Jennie some kind of birth control: "I understand," he tells her, "a number of things that you don't yet. It can be arranged. You don't need to have a child unless you want to. And I don't want you to" (158). Why was Lester's assurance so hazardous to publish? In 1873, the Comstock Law declared contraception to be both obscene and illegal. Lester might be referring to back alley abortions, but he is most likely suggesting he will use rubber condoms (available since the 1850s) or that Jennie use a vaginal sponge or Lysol douches, both of which were both sold as feminine "hygiene" products to circumvent their illegality (contraception will not be legal in the United States until 1938, when a federal judge lifts the obscenity ban on birth control). Whatever Lester has in mind, Jennie abjectly agrees to his demands and, in so doing, agrees "to serve him as lord and master," to be "his little girl" (Elias 70).[3] When Jennie tells her mother that she is going to live with Lester and asks her to keep Vesta, she insists that this is her only option: "No one will ever have me as a wife," she declares, and her mother does not disagree (161). As Susan Albertine points out, the price of "ascent/assent to material well-being" for the Gerhardts is "Jennie's body—a price the women silently agree must be paid" (63). In this poker game, women usually play against their will and for unequal stakes. For men, not much is to be lost, but for women, the stakes are their health, their reputations, their very social and economic survival.

Years pass and the Gerhardt family's condition improves thanks to Jennie's emotional and sexual sacrifices and her soi-disant husband's generosity. Lester comes to love Jennie "in a selfish way" (187) as his "soul-mate" (185) and Jennie "deeply, truly [learns] to love this man" (193–94), but even under these improved circumstances, she garners little self-respect or personal control, remaining, Dreiser observes, "as venturesome . . . as a mouse" (199). Driven by fear of Lester's disapprobation and by a conviction that she must protect Vesta from society's condemnation, Jennie makes complicated arrangements to keep her daughter a secret. Although Vesta seems to thrive, she remains "the little outcast" (181) and a "blotch on conventional morality" (183). Inevitably the day comes when she falls deathly ill, and Jennie, consumed by shame for having her, denying her, hiding her, and now she thinks, neglecting her, is desperate to get to her. Frantically, she confesses to Lester, and as she rushes to Vesta, she promises God that if Vesta survives, she will "take her to herself as a mother should" (205). When Vesta recovers, Jennie's shame, though not assuaged, is finally overridden and she keeps her promise: "Vesta must not be an outcast any longer . . . Where [I am], there must Vesta be" (206). Lester, of course, is irate that Jennie has deceived him and for awhile considers himself irremediably wronged, entirely forgetting, like a host of other men, his own past sexual exploits. Firmly "in the judgment seat" (212) and predictably unconcerned about applying the double standard, Lester now finds their home "tainted . . . low and common" (220). But when it comes time for him to leave, he is so impressed that Vesta's father is the late Senator Brander and by the "clever whimsicality" of the "bright and pretty" (220) "little waif" (222)—for Vesta is Pearl reincarnate—that he settles back into his comfortable life with Jennie and Vesta, feeling "as though the little girl belonged to him" and that she should share "in such opportunities as his position and wealth might make possible" (223).

Despite this temporary détente, social mores will not allow Jennie and Vesta the security Lester is willing to provide. When his sister surprises him with a visit and finds Jennie and Vesta living with him, she is sanctimoniously horrified. As a result, Jennie undergoes "a moral siege of her own." Although she understands vaguely that, in fact, poverty and fear rather than moral indolence have "surround[ed] her and [have made] her do differently from what she [has] wanted" (238), she does not have the wherewithal to critique "the callous cruelty of [the Kane family's] pharisaic morality of 'good form'" (Lingeman 15). Like many women then and now, she judges herself through the Kanes' eyes, and from their privileged pedestal: "She was really low and vile . . . How could it be otherwise?" (228). In a bid for redemption, she tries to leave Lester, but her "decisions [go] to pieces" when he insists that she "won't be any better off morally than [she is] now," that she "can't undo the past" (248). True to form, she acquiesces and they move on as a family to South Hyde Park, where she appears "more conspicuously, if not legally in the role of wife" (254). Vesta grows even more like Pearl: "sweet and gay, a lightsome, butterfly-type of child, always dressed in some extremely appropriate or childish novelty which set her off to perfection" (259). Beauty and docility protect Vesta and Jennie from expulsion from Lester's temporary Eden; Vesta's sugary, doll-like presence softens her illegitimacy, and Jennie's modesty and devotion to Lester distract from her status as his mistress. But as we have seen, no matter how angelic they might become, unwed mothers cannot shed the aura of impropriety that haunts them.

Jennie and Vesta may pass as "respectable" in their neighborhood, but Lester's father refuses to condone the arrangement, continually referring to Jennie as "a woman of the street" (276) and insisting she is only after the Kane fortune. Lester would like nothing more than to go on living with Jennie "as his sweetheart and handmaiden" and Vesta as his "gay plaything and . . . charming work of art" (279). However, to "his many distinguished friends . . . in the financial and social worlds," his contentment with impropriety suggests "that he must have a weak streak in him somewhere," and "people turn . . . quickly from weakness or the shadow of it" (280). Lester simply is not strong enough to defy convention's assault on the loving but unsanctioned domesticity that Jennie has created for him:

> To contravene the social conventions . . . to fly in the face of what people consider to be right and proper . . . is quite . . . difficult . . . to work out to a logical and successful conclusion. The conventions, in their way, appear to be as inexorable in their workings as the laws of gravitation . . . There is a drift to society . . . which pushes on in a certain direction, careless of the individual, concerned only with the general result. The drift for ages has apparently been toward the development of the home idea and the perfection of the family group, and, while this may have been a passing phase at the time that Lester and Jennie lived, much as its concomitant correlatives, the harem and the plurality arrangement of the Mormons, it was nevertheless dominant and destructive to anything in opposition. (283)

Social convention cannot be dodged, and a salacious, full-page story entitled "Sacrifices Millions for His Servant-Girl Love" is published in the Chicago Sunday newspaper complete with pictures of Lester, Jennie, their house, and the Kane factory (286). Mortified and "irritated beyond words" by the invasion of his privacy, Lester realizes that he should have married Jennie years before but still cannot bring himself to do so. Dreiser repeatedly describes Lester as vigorous and determined, but he is, in fact, paralyzed by lassitude. At age forty-six, faced with losing his share of his father's fortune, he continues to procrastinate, moping about life's mysteries, asking himself over and over again, "How should [I] do to play [my] part decently? How act?" (299). Jennie fares no better. During her years with Lester, she may be exposed to more of the greater world's complexities, but she remains the same Jennie: "brooding, mystified, nonplussed. Life [is] a strange, muddled picture to her, beautiful but inexplicable" (307). Despite her intuitive misgivings about their future, she lets Lester convince her of the foolishness of "little conventions in the light of the sum of things" and to trust in "goodness of the heart" (308), but finally, it is her ever-self-sacrificing "goodness," or what Lawrence E. Hussman calls "her programmatic self-immolation" (44), that brings about their separation.

When the Kane family lawyer pays her an unexpected visit to let her know that Lester's inheritance is contingent upon his leaving her, she takes the initiative herself and insists he leave her. Lester agrees partly out of fear of losing his money, partly because his ego has been wounded over imprudent business ventures, and partly because he knows that his social equal, Letty Pace, a wealthy widow, is waiting in the wings to "put things right for him" (361). Schwartz maintains that the novel relies on the archetypal fairytale "Snow White" as it reiterates the "competition of a young and an older beauty" (25). Indeed, the relationship between Jennie and Letty seems an obvious repetition of the struggle between the crafty dark queen and the angelic fair victim, especially when Jennie flees her gracious home in Hyde Park for a remote and charming cottage, replete with household pets—a horse, a puppy, a cat, a goldfish, and even a singing thrush (379).

À la Hester, Pearl, and Snow White, Jennie and Vesta set up housekeeping, and although Jennie is "depressed to the point of despair," she harbors no animosity for Lester: "Immersed in his great affairs he would forget . . . And why not? She did not fit in . . . Love was not enough in this world—that was so plain." Jennie is not obtuse. She is acutely aware of the limits her past imposes: "One needed education, wealth, training, the ability to fight and scheme. She did not want to do that. She could not" (366). Although Hussman's assertion that Jennie "is a woman battered by poverty and male dominance into a willing doormat" (48) seems unnecessarily abrasive, she does believe unequivocally that she is unworthy of Lester and that it is her due to agree to exile. When she comes across newspaper accounts of Lester's marriage, she is not angry; instead she persists in what has begun to feel like almost pathological self-torture: she follows the story tirelessly, "like a child, hungry and forlorn, looking into a lighted window at Christmas time" (383).[4]

As we read *Jennie Gerhardt*, some of my more credulous students relished these intermittent melodramatics, but the novel also provided us with revealing perspectives on the reach of ideology. In one of his persistent, long-winded soliloquies, Dreiser's narrator echoes Marx's famous conclusion, "Life is not determined by consciousness, but consciousness by life" (409) by contending that we adopt our values not because we create them but because we have been created by them. In Lester's predicament, the narrator speculates: "To have been reared in luxury, as he had been; to have seen only the pleasant face of society . . . like the air you breathe . . . It is so hard for us to know what we have not seen. It is so difficult for us to feel what we have not experienced" (368). Neither Jennie nor Lester can resist the clout of Lester's privileged class and culture. Even though he feels he is doing "the first ugly, brutal thing of his life," Lester is no match for "the armed forces of convention."

West notes that when Dreiser started the novel, he planned to let Jennie and Lester marry, but he eliminated the marriage upon the advice of a friend, Lillian Rosenthal, who insisted, "Poignancy is a necessity in this story . . . It can only be maintained by persistent want on the part of Jennie" (qtd. in West "Introduction" xi). Despite giving up on the marriage, Dreiser was still rebuked by Ripley Hitchcock, senior editor at Harper's, for not punishing Jennie enough for her life as the lover of two men and Vesta enough for her illegitimacy. Even though Dreiser had imposed a much harsher sentence on them than Hawthorne had on Hester or Pearl, Rosenthal and Hitchcock saw the idea of fiction as a moral imperative. As John Gardner explains in *Moral Fiction*, "The traditional view is that true art is moral: it seeks to improve life, not debase it . . . Art asserts and reasserts those values which hold off dissolution, struggling to keep the mind intact and preserve the city." Dreiser is clearly under the influence of traditionalists who want art to maintain the dominant, "to hold off, at least for awhile, the twilight of the gods" (Gardner 5–6). Both Hester and Jennie find sustenance and even some measure of joy in their jewel-like daughters, but Dreiser is compelled to remove all vestiges of consolation from Jennie. The archetypal poison apple awaits and when bitten by Vesta, it does its deadly work. Vesta falls into a deep coma, but with no noble prince in the offing, she dies. We learn later that she dies of typhoid, but no matter, Jennie's remaining source of affection and love is erased. From a modern perspective, this seems an especially cruel price for an unwed mother to pay, yet for some of Dreiser's contemporaries, Jennie's punishments were still lacking.

Vesta's death does afford Jennie a visit from Lester, who is full of regret, apology, and finally, an inkling of self-awareness. He professes that she has always been "the one woman in the world for him" (393), but he is too cynically entrenched in his new social and financial life, and too apathetic, to turn against the comfort it bestows. Supported by a trust Lester sets up for her, Jennie lives on, frugal, placid, and "always with [Lester] in thought, just as in the years when they were together" (409) but never again with the sunny disposition that once defined her. There are no more "beautiful mornings" for Jennie.

Years pass and ever true to what Carol Gilligan refers to as a particularly feminine "morality of care," Jennie adopts two orphans whom she dutifully raises with the same patient devotion she once showed Lester. Lester, on the other hand, phlegmatically drifts, "wining, dining, drinking . . . , travelling . . . finally altering his body from a vigorous, quick-moving, well-balanced organism into one where plethora of substance was clogging every necessitous function" (406). Deathly ill, he asks for Jenny, finally taking at least some stand against those who immediately object, insisting: "This is my death . . . I ought to be allowed to die in my own way" (411). Of course, she reverently attends him. His deathbed confession to her, that she is "the only woman [he] ever did love truly" and that they "should never have parted," is cold comfort, for as soon as he dies, she must fade quickly back into obscurity. She allows herself to attend his funeral, but sits in an inconspicuous corner of the church, all the time fearing she may be noticed by his wife and family. She need not have worried. Her part in his life has been so negligible that no one even bothers to notice her presence. Later that day, she stands behind an iron grating at the train station, still "caged in the world of the material" (16), hoping to get one last look at Lester's coffin. Even now, on a loading dock, class and propriety separate them. When the sleek, red train rolls in, "brilliantly lighted, composed of baggage cars, day coaches, a dining car set with white linen and silver, and . . . comfortable Pullmans," a trio of porters assist the Kane family procession on board. "The panoply of power had been paraded before her since childhood. What [can] she do now but stare vaguely after as it marched triumphantly by?" (417). "The wall" of convention—"the wealth and force which had found her unfit"—remains firmly in place.

Although Jennie is not for me just a "plaster saint" (Hussman 44), she is "one of the most extreme female self-abnegators in modern American fiction" (Gogol 142). She gains a measure of material security during the course of the novel, but from my contemporary feminist perspective, Jennie's bleak isolation seems far from Hester's austere but empowered self-liberation. Jennie remains a reiteration of the nineteenth-century "angel of the house," the self-effacing, all-giving archetype, but "with no place in men's culture" (Kucharski 23) and little "power as a woman" (Riggio x). Although "she is more polished now, she is still essentially a domestic worker" (Barrineau 133). She abandons her ambitions to become self-sufficient as a nurse or charity worker, and continues to live frugally, friendlessly, and it would seem, listlessly on Lester's trust. Although her two adopted orphans may sustain her emotionally for awhile, she knows they too will leave her, and "then what?" she asks.

Frustratingly for me, Jennie does not evolve into the self-directed Hester I so admire who at the end of *The Scarlet Letter* returns to the outskirts of Boston and finds direction, purpose, and respect when she willingly takes up the *A* and the vocation it bestows. Jennie is like Hester in that she believes "in giving" and will go on giving and giving, but she lacks the intellectual drive and critical decisiveness that would have allowed her to cease to drift, to pilot her own life with clear-headed resolve and a sense of well-earned reward.[5] Jennie can never revise the conviction implanted long before by Brander's seduction and Vesta's conception that she deserves her unhappiness, and Dreiser insists to the end that she must pay in enduring isolation, forever unacknowledged for her loyalty to the cult of selflessness, forever expected to bear the scar of social ostracism. If it is his purpose to hold a mirror up to reality, Dreiser refuses to embroider his scarlet woman's life with threads of self-awareness, empowerment, or achievement. Though Jennie does transform her life from homeless pariah to all-giving domestic angel, she cannot override the stigma of unwed mother. Although she is quite capable, there is never anything audacious about Jennie, never an inch of backbone. Instead she remains a banished angel, "a woman in black, heavily veiled" (414), "a marked example of the result of evil-doing" (Dreiser 94). She is sentenced to live out "an endless reiteration of days" (418), an outcast from what James Joyce calls "life's feast" (Joyce 98).

In his autobiography *Black Boy* (1945), Richard Wright tells the story of how as a boy he would use a charitable white man's library card to check out books. Ignoring the man's warnings that he would "addle his brains," he gave himself over to reading. When he came to *Jennie Gerhardt*, he relates his response:

[She] revived in me a vivid sense of my mother's suffering; I was overwhelmed. I grew silent, wondering about the life around me. It would have been impossible for me to have told anyone what I derived from [the novel], but it was nothing less than a sense of life itself. All my life had shaped me for the realism, the naturalism of the ... novel. (295)

My students and I also gave ourselves over to reading *Jennie Gerhardt*, though in far different circumstances than Wright. We live in a southern town, one that's not far in literal distance from the dehumanizing Jim Crow South where Wright came of age, but eons away from the racial prejudice that he grew up with. My students simply had to purchase the paperback at the university bookstore and dive into the novel, which they did with open-hearted compassion.

And I, with my economically and culturally privileged life in the South, cannot presume to claim the situated space from which Wright read, but I think my reading of *Jennie Gerhardt* was something like his. I too felt that all my life had shaped me for Dreiser's naturalism. Even though my own secret pregnancy occurred almost a century after Jennie's and my class advantages protected me from the bondage of poverty that made her so vulnerable, I was not unlike her. I too was consumed by shame for my capitulation, my pregnancy, my forever-altered body. I too was asked to keep secret the reasons for my absence and the truth of my daughter's birth. I too was marked by shame. I may not have been labeled "ruined," but I knew I was "damaged," and I cringed at the recoil of disgust I thought I would face if I were honest about my past. Now all my secrets have been told. No one has ever shown disgust, as Lester did, when I have told my whole story, but there have been those who have been angry when I've told the truth, angry that I duped them, that I took so long to tell them, that the past they thought they shared with me was based on falsehood, that they had unknowingly taken part in a travesty.

Yet I am without a doubt far better off than Jennie. I have not had to pay for a lifetime. Her loneliness is not mine. Rather than losing my daughter forever like Vesta, I have found Merideth, and I am able to watch her move through adulthood and her children grow. I have created a loyal and loving family; I stuck to my ambitions and built a rewarding career that I take pride in; I have formed a circle of steadfast friends; I sit at the feast of life. Still, Jennie's sorrow haunts my dreams. I understand her ongoing need to forever give, desperately hoping for an ever-receding redemption. There are those thousands like Jennie and Hester and me who were once told that we had done something unpardonable, something disgraceful. We were so convinced of our wrongdoing that even when the world we live in now tells us otherwise, abiding self-forgiveness remains beyond our reach.

CHAPTER 3

Edith Wharton's Female Enforcers

Another one of the novels Madame Lapaire loaned me at Florence Crittenton was Edith Wharton's *The Age of Innocence*, and I remember caring deeply about the book but also being, well, frightened by it. Sixteen and homesick, I identified much more readily with the adoring, demure, and entirely conventional May Welland than the desiring and desired misfit, Ellen Olenska. I wanted to go back to being an American good girl like May. The last thing I wanted was to be like Ellen, pushed out of my "tribe" and forced to live alone in a foreign country. Ellen's emancipation had no allure for me. I just wanted to go home. Even Paris couldn't attract me—at least not then. When I reread the novel years later, I was amazed by how much it seemed to change. Of course, it was I who had changed. Now Ellen became my wannabe heroine: mysterious, tragic, Bohemian, erotic. How I wished Newland Archer could have renounced stifling old New York and escaped with Ellen to that far-off country he imagined, a place for freethinkers, artists, and lovers, a place to cast off damning labels like "mistress," "fallen," and "ruined." But I understood Ellen when she tells him there is no such new world. Even when others know nothing of our secret labels, we still cannot shed them. They are too deeply engrained in our psyches. There are no thoroughly fresh starts. Still, I knew I would never be like Newland Archer: thwarted, haunted, and paralyzed by empty dignity.

In fact, I am neither Newland, nor Ellen, nor May. I don't have to read *The Age of Innocence* for personal guidance any more. I've charted my own alternative course. It's not Paris, though I have been there. More to my liking are the mountain ranges I've hiked—the High Sierra, the Rockies, the Cascades, the Tetons—the waterfalls, the glacial lakes, and the alpine meadows I've reached. I haven't evaded my uneasy past, but I have escaped the compulsory respectability of my parents' generation and the "tribe" of San Marino, where fastidious attention to appearances almost squeezed out my spirit. In my own home on a high ridge in the Appalachians, I'm about as far away from that old world as Ellen Olenska was from old New York. I don't know what Ellen did for all those years on her own in Paris, but I'd like to think she lived in loving fellowship as I do. I'd like to think she found gratifying work and faithful friends. And most importantly, unlike the forever repressed Newland Archer, I'd like to think she experienced the liberating pleasure of relinquishing secrecy. Living openly and forthrightly in the world can be exacting, sometimes excruciating, but most of the time, it is exhilarating because it is true. I don't lie, not anymore.

Such wide-open forthrightness is rare in Wharton's fiction. In her recent biography of Wharton, Hermione Lee observes: "reserve and concealment are everywhere ... Her characters often live double lives, and keep the most important fact about their past a secret not just for a few months or years, but forever" (11). Lee's words worked on me like a shockwave. I too had led a double life, keeping the most important fact about my past a secret! The momentary tremor spurred me on; now I was certain that if I had read more Wharton, I would surely find an unwed mother, a character keeping the same secret I had kept for thirty-five years. I was not disappointed, discovering not one but two female characters who, like me, had been privileged girls, but their privilege, like mine, did not prevent them from falling passionately in love or protect them from getting pregnant. In the novella *The Old Maid* and the short story "Roman Fever," Wharton's unwed mothers carefully guard their secret pasts—ardent sexual imbroglios that resulted in illegitimate daughters. In doing so, both characters must agree to live double lives.

Wharton was fascinated by social repression and, consequently, by the powerful undercurrent of desire that necessitated such obsessive authoritarianism. Novels like *The Age of Innocence* are charged with sexual intensity, intensity that may be kept in check but is never entirely extinguished. Perhaps it was Wharton's allegiance to upper-class propriety that made some of her critics find her fiction "inadequately realistic." As champions of the new naturalism, some critics grudgingly admitted that she was "undoubtedly affected" by Dreiser, but they judged her inferior "for turning her back on the truths of common life in order to write about the rich" (Bell 1, 15). But such conclusions are unfounded. If we look at the range of Wharton's fiction, we find that she did not turn away from the realities of the lives of women, whether they lived entrapped in the stodgy aristocracy of old New York or in more "obscure and straitened" lives (3). She never looked away from what her rival novelist Katherine Mansfield referred to as the "dark place or two in the soul" (qtd. in Bell 7), nor did she steer clear of "much darker stories of sexual love" (Bender 2). Millicent Bell argues that rather than "whispering the last enchantments of the Victorian age" (10), Wharton wrote novels that "had no real precedent in [their] boldness in treating sexual passion . . . except for *The Scarlet Letter*" (3). Unlike Rowson's *Charlotte Temple* and Foster's *The Coquette*, Wharton's unwed mothers are not so polluted by extramarital sex that they have to die after giving birth. But they do have to keep their seductions a secret or, like Ellen Olenska, suffer social expulsion. They keep their secrets well, but even so, the scarlet threads of scandal pursue them. To mark her "fallen women," Wharton uses new tropes to replicate crimson symbols of shame. In *The Old Maid*, the bloody sputum of tuberculosis stains the "ruined" maid; in "Roman Fever," a piece of red knitting sets her apart.

One might think, given the patriarchal paradigm my family followed and the authoritarian mind-set of my father, that he would be the decision maker concerning my pregnancy, but that was hardly the case. Instead, my mother took over. She called my aunt in Cleveland and after a short consultation, they immediately set their plan of exile in motion. I would fly to Cleveland, attend high school until we could no longer hide my expanding waistline, and then place me in a home for unwed mothers until my baby was delivered. I was on the plane for Cleveland the next day. When I had to say good-bye to my parents before heading down the jetway at LAX, it was my father who broke down weeping as we hugged and kissed. For the first time in my life, my father looked helpless and confused. My mother was not. In fact, she was still so furious that she couldn't bring herself to kiss me good-bye. Mortification had vanquished all compassion; seeing me go was apparently a relief. The complicated and expensive plans she and my aunt set in motion were carried out to a tee, and although some things went terribly wrong, the outcome they had hoped for was a success—my baby was delivered and immediately whisked away into the oblivion of closed adoption; the secret was ensconced; the family name was unsullied. My baby's birthfather and family were extraneous, neither informed of my pregnancy nor of the plan. Had my father wanted to intercede, he would have been directly overridden by those two unstoppable, steely women. They were not Victorian "angels of the house," but they were in their own ways loyal to the cult of domesticity as it was interpreted in the 1950s and early 1960s. They were affectionate wives and dutiful mothers, but like so many patriarchal women, they were determined to enforce the rules. And at all costs, the family must be safe from the disgrace I had invited in.

Wharton takes up a similar situation in *The Old Maid* and "Roman Fever." Unlike Hester's colonial Boston where the male elders sat in judgment, neither the patriarchs of old New York nor their sons mete out punishments to the young women who have not waited for marriage before having sex. Rather, it's their wives and daughters who do so with a mercilessness that surprises, though, given my experience, it should be expected. Like my father, the male characters of the novella and the short story are clueless when it comes to unwed motherhood. They remain on the margins, dupes to the machinations of shrewd women, like my aunt and mother, who they naively think they are protecting and controlling. As in my experience, even the birthfathers are not privy to the pregnancies they caused and never know that they fathered illegitimate daughters. Like them, my baby's father was so exempted from my mother's and aunt's cloak-and-dagger efficiency, that many years later, when I told him he had a daughter somewhere in Ohio, he didn't believe me. He could not accept that such an extravagant "covert operation" could have been pulled off without his knowledge. Like Wharton's male characters, he completely underestimated the resourcefulness of unforgiving women driven by an unquestioned convention.

Published in 1924 but set in the 1850s, *The Old Maid* is one of four novellas in the collection *Old New York*. Each of these tales addresses the tribal codes and customs of nineteenth-century New York's "ruling class," the rule-bound class that Wharton grew up in (Wharton 85). Intellectually inquisitive and artistically exceptional, Wharton was an anomaly in her high-society family. In order to escape her parents' conformity, she became the self-appointed and self-educated cultural analyst of her "tribe." She is described by Nancy Bentley Preston as a "'novelist-ethnographer,' trying to 'understand modern society through the lens of ethnographic estrangement,' analyzing it through reading the signs of 'tribal membership'" (qtd. in Lee 23). It's pertinent to this discussion that one of the ethnologists she read and eventually came to know was Bronislaw Malinowski, the social anthropologist mentioned in chapter 1 whose "Principle of Legitimacy" influenced debates on out-of-wedlock births for decades. Malinowski's moralistic position, that the most important moral and legal rule concerning kinship is that no child should be brought into this world without a father, went unquestioned by most social scientists, but

Wharton managed to complicate his moralizing attitude. By making good use of her ethnographic skills, she meticulously represented the moralizers of her milieu, the stifling Ralston clan of *The Old Maid* and the supercilious Slades in "Roman Fever," as overly conservative, narrow minded, emotionally immature, and incapable of originality.

Wharton was alleged to have a personal interest in illegitimacy, the integral theme of these narratives. According to her biographer R. W. B. Lewis, Wharton believed the rumor that she was the illegitimate daughter of a man she identifies in her memoirs as the "extremely cultivated English tutor" of her two older brothers (Lewis 535). She knew from family experience that deviating from the strict standards of sexual probity could mean social banishment. "Her cousin George Alfred had been 'vanished' from society and respectability on account of 'some woman,' who inevitably was blamed for his lapse" (Fishbein 404). Lewis ultimately concludes that the rumor of Wharton's illegitimacy was false; nonetheless, Wharton returns to the taboo subject of premarital and extramarital affairs over and over again in her fiction (*The Age of Innocence, Ethan Frome, The House of Mirth, Summer*). In her autobiography, *A Backward Glance*, she acknowledges her fascination with sexual transgression:

> The vision of poor featureless unknown Alfred [her cousin]and his siren, lurking in some cranny of my imagination, hinted at regions perilous, dark and yet lit with mysterious fires, just outside the world of copybook axioms, and the old obedience that were in my blood; and the hint was useful—for a novelist. (24–25)

Again, the master narrative of the fallen woman that has served authors so well in the past provides a compelling paradigm for Wharton's imaginative swerves.

There is good reason to conclude that compared to colonial America, when control over sexual behavior was fairly strong, premarital and extramarital sex were becoming more common as social and familial controls eased in the late nineteenth century. For example, in 1764, in the predominantly white population of Middlesex County, Massachusetts, there were an estimated 10 illegitimate births per 1,000 total births. By 1890, that number had more than doubled with 21 per 1,000 (Laslett, Oosterveen, and Smith 372). It must be noted that the Middlesex figures are only estimations based on incomplete court records. Data concerning illegitimate birthrates is hard to come by, partly because even in 1890, most births, legitimate or not, went unrecorded. And, of course, the other more compelling reason for the lack of data is due to the obligatory secrecy that goes hand in hand with un-wed motherhood. Fearful of social ostracism, separation, and/or outright punishment, unwed mothers have always worked hard to hide their preg-nancies and find ways to integrate unobtrusively their infants into their ex-tended families without betraying their illegitimacy. As noted by Laslett, Oosterveen, and Smith in their book *Bastardy and Its Comparative History*: "The easily counted events in American history tend to be those belonging to people who 'counted' at the time; these are not the people most likely to conceive children out of wedlock" (364). The last thing unwed mothers would have wanted was to be noticed at all, much less "counted." Yet we can draw some suppositions based on the illegitimacy statistics historians have collected and the continuing popularity of illegitimacy narratives in litera-ture: as female autonomy increased in the late nineteenth century, young women became more vulnerable to exploitation and illegitimacy.

In *The Old Maid*, Wharton takes up this theme, and like Dreiser, who had such enormous difficulties publishing *Jennie Gerhardt*, she had to jump several hurdles before publishing the novella. Despite the fact that she had just been awarded the Pulitzer Prize earlier that year for *The Age of Inno-cence*, a leading magazine still turned down *The Old Maid* because of "its powerful but unpleasant subject." Even with her reputation now well es-tablished, Wharton was unable to place it, complaining to friends that it was turned down because "its readers [could not] be told about illegitimate children." Finally *Red Book* magazine agreed to take it, but only with the provision that her next story would be "less strong" (qtd. in Lee 596).[1]

Ten years later she would be able to sell "Roman Fever" without diffi-culty for $3,000. Perhaps by then readers, who had negotiated the Twen-ties, flappers, the Jazz Age, the infidelities of *The Great Gatsby*, and the era's substantial liberalization in attitudes toward sexuality, were better equipped to read about illegitimacy. Both the novella and the story bear what Cynthia Griffin Wolff identifies as Wharton's "unique stamp—a scrupulous atten-tion to the interplay between individual character and the society that works to shape and constrain it" (x). Like *Jennie Gerhardt*, they are examples of cultural criticism, products of "an era [that was] critical of the pretensions of moral absolutism" (Fishbein 400). In *The Old Maid*, Wharton is espe-cially unsympathetic to the pitilessly imposed moral demand that unmar-ried women be "uncorrupted" virgins. In the *New York Herald Tribune*, a reviewer of *Old New York* observes, Wharton exposes "a small closed circle of tight security wherein men and women behave like toys in the discipline of a heartless social mechanism" (qtd. in Fishbein 399–400). In "Roman Fever" Wharton returns to the subjects that have preoccupied her since she started to write: "lifelong hidden love, maternal rivalry and deception, the constrictions of women's lives, the imprisonment of secrecy, [and] social conventions which continue to bind individuals" (Lee 725–26).

THE OLD MAID

The Old Maid begins with Delia Lovell Ralston, a young woman who by marrying Jim Ralston has been subsumed by the Ralston clan. The clan is so blinkered by New York elitism that its members can entertain only one conviction: "an acute sense of honour in private and business matters." They are "institutional to the core," having served for generation after generation as "the conservative element that holds . . . societies together as seaplants bind the seashore" (84). Delia lives according to the laws of the clan "as unthinkingly as one lives under the laws of one's country" (87). Since, as Wharton critic Pamela Knight observes, "identity is formed within social consciousness," it is no wonder that Delia cannot think beyond the limits of her tight circle. Old New York "society has taught [Delia] how and what to feel" (36, 37). And Delia is doubly oppressed, first by the rigidity of old New York noblesse oblige and, second, by the socially imposed doctrine of "separate spheres." According to Shari Thurer, the separation of public (male) and private (female) spheres confined bourgeois women like Delia to the home and to a code of conduct that emphasized ornate femininity, mannered refinement, moral superiority, and passionlessness (186–88). Unlike Jennie Gerhardt, who as a fallen woman at the bottom rung of the social ladder has to work, Delia has nothing more to do than develop her "feminine" skills in the refined glory of her exalted home. While Jennie performs low-grade labor where she is continually exploited, Delia's task in life is to live the Victorian ideal of womanhood: to appear helpless and decorative, to arrange social rituals, to demonstrate "virtue," and to ignore the poor Jennie Gerhardts of the world as they clean out the coal scuttles, scrub the staircases, and empty the chamber pots. While growing up in old New York, Wharton must surely have known many Delias, but she herself manages to escape the limiting confines of both the "cult of domesticity" and upper-class dogma. Instead, as an incisive social critic with insider knowledge, she uses her writing and this novella in particular to expose the extent to which clans like the Ralstons would hide under the guise of morality to preserve their social citadel, an edifice that seems no less puritanical than Hester's colonial Boston.

As a foil to Delia's dubious "angel of the house," Wharton creates her cousin: the shy, serious, and desperate unwed mother Charlotte Lovell. Although no one knows a thing about Charlotte's secret past, she is still not considered "marriage material" because she is so introverted and so poor. To be economically secure, Charlotte needs a husband. Delia, on the other hand, securely married and mother of two, has levered her "angelic" position as Jim's wife to gain some measure of social power in the Ralston tribe, power she enjoys wielding by way of exclusive, self-interested snobbery. The feminine perfection expected of Delia has exacted a high toll. She is frustrated, resentful, and inexplicably stingy. When she hears that Charlotte has received a marriage proposal from the highly respectable Joe Ralston, she feigns delight but is actually annoyed. Later, when Charlotte comes to her for advice, it's impossible for her to react with sincerity. Ironically, it is the high-minded and straitlaced Delia who serves as Wharton's "measure of the moral disease that has permeated the environment that spawned and nourished" her (Wolff xiii). The fallen Charlotte is merely her pawn.

In order to tell Charlotte's sexual story, Wharton has to risk the censorship that had long delayed *Jennie Gerhardt's* publication and forced the banning of Kate Chopin's *The Awakening*. Of course, she cannot explicitly describe sexual intercourse, but she does address the matter daringly by setting up a comparison of Delia's and Charlotte's first sexual encounters. Early in the novella Delia remembers her unhappy wedding night and her "startled puzzled surrender to the incomprehensible exigencies of the young man to whom [she] had at most yielded a rosy cheek in return for an engagement ring." Delia's mother had been of no help in educating her daughter, offering nothing more that "evasions, insinuations, resigned smiles and Bible texts." For Delia, sex with Jim has been nothing more than "flushed distress, confusion . . . and then, the babies; the babies who were supposed to 'make up for everything,' and didn't" (88). In describing Delia's sexual initiation, Wharton is probably drawing on her own wedding night. When she had sought advice from her mother a few days before her own disastrous marriage, her mother responded with "icy disapproval," making Wharton feel vulgar for asking and stupid for "not knowing what [she] had been expressly forbidden to ask about, or even think of" (qtd. in Lee 76).

Charlotte's sexual experiences are quite different, though they are never described outright and are introduced by an elaborately circuitous prelude. First, Charlotte tells Delia she has to call off her wedding to Joe. Delia is baffled, especially by Charlotte's reason: Joe has forbidden Charlotte to continue her charity work with foundling children. Delia's bafflement turns to horror when Charlotte's confession moves to sex. Charlotte cannot give up her work at her day nursery because one of the orphans is her daughter. She is a mother. Delia is at sea. How, she wonders, could Charlotte possibly had sex, given "the exposed . . . society to which they all belong"? Unlike Delia's miserable nights of sexual confusion, Charlotte's passionate sexual encounters in the beckoning seclusion of her grandmother's shadowy drawing room are described as "clandestine joys" in "Latmian solitude" (154). Delia's bewilderment does not last long. Like my mother and my aunt, she does not languish in uncertainty. She easily puts the puzzle together, recalling that moonlight sleighing party years earlier when Charlotte had supposedly caught cold, only to be hurried off to a remote village in Georgia to recover. When she returned a year later, Charlotte had changed from a pretty, healthy girl with a gay laugh to a pale, thin young woman. It was logical for everyone to blame the change on Charlotte's diagnosis—tuberculosis. But now Delia understands the other oddities about Charlotte's return: the "plain dresses of Quakerish cut . . . the same grey cloak and small bonnet" that Charlotte now insisted on wearing; the anonymous baby that had been handed over to the aunt's handyman by a mysterious veiled lady; and Charlotte's "sudden zeal for visiting the indigent."

Charlotte returns from Georgia a different person, almost a reincarnation of Hester Prynne in dress and social purpose, and like Hester, she prefers to venture out only in the dark so that she can escape what she feels is the world's "awful glare" (109). She never recommences "the light-hearted life of her young friends" (91). Her grandmother, who we must assume has carried out all the arrangements for Charlotte's secret confinement, now accommodates her somberness by helping her set up her day nursery for destitute orphans, one of which, Delia now sees, is Charlotte's daughter. Charlotte has carefully guarded her secret while caring for her baby, but she cannot depend on her grandmother forever; she needs money and without telling him the truth, has accepted Joe's proposal. But now he has unwittingly insisted she give up the day nursery. She cannot bear to surrender her daughter to the dangerous living conditions and anonymity of an orphanage; she cannot go through with the wedding.

When Joe first proposes to Charlotte and she accepts, she temporarily sets aside her drab, gray dresses, not for flashy new party dresses like Delia's, but for her dead mother's old, hand-me-down poplins. But like Hester, she cannot remove all residue of scarlet. She does not embroider an *A* on the breast of the remade dresses, but she does trim them with crimson velvet. Then, when she passionately confesses to Delia why she cannot marry Joe, she stains her dress with another trope: a "red trickle" of blood drips from her lips onto her crimson-trimmed poplin, marking her with the incriminating sign of her old "illness"—tuberculosis. Charlotte has actually recovered from tuberculosis, but thinking fast, Delia seizes on this scarlet stain. As patriarchal women have for generations, she sees it as her duty to make certain that Charlotte's unregulated sexuality not contaminate her clan. The red stain will suit her purposes, and Charlotte is her willing victim. She may no longer have consumption, but she is so consumed by debilitating shame that she is helpless to come to her own defense. Sure of his rejection, she is also too mortified to tell Joe Ralston the truth and too ashamed to turn to her baby's father for support; instead, she unsuspectingly agrees to all of Delia's machinations.

Delia, possessed by "all the traditions of honour and probity," quickly sets her plan in motion. First, she offers up the bloody stain on Charlotte's dress as the reason for calling off the marriage. It will stand for what cannot be allowed in: the sexual "contagion" that Charlotte carries (the broken hymen and illegitimate child) that would "implant disease in [the Ralston] race" (117). Joe accepts Delia's explanation with an alacrity that makes even Delia wince. Delia's husband Jim, completely in the dark about the real reason behind Delia's actions, praises her for her sagacity and promises to give her some money to help her support—in other words, control—Charlotte. Her scheming well under way, she sends Charlotte off to live in isolation with her "foundling baby" in a remote Ralston farmhouse on the Hudson. Charlotte's exile takes up again the recurring anecdote of many thousands of actual women who have suffered such a fate. In *Feminism and American Literary History*, Nina Baym notes that Hester as well as many other "sullied . . . madonnas" (Fiedler's term) elect to live in celibacy (13–14), as does Charlotte. She agrees not only to celibacy but to all the preparations Delia makes for her. Wharton resists the necessity that the unwed mother and her illegitimate child die, but there still must be sacrifice. A life of celibacy, dependency, and surrender insure that the fallen woman still pays.

Delia likes to see herself as Charlotte's savior, rising to the occasion for her and her baby as Dimmesdale did for Hester when the magistrates threatened to take Pearl away. But Delia's motives are far from generous. She has no genuine desire to help Charlotte; in fact, she is motivated not only by her fierce loyalty to Ralston "honor," but by her own secret, her long-held love for Clement Spender, a ne'er-do-well artist now living in Europe and the baby's unapprised father. If Delia can't have Clement, she will have his daughter. Charlotte is just a means to that end and her machinations continue. Years pass; Jim dies. Discontented and bored by the stultifying propriety of widowhood in old New York, Delia brings Charlotte and her daughter, now called Tina Lovell, back to New York. Her "own biological offspring never mean what [Charlotte's] child means to her" (Tintner 125); it is Tina that she wants for bizarre, vicarious, emotional nourishment. Rather than a Dimmesdale figure, Delia becomes an unnerving repetition of the jealous, manipulative Chillingworth, furtively pulling the strings of her class and privilege to challenge Charlotte's rightful position as Tina's mother and to undermine Tina's affection for Charlotte, who Tina believes is her aunt. Delia doesn't just envy Charlotte's "secret of her scanted motherhood" (137), she actually "hate[s] [her] for being Tina's mother" (132).

Tina is in some ways a reinscription of Pearl: "a brilliant and engaging creature" (129). But when she reaches adolescence, she is infected with a "disease" like the one the young and beautiful Jennie Gerhardt suffered from—a sexual magnetism so radiant that Tina effortlessly "attracts" men (143). Like Dreiser, Wharton does not explain this erotic "illness," but both Charlotte and Delia can see that "the first chapter of the mother's history was already written in the daughter's eyes; and the Spender blood in Tina might well precipitate the sequence . . . the girl [could be] lost" (167). As Ellen Herman notes, "Anxieties regarding eugenics were a prominent feature" in the 1920s (29), when Wharton is writing *Old New York*, so it is logical that Delia and Charlotte think that the sexual immorality of Clement Spender and Charlotte herself will have been passed on to Tina. The two women believe that if left unregulated, Tina's sexual heritability will put her "health," or we might say, her hymen, in jeopardy and thus ruin her "marketability" in marriage. Moreover, the shadowy implications of her mysterious parentage make her fair game in the illicit mating rituals of the tribe; the darkened drawing-rooms still serve as "moonlit forests" (154) for secret liaisons. Overly flirtatious, Tina's capital begins to "fall," and robbed of maternal authority, Charlotte can do nothing more than serve as Tina's unwelcome chaperon, "Aunt Chatty." Locked out of marriage long ago, Charlotte's position in the patriarchal hierarchy of old New York is nonexistent. Tina, who has grown up with a decided preference for Delia, holds her Aunt Chatty in disdain. When she cruelly brands Charlotte "an old maid" (130), Wharton manages to degrade Charlotte's "illness," that never forgotten scarlet stain, with the other contaminating imbrications of frigidity and spitefulness—a kind of affliction that utterly discredits her, locking her out of her secret daughter's social milieu.

Even though Tina appears to enjoy the same tribal privileges as Delia's children, Charlotte is well aware that she will have to pay for her illegitimacy, that she will not "escape disaster." Young men will fall in love with Tina, but they will find good reasons not to marry her. They will be suspicious of her "blood," concerned about her "stock." At the same time, Charlotte also knows that only marriage can provide the security Tina needs if she is to be saved from disgrace and exile or from the surrendered motherhood and prudish spinsterhood Charlotte has had to endure. She resolves to tell Tina the truth and take her away from the dangers of seduction and betrayal in old New York to a place "where [they] shall be among plain people, leading plain lives. Somewhere where [Tina] can find a husband, and make herself a home" (146). Boldly, she tells Delia, "Now it's my turn . . . It's I who must save her . . . She's lived too long among unrealities: and she's like me. They won't content her" (145–46).

Delia knows that Charlotte's plan will mean an irreversible "fall" for Tina from the "sweetened life" Delia has provided. To Delia's credit, she has come to understand that the mind-numbing restraints of old New York and the clan's insistence on conformity have kept her from the vivid life she was meant to live. She knows that by agreeing to be, at least on the outside, a dutiful, conforming, and acquiescent Ralston, she has "missed her vision." She resents her life, that of "a cloistered nun . . . doomed to dwell in shadows" (150). Again, she reminds me of Chillingworth and his monkish existence in puritanical New England. Just as he lived vicariously off Dimmesdale, Delia lives off of Tina's vivacity and charm. Without Dimmesdale to appease his bitterness, Chillingworth dies. Without Tina, Delia will lose the assuaging alter ego that has been sustaining her in her emotionally vacuous nunnery, for "she had been Tina, and Tina had been her own girlish self, the far-off Delia Lovell" (178). If Charlotte is allowed to prevail and take Tina away, Delia knows that she, not Tina, will pay most dearly. Again she takes up her plan and inserts herself between mother and child.

She begins by playing on Charlotte's guilt, calling her "a monster of in-gratitude" (147) and gains her advantage by moving to adopt Tina legally. As is so often the case, the push to adopt is motivated largely by the emotional needs of the adopting parent, in this case Delia; those of the birthmother are quite secondary. When Charlotte resists the adoption, Delia uses the rationalization that has been and still is used for endorsing adoption, the rationalization that almost always succeeds as it goes to work on a birthmother's conscience. I should know; it worked on me: a birthmother must do what's best for her child. Using the same tactics that a social worker once used on me, Delia convinces Charlotte that she must give up all her claims to Tina. If she doesn't, she will be sacrificing Tina's happiness for her own emotional needs. Since birthmothers are, after all, shameful, unworthy, and undeserving, adoption is best for the child. I had no sense of my maternal rights or any degree of self-respect, nor does Charlotte. Like me, she has nothing to parley in the argument. I thought I had to agree to whatever was demanded. Likewise, Charlotte has to agree to the adoption. I was expected to remain a secret birthmother forever. And Charlotte must remain nothing more than Tina's aunt, a "poor creature" whose ruling purpose will be "that her child should never guess the tie between them" (168). By way of adoption, Delia can keep Charlotte at her mercy, take Tina from her, and solidify their secret for a lifetime.

Legal adoption procedures were already in place to accommodate Delia's plan. Although few parents were willing to surrender children for adoption before 1900, it was common for poor children to be "placed out" as indentured servants, an arrangement that secured their services in exchange for food, shelter, and basic education until they were "released," typically at age eighteen. "Families requested children . . . 'to help around the farm' and 'to mind the baby'" (Herman 23, 26). And at the end of the nineteenth century, emotional motivations for exchanging children came more into play, so when Delia decides to adopt Tina, laws are available to formalize the arrangement. Her emotional rationalization anticipates the amended objectives of adoption practices in the twentieth century. By the time Wharton writes *The Old Maid*, "the modern adoption ideal rejected reciprocal economic obligations as a bogus basis for kinship and celebrated intimacy, emotion, and desire. In the rhetoric of modern adoption law and reform, 'human values' trumped material considerations" (Herman 28). Delia's "human values," her desires for intimacy and emotion, trump Charlotte's maternal rights. The adopting mother's motivations are found unquestionably commendable, and Tina becomes an official member of the Ralston tribe with all the privileges such membership bestows.

Delia is emotionally renewed by her victory. Wielding the power old

New York has bequeathed her, she secures Tina's marriage within the tribe. Elated, she watches her prepare for her wedding—the wedding that will entomb Tina in the insular mausoleum that has suffocated Delia. At this point Charlotte certainly has less power than Delia, but she is much more self-aware. She understands the deeper implications of her battle with Delia, that for Delia it was a battle born of emotional poverty, an unbearable need for revenge against Charlotte for her forbidden dalliance with Clement Spender and a covetous need for reparation by way of the brilliant daughter they conceived.[2] Wharton succeeds in making Charlotte her heroine; the shamed and exploited birthmother is the most sympathetic and honorable witness to the events. By adopting her vantage point, we see the moral relativism of old New York that has authorized the manipulative, vengeful, and unself-conscious Delia to win this contest. In so doing, Wharton undermines any trust in absolute morality. Instead she suggests that those who fall, like Hester and Charlotte, and are then forced to live on the margins of their communities, may become more self-aware, fair minded, and ethically judicious than those who remain protected by their insular, self-confirming enclaves.

Delia's victory as adoptive mother is sealed the night before Tina's wedding when Charlotte asks if she might be the one to have the mother-daughter talk with Tina about the sexual intimacy she will soon encounter. Delia agrees and even momentarily realizes the harm that she has done Charlotte, "the baffled pitiful . . . mother who was not a mother, and who, for every benefit accepted, felt herself robbed of a privilege" (176). Delia actually admits, albeit to herself alone, that she has done "a terrible, a sacrilegious thing" by interfering "with another's . . . right to love and suffer after [her] own fashion" (178). Although she may briefly regret her years of meddling, social convention is on her side, and it is too strong to allow Charlotte any recompense. As she approaches Tina's room, Charlotte realizes she cannot talk to her about sex without Tina realizing that she, Charlotte, has had sex. Shame silences her, as it has so many unwed mothers. She cannot speak.

Returning to Delia, who is waiting below, she admits: "I just stood in the passage, and tried . . . to think of something . . . something to say to her . . . without . . . without her guessing . . . It's no use. You were right; there's nothing I can say. You're her real mother. Go to her. It's not your fault—or mine" (179). Perhaps Charlotte is right; placing blame is indeed problematic. After all, it is old New York that will not let Charlotte stop dissembling; social appearances won't permit the truth. Secrecy, sexual hypocrisy, and jealousy continue to envelop her like poisonous smoke. Though Delia may catch a glimpse of the cruel sham she has perpetuated, she will not alter it. She is the enforcer of convention; she can't back down now.

Delia has the talk with Tina that Charlotte could not bear to broach. In our last image, Charlotte is outside Tina's closed door, eavesdropping on the conversation, listening to Tina promise Delia "everything, everything, you darling mother" (180). Despite her devotion, her knowledge, and her generosity, Charlotte will keep her shameful secret, playing out her role of "old maid," the forbidden outcast hovering outside closed doors, struggling to hear as others sit down to the feast of life.[3]

"ROMAN FEVER"

In *The Old Maid*, Charlotte is ostracized by social appearances and moral rigidity. She can find no respectable access to her daughter; she must capitulate to Delia's machinations. But in "Roman Fever," although we again find two women dueling for control, this time the one who is entwined with the scarlet threads of unwed motherhood finds a way to put her "fall" to good purpose. In this late, masterful, and often anthologized story, Wharton waits to reveal the true parentage of another illegitimate daughter until her last sentence. In the course of the story, she again makes "it clear that morality is little more than codified folkways, that society condemns in one era what it will condone in another" (Fishbein 402). Lee praises the story as Wharton's "most perfectly controlled and profound" (723), and given its unexpected concluding twist, it is one that gains new depth and meaning with each rereading. At first it seems to be about two well-mannered and thoroughly conventional dear friends, but in fact these women are Delia and Charlotte rewritten: they have been contending with each other for more than twenty years. This time, however, there will be a shift in the ruthless dominance one woman holds over the other.

The "two American ladies of ripe but well-cared-for middle age" are Mrs. Alida Slade, a lady of "high color and energetic brows," and Mrs. Grace Ansley, "the smaller and paler one" (3). They sit on a terrace overlooking the Roman Forum and the Colosseum while their daughters, both in their mid-twenties, spend the afternoon with two Italian aviators. As matronly neighbors on the Upper East Side of New York, each thinks she thoroughly knows the other, but in fact, their perceptions are wide of the mark; it is as if, suggests Wharton, they are visualizing one another "through the wrong end of her little telescope" (9). Both have been recently widowed, and Mrs. Slade finds her life "a dullish business" compared to the exciting one she had led as the wife of a famous lawyer, Delphin Slade. Her daughter Jenny is pretty, but she has none of the "vividness" that her mother once had as "an extremely dashing girl." Mrs. Slade finds Jenny boring and disappointing (9), but she admires Mrs. Ansley's daughter Barbara, a gaily spirited, brilliant girl. To Mrs. Slade, Barbara has much "more *edge*" than her parents, whom she considers "two nullities . . . museum specimens of old New York" (6). But when the perspective shifts and we see Mrs. Slade through Mrs. Ansley's eyes, we see a different woman—pushy and dissatisfied. Mrs. Ansley has always felt sorry for her. "On the whole," she thinks, Mrs. Slade "had had a sad life. Full of failures and mistakes."

As the women pass the afternoon, Mrs. Ansley begins to knit with a skein of crimson yarn, and Mrs. Slade begins to reminisce about the Rome of their pasts. She recalls how their grandmothers had to guard their mothers from the dangerous, miasmic nights when malaria, the eponymous "Roman fever," could be contracted. She remembers how their mothers had to guard them from a more sentimental contamination of the moonlight, an equally dangerous transmitter of "Roman fever," the seducer. But, she remarks, times have changed: Barbara and Jenny are out unchaperoned. Secretly Mrs. Slade is annoyed that Barbara will probably "catch" the Campolieiri boy, one of the best matches in Rome, and she jealously imagines the future Mrs. Ansley will enjoy with her sparkling daughter's Italian family. As resentful and stingy as Delia Ralston, Mrs. Slade sets out to humiliate Mrs. Ansley, remarking: "I was wondering how two such exemplary characters as you and Horace had managed to produce anything quite so dynamic [as Barbara]" (11). Mrs. Ansley will not take the bait; instead, she sits quietly knitting, pausing only to gaze thoughtfully at the Forum, "the great accumulated wreckage of passion and splendor at her feet" (12). Undaunted, Mrs. Slade presses on, extolling Barbara as an angel with "rainbow wings" while simultaneously betraying her festering irritation. As Mrs. Ansley passively knits her crimson yarn, Mrs. Slade's exasperation turns spiteful. She threatens Mrs. Ansley with a secret, a secret she has been hoarding since the last time they were in Rome twenty-five years ago. Alarmed by this ominous sortie, Mrs. Ansley looks at Mrs. Slade "as though she were looking at a ghost"; her knitting slides "in a panic-stricken heap to the ground" (15). But the now-seething Mrs. Slade will not be stopped despite Mrs. Ansley's obvious dread. Exultant, she tells her secret: it was she, Alida, not Delphin, who had written the love letter that Grace received twenty-five years ago. It was she who asked her to meet him at a secret late-night rendezvous in the Colosseum. She knew Grace was in love with Delphin and she needed to get her out of the way. She'd hoped Grace would catch the dreaded "Roman fever" at the Colosseum that night, and her machinations had worked. As Grace waited and waited for Delphin to show up, she caught a "bad chill." Two months later, she married Horace Ansley in Florence.

With "gladiatorial violence," Mrs. Slade, whose name, Rachel Bowlby notes, sounds like "slayed'" (41), completes her tale and seems to have won her battle again, though this time she is waging it for a dead man. She looks down triumphantly on her vanquished enemy, "a small bowed figure" with "her face streaked with tears" (16), so diminished that "the wind might scatter her like a puff of dust" (18). Dusk spreads over them and the "clear heaven overhead [is] emptied of all its gold." Still, Alida's vindictiveness is unsatisfied; she must inflict still more pain; after all, "girls [and middle-aged women] are ferocious sometimes." She delivers her final blow by confessing that she always could make herself laugh by imagining Grace alone and forlorn outside the shadowy Colosseum that night, "waiting around . . . in the dark, dodging out of sight, listening for every sound, trying to get in" (19). With that she uses up all her weapons, and she seems to have succeeded in defeating her old rival once again. Mrs. Ansley does not move for a long time.

Then, gradually she revives, turns toward her rival and deftly delivers her volley. No longer "knitting" the past into a prettified crimson screen, she boldly reveals her own extraordinary secret, the truth about that sexually charged, scarlet night in Rome. She had answered Delphin's letter. She had not had to wait alone that night at the Colosseum. Delphin was waiting for her. He had arranged everything. Alida had unknowingly brought about just what she had been trying to prevent—the lovers' passionate rendezvous. "I'm sorry for you," Mrs. Ansley concludes.

Mortified by Mrs. Ansley's passionate revelation, Mrs. Slade makes one more attempt at retaliation, this time by insisting that despite the secret rendezvous, it was she who had Delphin for twenty-five years. When it came to enforcing the inflexible matrimonial rules of old New York, Mrs. Slade had triumphed, or so she thinks. But Mrs. Ansley has the ultimate weapon, a fact that can invalidate all Mrs. Slade's slavish (and hypocritical) attention to propriety. Grace counters with simple forthrightness, declaring with dignity: "I had Barbara" (20). Now Mrs. Slade is indeed slayed. The result of her scheming was fever but not the fever she planned on. Instead, she brought on the ardent "fever" of lovers and the conception of the beautiful, brilliant Barbara. Finished with Mrs. Slade, Mrs. Ansley picks up her knitting and departs the terraced battlefield, vindicated and unrepentant. Rather than a fallen woman, Mrs. Ansley has achieved heroic dimensions.

For the first time since Hester Prynne assumed the scarlet *A*, we have a mother who, like Hester, has harbored an intense and secret passion for her forbidden lover, but unlike Hester, Grace Ansley manages to keep her pregnancy a secret until she can secure a marriage for herself and patrimony for her Pearl-like daughter. The marriage allows her to raise Barbara without scandal, without exile, and, it seems, without heartbreak. Though the secret rendezvous is an integral part of her emotional life, she has kept it carefully concealed from old New York. There are critics, such as Jamil S. Selina, who maintain that Mrs. Ansley is shamefaced and that the "half-guilty" manner in which she draws forth her crimson skein emphasizes a "gloom of guilt" that will eventually dissolve once "she is forced to acknowledge her guilty past" (Selina 99, 101). Alice Hall Petry also finds her "guilt-ridden" and "predisposed to fidget" (164). But I disagree. As the story builds and Mrs. Slade blunders through her version of the past, Grace dexterously knits her own design of secret "crimson" passion with startlingly efficient needles until it is time to reveal her secret—a meticulously crafted, empowering weapon. Knitting ceases to be a "symbol of complacent middle-age," and instead becomes "a complex personal emblem for Grace" (Petry 164), an evasion tactic with needles that serve as "effective psychological weapons against a woman who is deliberately tormenting her" (Petry 165).

In finally revealing her scarlet "truth," Mrs. Ansley does not allow the stain of illegitimacy to dim the coveted brilliancy of her gossamer Barbara. She knows that the prideful, supercilious Mrs. Slade will be far too humiliated to ever publicly admit that the late Delphin Slade conceived a dazzling child with the seemingly dull, diminutive, but indomitable Grace Ansley. Mrs. Ansley knows too well that in her society, her marriage provided the necessary foundation on which Barbara's well-being has depended, and she will not imprudently risk the legitimacy the marriage conferred on Barbara. Thus, even though the new information Mrs. Ansley provides seems to clinch the story with the utterance of what Bowlby calls "an age-old species of female secret," Mrs. Ansley does not actually admit that Delphin is Barbara's father. She only states the obvious: she had Barbara and, in "lovely literalness" (Bowlby 46), she says nothing about a father. The victory then of

"Roman Fever" is not only Mrs. Ansley's triumph over Mrs. Slade twenty-five years after Barbara's conception, but also the lifelong, mother-daughter bond that Mrs. Ansley, like her predecessor Hester, secured with Barbara, a bond that Mrs. Slade covets. If Barbara's biological father is in doubt, her mother "is superlatively certain" (47). In saying "I had Barbara" rather than "We had Barbara," Mrs. Ansley dismisses both Barbara's biological and adoptive fathers and emphasizes her victory not only over Mrs. Slade, but her successful manipulation of patrilineal regulations.

Although she has kept her premarital affair a secret, Mrs. Ansley has never allowed it to defeat her. Instead, she has taken from the constraining confines of patriarchy what she has needed—the patrimony with which "Ansley" legitimizes Barbara. Then using her needles capably to knit her empowered maternal position, she cunningly reveals her scarlet secret in order to defeat her enemy. In the confrontation, the moral ambiguity of Mrs. Ansley becomes less important, especially since it is Mrs. Slade who, in an unscrupulous effort to control Delphin and Grace, had dangerously manipulated events and relished doing so. Like Delia, she has been protected by social structures that allowed her to enforce protocol and maneuver people, but also like Delia, who takes no interest in her dull children, she has only been able to produce the "socially colorless" Jenny, who Tintner suggests is the "offstage victim of her mother's 'badness'" (76). When Mrs. Slade reveals her old plot in order to injure Grace yet again, her tactics fail; she doesn't hurt Grace and she earns our disapprobation. Her jealous cruelty makes it impossible to brand Grace's long-ago sexual transgression with any degree of high moral obloquy. Instead, she earns our admiration. Wharton has cleverly and seamlessly removed the immoral implications of premarital sex by characterizing both Grace Ansley and, in *The Old Maid*, Charlotte Lovell as far more generous of spirit than those who would enforce heartless codes of behavior.

Rachel Bowlby observes, "The name Barbara originates in the feminine form of the ancient Greek word for the non-Greek, non-civilized 'barbarian.'" Unlike the Greek citizen, the barbarian did not enter into a community that was defined by its "*logos*: logic, reason, and language." To Bowlby, Barbara is "a wild child, as yet unassimilated to patriarchal civilization" (48), as was Hester's Pearl, at least until she marries into European nobility. We don't know enough about the Barbara to speculate whether this wild child will agree to assimilate into what Bowlby describes as "the same old story of girls, in each generation, finding husbands" (43). But we can be certain that

Barbara's disputable paternity will not put her at a disadvantage. Bowlby fittingly concludes that "far from being victims of men, collectively or individually, the women of 'Roman Fever' are the drivers of the plots; it is they, not the husbands or boyfriends, who control what happens" (44). And Barbara we presume has learned how to drive the plot from her mother. After all, while her mother shrewdly outsmarts her would be "slayer," Barbara spends her day with an Italian "Marchese," and there's no doubt that should she want him, she will have him.

Wolff maintains that the moral ambiguities and the implications of social constrictions in Wharton's fiction are evidence of her lasting achievement as an artist:

> The dilemmas that she examines are not time-bound—not limited to the world of America's upper classes in the early twentieth century. They are dilemmas that beset all human beings and haunt all social arrangements. The explicit components of any given problem may differ from person to person and from age to age. Yet the fundamental configuration of the problem will remain the same. (xx)

Although it is risky to read history and culture synchronically, Wolff's observations appear valid. Certain dilemmas are fluid, not time-bound. Though never identical, they seem to endure, erratic, volatile, and unresolved. The ordeal of unplanned pregnancy outside of wedlock will continue to beleaguer women of all classes throughout the twentieth century and on into the twenty-first. While it may be true that the "disorder which may unfairly penalize some wayward spirit in a given era" may someday, in another era, "afford the same creature refuge" (Fishbein 403), the stigma attached to the unwed mother has not entirely dissipated, and women continue to be appraised by their sexual appeal (or lack thereof). Wharton is not the first to invest the unwed mother with dignity and insightfulness; Hawthorne does also. But in "Roman Fever," Wharton takes the imaginative and ethical swerve away from the guilt and shame that is heaped on Charlotte Lovell and Charlotte Temple, on Jennie Gerhardt and Eliza Wharton. Taking up her needles, she knits a new tale for the scarlet woman, one that is not only passionate but also triumphant. In so doing, she creatively readies the narrative design for the next writer who will take up the story of the unwed mother and her illegitimate child.

CHAPTER 4

The Scarlet Women of William Faulkner's The Sound and the Fury

Students trickle into my American Modernism seminar, take their seats at the long table, take their books out of their backpacks, lean back in their chairs, and stare at me. Some look grumpy, some are clearly baffled, others are apprehensive; no one looks satisfied. It's our first class meeting after I assigned the Benjy section of *The Sound and the Fury*. I always empathize with my students' first bewildered responses to William Faulkner's masterpiece, and I try never to be "the sage on the stage," especially because I know from years of experience that we will all be more productive if the novel is a field in which we all labor. But, as I sit at the head of the table, I also feel something like the grinning, self-satisfied Cheshire cat on his mushroom. When it comes to *The Sound and the Fury*, I do have a rough map of the maze I've asked my students to enter, though this did not come quickly or easily.

I can vividly recall the exciting perplexity that accompanied my first reading of the novel. I was just starting my first semester at Oregon State University. Though I'm usually not particularly good at standardized tests, I had placed out of freshman composition and was told to enroll in an honor's English seminar instead. Looking back, I am pretty sure this was not the best prescription for my writing competence. I was imaginative, but I had little confidence about structure or development. After all that sentence diagramming at Florence Crittenton, my grammar skills were respectable, but my rhetorical skills were embryonic. I can't remember any discussion of logical fallacies until years later when I started teaching my own Freshman Composition course and was expected to explain concepts like *non sequitur* and *ad hominem*. They were all Greek to me. But at OSU, as the brilliant, crisp days of fall unfolded in Corvallis, Oregon, my sketchy background in composition did nothing to prevent my immediate immersion into Faulkner's Jefferson, Mississippi, and the doomed Compson world. I loved the novel, even if it was baffling and frustrating. Much like me with my Cheshire cat grin, our professor smiled at our apprehensive confusion and proceeded to reverentially explain that *The Sound and the Fury* is *the* great American novel—not *Moby Dick*, not *Huckleberry Finn*, and not *The Scarlet Letter!* I'm not going to try to defend his claim, but without question, the novel is a narrative tour de force. To inhabit Benjy's intricately complicated mind and follow his achronological meanderings is one of the greatest reading experiences the genre has to offer.

It has taken me more readings than I can count to fully appreciate the narrative achievements of the novel, and surely I have not grasped them all. But it wasn't Faulkner's narrative technique that pulled me into novel that first time, as if I were a hooked trout befuddled by the barb that was pulling me willy-nilly through painful pages and pages of mystifying prose. Even now, as I reread it once again, it's not the narrators that capture me: not Benjy's purity, or Quentin's nihilism, or Jason's misanthropy. It's Caddy. It's always Caddy. I fell in love with her in the fall of 1966, and I've remained more faithful to her than she ever would have been to me. My purpose, then, in this chapter, is not to dissect Faulkner's narrative wizardry, worthy as that project surely is. Instead I go back to Caddy—my twin, my doppelgänger. I go back to the character Faulkner weaves as he picks up the symbolic threads of the archetypal scarlet woman and embroiders a new story of a woman's fall, Caddy's fall from Benjy's Eden, Quentin's agony, and Jason's fury.

On Easter weekend, April 1928, Benjy Compson is turning thirty-three. He and his caretaker, Luster, are walking along a fence that divides the Compson place from the golf course that borders it when they hear a golfer innocuously call, "Here, caddie." Instantly, Benjy begins to moan for his lost sister, Caddy, whom he desperately loves. But Caddy is not just greatly loved by Benjy (and by me). She is also the beloved and torturous obsession of her brother, Quentin, and the maddening fixation of her other brother, Jason. Her erotic attraction is established early on in a famous scene when, at age seven, she boldly disobeys her father and climbs a pear tree to spy on the adults gathered inside for a funeral. Quentin, Jason, and Benjy (still called Maury at this point in the novel), as well as Dilsey's children, Frony, Versh, and T.P., are standing under the tree, watching her ascend:

"Push me up, Versh." Caddy said.
"All right." Versh said. "You the one going to get whipped. I aint." He
went and pushed Caddy up into the tree to the first limb. We watched
the muddy bottom of her drawers. Then we couldn't see her. We could
hear the tree thrashing. (25)

Faulkner himself claimed that his story began with this mental picture,
"the muddy seat of a little girl's drawers in a pear tree where she could see
through a window . . . and report what was happening to her brothers on
the ground below." The image is charged with erotic and voyeuristic implications, but Faulkner maintains that it wasn't until later that he "realized the
symbolism of the soiled pants" ("Interview" 233). In a 1933 "Introduction"
for a new edition of the novel that was never published, Faulkner declares
that this mental picture was "the only thing in literature which would ever
move [him] very much" (227). Clearly Caddy and her prepubescent sexuality fed Faulkner's imagination and inspired the novel, yet Michael Millgate
argues that although "the novel revolves upon Caddy . . . Caddy herself escapes satisfactory definition" (98). Minrose Gwin goes further, maintaining
that although we can hear Caddie's voice for much of the novel, we cannot
fully understand what she is saying (34). I would agree, and acknowledge
that Caddy's incomprehensibility may have much to do with why I love her.
She is my unattainable lodestone, a captivating cipher I can't quite figure
out and don't dare emulate, but with whom I secretly identify. She shares
some of those bad-girl qualities that have led me to my most devastating
consequences: my impetuousness, my blustery insolence, my pull toward
sexually exciting risk, my difficulty with staying put, my exasperation with
stodgy convention. Rather than contradict me, Caddy appeals to my stormy
side, the side that I often squelch in order to be the good wife, mother, and
teacher that I know I'm expected to be. No wonder I love her.

Narrators make five attempts[1] to tell Caddy's story, yet none of them can
adequately "capture" her. As John T. Matthews notes, Caddy "climbs out of
the book . . . [She] is the figure that the novel is written to *lose*" (23). Faulkner
does not give her the opportunity to narrate, explaining years later that she
was "too beautiful and too moving to reduce telling what was going on"
("Class Conference" 235). Instead, he creates "a beautiful and tragic little girl"
(Faulkner "Introduction" 228) who becomes a beautiful but fallen woman as
seen through the eyes of her three brothers, then from the perspective of an
authorial "spokesman" with some omniscience, and finally in the "Appendix,"

which Falkner writes years later for *The Portable Faulkner*, from the perspective of yet another narrator with limited omniscience.[2] By relinquishing illusions of authority and admitting that we will never know the true Caddy, we can be better attuned to moments when Caddy is actually present in the text and her chimerical trace when she is not. Although for some critics, Caddy remains "little more than a blank counter" (Bleikasten 423), I maintain that by paying close attention to what we do hear and see of her, we can watch her emerge as a complicated, conflicted, twentieth-century, female-subject-in-process who decimates the "angel of the house" stereotype.[3]

As each narrator fails to master Caddy, each is influenced by the master narrative of the fallen woman, the narrative that to some extent controls Caddy and also impinges on her illegitimate child, Miss Quentin.[4] Faulkner gives us the opportunity to witness these two "scarlet" women or, I maintain, "modern" women, in a very different historical and geographical context than Wharton's old New York or Hawthorne's colonial Boston. "The degenerate New South" (Roberts 57), circa 1900 to 1928, is changing, especially the Victorian, aristocratic, moral attitudes of bygone plantation ideology. Nonetheless, aspects of what Richard King calls that "collective fantasy" still hold; many white, paternalistic, southern men remain hell-bent on defending the "altar of femininity" (Richard King 249, 251) and the antiquated standard of white female purity. But Caddy, who comes of age on the cusp of dramatic social change, is like "that damn honeysuckle" her brother Quentin connects with her: she cannot be ignored and she will not be restrained. Her verdant "sexuality is freed to both envelop and disrupt the narrative as it envelops and disrupts the Compsons' position as aristocrats" (Roberts 117).

I

The story of the Compson family demise begins with the initially puzzling but most reliable narrator Benjy, a mentally disabled boy/man whose neurasthenic mother changes his name from Maury to Benjy when she realizes he will always be delayed. Benjy has very little attachment to his mother; it's his older sister he wants, and his desire is unappeasable. He wants Caddy everywhere and for everything. He wants her to feed him, dress him, play with him, soothe him, and sleep with him. Benjy is oblivious of the structure of time; hence his "memory has no memories. He cannot remember, nor can he forget." Even in the later sections of the novel, after Caddy has been gone for years, for Benjy "it is as though Caddy had only departed a few seconds ago" (Bleikasten 424). His unreflective narration revolves around "a series of frozen pictures offered without bias" (Kartiganer 8) that involve either Caddy herself or her trace. Once we figure out how his mind works, his narration is straightforward, though chronologically fractured: "he repeats the events . . . with camera-like fidelity" (Millgate 91). Benjy craving for his sister's asexual yet intensely intimate physical presence is acceptable as long as they are children. But as they both physically mature, his constant desire for Caddy's affectionate proximity is threatened by her sexuality and by the other young men her emerging erotic appeal attracts.

Benjy's world is highly sensual. He's attuned to touch, sound, flashing lights, and smells of all kind. He knows Caddy best by the way she smells. For Benjy, young Caddy has the comforting smell of "leaves" (5) and of "trees in the rain" (12), but when she reaches puberty, things change. As we witness Benjy react to her changing body, we can gauge her transformation from the bold, impertinent tomboy with muddy drawers to a fully eroticized, sexually active young woman who defies her preoccupied parents and their collapsing customs. It begins when, at fourteen, she puts on perfume, after which Benjy cries inconsolably until she washes it off (27). But it's not just Caddy who is changing. When Benjy turns thirteen, he is told he must sleep alone, upon which announcement he cries so piercingly that Dilsey relents and brings Caddy in to him. But Dilsey is aware of the immature yet nonetheless unconsciously sexual nature of Benjy's desire and insists that Caddy sleep in her bathrobe with a blanket between them (29). From here on, Benjy's dependence on Caddy "is subject to constant threats which he fends off to the best of his ability" (Vickery 283). One night after he finds her making out on the swing with Charlie, he succeeds in putting an end to the tryst by wailing at full volume until Caddy abandons Charlie, washes out her mouth, removes the lingering odor of Charlie's kisses, and restores the smell of trees. On another occasion, the summer that Mr. Compson sells Benjy's pasture so that Quentin can go to Harvard, Caddy, who we assume has just had sexual intercourse with Dalton Ames, rushes into the house, trying to avoid her mother and father's notice. But she can't get around Benjy's acute sense of smell, and now that his voice has changed, Benjy's wails have turned to bellowing roars. Hysterically, he pulls at her dress and pushes upstairs to the bathroom, "his voice hammering back and forth as though its own momentum would not let it stop" (79). His attempts to restore the asexual intimacy of their childhood inevitably fail as Caddie becomes more and more defined by her sexuality. On her wedding day, when she puts her arms around him to comfort him one last time, he "can't smell trees anymore" and commences once again his unrelenting bellowing (26).

Benjy's desire for Caddy never abates; years later, after he chases a schoolgirl who reminds him of his long-gone sister, his older brother, Jason, has him castrated.[5] But castration does nothing to deaden his desire for Caddy. For the rest of his life, Benjy will pine for her physical presence, for her touch and her smell, finding a small measure of comfort in a not uncommon fetish, her slipper. The night that he relives most frequently is the night he and his brothers first looked up at Caddy's muddy drawers as she climbed the tree and later when they watched as Dilsey wadded up those same drawers and scrubbed "Caddy behind with them," while chiding that the mud "done soaked clean through onto [her]" (48). He summons up the sensory impressions of lying in bed as "Caddy held me and I could hear us all, and the darkness, and something I could smell. And then I could see the windows, where the trees were buzzing. Then the dark began to go in smooth, bright shapes, like it always does, even when Caddy says that I have been asleep" (48). That this passage shifts from past to present tense should not surprise, for Caddy is absent/present: "literally nowhere . . . [but] metaphorically everywhere" (Bleikasten 425). For Benjy, "the past takes on a sort of super-reality; its contours are hard and clear, unchangeable. The present, nameless and fleeting, is helpless before it" (Sartre 267). Caddy remains inevitably elusive yet always beckoning, and Benjy, "impervious to the future," will never relinquish her (Faulkner "Interview" 231).

II

Unlike Benjy, once Quentin reaches adolescence, his despairing love for his sister is consciously sexualized if not overtly acted upon. Caddy is as essential to him as she is to Benjy, and like Benjy, he cannot reconcile himself to losing her to other men. But Caddy, driven to defy authority of any kind, jumps at the opportunity for sexual rebelliousness. In so doing, she "runs . . . out of [Quentin's] and Benjy's world," abandoning Quentin's imaginary "paradise" for the "rife animality of sex" (Vickery 285). Benjy cannot control her; Quentin cannot control her; her father cares not to; Caddy herself seems to have both claimed her own body, in that she will do with it as she pleases, and surrendered it, in that she offers it without thinking to whoever desires it. But her passivity does not fit the template for the heterosexual master narrative of romance, which is premised on female submissiveness and male aggression and dominance. Though Quentin may want to maintain male dominance and remain loyal to the distinctions, such as male/female, good/ bad, and pure/fallen, that inform the traditional romance narrative, Caddy moves far beyond the condoned pleasures this narrative permits. Rather than be the "nice girl" who learns to resist sexual desire, Caddy becomes the bold, unfettered "bad girl," abandoning herself to taboo, unregulated sexual desire. Her sexual defiance is not necessarily new to the master narrative of the fallen woman, but it is new to this survey of fallen women in American literature. Until now, the ruined women we have encountered have been seduced either by duplicity and trickery (as in *The Power of Sympathy*, *The Coquette*, *Charlotte Temple*, and *Jennie Gerhardt*) or by moments of surrender to a grand passion (as in *The Scarlet Letter*, *The Old Maid*, and "Roman Fever"). Caddy is our first "bad girl," or we might say, our first modern woman who enjoys sex and has it as often as she likes with whomever she pleases. For me, her example is both appealing and appalling since I know all too well that female sexual freedom is rarely free. We may claim sexual liberation but as Caddy (and I) must learn, at considerable cost.

According to Caddy's cynical, dipsomaniacal father, all women bear the mark of the fallen woman—menstruation—or what he refers to as the "periodical filth between two moons" (81). Like the bloody sputum that Delia uses in *The Old Maid* to finalize Charlotte's fall, menstrual blood is embroidered by Jason Compson Sr.'s misogyny with shades of shameful fecundity and inevitable promiscuity. Caddy's blood becomes the "source of trouble" for the Compsons as her adolescent, unrestrainable body threatens their precarious stability. According to Fiedler, Caddy is one of Faulkner's stereotypical females, the "febrile . . . sexually insatiable daughters of the aristocracy" (321). Caddy is, in fact, both febrile and insatiable, but she is also so multifaceted and enigmatic that it is shortsighted to stereotype her. Nonetheless, her sexual eagerness is corroborated by her actions. For example, when Quentin angrily asks her why she let her lover kiss her, she replies defiantly, "I didn't let him I made him" (84). Quentin responds by slapping her and in so doing, he bruises her face. He watches as the bruise spreads and the red shape of his hand emerges on her cheek, "coming up through her face like turning a light on under your hand . . . my red hand coming up out of her face" (84–85). To obliterate her lover's residue, Quentin in effect marks her with his own "brand," and its scarlet outline functions as "an emblem of her defilement. An indelible stain on her honor" (Bleikasten 427). Once again, the color red breaks the surface of the narrative, staining the fallen woman. From Persephone to Caddy, it has seeped into their stories, marking them as indelibly defiled.

Caddy is herself confused by her disruptive sexual desire and willingly assumes the burden of guilt for what southern, patriarchal tradition condemns as perversity—uncontrollable female desire. "There was something terrible in me terrible in me," she tells Quentin, and the sexual climaxes she reaches with her lovers only seem to confirm this. Rather than finding pleasure in intercourse, she finds death: "I died last year," she tells Quentin. "I told you I had but I didn't know then what I meant I didn't know what I was saying . . . but now I know I'm dead I tell you" (78). Caddy connects sexual intercourse and orgasm with death, as Freud says we all do unconsciously. Nonetheless, she tells Quentin she would "die" for her lover "over and over again" (95). In a crucial scene, Caddy runs away from her lover and from Benjy, who had sought them out and is wailing accusingly. Quentin follows her to the river branch where he finds her—Ophelia-like—lying in the shallow water. He remembers the long-ago night of their grandmother's death, the night Caddy got her drawers muddy, the night that established her as the object of his unbearable sexual desire. Like Caddy, he too cannot separate sex from death; aroused but impotent, he takes out his knife in frustration, intending to kill Caddy and then himself. The suggestion that he is, in fact, trying to have sex with her is not subtle. Caddy, also consumed by guilt and confusion, seems willing to acquiesce to either sex with her brother or death. She tells Quentin, "[I'll] do anything you want me to anything" (99). But Quentin fumbles with his "knife"; the moment is lost, and he ends up taking her back to her lover and shaking his hand like a gentleman.

Although Quentin may not agree with his father's condemnation of women in general, that "no woman is to be trusted" (67) because "they have an affinity for evil . . . for drawing it about them instinctively" (62), he demonstrates his egregious racism when he berates Caddy for having sex "like nigger women . . . in the pasture the ditches the dark woods hot hidden furious in the dark woods" (59). Until Caddy, white women in southern literature have been denied sexual appetites, which have been displaced onto black women (King 254). Quentin's racist insult repeats "the creed of Faulkner's culture," which associated black women with animal sexuality (Roberts 79). Given the culturally sensitive awareness we have fortunately acquired, passages like this one are almost unrepeatable; nonetheless, Quentin's unpardonable comparison reveals Caddy's brazen sexual avidity.

No matter what insults he hurls, Quentin cannot rein in his sister. When he asks her how many sexual partners she has had, she answers "I dont know . . . too many." Caddy's potential for autonomy seems almost entirely obliterated by her sexual extravagance. The only way Quentin can figure out how he might win her back is by sexual domination, but since that had failed in the flesh, he turns to language. He will verbally, if not physically, dominate her with words. Thus, he insists, "you thought it was them but it was me listen I fooled you all the time it was me you thought I was in the house where that damn honeysuckle . . . the swing the cedars the secret surges the breathing locked drinking the wild breath the yes Yes Yes yes . . . [I'll] make you say we did [I'm] stronger than you [I'll] make you know we did" (94). But saying they had sex, even if he could make Caddy say it too, does not make it so.

Caddy's father brands Caddy as inevitably ruined just because she is female. Her mother brands her as such because she has the "blood" of the Compsons rather than the Bascombs. One of her lovers, Dalton Ames, tells Quentin that "all women are bitches" (102). Faulkner himself describes her as "doomed" and unable to be cleansed of the symbolic "mud" that soiled her "body, flesh and . . . shame" ("Introduction" 231). As Vickery notes, "Dilsey's determined scouring of Caddy's bottom shows [that] the stains of one's experience are not that easily removed" (285). Though a contemporary reader may see Caddy as courageously breaking with traditional patriarchal patterns that oppress, and is so doing, demonstrating "just how moribund those patterns have become, how irrelevant both to modern conditions and to the needs of the human psyche" (Millgate 97), it can't be denied that Caddy sees herself as ruined.

Faced with the incontrovertible fact of Caddy's inevitable pregnancy, Quentin accuses her of not knowing who the father of her baby is. She does not deny it. Once again, in a futile attempt to isolate and control her, Quentin tries to rewrite the past and make himself the father: "making unreality a possibility, then a probability, then an incontrovertible fact, as people will when their desires become words" (75). In so doing, he tries to convince his father (and himself) that he has committed incest with Caddy. His is a desperate bid to stop the life changes—puberty, sexual desire, marriage, and maternity—that have removed and will continue to remove Caddy from his obsessive possessiveness. Mr. Compson will not be persuaded (49–50, 94). With roundabout cynicism, he tries to convince Quentin that his virginity and Caddy's "unvirginity" are of no consequence, that "women are never virgins" (73–74). Here Mr. Compson actually makes sense as a shrewd critic of patriarchal standards. He understands, argues Vickery, that "virginity is merely a transient physical state which has been given its ethical significance by men" (284). He recognizes that the connection of virginity with morality is "an invented script, . . . a produced structure, not an inalterable essence" (Weinstein 433). But Quentin will not be dissuaded. He cannot restore his sister's virginity, but he can reclaim her if he can convince his father of the incest, and so he continues his desperate narrative: "we did . . . we did a terrible crime it cannot be hid . . . Ill tell you Father then itll have to be . . . then well have to go away amid the pointing and the horror the clean flame" (94). Like Benjy, he cannot bear to lose his sister to another man, whether that man is Charlie, or Dalton Ames, or Herbert Head. Rather than losing her, he prefers hell, "because if it were just to hell . . . Nobody else there but her and me. If we could just have done something so dreadful that they would have fled hell except us . . . If we could have just done something so dreadful" (50–51). But Quentin's frantic words cannot make it so.

Pregnant with an unidentifiable man's baby, Caddy can think of no other option than to marry the detestable Herbert, the "blackguard" who was "caught cheating at midterm exams and expelled" from Harvard. Caddy has no choice. Maternity takes away her sexual freedom, entrapping her in the patriarchal expectation of monogamous marriage and when that fails, banishment. Neither her father, mother, Quentin, Benjy, Jason, nor Dilsey can control her, but southern patriarchy still wins out. Like the other fallen women we have encountered, once she is pregnant, she is powerless to choose a future other than maternity. Thoroughly entrapped now by her sexuality, Caddy can only think of herself as "cursed" (100). "She cannot wash off or throw away her desire" (Gwinn 46) and believes that her only means of escaping the "curse" is to agree to marry a man she loathes. And Quentin, who can do nothing to stop her and cannot bear to think of the time when losing her will not hurt, sees no option but suicide. In this version of the fallen woman, unwed motherhood, even when ostensibly "put right" by marriage, still spells doom.

III

The third brother, Jason, "the brother Caddy never value[s]" (Clarke 22), is just as obsessed with Caddy as Benjy and Quentin, and he too lives an utterly frustrated existence, irate because her failed marriage destroys his chance for a job in Herbert's bank. While appearing to ignore her, Jason pursues her relentlessly, or if not literally her, a representation of her in his life (Matthews 92). But Jason's pursuit is as thwarted as Benjy's and Quentin's. He can manipulate Caddy, exploit her, and cheat her, but he can't completely control her, nor can he keep her illegitimate daughter in check. Both are valuable commodities in Jason's scheme, pawns that he positions and repositions on his complicated and unlawful moneymaking game board. But just as he can't fully control his pawns, he also cannot entirely control his own narrative, and Caddy's voice is heard intermittently throughout as she "speaks [of] the tragic results of the cultural objectification of real people and the disastrous effects of a system of barter which makes women commodities" (Gwin 56). The endgame will reveal all.

Jason's section takes place the day before Benjy's birthday on April 6, 1928, almost eighteen years after Quentin's suicide. We learn that Caddy's marriage ended abruptly after she gave birth to her daughter, the daughter she names Quentin (and I refer to as Miss Quentin). After "Herbert threw her out" (138), Caddy surrendered her infant to her father, who brought the baby back to the Compson home, where she has been raised with patience by Dilsey and with malice by Jason. Faulkner maintains, "She [has] never been offered love or affection or understanding" ("Interview" 233). Mr. Compson dies only a month after bringing her home. Caddy, the disgraced unwed mother, is exiled, and made to promise that she will not return to Jefferson. Perfidiously arrogant, Mrs. Compson insists that Caddy's name never be uttered in the house again. Although Caddy faithfully sends a monthly check for her daughter's care, Mrs. Compson insists the checks "of [that] fallen woman" (138) be burned. Bent on revenge, Jason, a Chillingworth figure if there ever was one, finds a way to pocket Caddy's money. Hoarding it in a locked box in his bedroom, he uses it sparingly to buy a car, play the stock market, and maintain a mistress. But no amount of money can satiate his craving; only the ongoing, pitiless exploitation of his sister's illegitimate child provides him passing satisfaction.

Jason's loathing for Miss Quentin is established in the very first sentence of his section and he repeats it at the section's conclusion: "Once a bitch, always a bitch" (113, 165). Her illegitimacy marks her in ways that are very different from any of the illegitimate daughters we have encountered thus far in American fiction. At seventeen, Miss Quentin is not Hawthorne's radiant Pearl, or Dreiser's angelic Vesta, or Wharton's charismatic Tina or dazzling Barbara. She is a vulnerable and desperate girl, living in an exceedingly dysfunctional family. She rebels like many teenagers: she wears heavy makeup and provocative clothes, skips school, and forges her grandmother's name on her report card. But her reckless rebelliousness goes beyond typical teenage disobedience. She defies every one of Jason's commands, flouts her promiscuity, and insults Dilsey, the one person who sincerely cares about her, even as Dilsey tries to protect her.

Jason repeatedly rubs in the sad circumstances of her birth. He believes Caddy's sexual voraciousness runs through Miss Quentin's veins. He insists, "You cant do anything with a woman like that, if she's got it in her. If it's in her blood, you cant do anything with her. The only thing you can do is to get rid of her, let her go on and live with her own sort" because "blood always tells. If you've got blood like that in you, you'll do anything (146, 149). Jason has told her for so long that she was born corrupted[6] that she comes to believe it too. When he chastises her for "slipping up and down back alleys with one of those damn squirts," she replies: "I'm bad and I'm going to hell, and I don't care." Later she adds, "Whatever I do, it's your fault . . . If I'm bad, it's because I had to be. You made me" (119, 162). In many ways, she is right. Jason's psychologically destructive influence over his "own blood niece" (158) has been poisonous. Her grandmother also believes she is "contaminated" by her "heritage," and has decreed that she "grow up never to know that she had a mother" (125). Miss Quentin accepts their version of her as tainted by her mother's precedent. But it's not Caddy's "blood" that has turned Miss Quentin "bad," or fallen, or damned. Rather, it's her malicious uncle's abusive "guardianship" that has made her such a desperately reckless teenager. And, like her long-dead uncle for whom she was named, she has a compelling death wish, declaring at one point that she is sorry that she "ever drew breath" (118).

Although he is unable to control Miss Quentin, Jason can control Caddy's access to her. Even though Caddy knows the money she is sending is not being given to Miss Quentin, she is made helpless by her required exile. Dispossessed from her position in the family by her fall and her ongoing shame, which Jason uses as a weapon that stings, she relinquishes control. For Jason, she becomes "like some kind of a toy that's wound up too tight and about to burst all to pieces" (131). Because he is "wholly in the world [and] acutely sensitive to social values" (Millgate 99), Jason can manipulate her like a marionette, pulling the strings of her longing and her shame any way he pleases. Although we know little of the actual circumstances of Caddy's life away from Jefferson—how she makes her money or why she cannot keep Miss Quentin with her—we do know that she does not believe that she has the psychological resources to raise her daughter. She agonizingly confesses to Jason, "I'm insane. I cant take her. Keep her. What am I thinking of" (131). Maternity, as Philip Weinstein observes, is a sort of "Waterloo" for Faulkner's women, none of whom can take it on without diminishment. "Once his pregnant women *deliver*," Weinstein maintains, "they cease to be figures of empathy or desire" (440). Certainly this is the case for Mrs. Compson, and critic Deborah Clarke maintains that Caddy merits "no consideration as Mother of the Year." Clarke argues that "her abandonment of her daughter to Jason . . . seriously undermines both her idealized status and her maternal position" (21). Nonetheless, I continue to read Caddy's inability to keep and raise her child with compassion. I know the powerful social forces that keep unwed mothers and their illegitimate children apart. And regardless of critical disapproval of Caddy's failure to mother, she persists as the object of both Benjy's and Miss Quentin's desire for maternal devotion and as the compelling object of Jason's revenge.

Jason has in the past been impressed that Caddy "dont mind anybody" (127), so when she begs him to be sure Miss Quentin "has things like other girls," he takes a great deal of satisfaction by establishing conditions that will make her "mind" him: "Sure," he tells her, "as long as you behave and do like I tell you" (128). By using guilt and guile, Jason "insinuates himself into a heavily disguised, disfigured intimacy with Caddy" (Matthews 101), manipulates his mother and Dilsey, and gains the control over Caddy that he always wanted and now malignantly deploys. She "minds" him and he successfully uses, as Faulkner notes in the "Appendix," his "niece's illegitimacy to blackmail [her] mother" for seventeen years (212). But Miss Quentin's obedience is another matter.

As she becomes identified as a "scarlet woman," the signifiers that identify her shift to more obvious signs of willful, sexual provocativeness. For Caddy it was the symbolic muddy drawers, but for Miss Quentin, they are, in Jason's words, "a face painted up like a dam clown's . . . hair all gummed and twisted and a dress that if a woman had come out doors . . . with no more than that to cover her legs and behind, she'd been thrown in jail" (145). The color red also stands out on a male character for the first time in our analysis. One of Miss Quentin's boyfriends, a "drummer" (or pitchman) for a traveling show, sports a distinctive red tie, a tie that critic Michelle Ann Abate maintains, marks him as homosexual (293).[7] When Jason spots Miss Quentin with the "drummer," his reaction lends credence to Abate's claim. He declares: "I saw red. When I recognized that red tie, after all I had told her, I forgot about everything" (149). In Jason's homophobic American South of the 1920s, the red tie acts something like Hester's scarlet A did in New England of the 1650s: it marks him as an outsider, as sexually deviant and debased. But also like Hester's A, neither the drummer's red tie nor Miss Quentin's provocative clothing are disempowering. Rather they are markers for their sexual audaciousness, for the gutsy impudence of Miss Quentin that releases her from the southern coterie of demure, ladylike "good breeding," and for the freewheeling daring of the drummer that dumbfounds Jason and leaves him ripe for Miss Quentin's revenge. For both Miss Quentin and the drummer, clothing is a means of flaunting convention, a sign of rebelliousness and freedom, a sign that they will neither play by Jason's rules nor abide by Jefferson's customs. As the latest rendition of the illegitimate child, Miss Quentin reverses vulnerability, flings off the social trappings that would condemn her to stultifying decorum, and seizes the offensive. Rather than be threatened by the taint of sexual impropriety that jeopardized Tina in *The Old Maid*, Miss Quentin puts it to good use, abetted by the color red.

III

In the final section, often referred to as the Dilsey section, we learn from the limited-omniscient narrator that Miss Quentin has learned something important from her uncle: how to be a clever thief. Not unlike her headstrong mother, she easily climbs the blossoming pear tree, not to spy on the adults but to break into Jason's locked room. There she finds his locked box, and takes back at least some of the money that her mother has been sending over the years. By climbing down the same tree that once gave her mother a perch of temporary superiority, Miss Quentin, far from helpless, manages to escape her dysfunctional family and the cruel revenge plot Jason had been writing for her. She springs the trap, grabs the bounty, and takes off with her "drummer" for the unknown. Rather than repeat her mother's mistakes, Miss Quentin has been using contraception, as evidenced by the box of Agnes Mabel Becky condoms Luster finds under a bush near the swing (32). And, if indeed the man with the red tie is gay, Miss Quentin has chosen her accomplice well by escaping with a man with whom she will not likely be romantically involved. She gets out of her uncle's house without pregnancy limiting her choices, before she is shamed into exile. From Dilsey's final vantage point we gain a more reliable perspective, one that corrects Jason's venomous version of Miss Quentin. She takes what is hers and runs we know not where; Jason is powerless to stop her.

IV

In his "Appendix," Faulkner tries one more time to tell the Compson saga and in so doing, gives us more, although conflicting, information about Caddy and Miss Quentin.[8] We learn that Miss Quentin escapes much like her ancestor Charles Stuart Compson, who also "fled by night, running true to family tradition" ("Appendix" 205), once did. Of Caddy, whom Faulkner describes even as late as 1957 as "the beautiful one . . . my heart's darling" ("Class Conference" 236), we learn what we suspected, that like her father, "she [had] placed no value whatever" on her virginity: "the frail physical stricture which to her was no more than a hangnail would have been" (208). We learn that she married a Hollywood moving picture magnate in 1920, when Miss Quentin would have been nine years old, and divorced in 1925. More mysteriously, we learn that in 1940 while she was living in Paris, which was under German occupation at that time, she vanished only to show up photographed in "a slick magazine," riding down the main street of Marseilles. It is a picture "filled with luxury and money and sunlight"; Caddy is in "an open powerful expensive chromiumtrimmed sports car, hatless between a rich scarf and a seal coat, ageless and beautiful, cold serene and damned; beside her a handsome lean man of middleage in the ribbons and tabs of a German staffgeneral" ("Appendix" 210–11).[9] Once again Caddy is playing with fire, and Faulkner has found a way for his untamable fallen woman to fall even further by becoming the mistress of a Nazi.

For Fiedler, Faulkner's dis-ease with female sexuality trumps both Fitzgerald's and Hemingway's chauvinism. He maintains that Faulkner gives "the impression of the village misogynist swapping yarns with the boys at the bar in order to reveal a truth about women which shocks even himself" (321). As if to corroborate Fiedler's conclusion, Faulkner can't resist adding unnecessary sexist trivia to his "Appendix," providing "images of the anti-virgin," or what Fiedler describes as "mindless daughters of peasants, whose fertility and allure are scarcely distinguishable from those of a beast in heat" (Fiedler 321). Faulkner chooses to include an unneeded description of the bus terminal where Melissa Meek, the Jefferson librarian who discovers Caddy's picture, returns after visiting Dilsey. The platform, Faulkner observes, is crowded with soldiers and "the homeless young women, their companions, who for two years now had lived from day to day in pullmans and hotels . . . pausing only long enough to drop their foals in charity wards or policestations and then move on again" ("Appendix" 211). It is a mean, excessive detail, yet telling of Faulkner's enduring preoccupation with female sexuality, extramarital sex, and illegitimacy.

For Miss Quentin, "fatherless nine months before her birth, nameless at birth," it is no surprise that Faulkner pessimistically projects a future in which the pitchman (no longer referred to as "the man with the red tie") with whom Miss Quentin runs away is "already under sentence for bigamy" and that she is "doomed to be unwed" ("Appendix" 214). An unmarried woman still spells calamity in Faulkner's heteronormative world as surely as it did for Charlotte in Wharton's "The Old Maid."[10] That Miss Quentin vanishes from Jason's, her grandmother's, Dilsey's, and, we assume, from Caddy's life may similarly suggest misfortune, but her portentous escape can be read as a successful bid for freedom from an oppressive, cruel, vindictive uncle who has held her hostage all her life as he has blackmailed her banished birthmother.

For most Faulkner critics, Caddy remains unsavable. According to Cleanth Brooks, her future as the "homeless . . . sexual adventuress adrift in the world" can be read "as a parable of the disintegration of modern man. Individuals [like Caddy] no longer sustained by familial and cultural unity are alienated and lost in private worlds" (342). Certainly she is alienated from the Compson domain, meager as it is, and by placing her in a Nazi's car, Faulkner suggests she is morally lost. Branded forever by signs of transgression that mutate from her infamous muddy drawers, to the unrestrainable honeysuckle, to her menstrual blood, to the red outline of Quentin's hand on her slapped face, to the swastika emblazoning her Nazi general, Caddy is swept "into dishonor and shame" ("Introduction" 230) and, insists Faulkner, she "*doesn't want to be saved hasn't anything anymore worth being saved for nothing worth being lost that she can lose*" ("Appendix" 212). Like Hester, she cannot escape her sexual "branding," which becomes inextricably entwined with her beauty, her desirability, and her livelihood. And so it follows her from childhood and adolescence in Jefferson into adulthood in Hollywood, and onto Paris and Marseilles, the last place we see her.

Faulkner notes in his unpublished "Introduction" to the novel that the branch where the children played and where Caddy wet her clothing becomes "the dark, harsh flowing of time sweeping [Caddy] to where she could not return to comfort" Benjy, or Quentin, or her father, or her mother, or even her daughter (230). Without the centrifugal force that Caddy created, the Compsons begin their gradual disintegration. Quentin and Mr. and Mrs. Compson die, Benjy is sent to an institution in Jackson, Dilsey goes blind, Jason never gets his revenge, and Miss Quentin vanishes. The novel "yearn[s] for an ending" (Matthews 104) but the representations of desire resist resolution and will not be extinguished even at the novel's conclusion. The retelling of the fallen woman's master narrative insists on difference as it endures.

Caddy and Miss Quentin do not diminish the significance of the fall, but they do escape the patriarchal and misogynistic confinement of the Compson domain and the obsessions of the men who would imprison them in the past's idealization of feminine purity and helplessness. If Caddy and Miss Quentin are read in this way, argues critic Sally Page, the novel can be considered "a powerful indictment of the idealization of virgin purity and a moving portrayal of the destructiveness this idealism precipitates" (48). Because Benjy insists on the literal purity of unconditional love, he is devastated when Caddy has to relinquish her role as his ideal nurturer and protector because of her sexual fall. Because Quentin insists on symbolic purity of the ideal southern belle, he is destroyed when Caddy falls into sexuality and maternity. Because Jason insists on the metonymical purity of money as ideal compensation for Caddy's fall out of matrimony, he is thwarted, if not destroyed when Miss Quentin takes back at least some of money he has stolen from her. But why not validate Caddy on her own terms, not those of her brothers and, in so doing, honor "the feminine energies" (Roberts 111) of the novel? Why not applaud Caddy for daring to transgress, for giving herself to whom she pleases, for not acting "as an object of transaction but as a transactor" (Roberts 112)? Why not admire Miss Quentin's clever decision to enlist the help of the "drummer," escape her vicious uncle, and regain what is hers? After all, she gives Luster his precious quarter before making her getaway and her generosity suggests that she will be not repeat Jason's miserliness. Also, "unlike her mother, she leaves no hostage behind" (Millgate 103). We might not be able to see her as conclusively heroic, but for me, her getaway is exhilaratingly triumphant. As I write this, I can hear my dissenters insisting:

That's not what Faulkner meant at all. We can't congratulate Caddy on her escape or characterize Miss Quentin as a jubilant Huck Finn, taking off for the new territories. We cannot celebrate these fallen women. They are doomed!

Yet I've learned from feminist scholars to be "a resisting reader" (Fetterly 1035), to see "with fresh eyes" (Rich 18), "to look at life and letters from a new coign" (Heilbrun 39), to listen for voices of alterity (Gwin 34), to "Tell all the Truth but tell it slant" (Dickinson). Thus as I wrap up, I applaud Caddy's and Miss Quentin's escapes from the chauvinistic tyranny that tried to confine and define them and celebrate their bold disobedience. I admire their sexual autonomy and pay tribute to the ways they, like Hester, appropriate the tropes that would brand them scarlet women. Far from reading Miss Quentin's escape as the end of the old Compson line, as Dilsey seems to do when she remarks, "I've seed de first en de last" (185), I read her breakout as a promising new beginning. Together, Caddy and Miss Quentin creatively carry the narrative of the fallen woman into modernity, embroidering the scarlet archetype with erotic possibility and irrepressible audacity.

I would like to be end on this celebratory note, yet ultimately, I must admit that *The Sound and the Fury* will never end happily for me. I must return to the birthmother, to Caddy, always Caddy, and the pain that I know lies just beneath the surface of her adventurous spirit. In my own compulsion to repeat, I always return to one heartbreaking scene. It may not stand out for most readers, but the scene still haunts me long after I've labored to put my congratulatory spin on the novel's ending. It's that terrible moment that Jason narrates; it's the night Caddy returns to Jefferson after her father's death. She does not dare attend the funeral, but after it's over and everyone's gone, Jason finds her standing over the grave, her black veil obscuring her face. She offers him fifty dollars if he will arrange to let her see her baby. Predictably, Jason insists on a hundred dollars and that he be paid up front. And, since his consuming purpose in life is to cheat her, he proceeds to do so. He goes home, makes an excuse to Dilsey to take Miss Quentin to her grandmother, wraps her up in a raincoat, puts her in the horse-drawn hack, and gets the hired hand, Mink, to drive them to the depot. When he sees Caddy, "standing on the corner in the light," he has Mink drive up close. He describes the moment:

> I took the raincoat off of her and held her to the window and Caddy saw her and sort of jumped forward. "Hit 'em, Mink!" I says, and Mink gave them a cut and we went past like a fire engine. "Now get on that train like

you promised," I says. I could see her running after us through the back window. "Hit 'em again," I says. "Let's get on home." When we turned the corner she was still running. (129)

I am always there with Caddy on the outskirts of the cemetery, on the margins of town, all the gates closed, all the doors shut, all the shutters drawn. I am always there with Caddy, standing on a lonely corner under a dim streetlight, anxiously waiting for my baby, only to have her snatched away before I'm even sure what I saw. I am always there with Caddy, running after the speeding hack, desperate to hold my daughter. I am always there with Caddy, alone on the dark, deserted street, the clatter of the hack receding into the night. I am always there with Caddy, my footsteps the only noise now as I turn back to the miserable station, without hope, without surcease, without love.

CHAPTER FIVE

The Unwed Mother Triumphant
Alice Walker's The Color Purple

When students read *The Sound and the Fury*, they are almost always intimidated and then impressed by Faulkner's narrative techniques: fascinated by Benjy, bewildered by Quentin, repelled by Jason, sympathetic of Dilsey. They recognize the novel as an American classic except when it comes to Faulkner's racism and sexism. Then they balk. How can we respect a novel that demeans blacks and disparages women? As their teacher, how can I help settle this dichotomy? First, we begin by discussing the influence of the racist and sexist ideology and discourse of the post–Civil War, segregated South. Faulkner's situatedness in this context led him to opt unselfconsciously for debasing stereotypes throughout the novel. In creating Dilsey, for example, he repeats with slight revisions the stock type Mammy, a noble, generous, faithful, and subservient woman who endures when the Compsons do not, but his revision is inadequate and disconcerting for its obvious racial and sexist bias. Still, is it possible to appreciate Dilsey and at the same time refuse to excuse Faulkner's racism in creating her? To help them manage rather than solve the dilemma, I ask them to employ W. E. B. Du Bois's sense of "twoness." Following Du Bois's example, we try holding two irreconcilable thoughts simultaneously: respect for Dilsey and disrespect for Faulkner's dependence on caricature. Du Bois's method works well for them. We appreciate the novel and at the same time, we are upfront about its racism and sexism. But it doesn't solve the problem completely. We need to find other productive ways to critique chauvinism. We need to read more. We need to read other novels about women and in particular black women of that era that will serve as a corrective lens to Faulkner's myopia. And so we turn to Alice Walker's *The Color Purple*, an always highly respected southern novel that also takes place in the South of the early decades of the twentieth century but from a very different perspective than the one that informed Faulkner in Oxford, Mississippi, 1929.

However, before we turn to *The Color Purple* and to its protagonist Celie, our next fallen woman, it's useful to talk about ways to situate not only our authors but also the characters they create. In their essay "Revising Critical Practices," Felicity Nussbaum and Laura Brown give us ways to situate female characters as we continue our reading and attempt such critical analysis. Nussbaum and Brown's insights are not only relevant when talking about Dilsey, or Caddy, or Miss Quentin, or Celie, but also when discussing all female characters in literary history. Nussbaum and Brown maintain:

> "Woman" must be read as an historically and culturally produced category that is situated within specific material conditions and is interactive with the complicated problems of class and race . . . certain regimes of truth, of discourse, and of subjectivity are limited by the category of gender. (15)

We have repeatedly seen in over a century of American literature, fallen women pay greatly for their seductions, but always in different and sometimes radically different contexts for which we must account. Each exists in a specific historical moment, and her circumstances in that moment are never simply the result of her gender. Rather each exists in a complex maze of conditions that include her class and her race as well as particular cultural assumptions and social truths that go beyond gender. Nussbaum and Brown help us see the extent to which literary texts like *The Old Maid* and *The Sound and the Fury* possess their own, unique ideology.

Even after grappling with Du Bois's "twoness," students want to know how racial and sexist biases could remain so ingrained even in an intellectual like Faulkner. Katie Cannon, in her book *Black Womanist Ethics*, helps us better understand the historical persistence of racism and sexism by giving us a chronological context that also better prepares us for our reading of *The Color Purple* and the twentieth-century oppression Walker confronts. For three centuries before the Civil War, slavery was justified through the twisted logic of a hierarchy inherited from the "great chain of being" of the Middle Ages. On this chain, "Blacks were assigned a fixed place as inferior species of humanity ... a species between animal and human." As slavery became the rule in the South, white colonists were "caught in the obsessive duality of understanding the slave as property rather than a person." In order to justify treating persons as property, slave traders and southern slave owners proffered racist rationalizations, and eventually a racist ideology "that proclaimed Blacks as lazy, cunning, lewd, impure, naturally inferior, full of animality and matriarchal proclivities, incapable of life's higher thoughts and emotion, and thus incapable of equality with whites" (Cannon 41). As we know all too well, that ideology was not eradicated by the Emancipation Proclamation or the Civil War.

Black women in this ideological hierarchy fared even worse than black men. Slave traders had once outrageously insisted that "the black female was sexually aggressive and sometimes mated with orangutan males" (qtd. in Cannon 41). Such contemptible claims were readily accepted as fact so that even when chattel slavery ended during the Civil War, long-established assumptions about race and gender did not. "The patterns of exploitation of black women as laborer and breeder were only shaken by the Civil War. By no means were they destroyed" (Cannon 46). Faulkner's post–Civil War South remained fixated on the racial dualities of white/black, master/servant, property owner / laborer. White southern men demanded the codification of white patriarchal superiority: white over black, male over female, white "belle" over black "wench." "Jim Crowism" became a calculated, invidious state policy, and white terror organizations such as the Ku Klux Klan engaged in illegal violence to supplement the policy. White southerners clung to self-serving narratives that justified a way of life where clearly delineated divisions between classes, genders, and races were ruthlessly maintained.

The disastrous holdovers from the accusations of the long-gone, odious slave traders lingered: "Black women were held to be (in contrast to white ladies) promiscuous, sensual, earthy"; "'polluted' instead of 'pure'" (Roberts xv). Just as the imposed sexual designation of black females as sexually aggressive had provided justification for white rape of black female slaves, it later justified the routine sexual exploitation of poor black women and girls in the post–Civil War South and beyond. In her book *Black Feminist Thought*, Patricia Hill Collins suggests, "The creation of Jezebel, the image of the sexually denigrated Black woman, has been vital in sustaining a system of interlocking race, gender and class oppression" (174). But the stereotype of the wanton Jezebel has not only supplied rationalization for white male sexual domination; it has also ironically provided justification for black male sexual exploitation of black females. Perhaps the most sinister example of historical racism combined with cultural sexism is the double bind of black females whose bodies have not only been defined as "naturally" sexual but also have rarely been granted the public legal protection that white females are usually extended. In an ideology that defines black females as intrinsically sexually available, black women and girls are doubly oppressed.

In Faulkner's fiction, the prescribed dualities and delineations are beginning to crumble, but not necessarily, as my students come to see, in positive ways. Diane Roberts observes that in novels like *The Sound and the Fury*, "Women can slip toward masculinity, ladies can slip toward whorishness, white can slip toward black" (xiv). When Caddy begins to perform both feminine and masculine sexual roles by being both sexually submissive and sexually aggressive, she crosses all kinds of boundaries and, in so doing, she imperils not only the Compson "name" but also the symbolic order on which the South has sustained itself. She rejects her designation as an upper-class, white southern lady but, in so doing, she falls to the opposite pole of the binary, and thereby debasing racial slurs are immediately applied to her by Quentin and later by Jason. The appalling racism and sexism of southern ideology are in full view.

In previously discussions of *The Old Maid* and *The Scarlet Letter*, the stigma of sexual proclivity—an attribute of the scarlet woman—might tarnish a white woman like Charlotte or Hester, but they resist it with nun-like severity. Caddy, on the other hand, embraces sexual avidity with hedonistic abandon. Nonetheless, shame and social opprobrium for lack of sexual restraint are imposed on all three, but only *after* their falls. In *The Color Purple*, Alice Walker lets us see how the racialized rendition of the scarlet woman, the Jezebel, can be imposed much earlier on poor, black females. Black girls, like the novel's protagonist Celie, may be obliged to bear the designation almost from birth and contend with its endangering consequences. As we move now from Caddy's sexual rebellion to Celie's sexual exploitation, Walker will reveal what Faulkner failed to show, the damaging racial and sexual assumptions about black females that leave black women and girls excruciatingly vulnerable to socially tolerated male violence.[1]

When we first meet Celie, she is growing up during the first few decades of the twentieth century in a rural Georgia community, one where lynchings are not uncommon and whites pay no real penalties for raping black women and murdering black men.[2] Rather than providing her with any measure of paternal protection, Celie's "Pa" has raped her repeatedly. Unprepared and unattended, she has given birth to two of his children, and he has taken both babies from her shortly after their birth, claiming to have killed them in the woods. He has felt no compunction about forcing a girl barely beyond puberty to have sex with him; rather he feels justified, telling Celie, "You gonna do what your mammy wouldn't" (1). The rapes stop only after he finds a replacement, another girl Celie's age whom he also abuses, leaving her to "walk round like she don't know what hit her" (4). In the dominant ideology of Celie's Jim Crow South, poor black women's bodies are objects to be used and discarded.

Celie is not banished to the margins of a community in the same way that Hester was in colonial Boston, but she is sent away from the only home she knows, inhospitable though it may be, after her children are taken from her. When "Pa" has finished with her and wants unimpeded sexual access to her younger sister Nettie, he disposes of Celie, Nettie's only protector, by giving her to Mr. ——, who needs someone to take care of his children. After all, she is his to give in the exchange of women, though we learn that value in this particular exchange has ironically increased because she is not a virgin. "Pa" explains to Mr. ——, "She ain't fresh . . . She spoiled. Twice" (7); but he adds, "God done fixed her. You can do everything just like you want to and she ain't gonna make you feed it or clothe it" (8). Rather than lower her value on the marriage market, rape and pregnancy have increased her worth by making her infertile. She will be the sexual workhorse Mr. ——needs but will not produce anymore unwanted children. Mr. —— hesitates; he still prefers Nettie who, because she hasn't been raped yet, is referred to as "fresh." When "Pa" throws a cow into the deal, he grudgingly accepts. Critic Lean'tin Bracks observes that Celie "willingly takes Nettie's place with Mr. —— . . . because she sees little value in her own person . . . [H]er position as a site of racialized and sexualized dominance codes . . . does not allow [her] to fight for a more equitable role in life" (92). Certainly racism and sexism leave Celie powerless to determine her own future, but she has also been wounded by acute trauma that leaves her psychologically immobilized. Her infertility, undoubtedly caused by medical neglect, is only a small hint of the deep emotional wounds she bears, open wounds caused by rape, by excruciating childbirths, and by the wrenching loss of both her babies. All are exacerbated by her helplessness, so it is no wonder that she goes from "Pa" to Mr. —— willingly. She has no cultural or psychological means of resistance. In the new domestic prison, Mr. ——'s farm, she automatically takes on the responsibility for his undisciplined children as well his house and fields. She distracts herself while Mr. —— is "on top of [her]" (12) by thinking about Nettie and Mr. ——'s mysterious lover, Shug Avery. She does her best to be invisible, easing her loneliness by secretly writing letters to a God who never answers.[3]

Both "Pa" and Mr. —— sexually bully women as a way to claim power in an oppressive white society where blacks are disenfranchised and black men have little means of defining themselves through financial avenues. Although they must not be pardoned for their cruelty, feminist critic bell hooks provides a way to comprehend their need to dominate women. In her book *Black Looks*, hooks discusses black ideology, in particular phallocentricism, the "model where what the male does with his penis becomes a greater and certainly a more accessible way to assert masculine status" (94). Her explanation helps us see why many of Walker's black male characters are hardened chauvinists:

A sexually defined masculine ideal rooted in physical domination and sexual possession of women could be accessible to all men. Hence, even unemployed black men [or economically exploited men] could gain status, could be seen as the embodiment of masculinity, within a phallocentric framework. (94)

Aggressive phallocentricism gives Pa and Mr. —— masculine status through sexual domination, since racism and poverty prevent them from attaining that status through gainful wage earning. The battered bodies of black women like Celie, who has no means of resistance, provide ill-gotten salve for the wounded egos of desperate, oppressed black men. Cynthia Cole Robinson notes that Walker's own father, with whom Walker herself had a less than favorable relationship, "taught his sons the way in which he thought masculinity could be achieved, through sexual conquest. As a result, [Walker's] brothers would go on sexual escapades on the weekends, which led to many illegitimate children . . . whom they did not provide with financial assistance" (300). Walker herself responds to the criticism she has garnered from her negative portrayal of black men:

At the root of the denial of easily observable and heavily documented sexist brutality in the black community—the assertion that black men don't act like Mister, and if they do, they're justified by the pressure

they're under as black men in a white society—is our deep, painful refusal to accept the fact that we are not only descendants of slaves, but we
are also the descendants of slave *owners*. And that just as we have had to
struggle to rid ourselves of slavish behaviors, we must as ruthlessly eradicate any desire to be mistress or "master." (Qtd. in Collins 186)

"Pa" and Mr. —— are despicable characters, but the way they treat black
women is learned behavior that has been socially promulgated by the cultural institutions of slavery, male superiority, and female degradation. It can
be ended only by cultural awareness, self-awareness, and accountability.

Celie doubts early on that her "Pa" actually killed her babies. She suspects he may have sold her son "to a man an his wife over Monticello" (3),
but she is never in any position to try to find him. By coincidence, when she
is in town one day, she recognizes her daughter shopping with her adoptive
mother. To Celie, "she look just like me and my daddy. Like more us then us
is ourself" (13). The falsehood that babies can simply be taken away from
birthmothers without causing deep psychological harm is demonstrated to
be just that—a fallacy. Celie has never forgotten her children, and when
she see her daughter, she uncharacteristically abandons her fears and dares
approach the woman the child is with, saying to herself, "My heart say she
mine." When the child's name does turn out to be Olivia, the name Celie had
embroidered on her baby's diapers, she is proved correct. Olivia has been
adopted by Reverend Samuel and Corrine, his wife. Subsequently, when
Nettie is almost raped by Mr. ——, Celie sends her to Corrine and Samuel,
hoping she will find safe haven with the same people who have Olivia. She
won't see Nettie or Olivia again for thirty years.

Celie's sister-in-law, Kate, cannot protect Celie from Mr. ——'s abuse,
but she does decide to buy her some material for a new dress. Celie asks for
the color purple, a color a queen might wear. Not surprisingly, there is no
purple, and although there is plenty of red available, Celie doesn't dare adorn
herself with Hester Prynne's symbolic scarlet—not yet. Although she is labeled "spoiled," her alleged "ruin" has not granted her the isolation and protection that the scarlet *A* once afforded Hester. Celie is emotionally isolated
but her body is not her own; it is Mr. ——'s sexual tool that he penetrates,
beats, and puts to work. She has neither the regal presence the color purple
connotes nor the sexual avidity the color red suggests, so it is no surprise
that Kate insists she choose blue or brown. When Kate tells Celie she's "got
to fight" Mr. ——, Celie dismisses the notion. She is defenseless against

the black man who treats her no better than white plantation owners once treated slaves. The best she can hope for is to stay alive by being obedient. The utterly powerless position of poor black women in this era of southern history is made devastatingly clear when Harpo, Mr. ——'s son, asks Mr. —— why he beats Celie. Mr. —— replies that that's "All women good for" (22). Celie survives his sanctioned brutality by dehumanizing herself: "I make myself wood. I say to myself, Celie, you a tree" (22).

When Harpo brings his new wife, Sofia, home, Celie witnesses her first example of an uppity woman who refuses to don the mantle of deferential slave. Sofia is a physically powerful woman who works hard and feels entitled to respect. Celie, on the other hand, is so dominated by misogyny that when Harpo asks her how to tame Sophia's defiance, Celie can only think of one thing to do: "Beat her" (36). Harpo cannot temper Sophia's spunk, but when she punches out the white mayor and talks back to his wife, she is ruthlessly beaten and thrown in prison. The only way the family can gain any leniency for Sophia is by sending Squeak, Harpo's girlfriend, to plead Sophia's case. They dress her up in the trappings of a proper "white woman," even giving her "a little black bible" to carry (93), but the sheriff, her white uncle, still assumes she's a Jezebel and rapes her (95). No matter how much strength, or propriety, or deference black woman like Sophia, Squeak, and Celie demonstrate, they cannot get a purchase on respect or, for that matter, on individual identification. They cannot seem to extricate themselves from the "historically and culturally produced category" (Nussbaum and Brown 15) of drudge, the dehumanizing designation left over from slavery that allows them be worked, beaten, and raped with impunity by men, both white and black, with power.

Walker is not content to expose the condoned brutality in these families and this community; religion is also implicated. Rather than serve as a benevolent congregation for Celie, her church has done nothing to lessen her isolation and safeguard her from "Pa" or Mr. ——. Instead the parishioners have marked her as a fallen woman. Like the women of Hester's Puritan community, the women of this congregation judge her especially harshly, blaming her for her pregnancies. The preacher does nothing more than exploit her willingness to work as his church's scrubwoman. Despite being shunned by those who should defend her, Celie dutifully trusts that heaven will be her reward. When Sophia is arrested, she imagines that God, "lookin like some stout white man work at the bank," will be "coming down by chariot, swinging down real low and carrying ole Sofia home" (90–91). Religion in Celie's life is used as it has been used for centuries: to mollify the abused and exploited and encourage meekness. In Celie's case, religion discourages her from developing a will of her own; instead, it keeps her beholden to a husband who is not held accountable for his violence—not by the church, not by his family, and certainly not by the state where racial persecution is the norm and laws are in place to deny him (and Celie) dignity.

But Celie's life changes dramatically when Shug Avery arrives in the guise of the archetypal scarlet woman; Celie gains a friend who comforts her and, more importantly, intervenes for her. Shug is a successful blues singer, the "Queen Honeybee." Cheryl Wall observes in her book *Worrying the Line* that when Walker invented Shug, she drew on the lives and art of blueswomen like Bessie Smith, a "woman who left home and succeeded in the world on her own terms," free of the bonds of traditional marriage, the constraints of "ladyhood," and the authority of the church (147, 142). Celie knows that Shug is Mr. ——'s great love and the mother of three of his children (and thus, also an unwed mother who surrendered her children to her parents to raise), but when Mr. —— brings her home for Celie to care for, far from being jealous or humiliated by Shug's presence, Celie is ecstatic. She has been fantasizing about Shug for years, and when she sees her naked for the first time while helping her bathe, she declares, "I thought I had turned into a man" (49). Shug's beauty and her sexual appeal are electrifying for Celie, and her lifelong loyalty to Shug is confirmed when Shug offers her a deep and intuitive friendship. Shug is a magnetically seductive woman who indulges the sensual, enjoys attracting men, and is a talented singer. When she sings in Harpo's new juke joint, she gladly dons the guise of the scarlet woman with a "tight red dress" and "little sassy red shoes" (73). Flaunting her sexual allure is part of Shug's artistic performance. Rather than inciting male sexual desire that degrades and endangers, her art permits her a significant measure of respect, independence, and self-direction even in the Jim Crow South.

Shug is more than just an example of a talented and capable black woman for Celie. Up to this point in our survey of fallen women, not one has had a compassionate female friend to advocate for her. Rather, we have seen women like Delia of *The Old Maid* and Alida Slade of "Roman Fever" turn into cruel enforcers of patriarchal ostracism and punishment. Shug is different. She actually listens to Celie, which, as Collins points out, "enables [Celie] to transcend the fear and silence of her childhood" and find "the language to tell of her sexual abuse" (163). And as soon as she tells, Shug intercedes. She not only stops Mr. —— from beating Celie, she also teaches her about female sexuality. Lauren Berlant refers to Shug as "the novel's professor of desire and self-fulfillment, and as such her 'example' is not only symbolic but technical, practical" (214). Although Celie has been labeled by men as "spoiled," her actual sexual experience has been so thwarted by the rough treatment of "Pa" and Mr. ——— that she has never understood her sexual anatomy or experienced sexual pleasure. By inviting Celie into female-centered discourse and by teaching her about her body and its pleasures, Shug subverts phallocentric discourse in ways Michel Foucault suggests in *The History of Sexuality* are possible: "discourse can be both an instrument and an effect of power, but also a hindrance, a stumbling block, a point of resistance and a starting point for an opposing strategy" (101). Shug has an opposing strategy and gives us a starting point for opposing phallocentric sexual designations of women's bodies by using women's language to describe women's bodies and women's sexuality. In *The Sound and the Fury*, a novel that is also highly concerned with women's bodies, Mr. Compson tries to persuade Quentin that "virginity" is an arbitrary, man-made designation. Shug takes this a step further. She rejects the patriarchal definition of "virgin" as a female with an unpenetrated hymen and instead redefines "virgin" to mean a woman who has not had an orgasm. In women's discourse, Celie is still a virgin. According to Molly Hite:

> [Shug replaces] conventional terminology for the female genitals, shifting the emphasis from a hole that requires plugging to a button that gets hot and finally melts . . . [her] redefinition of the word "virgin" is equally threatening to patriarchal control over women's bodies, in that it places priority not on penetration . . . but on enjoyment, making the woman's own response the index of her "experience." (128)

When Celie, with Shug's guidance, looks at her genitalia for the first time in the mirror, she claims her body as her own dominion, saying simply but conclusively, "It mine" (78). And when she and Shug become lovers, their shared erotic pleasure represents not only Celie's arrival at deserved female *jouissance* but also the lovingly, generous sharing of *her* body. The body, which was time after time taken from her against her will, is now hers to share with the woman she loves.[4] In so doing, "Celie transforms herself from sexual object to sexual subject" (Wall 151). Again, Walker takes a liberating swerve from the master narrative of the fallen woman: Celie is not relegated to the life of the cloister, like Hester and Charlotte, or to a life of indiscriminate sexuality with corrupt men, like Caddy. Rather, the self-defensive, stony woodenness of her body as a tree is transformed and imbued with supple, radiantly animated eroticism.

But Celie's journey is far from over. Like most birthmothers, Celie cannot forget the two babies that were stolen from her years earlier, and I use the word "stolen" purposefully. Celie didn't lose her babies, or give them away, or relinquish them, or surrender them. Those words are inadequate and misleading to describe Celie's and other birthmothers' experience. Those words suggest a birthmother had some say in the matter. Celie's babies were stolen from her, and I understand how that feels. Although the morning my daughter was taken away from me was much different, I too can use the word "stolen." I didn't give birth at home, and I wasn't alone; I gave birth among strangers with only last-minute anesthesia. I knew that there wasn't a chance I would be able to keep my baby, but when I begged just to hold her, I was denied even that. She was taken away from me against my wishes, never to be returned until I found her myself decades later. My experience and Celie's are like other birthmothers who stress that they did not willingly "give away" their babies. Our relinquishments were involuntary. We had to surrender them; powerful people and institutions told us so. In this sense, Walker gets a birthmother's experience right, much more so than in her novel *Meridian*, in which Meridian relinquishes her son and then actually forgets about him. As Elaine Tuttle Hansen notes in her book *Mother Without Child*, when Meridian freely chooses "what a real mother could only be forced to accept," she is not representing the experience of real birthmothers (66–67). Torment-free choices and the balm of forgetfulness like Meridian's are a myth, one that needs to be challenged. Celie's experience is more credible. Her babies were stolen, and she never forgets.

When Shug discovers Nettie's letters from Africa, which Mr. —— has been hiding for years, we learn the truth about Celie's children. "Pa" had taken them both to Samuel. Like many adopting parents who want to deny that a heart broken birthmother is out there somewhere, Samuel and Corrine ignored the shady circumstances of the babies' origin. They were the answer to their prayers. They could not have children, so "'God' sent them Olivia and Adam" (133). They raised them and when they went to Africa as missionaries, they took the children and Nettie with them. When Celie first learns her children are alive, she is, like so many birthmothers hobbled by disgrace. At first, she feels shame more than love, especially since she believes they were incestuously conceived, and she has been told "children got by incest turn into dunces" (148). It's not until she reads further in Nettie's letters and learns that her biological father had been lynched and the man who raped her was her stepfather that her shame begins to dissipate and her acute longing, coupled with lethal hostility for Mr. ——, breaks the surface.

To keep her from killing Mr. ——, Shug takes a lesson from Hester and has Celie take up her needle. Celie begins making pants, avoids murder, and acquires a profession. Shug also gives Celie a new way to think about God. The curse that the biblical God puts on the "fallen" Eve in the book of Genesis sets the seal of patriarchy on Western religion and ensures that centuries of female repression will follow. By depicting Eve as the one who causes the fall of man in her quest for knowledge, the seeds for phobia against women are sewn. Especially dread-inducing are women who sexually exceed the control of patriarchal paradigms. As we saw in *The Scarlet Letter* when Hester is pilloried, it is on the order of the Puritan clergy. The fallen woman becomes a primary target for punitive religious practices. Far more than state institutions, organized religions have felt compelled to enforce the punishment of seduced or raped women, insisting on their humiliation and banishment, first from Eden and then from their homes and communities. In the name of religion, women have been pilloried, whipped, stoned, even burned at the stake. How can Walker and Shug redeem religion for women?

To find an internally sustaining spiritual foundation for women, Shug has to reject Christianity and rewrite religion's master narrative with what Wall refers to as "a global spiritual consciousness that was historically unavailable to the [female] figures who inspire the [novel]," women like Zora Neale Hurston and Bessie Smith (141). Celie's "God" has been a "big and old and tall and graybearded and white" man who "wear white robes and go barefooted" and has eyes "sort of bluish-gray. Cool. Big though. White lashes" (194). Celie's church has been complicit in her oppression by branding her a fallen woman and remaining morally indifferent to the violence perpetrated against her. The congregation has stigmatized and isolated her for what was done to her rather than benevolently empathizing and protecting her. There's little hope for redemption in this version of Christianity and so Shug urges Celie to "chase that old white man out of [her] head" (197).

Walker turns to Emerson, pantheism, and what she identifies as "*animism*—a belief that makes it possible to view all creation as living, as being inhabited by spirit" (qtd. in Harrison 106)—to construct a belief system for Shug and Celie in which people, nature, and God coalesce.[5] In Shug's metaphysics, isolation is eradicated; unity is a given. Her God is neither severe nor imposing; "ain't a he or a she, but a It" (195). Ultimately, materiality is crucial to Shug's kingdom, and she echoes Emerson when she maintains, "I believe God is inside you and inside everybody else ... God is everything ... One day when I was sitting quiet and feeling like a motherless child, which I was, it come to me: that feeling of being part of everything, not separate at all" (195–96). Like Emerson's amalgamate awareness that allows him to see that "the currents of the Universal Being circulate through [him]," in Shug's all-inclusive perception, living things are so entirely connected that she claims, "if I cut a tree, my arm would bleed" (196). No one is fallen; no one is a "Jezebel," no one is cast out; and most importantly, everything deserves admiration. Shug insists, "it pisses God off if you walk by the color purple in a field somewhere and don't notice it" (196). In Shug's holy garden, "Everything want to be loved," even trees, whose wooden solidity Celie once emulated in order to endure Mr. ——'s beatings. Like people, Shug says, "trees do everything to git attention ... except walk" (196). Shug practices an integrated pantheism in which the material is sacred. The importance of bridal virginity and marital conception drop away; rather than damned, the sexually awakened female body is revered.

Nonetheless, Celie finds it hard to "git man off [her] eyeball" (197); it is hard to think outside the institutionalized, dominant ideology even when it's pointed out that this belief system has debased women's bodies and strangled their spirits. Shug advises Celie that whenever she prays and "man plop himself on the other end of [her prayers], tell him to git lost ... Conjure up flowers, wind, water, a big rock" (197). As Celie becomes more critically aware, she realizes the injustices that have been heaped on her; she seethes with anger. When she conjures up a rock, she wants to throw it.

Shug proves that she is a genuine friend, one who will not close her eyes to another's pain, by taking Celie out of Mr. ——'s domestic trap. In her essay "Black Women's Literature and the Task of Feminist Theology, " Delores Williams describes Shug's role as that of "a catalyst: a liberated, self-confident black woman who accelerates the movement of another woman away from the psychological, sexual, and emotional abuse that has plagued her" (96–97). Shug can and does help Celie shed her passivity and change the constraining parameters of her life permanently. For the first time, Celie begins to take control of her life.[6] She cannot shed her bleak past, but she learns from Shug, the scarlet woman herself, how to color her future with hues of her choice. Again Celie reminds me of Hester, who finds a way to mitigate the humiliation of her scarlet *A* with lavish embroidery and her unpromising future with self-determination. Celie will do the same, embellishing her potential with passion and skill.

When Mr. —— hears Shug and Celie are leaving for Memphis, he sums up Celie's social disadvantages, obstacles that he has erected to keep her unprepared for life outside his incarceration: "Nothing up North for nobody like you . . . You too scared to open your mouth to people. All you fit to do . . . is be Shug's maid. Take out her slop-jar and maybe cook her food . . . You black, you pore, you ugly, you a woman. Goddam . . . you nothing at all" (205–6). But Celie is no longer silenced. She opens her mouth and "the air [rushes] in and [shapes] words." Leveling a curse on Mr. ——, she proclaims: "The jail you plan for me is the one in which you will rot . . . Anything you do to me, already done to you . . . I'm pore, I'm black, I may be ugly . . . But I'm here" (207). Celie acknowledges the social and economic circumstances (poverty and race) that have impeded her, but recasts the coercion that subjugated her (rape, abuse, enslavement) not as inevitable but as escapable. She may not be able to set aside her losses, but she routs the disempowering shame that has kept her locked in crushing domesticity. Stepping out of a prison of sexist subservience and sexual slavery, she starts anew, and we are meant to celebrate her emergence without the equivocation that accompanies Miss Quentin's escape from Jason's stranglehold or the losses that come with Caddy's leaving. Faulkner is not ready to let his scarlet women get away scot free. Although Walker exonerates Celie from any hint moral ambiguity, she is still Faulknerian when it comes to the past. Like all our preceding unwed mothers, Celie's painful past won't let her go.

Still, life in Memphis allows Celie freedom for the first time in her life. Like Hester, she employs her artful needle and establishes her own business: Folkspants, Unlimited. Corroborating Virginia Woolf's maxim that "five hundred a year . . . means the power to think for oneself" (106), Walker observes, "Without money of one's own in a capitalist society, there is no such thing as independence" (*In Search of* 90). With Folkspants, Celie can do gratifying, skilled work and make money. As Shug puts it, "You making your living, Celie . . . Girl, you on your way" (214) and Celie herself declares, "I am so happy. I got love, I got work, I got money, friends and time" (215). The only thing she is waiting for is Nettie and her children's return from Africa. When the man Celie had called "Pa" dies, she inherits his house, his land, and his store. Again, Shug praises her: "You doin' all right, Miss Celie . . . God know where you live" (246).

Walker underscores the irrevocable ties between biological children and their birthmothers by way of Shug. As mentioned, Shug's parents had raised the illegitimate children she had with Mr. ——, a common practice in black communities. In her book *Wake Up Little Susie*, Rickie Solinger makes note of the differences in family and community responses among blacks and whites to out-of-wedlock pregnancy, differences we see played out to some degree in *The Sound and the Fury* and *The Color Purple*. "The black community organized itself to accommodate mother and child while the white community was totally unwilling and unable to do so. The white community simply organized itself to expel them" (6–7). In *The Color Purple*, Shug and Celie's black community take in their illegitimate children, though, as we know, this is kept from Celie. In *The Sound and the Fury*, Dilsey wants to take in Miss Quentin and Caddy; but the Compsons are totally unwilling to do so. Caddy is expelled. Shug is spurned by her parents as well, and though they accept and accommodate their grandchildren, she too has been expelled for her "evil life." Now her parents have died and her children have grown up and dispersed, but Shug is not Meridian. Despite beauty, popularity, and a successful career, she has never completely recovered from leaving them behind. When her new man, Germaine, wisely insists that she "would prob-ably feel better in [her] life" (268) if she made contact with her children, she decides to do so. Two of them don't want to see her (she's too far fallen), but one son has always wanted "to see his mama no matter what" (267), so they head to Arizona, where they find him working as a schoolteacher on an In-dian reservation. Shug acquires a large measure of peace from this reunion, and Walker's shows the ambivalence birthmothers harbor concerning the adoptive parents who raise their children. Separated from my own daughter by a closed adoption, I worried incessantly as the years passed: "She's two," I would think. "Does her mother spank her if she wets her pants?" "She's six. Does her father yell at her when she's scared of the dark?" "She's eleven. Do they slap her for talking back?" When I finally found her, I was relieved to learn that my worry had been for naught. Hers was a good adoption; her adoptive parents were more than capable, and although they divorced when she was seven, her single mother raised her and her younger brothers with patience and affection that never faltered. Did I appreciate her devotion? Absolutely. Did I begrudge? Terribly. Like me, Shug is grateful that her par-ents had loved, cared, and educated her children well, but understandably, she's bitter that they tried their best to turn them against her.

Celie has one more important step to take in achieving autonomy. She is crushed when Shug "falls" for Germaine. Nonetheless, she gathers her forces and demonstrates an extraordinary emotional stoicism, not unlike Hester Prynne's. She asks herself, "Who am I to tell her who to love?" (269) Her question is not motivated by self-loathing. She had once believed "Pa" when he said she was "spoiled." His label left her socially condemned and isolated, with no means of revising that designation. Without Shug's intrusion and insistence that Mr. —— end his brutal reign, Celie's chance to redefine herself could not have begun. Walker is being realistic here. Sometimes women need others to help us get a new start. I know I needed the strong emotional safety net of a compassionate, dependable, committed partner before I could begin to tell my secrets, rout out my shame, shed decades of self-loathing, and begin the process of redefining myself. There's no shame in needing help, and like me, Celie had needed an advocate. She needed someone like Shug to extend her the emotional and economic stability required if we are to refashion ourselves and construct healthy, unassailable identities undergirded with self-respect. Ironically, the emotional and financial resilience Celie builds allows her to release Shug, the friend who made her resilience possible. She remarks, "Shug got a right to live too" (269). She understands that she must grant Shug the same opportunity for self-determination that Shug helped her establish for herself. We know that Celie has achieved a sturdy sense of emotional autonomy when upon learning that Shug might be coming back home, she is strong enough to respond: "If she come, I be happy. If she don't, I be content" (283).

Celie's stoicism allows her to accept the possibility of Shug's rejection with equanimity, but that emotional self-possession does not assuage her constant longing for her sister and her children. When she is notified by the Department of Defense that Samuel, Nettie, Adam, and Olivia are believed lost when the ship returning them from Africa is sunk by German mines, she is devastated. She loses her children and her sister all over again.

Initially, Olivia and Adam do not suffer from the stigma of illegitimacy, yet psychologically damaging complications do emerge. Samuel had known Celie's stepfather during an earlier, licentious time in his life, which explains why "Pa" leaves the infants with him. When Nettie shows up at Samuel and Corrine's house shortly after the children, Samuel assumes Nettie is their mother and is following them. Knowing that the children's father "had always been a scamp" (176), he takes Nettie in to protect her and then, goes on to Africa. Because of the striking resemblance between Nettie and the children, Corrine suspects that Adam and Olivia are Nettie and Samuel's biological children. As her suspicions grow, she withdraws her affection for the children. Illegitimacy has a sadly negative effect: the children's ambiguous origins cause their adoptive mother to reject them. Born outside of the prescribed rules of patriarchy, they suffer. Nettie eventually convinces Corrine that she, Nettie, is not the children's mother by reminding Corrine of the long-ago day when Celie had recognized Olivia in town. "[Celie] was so much like Olivia!" (187), Corrine remembers, that she was afraid Celie would take Olivia back. Corrine dies before she can repair her relationship with her adopted children, which is, of course, unfortunate. But that loss is mitigated when Nettie tells the children, now young adults, that she is their aunt and that their birthmother, Celie, lives in America.

Their immediate reaction is something like my other three children's' reaction when they were told I had surrendered my first baby, their half sister, to adoption. My ex-husband told them this because he was angry with me. He told them in spite; he told them in order to hurt me. And you might expect that they would have felt threatened by this revelation, that they would be both fearful and angry. After all, they might have thought, "If she gave one child away, she might give us away." I had been afraid to tell them about their sister, the baby I had wanted to keep so badly, that I still wanted, that even they couldn't replace. But their reaction was far from fear or anger. Rather than threatened or afraid, they were concerned about me. They knew me; they knew how devastating the loss of their sister must have been. My ex-husband's plan to turn them against me backfired. Instead, they came to me lovingly, with compassion and concern. Celie's children react similarly. Nettie knows nothing about Celie's good fortune. As far as she knows, Celie has lived the last thirty years under Mr. ——'s cruel reign. Celie's children are "instantly alarmed" about their birthmother. They want to find her, to help her. The family immediately plans its return to America.

Shug does return to Celie and to Celie's home, where "everything . . . [is] purple and red cept the floor, that painted bright yellow" (284). Celie has made the color purple, "a sign of indomitable female spirit" (Abbandonato 206), her own. She has taken the color red, a sign of female sexual desire and has purged it of the denigrating connotations that have stained scarlet women from Persephone to Hester and beyond. Now Celie uses red to ignite her color palate so that it reflects her expanded identity, shot through with liberation, pleasure, capability, and wonder. Walker rewards this deserving woman in ways that fallen women and unwed mothers have not yet been. Not only does she grant her Shug's sexual love and devotion, a gratifying friendship with Mr. ——, now "a man, not a master" (Wall 148), but also her family restored: the return of her children and Nettie, and new members as well, Samuel and Tashi, Adam's African wife.[7]

Unlike Hester Prynne and Jennie Gerhardt, Celie is not relegated to the lonely margins of the community, nor is she sidelined like Charlotte as an old maid or demonized like Caddy as a lost philanderer. Hawthorne, Dreiser, Wharton, and Faulkner faced intractable ideologies that constrained narrative possibilities for their female protagonists. They all felt compelled to choose some level of punishment for their unwed mothers. As a writer in the 1970s, Walker had more choices.[8] She could portray the brutal reality of Celie's life unvarnished, but also allow her social transformation. In her study of the novel as genre, Margaret Cohen delineates the specifications of what she calls the "sentimental social novel." These narrative use "the novel's power to intervene in public life" by combining "the descriptive power of realism with the transformative power of idealism" (qtd. in Hedrick xiv).[9] *The Color Purple* is just such a novel. Celie's life is grimly realistic, but she is rewarded with an idealized vision of justice and recompense: her father's house is returned to her; her lover is restored to her; she takes her rightful, respected place in a lovingly redeemed extended family; and her children come home. When Nettie reintroduces Celie to Adam and Olivia, she says, "These *our* children" (286; emphasis added), but Celie makes a point of saying, "I hug *my* children" (287; emphasis added), and they are hers to claim with joy. What was lost is found, what was stolen is restored.

We have been waiting a long time through centuries of literary history for a transformative narrative like Celie's that redefines punitive cultural scripts for fallen women. Like all birthmothers, Celie had to pay for her unasked-for maternity and the costs to her have been immense: years of loneliness, years of not knowing her children's fate, years of pain, humiliation, shame, fear. But Walker can and does imagine a new ending for the unwed mother and her illegitimate children.[10] As both novelist and social critic, Walker creates a new designation for women, the designation "womanist" that she defines as

A feminist of color ... who loves other women, sexually and/or nonsexually. [Who] appreciates and prefers women's culture, women's emotional flexibility ... and women's strength ... [Who is] committed to survival and wholeness of entire people, male and female. (*In Search of* xi)

Literature has needed a writer like Walker, a writer who loves and appreciates women. And women have needed her commitment to social justice and her dedication to the survival and wholeness of women—birthmothers especially who have, like Celie, been denied the experience of nurturing and loving their own children. We have needed an imaginative, farseeing womanist to think beyond limiting narrative structures, to crack open ideological paradigms, to resist damning archetypes, to liberate characters like Shug and Celie, to add the color purple to the deepening, rich hues of a triumphant scarlet woman. We have needed an artistic, unwavering, transformative womanist to give us, finally, our first happy ending.

Happy endings. Are they really possible for birthmothers? Does reunitement compensate for years of separation, missed opportunities, worry, fear, longing, sorrow? When my daughter and I were reunited, I thought it was my happy ending. I'll always remember the vivid details from the day I saw her again, thirty-five years after her birth. It was one of the most thrilling, most fulfilling, yes, one of the happiest days of my life. When I think of her opening her front door and my catching my first glance of her, my heart starts pounding all over again. I couldn't stop staring at her that day. She was a sight for a sore heart. We look extraordinarily alike, same body type, same height, same hearing loss, even the same haircut. I knew she was mine and I was hers.

But did I get *my* daughter back that day? I still wince when I read Nettie's first words to Celie, "These *our* children," because I know what she means. They are hers. And I know when Celie says, "I hug *my* children," she's making a claim that can't be honored. My first daughter will never be *mine*. She belongs to her adoptive family, her brothers, her father, her mother's memory. They have a rightful claim to her. Don't misunderstand me. My daughter has been magnanimous. She has lovingly welcomed me into her home, her family, her community of friends. She's traveled hundreds of miles to visit me regularly. Her children call me "Grandma." She let me be one of the first to enter her hospital room the day her youngest was born. She lovingly cares for my children, her half-siblings, and their children. Whenever we talk, she tells me she loves me. I am always grateful. How greedy to want for more.

But the wounded heart is insatiable. I know now that the loss I suffered cannot ever be erased. When a mother loses her newborn baby, her pain is incurable, as is mine. Those years apart are forever gone. My sorrow abides as does my yearning. This experience is not uncommon. I have met many birthmothers who like me are thankful for their reunitement but struggle with unrelenting, unquenchable longing. I have seen women ask for so much that rejection replaces gratitude and connection. I will try never to let that happen. I accept my place as, well . . . Aunt? Sister? Friend? It's hers to define. I stand and wait, here on my mountain ridge, my flowers blooming, my vegetables ripening, my words flowing, grateful always grateful for whatever happy ending I can write. My first daughter. She is not mine, but I am hers.

CHAPTER 6

Illegitimacy and Sexual Violence

For the first few years after I surrendered my daughter to adoption, I drifted from one boy to the next, unable to stay in a steady relationship for long. There were lots of dates and some heavy petting in "mattress rooms" at fraternity keggers, but I was still too ashamed of my altered body to want to share it fully with anyone. White stretch marks streaked my breasts and snaked around my hips, and even though somehow my stomach had expanded without leaving telltale marks, I was sure that just by touching my vagina, any boy would know I have given birth. Now I know that my body wouldn't have given me away, but at the time I had been so psychologically seared by my own version of Hester Prynne's scarlet *A* that I felt as if I glowed with hot, shaming evidence of my fallen state. My obsession with secrecy coupled with a well-founded fear of pregnancy kept me from any kind of intimate commitment for awhile. Then I met a boy. He was twenty years old, and he was a young, confused, obsessive boy, but he loved me, or so he thought. He said that he had to have me, that we should be having sex, that everyone else was. And in our milieu he was probably right. My roommates were; his roommates were. It was, after all, the late sixties, and when we marched, we carried placards that read "Make Love, Not War!" I was too shy to seek out a prescription for birth control on my own, but when my roommate Elaine heard a rumor that we could get the pill at the student health center, we rode our bikes across campus to see if this could possibly be true. We returned home that afternoon, each with our own prescription and a little white starter pack of freedom. We lit some incense, popped our first pill, and turned up "Lay Lady Lay" as loud as we could until our neighbors started pounding on the wall next door.

My new boyfriend was a fine-looking hippie, scruffy beard, untrimmed hair, and tattered clothes. He invited me to be part of his circle, a hardy group of engineering students who lived together in a seedy old house in Corvallis. When they weren't studying, they would made huge pots of cabbage stew, pass around a joint, set the record player on repeat, and eat everything with relish as The Doors sang "Light My Fire" over and over again. On weekends, they would pack their pristine outdoor gear into their decrepit cars and head for the mountains. I was in love with the lifestyle and its immense possibilities more than the boy. Together we climbed many of the Cascade peaks. They taught me how to rope up, how to cross a glacier tethered to one another, how to glissade down a mountainside with my ice ax as rudder. They sang "Happy Birthday" to me on the summit of Mount St. Helens eleven years to the day before it would erupt and become an entirely different mountain. I loved the group and my place in it so much that I agreed to marry the boy even though I knew better. He had a fanatical perfectionism that I couldn't begin to measure up to. He was exacting, impatient, and sometimes easily enraged. Before we could set the date, I knew I had to confess my secret, and when I haltingly did so, his response surprised even me. Rather than sympathetic, he was apoplectic—mean, insulting, and unforgiving. His reaction should have given me all the certainty I needed to end our relationship, but since I had never really forgiven myself for having sex, for getting pregnant, and, most of all, for surrendering my baby, his response seemed right on the mark.

Our marriage lasted six miserable months, and I was in dangerous territory. Like that unpredictable mountain, Mount St. Helen's, he would erupt into violence without warning. When I left the kitchen cupboards open, he threw me across the kitchen, and then straightened the dish towels and alphabetized the spice rack. When I scratched one of his albums, he twisted my arm back until I screamed and then broke the record into smithereens. He told me he got no pleasure having sex with me. Having a baby had ruined my vagina, he said; I needed to have it repaired; it wasn't tight enough. Then a clean-cut, well-dressed Latino man who managed the restaurant where I was waiting tables told me I was the most beautiful woman he'd ever met. After months of cruelty and shattered self-esteem, the contrast was so powerful that I simply abandoned any judgment I had left. I was "putty in his hands." When he offered to spirit me away, I jumped at the chance. When I told him that I had a little girl somewhere in Ohio and his first response was, "Let's go find her," I fell in love. This is the same man who seven years later would spitefully tell our three small children that I had given their baby sister away and then offer a quarter to the first one to cry. But in those first giddy days of my great escape, I once again ignored all warning signs, and we headed out for the Big Apple. We didn't make it in New York, and I had to turn to my worried, aggravated parents for money. But I was happy because I was pregnant. And this time, this baby would be mine. Ten months after our getaway, I gave birth to our son. Although my savior had helped me escape from a sadistic man and together, we started a family, I eventually had to learn that he too was more than capable of resentment, possessiveness, and cruelty. When the shouting escalated to shoving and then to a punch in the face and my first black eye, I had to escape once again, but this time with my three children in tow.

Why had I fallen for such punishing men? In the world of pop psychology, there's an obvious answer: Yes, I clearly had an overwhelming need to atone over and over again for my mistakes. But I want to look beyond that obvious need for punishment; I want to look at the vulnerability that shadowed me, one that accompanies so many unwed mothers as they try to resume their lives after giving birth. Shame and loss can leave birthmothers who are forced to surrender their infants hobbled by disempowering guilt, meager self-worth, and substantial emotional needs. Such neediness puts women in jeopardy. My willingness to pair up with volatile, mean-spirited men is not anomalous. Women are endangered by unwed motherhood, whether they surrender their babies or not. They are marked. I thought my own secret past was a stain that I would never be able to wash away, but I was lucky. I had a profession and friends, and my sister was willing to take me in when I decided to not just leave my husband but leave the state. I was able to get myself out of danger and my children too. Although we didn't suddenly enter the promised land, few ever do. But we were able to start a new life, though inevitably, I was drawn back into past patterns and immediately started up with an inappropriate new man. My emotional neediness was far from appeased.

My children turned out fine. They're grown, independent, capable, loving, and loved. We got lucky. But the stain of the unwed mother can bleed into the next generation. It can leave stigmatized children unprotected, easy prey for manipulative, corrupt adults. The alarming connection between unwed motherhood and family violence is a social reality, one that has been reflected in the ongoing narrative of the fallen woman.

"ONE HOLY NIGHT"

In a 1988 interview, Sandra Cisneros discusses the difficulties of growing up as a Mexican American, "always straddling two countries . . . but not belonging to either culture," but she has tried to use that sense of in between to define a middle ground where revision and reinvention of cultural and sexual roles might be possible (qtd. in Doyle 54). Her efforts have been successful in, for example, her novel *The House on Mango Street*. However, in the short story "One Holy Night," she cannot revise or reinvent the cultural and sexual role of the fallen woman. That master narrative is just too ensconced to be reinvented even on the promising middle ground between Latino and American culture. The story's narrator conforms, yet again, to another damning rendition of the scarlet woman, one that is all too similar to the versions we have seen reenacted on our journey through American literary history, including the exile of the unwed mother. Although the narrator is just a thirteen-year-old girl, once she's pregnant, she too is sent away as I was, not to the unfamiliarity of a Florence Crittenton Home, but to San Dionisio de Tlaltepango, a "town of dust" in Mexico to live with a "wrinkled witch woman who rubs [her] belly with jade, and sixteen nosy cousins" (27). In this way, she reverses and repeats the path her mother had taken years before when she was sent "to the United States so that neighbors in San Dionisio de Tlaltepango wouldn't ask why her belly was suddenly big" (33). The unnamed girl's narration is delivered "in the form of *testimonio*" as she bears witness to "the events that led up to her 'Holy Night' with an older man and her subsequent exile" (Brady 136).

The story starts in the Hispanic community of a Texas border town. The narrator recounts the consequences of having been sent out to work alone by her *abuelita* to sell cucumbers from a pushcart. Although unwilling to shoulder any of the blame for the seduction, the narrator's *abuelita* has imprudently put not just cucumbers but her granddaughter on public display for public consumption. Only in retrospect does the narrator herself see that the unrestricted location of the cucumber stand and her own naïveté left her ripe for sexual exploitation. She observes, "I don't know how many girls have gone bad from selling cucumbers. I know I'm not the first. My mother took the crooked walk too" (27–28).

Both mother and daughter are branded as fallen, and though they can cross and recross geographical boundaries, they cannot escape the cultural

sexism that follows them. Given the patriarchal values that traverse borderlands and the antiquated but not obsolete value of virginity, the narrator
must accept, as her mother had before her, that she is "bad." Even as young
as she is, she understands there are certain gradations of "bad," and insists
that she is "not like the Allport Street girls, who stand in doorways and go
with men into alleys" (28). In other words, she is an unwed pregnant teenager but she is not a prostitute. She is ruined, but not that ruined. She has
fallen, but not disastrously so. After all, she maintains, she was in love with
her seducer: Chaq Uxmal Paloquin, a man of Mayan blood, of the "people
of the sun . . . of the temples," a man who persuades her he "will bring back
the grandeur of [his] people . . . from those who have pushed the ancient
stones off their pedestals" (29). When I read about Chaq Uxmal Paloquin, I
can't help but remember my own gullibility, how puppy-dog eager I was to
believe in the men who claimed they loved me, how willing I was to follow
them to darkened rooms, throwing caution and reason away for easy words
of affection.

Chaq is irresistibly seductive for a girl of thirteen, especially when he
brings her Kool-Aid as she sells cucumbers and mangos from her cart. She
minimizes his manhood by calling him "Boy Baby," the name the street people have given him because he is seems "boy and baby and man all at once"
(28). He is vague about his past, his age, and his future, but she does not ask
questions, content instead with his explanation that "the past didn't matter," that the "past and the future [are] all the same to his people" (29). One
night he takes her back to his single room where he shows her his guns—
twenty-four in all—and tells her that he had promised his father he would
"bring back the ancient ways" (30), but she is far from alarmed. She is his
perfect audience: gullible, trusting, fascinated, awed. Girls the world over
are susceptible to the cultural myths and illusions that patriarchal ideology
promotes: love at first sight, rescue by a knight, and the triumph of true love.
She is no exception. Her descriptions of this "man and child," lying down
among his "great and dusty guns" to "[weep] for a thousand years" (30), are
as bellicose as his dreamy, quixotic stories. When she first tells of the one
and only time they have intercourse, she uses the starry-eyed language of romantic fantasy: she comes "undone like gold thread, like a tent full of birds"
(28). Then with "the moon, the pale moon with its one yellow eye, the moon
of Tikal, and Tulum, and Chichen" looking on, "something inside [bites her]
and [she gives] out a cry as if the other, the one [she] wouldn't be anymore,
leapt out" (30). She is initiated, she believes; she is "Ixchel," Chaq Uxmal

Paloquin's queen. She lets the myths of Mexican history and the romantic flourishes of Mexican legends shape Chaq's identity and turns her seduction on a dirty cot, "under one bald bulb, in the back room of the Esparza garage" (29) into a chimerical transformation.

Although the narrator has learned well the values of heterosexist patriarchy that dominate Mexico and America, and she knows that she should feel disgraced by her seduction, at first she registers no shame, perhaps because of the fantastical aura she gives her "initiation." Her smugness prevails, for a while at least, and shows just how innocent she had been before her night with Chaq. Now she marvels Eve-like at the knowledge/experience she has gained. Now she understands why she has never been allowed to sleep over at her friend Lourdes's, whose house is full of brothers; now she understands why the girls in movies always run away from soldiers; now she knows what happens when scenes in love stories begin to fade, why brides blush, and "how it is that sex isn't simply a box you check M or F . . . on the test we get at school" (31). But the marvelous is temporary. When she realizes that she might be pregnant, she learns what all unwed mothers know: "The truth has a strange way of following you, of coming up to you and making you listen to what it has to say" (29). The enchanting promises of romantic love made in myths, movies, and love songs have left her woefully unequipped for the real consequences of intercourse; all their promises vanish. She replaces all her highly romantic descriptions of her seduction and with a gritty version of first-time sex: "The truth is, it wasn't a big deal. It wasn't any deal at all. I put my bloody panties inside my T-shirt and ran home . . . [wondering] why the world and a million years made such a big deal over nothing" (30). In obviously material ways, my adolescence in privileged San Marino was different from the narrator's life in her Texas small town, but our first sexual experiences are excruciatingly similar: the pain, the blood, the confusion, the embarrassment, the incredulous feeling that this can't be it! This can't be what all the fuss is about. And like her, I remember "praying for the moon cycle to come back, but it would not" (32), not for her, not for me. I still cringe when I remember another night, the night I had to tell my parents the truth about my "one night" on a nubby avocado couch in my boyfriend's darkened living room—the night that turned into tragedy: no birds, no moonlight, no magic. She too must face that other night when she must tell her grandmother the unsentimental truth about her "one night" with Chaq on a cot covered with newspapers in a room that was once a closet.

Mary Pat Brady notes with interest the story's "discursive refusal to characterize the narrator's sexual encounter as rape, even though it involves a young vulnerable, clearly naïve girl and a much older man" (138). Although the narrator expunges all the mysterious beauty of her seduction from her narrative, she never uses the word "rape"; no one does. Her uncle blames America. Her grandmother blames "the infamy of men." But her indictment is problematic, for as Brady observes, it assigns to all women "a certain helplessness that ensures the continuity of the violence of patriarchy and the inevitability of men exploiting their physical dominance over women" (139). The narrator refuses to cry "rape," or to blame men or America. She refuses to make Chaq the enemy. Instead she emphasizes her own agency and builds a case for her own culpability. Not unlike Hester Prynne, she bravely takes full responsibility for her seduction and her pregnancy, and doesn't flinch when her grandmother calls her "a *sinverguenza*," a hussy without shame (32).

When *Abuelita* tries to find Chaq, believing foolishly that he can "correct [her granddaughter's] ruined life" (33), his real persona is revealed by his sister, a Carmelite nun. "Boy Baby" is not a boy; he is thirty-seven years old. His real name isn't Chaq; it's Chato, which means "fat-face." He has no Mayan blood. Though the narrator has been trying to hold onto her "holy" image of "Boy Baby," these details begin to desecrate that picture. Now even if she doesn't, we must use the term "statutory rape" to describe what has happened, but there's more unnerving news. His sister sends a newspaper clipping, a photo of him "looking very much like stone, police hooked on either arm," and a story about which we are given only enigmatic details: He has been arrested "*on the road to* Las Grutas de Xtacumbilxuna, *the Caves of the Hidden Girl . . . eleven female bodies . . . the last seven years*" (34). Chato has done appalling things with his twenty-four guns to eleven women. Not only has our deceived, unsuspecting narrator been raped and abandoned, romantic myths of princely seducers have dangerously deluded her. She was in greater peril than she could have imagined. Other girls had paid with their lives for trusting those myths.

Knowing the truth about Chato leaves the narrator more embittered than relieved. When her girl cousins ask her what it is like to have a man, she replies, "It's a bad joke. When you find out you'll be sorry" (35). The baby she carries feels like something foreign and ominous to her, "like a ring of water inside me reaching out and out until one day it will tear from me with its own teeth . . . it's the ghost of [Chaq] inside me that circles and circles, and will not let me rest" (34). Though its conception made for a romantic story, now the child she conceived is more like a creature in a horror story, an aggressive vampire-baby waiting to gnaw its way out of her body. Yet even as she distrusts the baby and fears childbirth, she clings to the patriarchal ideal of the nuclear family in her future, claiming that someday she will have one composed of a perfect man (with "man-bones," "man wrist and man-jaw thick and strong, all salty dips and hollows"), her baby, whom she plans to name Alegre, meaning glad, bright, gay, and four more children, two boys—Pablo and Sandro—and two girls—Lisette and Maritza (34–35). Again she lets roseate, romantic, culturally endorsed illusion color the reality of her situation. Rather than anticipate the demands of an actual infant, she pictures her newborn baby like a bright new doll that will eventually be followed by four more perfect doll babies. Although she is isolated, young, inexperienced, uneducated, and completely dependent, the material conditions of her life are still overshadowed by useless dreams of happily-ever-after, fantasies that not even her most sensible, realistic, focused efforts could make come true. But she can imagine nothing beyond or opposed to the parameters that the dominating paradigm culture affords: the role of wife and mother.

At the story's end the narrator remains proud, still resisting the humiliation of unwed motherhood by muting her shame with rose-tinted visions of a future within acceptable patriarchal limits. But she no longer idealizes love. Like so many fallen women, her sense of romantic love is obliterated. She tries on a couple of comparisons: "Love is like a big black piano being pushed off the top of a three-story building and you're waiting on the bottom to catch it," or, "It's like a top , like all the colors in the world spinning so fast they're not colors anymore and all that's left is a white hum." But she ultimately decides that love is like the crazy man who lives upstairs and can't talk. He "just [walks] around all day with this harmonica in his mouth." He doesn't play it; he just breathes through it, "all day long, wheezing, in and out, in and out" (35). It's a dismal association: love is the hum of a crazy man, discordant, incomprehensible, and as empty as mouthful of air. With that Cisneros turns a young girl's dreamy first seduction into a near-miss murder, even as she reiterates the script of punishment, of pregnancy in exile and an ominous maternity. Our narrator will live, we presume, but we are left with a modern version of the lethal danger girls and women face while in the hands of their seducers. We are left with *Abuelita*'s legitimate distrust of "the infamy of men" and a cynicism when it comes to love that no amount of bright, *alegre* embroidery can ameliorate.

BASTARD OUT OF CAROLINA

Dorothy Allison offers no such beautifying or healing needlework. Her novel *Bastard out of Carolina*, published the same year that Cisneros published "One Holy Night" as part of a collection of short stories, *Woman Hollering Creek*, all of which are about "how and why we mythologize love" (Ann Beattie). Allison also lays bare the risks women face in the pursuit of romantic love and family security, especially unwed mothers and their illegitimate children. Like the narrator of "One Holy Night," Allison's first-person narrator, Bone, gives her own *testimonio*, asking us to bear witness to the abuse she endures as a girl.

The first time I read the novel, I was about as far away from the deprivations and dangers of the novel's setting than one can get. I finished it on a summer afternoon fifteen years ago as I sat on the beach at Aquinnah on the island of Martha's Vineyard. Bathing suits are optional there and all around me were relaxed children and adults, some nude and some not, sunbathing, playing in the sand, building cairns, and cavorting in the ocean. The day felt wonderfully innocent. As far as I could tell, there was no hint of predatory sexual danger, voyeurism, or inappropriateness. The sheltered harbor of our material advantage provided all our bodies with protective layers of respect and safety. The only fears on the beach involved occasional jellyfish and harmful sunburns.

This is not the universe of Allison's, which takes place in early 1950s rural South Carolina, so I was separated from its two main characters—Bone, an illegitimate child, and Anney Boatwright, her mother—by close to fifty years, hundreds of miles, and significant privilege. Nonetheless, as I read, I became so empathically linked to their hard, cruel lives that when the novel came to an end, I put it down and wept. Even a gasp-inducing dive into the chilly Atlantic couldn't snap me out of Allison's devastating fictional world. It took several fitful nights, disturbed by the forlorn dreams that have haunted me since Florence Crittenton, but I did find my way back to the lighthearted mood of Martha's Vineyard, the peaceful haven where I was teaching that summer, enjoying my days of creative energy and savoring moments of luxurious lassitude. But why such an emotionally flooded response to the novel? There are obvious answers: like Anney Boatwright, I was an unwed mother; I had an illegitimate daughter. But that's where the similarities would seem to end. My affluent parents had made sure that my illegitimate daughter was taken from me only minutes after her birth, and I would not see her again for thirty-five years. But desperately poor Anney gets to keep her daughter. She loves and nurtures her as best she can. I have never stopped regretting that my daughter and I were separated for so long. I've always believed that she and I were robbed of one another, that we would have been better off together. And, I've always steadfastly insisted that I would have raised her responsibly and lovingly had I been given the chance; but Anney Boatwright's tale disturbs all my untested self-assurance.[1]

Allison represents unflinchingly the dangers that come with adolescent sexuality, teenage motherhood, and the vulnerability of illegitimate children as their young mothers try to create families that will lovingly coalesce and prosper. The 1950s version of Hester's punishing scarlet *A* is an onerous burden for Anney. Of course she's not expected to wear an actual *A*, but she is presented with a humiliating brand nonetheless—her daughter's birth certificate. Just as Hester's *A* is passed onto Pearl, who becomes "the scarlet letter endowed with life" (Hawthorne 90), Anney's punishment is passed on to her illegitimate daughter, Bone, when she is branded "illegitimate" by the state of South Carolina in large red letters across her birth certificate. Like Pearl, Bone becomes an embodiment of her mother's illicit sexuality, but unlike Pearl, who seems to emerge from illegitimacy unscathed, Bone cannot elude the institutional and psychological implications of the label she inherits. She must bear it in appallingly injurious ways.

Bastard out of Carolina is a semiautobiographical novel in which Allison is able to map out a version of her own abuse and its sources. She shows us how illegitimacy, driven home by the red brand illegitimate, takes on more menacing significance in the mind of a mixed-up father surrogate and gives him license to abuse. Critic Ying-chiao Lin observes, "The history of an abused person is always set within the rhythm of a larger social context" (3) and Bone's abuse is located in a family context that these days is not unusual—the melded family. Her predicament cannot be dismissed as just bad luck or only a harrowing story. Bone's maltreatment requires that we generalize about the dire social challenges many unwed teenage mothers must face, challenges that put the well-being of their illegitimate children in question. Allison paints a vivid picture of a social system that continues to leave unprepared young mothers vulnerable and their children susceptible to the social pathology of child abusers.

Allison's novel also makes clear Patricia Hill Collins's argument that systems of oppression are interdependent. For teenage mothers, discrimination begins immediately: it is generally assumed that young mothers cannot be good mothers. Such age discrimination is compounded by the moral disapproval and social shame that have historically been associated with out-of-wedlock motherhood. The oppression of unwed mothers is further guaranteed by the economic deprivation that almost inevitably accompanies the loss of educational opportunities once their childcare responsibilities take precedence. The American dream of upward mobility evaporates for the majority of teenage mothers and their children. For Anney Boatwright, achieving the post–World War II version of the dream is not even a remote possibility. Systems of oppression intertwine with poverty, class discrimination, and the social designation "white trash,"[2] leaving Anney with no hope of achieving the material and social well-being that she and Bone deserve.[3]

Anney is fifteen when Bone is born in the early 1950s. For the first time in American history, "unmarried white mothers . . . were expected to put their babies up for adoption" (Solinger 149), but perhaps due to her rural isolation and poverty, the postwar values that changed the choices available to unwed mothers had not reached Anney. The novel never suggests she considers adoption. She intends to keep her baby, "as most unwed mothers, black and white, had done throughout American history" (Solinger 149). Although Anney wants Bone, that doesn't mean the state of South Carolina or American culture at large wants her. An experienced obstetrician describes the degree to which children born out of wedlock were unwanted: "Our culture is actually hostile to the illegitimate child whom it sees . . . as a burden and as a menace to the monogamous family" (qtd. in Solinger 151). In fact, by 1960, a number of state legislatures, including that in Anney's neighboring state, North Carolina, "supported preventative, punitive actions against women who might in the future conceive another child defined by these states as 'unwanted.' These states enacted . . . laws mandating imprisonment or sterilization of women who had more than one illegitimate child" (22–23). When North Carolina state senator Luther Hamilton argued for sterilization, he did so on moral grounds: "We are," he said, "breeding a race of bastards" (qtd. in Solinger 55). It's stunning to realize that not long before my own first daughter was born, it was still commonly believed that "the biology of illegitimacy stamped the baby permanently with mental and moral marks of deficiency" (Solinger 151). In this benighted climate, what hope is there for Anney and Bone?

As first-person narrator, Bone tells the story of her premature birth, brought on by a car crash caused by her drunk uncle that leaves Anney unconscious for days. When an impatient state clerk won't wait for Anney to wake up and supply the birthfather's name, Bone's birth certificate is stamped "illegitimate." Depriving Bone of a father's name, the red letters establish unsparingly Anney's and Bone's disenfranchised status in patriarchal culture.[4] For Anney, the letters "burn her like the stamp she knew [people had] tried to put on her. *No-good, lazy, shiftless* . . . She'd [do] . . . anything to deny what Greenville County wanted to name her. Now a soft-talking black-eyed man had done it for them—set a mark on her and hers" (3–4). For Bone, the red letters mean "born to shame" (Allison 206) and her "bastard" status, observes J. Brooks Bouson, leads her to years of deep self-contempt. For Bouson, the novel is "mired in shame" and the "devastating effects of stigmatization" (104). For Andrew Morrison, Bone's life is marred by what her calls "shame vulnerability"—that is, a "sensitivity to, and readiness for, shame" (206). Together, Anney and Bone are publicly marked. "Anney is marked as a socially undesirable and tainted woman" and "her social stigma ends up affecting and infecting" Bone (Bouson 105). In *The Color Purple*, while Celie is still a girl, she is unjustly socially marked as "spoiled," and the psychological consequences are devastating. In *Bastard out of Carolina*, Bone is similarly marked, forced to grow up with what Rosemarie Thomson refers to as "a spoiled identity" (207).

The state may name Bone "bastard," but her notorious uncle, Black Earle Boatwright, names her "Bone" because when she's born, she's "no bigger than a knucklebone" (2). Her grandmother dismisses the birth certificate's red lettering, insisting, "Ain't no stamp on her nobody can see" (3). And yet Bone is clearly stamped as "other" in the Boatwright clan, her only extended family. Her blue-black hair and her black eyes mark her as an outsider right from the start. She looks nothing like her blond mother or the other brown-eyed Boatwright women; in fact, she does not "look like anybody at all" (30) except maybe her Cherokee great-grandfather who, her grandmother insists, was "Not a Boatwright, that's for sure" (27).

There's no scarlet *A*, but the red word illegitimate is impossible to remove. When Anney tries to get the birth certificate changed, the male clerk, "who represents the callous patriarchy of the state" (King 126), refuses to remove the stigmatizing stamp, declaring patronizingly, "Well, little lady . . . This is how it's got to be. The facts have been established" (4). The women working in his office are as unforgiving as the women of Hester's village centuries before; staring unforgivingly at Anney, they shake their heads and whisper, "Some people" (4). The "relationship between social formations and structures of feelings" (Fox 14) is made clear by reactions to the certificate. It may be just a sheet of paper, lying deep in a file cabinet, but its "official" authority bestows self-righteous superiority on the state workers and social inferiority and shame on Anney. Year after year, she returns to the courthouse to have the certificate changed, only to be met by unbending institutional policy and an ongoing dose of public humiliation. Her attempts to undo the past become a shaming ritual not unlike the pillory Hester was made to endure: year after year Anney is re-exposed to public disgrace.

At the conclusion of *The Scarlet Letter*, Hester offers consolation to the "wounded, wasted, wronged, misplaced, or erring and sinful" women who seek her out, assuring them that "at some brighter period, when the world should have grown ripe for it, . . . a new truth would be revealed, in order to establish the whole relation between man and woman on a surer ground of mutual happiness" (201). That brighter, ripened world is clearly not Greenville, South Carolina. Anney attracts some of the same scorn in the 1950s that Hester attracted in the 1650s. Understandably, she wants to escape the denigrating social shaming and financial struggles an unwed, single mother must confront, and marriage is her best opportunity. At nineteen, she marries Lyle Parsons, "one of the sweetest boys the Parsons ever produced," and Anney believes he "loves Bone" and "wants to adopt her when [they] get some money put by" (6). They are poor, but Anney seems to have successfully escaped the damning effects of unwed motherhood, especially after their daughter Reese is born. But her security is short-lived; Lyle dies in a car crash and Anney is left bereft, or as Bone puts it, "all butter grief and hunger." Now with two babies, she has to work even harder to support them, and "more than anything else in the world, [she wants] someone strong to love her like she love[s] her girls" (10). "Family values" are entrenched in post—World War II America, and "family" almost universally means mother *and* father, husband *and* wife.

Male superiority is a given, and in the infamous Boatwright clan, there is no exception to that rule even though Bone's uncles are more like rambunctious teenagers than grown men. Bone realizes early on that "Men could do anything and everything they did, no matter how violent or mistaken, was viewed with humor and understanding" (23). Entangled in poverty, the uncles have almost no economic power. They are educationally unequipped for white-collar jobs, and there is little steady blue-collar employment in Greenville, so they are unable to provide material well-being for their wives and children. Still they engender a great deal of respect. How so? Like Mr. —— in *The Color Purple*, they achieve their prominence in a crude manner, by asserting their masculinity. They use their brute strength and their penises to gain status in the phallocentric system they live in. By enacting a rebellious bravado that involves drinking excessively, carousing destructively, and philandering, they feign both autonomy and mastery, qualities that, in fact, they cannot hope to achieve. Restricted from capitalist social success by poverty and poor education, they find ways to assert themselves as pretend patriarchs in their families and in their community through dangerous and often unlawful escapades.

Bone's aunts and her mother are different; they are "old, worn-down, and slow, born to mother, nurse, and clean up after the men" (23). The Boatwright women are not as oppressed as Celie, but while their husbands, brothers, and sons are given carte blanche to shirk economic and family responsibilities of all kinds, the women stoically endure, making excuses for the sexual licentiousness from which the Boatwright men will not refrain. Ruth even speaks admiringly of her brother Earle, whose wife actually does leave when he won't stop "messing around with girls he would never have married and didn't love" (24). Ruth boasts: "Earle's got the magic . . . [That] man is just a magnet to women. Breaks their hearts and makes them like it" (24). Even though he is "trouble coming in on greased skids" and consistently acts like an insatiable, aggressive child, he garners respect from his peers, and all the Boatwright women pamper him, "their cheeks wrinkling around indulgent smiles while their fingers [trail] across [his] big shoulders" (24). Bone admires her unruly uncles, but she identifies with the Boatwright women. She likes "feeling a part of something nasty and strong and separate from . . . the whole world of spitting, growling, overbearing males" (91). The grandmother, aunts, and mother are strong and resourceful, but their readiness to excuse their men for their cavalier destructiveness puts them all in danger.

The moral laxity that is afforded the Boatwright men is also granted to other male characters of the novel. Indeed, Bone's grandmother holds the fact that Bone's birthfather has "never been in jail a day in his life" against him. It makes him "a sorry excuse for a man" (25). After Lyle's death, Earle introduces Anney to Glen Waddell, the black sheep of his middle-class family, a seventeen-year-old boy with "a hot temper, bad memory, and general uselessness" who aspires to be like the Boatwright men (12). Anney is all neediness, emotionally, economically, and sexually. She needs Glen "like a starving woman needs meat between her teeth" (41), and he does manage, Bone observes, to turn her "from a harried, worried mother into a giggling, hopeful girl" (35). She quickly becomes pregnant and needs to marry him before she starts showing (43). Even though almost all the Boatwright's have significant reservations about Glen—Bone's grandmother tellingly compares him to a "junkyard dog waiting to steal a bone" (37)—the penalties are too great for Anney to even consider having another baby out of wedlock.

When she accepts Glen's marriage proposal and he tells Bone and Reese to call him "Daddy" because "You're mine, all of you, mine" (36), his words have an ominous ring. He claims that he wants to adopt the girls, and, as Shawn E. Miller points out, "a loving adoptive father might conceivably enrich the limited system of orientation available to Bone" (142), but Glen is no such father. The "family" he forms is a "perverted exercise of paternal power" that grants him the authority to "distort and deform" his stepdaughter (Lin 3). He begins to abuse Bone the night Annie delivers his stillborn son, the boy he so desperately wants in order to secure his place in patriarchal lineage. As he and Bone wait in the car, Glen masturbates between Bone's legs, leaving her sore and bruised but unwilling to tell anyone what happened because she doesn't want to add any more suffering to her mother's latest loss. She even begins to doubt that the abuse happened at all because she too wants what her mother wants and what ideology has already taught her she should want—a "normal," two-parent family. Bone wants a father who will hold her gently. She wants "to be locked with Reese in the safe circle of [her mother and Glen's] arms" (52). She wants "to be like the families in the books in the library" (209). Although she can't bring herself to call him Daddy as he wishes, she does agree to call him Daddy Glen.

Depressed, overworked, and baffled by Glen's emotional needs, Anney gives over all her control to him. She agrees (until their poverty makes it impossible) not to "work outside the home" (98) because the Waddell men disapprove of working women. She lets Glen move them physically away from the rest of Boatwright family and the protection they might offer. Then she stands by as he irrationally insults Reese's grandmother, Lyle's mother, who only wants to bequeath Reese some property. Anney explains to Bone that she has to let Glen take of things. "He needs to do it," she says, "and I've got to let him" (57). Anney knows it's up to her to shore up Glen's fragile masculine pride. The patriarchal ideology that informs both Glen and Anney as to the designation of authority in family politics does indeed demand that she acquiesce. The bungling Boatwright uncles sense that all is not right with Glen, but rather than intervene and confront him, Bone overhears them making fun of his temper, his overly large hands, and his penis. Their teasing is portentous: "He gets crazy when he's angry," they remark. "Use his dick if he can't reach you with his arms, and that'll cripple you fast enough'" (61).

At first Bone is vague in her narration about what Glen's hands do her; she describes them as restless hands that are always reaching for her, "trembling on the surface of [her] skin" (105). But when she is ten, his abuse escalates and he beats her badly with a belt and then tells Anney that Bone called him a bastard (which she did not) and so he had to beat her until her backside is covered with stinging red welts. The novel's title becomes ambiguous if we stop to consider that Glen is the real "bastard out of Carolina," not Bone, though the novel never makes that explicit. According to Esther Saxey, "physical and sexual abuse has little vocabulary" (44), and indeed, Bone is silenced by Glen's violence, unable to find the words that could effectively represent his actions and her reactions. She acknowledges, "[Daddy Glen] never said 'don't tell your Mama.' He never had to. I did not know how to tell anyone" (108–9). Although she tries to avoid him, he inevitably catches her, beats her, or molests her, "his hands shaking as they moved . . . endlessly, over my belly, ass, and thighs." Bone endures these encounters "rigid, ashamed . . . afraid of making him angry" (108).

Anney is in treacherous denial. For much of the novel, we can believe she does not know about the sexual abuse, but when Glen beats Bone while she's home, her unwillingness to stop him is unforgivable though, unfortunately, not atypical. She repeatedly lets Bone down, doing nothing more than standing outside the locked bathroom door until the beating is over. Afterward she washes Bone's face, chastises her for being stubborn, and begs her not to make Glen mad. In effect, she revictimizes Bone by shifting blame for Glen's brutality onto Bone (Bouson 110). But Bone knows: "It was nothing I had done that made him beat me. It was just me, the fact of my life, who I was in his eyes and mine. I was evil. Of course I was" (110). Bone intuitively knows it's "the fact of her life," her illegitimacy, that leaves her unprotected against Glen's abuse. Anney is not evil, but her teenage pregnancy and ongoing poverty have left her critically ill-equipped to safeguard her daughter. Her emotional need for Glen as her husband and as her daughters' father makes her overlook the signs of his pathology. At the same time, Bone's fatherlessness makes her easy prey for this evil man. Left defenseless outside the protective boundaries that patriarchy customarily sets up around girls, Bone ingenuously consents to her abuse, blames herself, and accepts the false identity her sadistic "daddy" assigns her. Throughout the novel, he calls Bone "little bitch" (106), "a cold-hearted bitch" (130), a "*goddam little bastard*" and a "little cunt" (284). Anney stands by. Having capitulated to the reigning ideology that automatically authorizes Daddy Glen as the "man of the house," she fails Bone again and again.

Bone becomes even more ashamed of herself as the beatings get more violent. Daddy Glen brings out the color red all over her body, but she hides the welts and bruises "as if they were evidence of crimes [she] has committed" (113). Judith Herman explains how this comes about:

The child entrapped in this kind of horror develops the belief that she is somehow responsible for the crimes of her abusers. Simply by virtue of her existence on earth, she believes that she has driven the most powerful people in her world to do terrible things . . . her nature must be thoroughly evil. (105)

Even when a doctor finds that her collarbone has been broken twice and her tailbone once, she cannot bring herself to answer his questions of concern. Simply by existing, she drives the most powerful person she knows to do terrible things, for which her mother holds her responsible. She believes she is complicit; she believes she has not just done bad, she is bad. Allison takes us to a horrifying place, but by going there, we come to understand why abused children are too afraid and too ashamed to tell on their abusers. Bone also knows intuitively that she must protect her mother. As she watches Anney defend Glen when the frustrated doctor confronts her, Bone is "more terrified of hurting [Anney] than of anything that might happen to [herself]" (118). She can't remember a time when her mother hasn't look tired, sad, and scared (207); she won't add to her anguish. Consequently, Daddy Glen and Bone form a wretched alliance: he doesn't stop abusing her but he tries not to leave marks on her body; she tries to make sure Anney never again finds out what he is doing to her. Lin observes, "The act of saving her mother from knowing of her suffering places Bone, through a sort of reversal, in a motherlike role and the mother in the role of protected daughter" (11). Bone even thinks of herself as Anney's mother, musing, "It was as if I was her mother now, holding her safe, and she was my child, happy to lean on my strong, straight back" (118). Just as the stigmatizing onus of illegitimacy swings back and forth between mother and daughter, so does social responsibility. Anney has never overcome her unprepared initiation into unwed motherhood, and now her child must compensate for her mother's failures.

Religion comes to Bone by way of the lure of salvation. Brimming with shame for her illegitimacy and all its painful consequences, she gives herself "over to the mystery of Jesus' blood." In an effort to wash away her sense of guilt and survive her home life, she manages to be saved fourteen times in fourteen different Baptist churches. Each deliverance is intensely alluring, a "moment of sitting on the line between salvation and damnation with the preacher and the old women pulling bodily at [her] poor darkened soul" (151). But afterward, she always stumbles out into the sunshine unsaved, "Jesus' blood . . . absent, [and] the moment cold and empty" (152). Patriarchal religion can offer Bone no more salvation, or safety, or vindication than it offered Hester in *The Scarlet Letter* of Celie in *The Color Purple*. Though Bone hopes for "God's retribution on the wicked," she finds nothing more than a preacher "so full of himself he crowds out all the air . . . [and] old biddies sweating talcum powder and perfume" (173). Patriarchal religions too often endorse family arrangements in which men are granted unquestioned dominance and unaccountable priests and pastors are given free reign. In so doing, organized religion seems consistently ill-fitted for protecting "the least of these," for helping the legions of Mary Magdalenes, for shielding the Celies and Bones of our world.

Girlhood friendship also fails to give Bone any positive counterbalance to her self-loathing. Although there is a Pearl in Allison's novel, whose mother—like Hester—actually supports the family by sewing and embroidery, this Pearl is nothing like the lithesome, sprightly Pearl that Hawthorne created. Instead Allison gives us Shannon Pearl, an unfortunate albino child who is, like Bone, treated viciously by others. Rather than bond over their shared adversity, Bone and Shannon Pearl cruelly turn on each other. Their weapon—name-calling—is one they have learned from adults. Shannon Pearl reiterates Bone's illegitimacy, telling her that everyone knows all the Boatwrights are "drunks and thieves and bastards," and Bone's rejoinder, "white-assed bitch," makes Shannon Pearl cry. The name-calling escalates dangerously, and when her cousin calls her a "fat old hog," Shannon Pearl pours so much lighter fluid on a barbecue grill that she is consumed by flame. Her hellfire death drives home just how lethal the power of name-calling can be. For Bone, being repeatedly identified as bastard could prove deadly.

The most contented of all the Boatwrights, Bone's Aunt Raylene, is also the only Boatwright to resist compulsory heterosexuality and, in so doing, subvert the patriarchal values that are so precarious for Boatwright women. At seventeen, she had run away to work "like a man, cutting off her hair and dressing in overalls" and calling herself Ray (179). When she came back, she had taken up living alone outside of town, "completely comfortable with herself" (182). Raylene is something like Hester, getting by contently on the outskirts, avoiding the disapprobation of the community. After the doctor discovers Bone's broken bones, Anney sends her to stay with Raylene, whose patriarchal nonconformity makes her Bone's most dependable mother substitute. Informing Bone that "trash rises all the time" (180), Raylene shows her how to drag junk from the river and repair it. Bone is still not yet completely aware of her own sexual orientation, but she falls in love with Raylene's way of life. The critic Deborah Horvitz observes, "Raylene's metaphor (and her actual work) of making beauty out of trash resonates deeply with Bone, connecting her own and Raylene's lesbianism and artistic creativity with comfort and safety" (253). Bone works hard for Raylene, and Raylene praises her. In opposition to Daddy Glen's annihilating criticism, Raylene's nourishing attention and lesbian alterity helps Bone construct a more stable subjectivity outside the corrupted patriarchal matrix.

Given Daddy Glen's unrelenting abuse, we would assume that Bone would never again look to him for affection and confirmation and that her mother's love would become the most necessary ingredient for her psychological well-being. But Anney's ability to mother is always compromised by either her preoccupation with Glen or her draining, physically demanding jobs. Although Bone loves her mother and her aunts acutely and they in return love her, they are no match to the reigning paradigm that constructs our desires and dreams. Bone craves "a father's love," musing almost romantically, "If he loved, if he only loved me "(209). Anney cannot relinquish her desire for the ideal husband; Bone cannot abandon her dream of the ideal father.

Finally when Bone gets drunk with her cousins at her aunt's funeral and Raylene tries to help her in the bathroom, she discovers bloody stripes on Bone's thighs and buttocks, the evidence of one of Glen's particularly vicious beatings. The uncles are involved immediately, and although they don't kill Glen, they do put him in the hospital. Bone tries to take responsibility for the beating, insisting, "I made him mad. I did," and Anney tries to explain what's been happening: "I couldn't stop him, and then . . . I don't know . . . He loves her. He does. He loves us all. I don't know. I don't know. Oh God . . . I love him. I know you'll hate me. Sometimes I hate myself, but I love him. I love him" (246–47). The violent Boatwright revenge does nothing to extinguish Glen's passionate rage. Bone is no safer than before.

Bone falls "into shame like a suicide throws herself into a river" (253). Even though several adults tell her that what has happened is not her fault, the one person who won't say this is Anney. All she can do is promise that she won't live with Glen again until she knows that Bone will be safe, and Bone knows that won't ever be the case. In a strong voice and clear words, she says what she must: "I know you'll go back, Mama, and maybe you should. I don't know what's right for you, just what I have to do. I can't go back to live with Daddy Glen. I won't . . . I could go stay . . . with Raylene . . . I love you . . . but I can't think of anything else to do" (276–77). Bone has been relentlessly driven to this impasse with Anney. Twelve years after her birth, she gives her mother permission to give her up, to relinquish her to the care of others—to be "adopted," in a way, by Raylene.

When Bone refuses to come home with Anney, Glen's mania is unleashed again. After all, he considers her his property, and he cannot / will not give up the patriarchal license that still scandalously authorizes him. While Bone is staying at her Aunt Alma's, Glen shows up, demanding that Bone tell Anney that she wants to come home. When she refuses, he insists, declaring, "You don't say what you do. I'm your daddy. I say what you do" (282). When she still refuses, his next accusations tell the story from his distorted perspective:

> You're the reason. She loves me, I know it. But it's you, you're the one gets in the way. You make me crazy and you make her ashamed, ashamed of you and ashamed of loving me. It ain't right her leaving me because of you . . . *You Goddam little bastard!* . . . Just die and leave us alone. If it hadn't been for you, I'd have been all right. (283–84)

In his own crazed way, Daddy Glen articulates Bone's illegitimacy and her resultant defenselessness in the nuclear family. She does "[get] in the way," complicating his relationship with Anney; she does "make [him] crazy," arousing his rage and perversity; she does "make [Anney] ashamed of loving [him]," for colluding with her daughter's abuser. Even though Bone has verbally released her mother from responsibility, Anney has remained torn and Glen can't bear her uncertainty. But he is badly mistaken to think that Bone's death would solve his problems, and it's a clear sign of his pathology that he blames her for his misery. Glen has employed a classic defensive mechanism, displacing all his anger and resentment onto a helpless stand-in, Bone. Some might see him as a psychologically damaged man, harmed by his father's rejection, disabled by humiliation, and hopelessly susceptible to uncontrollable, sociopathic rage. But in this novel, there is no sympathy and no defense for the Daddy Glens of our world.

Most appalling, perhaps, given the litany of damage Glen inflicts, is that he has arrogantly used his stepdaughter in a frenetic attempt to exorcize his demons because he can. No one has stopped him, and he is not done yet. Now he beats Bone even more brutally, dislocating her shoulder, breaking her wrist, choking her, raping her, all the while screaming, "Now . . . You'll learn . . . You'll keep your mouth shut. You'll do as you're told. You'll tell Anney what I want you to tell her . . . I'll teach you. I'll teach you" (285).

Glen is still on top of Bone when Anney finds them. Lying helpless on the kitchen floor in a slippery pool of blood, unable to talk, unable to move, Bone listens to Glen defend himself, sobbing, "No, darling. No! It's not what you think." She finds herself wondering, "Would she think I wanted him to do that? Would she think I asked for it? What would he tell her?" (287). Bone has assumed the blame for her abuse for so long that even though this time she has been viciously raped, she thinks she may be held responsible for it. As Anney gets her into the car, Glen pleads: "Kill me, Anney. Go on. I can't live without you . . . Kill me!" (290). To Bone's amazement and the reader's horror, Anney pauses for a minute to hold him, comfort him, and cry over him. As Bone waits for her mother, she speculates with good reason, "Could she love me and still hold him like that?" The once necessary, sustaining connection between Bone and her mother shatters. Anney finally extricates herself from Glen's embrace and leaves him there in the yard, but when she gets Bone to the hospital, she drops her off without giving her name or Bone's and disappears. It's clear she's going back for him. The doctors and nurses treat Bone's arm, shoulder, and cuts, but when the sheriff asks her who assaulted her, she still won't tell on Daddy Glen. She replies, "I want to go home . . . I want my mama" (297). No one seems to know that she has been raped. Anney is gone and Bone will not speak.[5]

Raylene takes Bone home to her house on the river, and on the way tells her story. Once she had made the woman she loved choose between her and her baby. The woman stayed with her baby, a choice that almost killed Raylene. Bone marvels at the story of the woman who chose her child over her lover. Although her battered, broken body aches, it's her heart that hurts the most. She knows that will not be her story. Knowing that Anney will choose Glen makes her angry and "so old [her] insides turned to dust and stone" (306). When Anney shows up at Raylene's days later, she tries to explain to Bone that she never imagined he would hurt Bone "like that." Even if we believe her, the novel makes us confront "the potentially cataclysmic repercussions of lying to oneself and refusing to bear witness to one's own story" (255). Anney's ongoing denial has proved almost fatal for Bone, and although she still insists she loves Bone, that she is "not gonna let [her] go," she does just that. She disappears into the night with Glen, bound we know not where.

The only thing she leaves behind for Bone is a new birth certificate. She does manage to have the scarlet letters—illegitimate—removed. Despite innumerable offenses, Bone still empathizes with her flawed mother. Even with Anney's heartbreaking betrayal, Bone can compassionately identify with her losses:

Who had Mama been, what had she wanted to be or do before I was born? Once I was born, her hopes had turned, and I had climbed up her life like a flower reaching for the sun. Fourteen and terrified, fifteen and a mother, just past twenty-one when she married Glen. Her life had folded into mine. What would I be like when I was fifteen, twenty, thirty? Would I be as strong as she had been, as hungry for love, as desperate, determined, and ashamed? (309)

Lin suggests that the "hidden motive that prevents Anney from being a caring and protective mother, that allows her to in effect betray her own daughter . . . centers around [her] debased self-image" (16). Her own sense of illegitimacy keeps her from safeguarding her innocent daughter. Bone seems to understand this. She knows that her mother has suffered under the shameful stamp of unwed motherhood. Perhaps she even comprehends that the new, purified birth certificate is more legitimizing, redeeming, and necessary for Anney than it is for her. Bouson sees it as "at best a misguided attempt to ease her daughter's shame" (117). For even though this sheet of paper is now unmarked, Bone has been deeply marked by her shame, abuse, rape, and rejection, for always. We assume Raylene will care for Bone lovingly and Bone knows she can trust her, but shame, undeserved, unjustifiable, but unrelenting shame, is branded into her selfhood. Not even thirteen yet, she knowingly declares, "I was already who I was going to be" (309).

Most critics want to argue that even though the ending of the novel is devastating, we can predict recovery for Bone. We feel she will never acquiesce to another Daddy Glen, that she will be stronger than her desperate mother, that through the power of storytelling, she will successfully construct herself as a heroic "bastard." Allison herself maintains that "the peak of the story is that Bone gets angry . . . and begins to hold people responsible"; her anger promises "the possibility of healing . . . [and surviving] the worst things in the world" (qtd in Ng 3). Vincent King maintains that Bone "is no longer a bastard; she has finally escaped the state-given name" (135). Katrina Irving argues that Bone rejects the unsullied status the new birth certificate grants when she chooses a title for her story, *Bastard out of Carolina*, that "defiantly claims the negative epithet from which her mother had attempted to deliver her" (101).[6] Such defiance is certainly salubrious and bodes well for her, but I would suggest that even as Bone appropriates "bastard," she knows there's no escaping the shadow it has cast. One can only re-embroider it.[7]

Anney, the unwed mother who at fifteen keeps her baby and loves her fiercely, ultimately gives her away anyway. She has to choose between a life without Glen, once again a disadvantaged single mother in need, or a life with Glen, the man against all logic she can't stop loving. She chooses the man, the damaged, destructive, but for her, necessary man. She chooses a system under which women suffer physical, emotional, and economic abuse and children are demeaned, beaten, raped. Spousal love trumps maternal love. Anney cannot declaim, as Hester once did, "She is mine. Ye shall not have her." In Bone's words, Anney is too "hungry for love."

I know something about being that hungry, which leads me to a story I have to tell about that link between unwed motherhood and violence. After my first marriage to the hippie mountain climber, who turned sadistic and violent, and my second marriage to the would-be Prince Charming, who turned possessive and violent, I mentioned that I started over with the help of my loyal sister in a new state with a "clean slate" (well, if not clean, at least a slate I thought I had carefully erased), but that I also straightaway took up with another man. He wasn't Daddy Glen, but he did get fired. We couldn't afford day care for my youngest, and while I went to work, he stayed home with her. God, I hate to tell this part . . . Kezia wasn't a baby anymore, though I still thought of her as such. She was four years old and didn't need a nap, but Langdon, my new man, wanted some time to himself and told her to turn off *Sesame Street*—she had already watched it twice that day—and go to her room. When she ignored him, he threatened her. When she still dawdled, he took off his belt and spanked her with it, and then he said, "Don't tell your mother or I'll do it again." She'd never been spanked; none of my children had. I prided myself on that, but that was unmerited pride. My own emotional neediness and tarnished self-image had pushed me once again into a hasty, foolhardy romance, and this time I had put my little girl in harm's way.

Am I no better than Anney Boatwright? I'd like to say I redeemed myself as best one can in that situation. When I got home from work that evening, all three kids were waiting outside for me. Kezia, my smart and feisty little girl, had already told her sister and her brother that Langdon had spanked her with his belt as soon as they got off the school bus, and they were beside themselves to tell me about it. I came in the back door, put down my things, and uttered those dramatic words, "Get out." He left for California the next day and we only saw him one more time when he came back for his boat.

In creating Bone's battered life, Allison uses stark realism to testify, as Sarah Eden Schiff maintains, "to the lived experience of people whose very presence undermines the narratives that [Americans] hold so dear" (551–52), narratives of triumph over adversity, poverty spun into gold, decency over decadence, moral good over evil. My daydreams about keeping Merideth and raising her and her brother and sisters with love and determination have everything to do with those "American dream" narratives. I want to believe that hard work and a good heart will allow anyone the opportunity to achieve the comfort and the security I enjoyed the day I finished Allison's novel on the beach at Aquinnah. It had been twenty years since Langdon had used his belt on Kezia, but that terrible memory came crashing back. I've learned since then that the "American Dream" can indeed be bad faith, a dubious promise that's unattainable for most. Would Merideth and I have been as burdened by illegitimacy as Anney and Bone were? Would she have been unjustly penalized for the circumstances of her birth? Could I, an unwed mother, have been in such desperate straits that I could have fallen for a Daddy Glen? Would I have chosen a man over my daughter? I want to answer emphatically "No! Never!" But Dorothy Allison and my own experience have shown me just how the psychologically impairing and emotionally devastating the consequences of unwed motherhood can be.

I have always thought of Mount St. Helen's as my mountain. Since that first climb on my twenty-first birthday and its subsequent eruption on my thirty-second, I've returned to it many times to pay tribute to its fearful magnificence. Since that first cataclysmic 1980 eruption, there have been intermittent aftershocks for over thirty years now, sometimes just a rumble, sometimes an actual explosion of steam and debris. My past hangs on to me like that. Every once in a while, it rumbles through me, destabilizing all my accomplishments, all my security, shaking the very ground I've built a life on.

CHAPTER 7

Birthmothers in Exile

Since standards of morality are culturally produced, it makes sense that these standards would operate differently in diverse cultures. In the production of American culture, stories such as *The Coquette, The Scarlet Letter, The Sound and the Fury,* and *The Color Purple* are attempts not only to reflect American moral standards, but also to produce, revise, even subvert moral standards, or to use a term Richard Rorty employs in *Achieving Our Country,* to "forge a moral identity" (13). In this sense, each text has forged the moral identity of appropriate and inappropriate sexual intercourse, focusing especially on the moral character of unmarried women and their illegitimate children. Each of the texts has demonstrated the significance of lost virginity and the severe, sometimes deadly consequences of extramarital conception. Readers cannot help but take a position about the ethical or unethical treatment of the seduced woman, the unwed mother, and her illegitimate child. We may adhere to the moral tenets established by religious, patriarchal, and conservative ideologies and condemn her as a fallen woman, a scarlet woman, or a Jezebel. We might acquiesce to her punishment as inevitable even when we sympathize with her. This is certainly the moral identity that the earliest novels, *The Power of Sympathy, The Coquette,* and *Charlotte Temple,* hope to inspire. Or we may choose a more forgiving moral position, one that questions the religious, patriarchal, or family codes that automatically impose "Thou shalt" and "Thou shalt not" on powerless, exploited women. Rather than condemn the fallen woman, we might absolve her and hold others accountable for her seduction, condemning those who unjustly penalize her and her child. Certainly this is the more common progressive position, especially for contemporary readers of *The Scarlet Letter, Jennie Gerhardt, The*

Old Maid, or *The Color Purple*. Or we may be ambivalent—sympathizing with Caddy Compson of *The Sound and The Fury* and Anney Boatwright of *Bastard out of Carolina* but unable to condone their desperate decisions. Unwed motherhood crosses every social barrier American culture has constructed; unmarried girls get pregnant whether they grow up in New York City, the Mississippi Delta, a California suburb, or rural North Carolina, whether they are white, black, Latino, Asian American, American Indian, Catholic, Jewish, Amish, Muslim, privileged, disadvantaged, wealthy, poor, educated, or not. No one segment of American culture is exempt from extramarital sex. Given this pervasiveness, we might expect the communal and familial responses to unwed motherhood and illegitimacy would be as diverse as our population. We might also assume that since each text tells a different woman's story, her unique history, location, class, race, and religion—to name only a few—would intrude as dissimilar socially determining strands producing distinctive intertwining moral consequences within the subcultures of the United States. But I have been surprised by a troubling repetition in these narratives. Though our sympathies for literary unwed mothers may shift from era to era, place to place, and protagonist to protagonist, the consequences our characters face for extramarital conception remain unswervingly punitive. American literature seems to uphold Malinowski's "Principle of Legitimacy," that illegitimacy is a universal and inviolate taboo in any society.

Given this disconcerting uniformity, I began to search for narratives that forge a different moral identity. I wanted more forgiving narratives that suggested more permissive norms, narratives that did not categorize nonmarital sex as morally wrong, that did not punish the unwed mother, that did not exile her or force a painful separation between her and her child. This was more difficult than I first anticipated. The historical context explains why: "Before World War II," observes historian Ricki Solinger, "social, religious, and education leaders did *not* . . . suggest that there were steps [unwed mothers] could take to restore . . . their place in the community. What was lost could not be regained; what was acquired could not be cast off." Once fallen, forever fallen. Although there was no condemning scarlet *A* for an unwed mother or her illegitimate child to don for a lifetime, Solinger maintains that "illegitimacy was a shame that carried with it shamed motherhood" (152). While the norms held in the United States in the early decades of the twentieth century may have become more permissive about nonmarital sexual behavior, out-of-wedlock birth remained a disgrace. So it seems that

unless I moved to very contemporary narratives, moral disapproval and punitive shame would remain givens when it came to the fallen woman's master
narrative if the fallen woman becomes an unwed mother. But what about the
need for secrecy and compulsory exile?

Solinger also points out that until the end of World War II, unwed
motherhood was almost always managed as an internal family matter, and
the circumstances of the out-of-wedlock birth were often kept a family secret. As we have seen in our literary texts so far, girls such as Jennie Gerhardt
and Charlotte Lovell are certainly seen as immoral and pay for their moral
failure, but they are not permanently evicted from their extended family.
Nonetheless, we have also seen families like the Compsons and Celie's family who do insist on separation of mother and child; or the extended family
can become the site of horrific punishment for the illegitimate child, as in
Bastard out of Carolina. But until after World War II, "unwed mothers did
not look to complex networks of overlapping social agencies to meet their
needs" (Solinger 152) and this seems to be the case in the fiction as well.
Although the elders of colonial Boston try to step in and remove Pearl from
Hester's care, Hester makes sure that will not happen. We do not again see
the attempt at intervention by a community agency in any of the fiction
that follows. Instead, each new narrative repeats almost without exception,
though always with its own unique swerve, some version of an ongoing scenario of seduction, pregnancy, birth, and secrecy that often involves punishment and exile. Such consistency is disconcerting, especially since my purpose is not to prove the omnipresence of the fallen woman master narrative
but to demonstrate the creative and illuminating ways writers subvert its
authority and lessen its punitive spirit.

Clearly, if I were going to refute this dominating master narrative, I
would have to find fiction that would help me do so. And so my reading
became a sort of treasure hunt in search of novels that forge a more accommodating morality, novels in which unwed motherhood is not tragic, novels
in which illegitimacy is managed in caring, extended families, in families
that do not insist on secrecy or on the separation of mother and child and
in communities that do not become the site of punishment for the unwed
mother or the illegitimate child.

My quest led me to Reynolds Price's *Kate Vaiden* and Louise Erdrich's
Love Medicine. I turned to both enthusiastically, anticipating narratives from
diverse subcultures of America, representing committed extended families
lovingly caring for illegitimate children in places where birthmothers were

not forced to bear the burden of shame. In short, I was hoping they would subvert the condemning moral standards of the master narrative and help forge a new, more forgiving moral identity for the unwed mother and her illegitimate child. And I did find the extended family members caring as best they could for illegitimate children, but frustratingly once again, I found condemnation. Each novel takes a disturbing moral twist that cancels its potential for narrative subversion. Neither birthmother is punitively exiled by their family or community. Both voluntarily leave their sons in ostensibly good hands in order to pursue their own quests unburdened by the responsibilities of single motherhood. But their journeys are so heartbreakingly lonely that the narratives serve once again as examples of exile and punishment, self-imposed though they may be.

I am acutely aware that by drawing analogies between culturally distinct narratives and the larger cultural narrative of unwed motherhood, I risk conflating these narratives, and erasing their particularity. That is, of course, not my intent. Instead I hope to demonstrate the way that the following narratives repeat the master narrative about the lived experience of unwed motherhood in different cultural locations. In so doing, we will also see the long reach of conventional moral standards.

KATE VAIDEN

In his 1986 novel *Kate Vaiden*, Reynolds Price demonstrates the southern sense of humor for which he became famous, respected, and beloved in my adopted state, North Carolina. Price, who died in 2011, was raised and remained a North Carolinian, and sets most of his fiction in the state as well. *Kate Vaiden* is no exception, with much of it taking place in 1940s Macon, the small town north of Raleigh where Price was born. Macon has a centrifugal force for Kate, the first-person narrator and protagonist. She leaves it several times, but she always comes back. It's the place where, to use her words, she "had lost or thrown away" her infant son, whom she hasn't seen for almost forty years, since the day she put him down for a nap and vanished.

Kate's story has a great deal to do with suicide, and although this is not a focus I will pursue, it must be mentioned that by the time she is eighteen, she has lost her mother and father to murder/suicide, as well as her first love, Gaston, and the father of her baby, Douglas Lee, to suicide. Hers is an unsettling inheritance and critics such as Joseph Dewey have argued convincingly that because of these terrifying occurrences, Kate "comes to learn [suicide's] persuasive argument—the necessity of sacrificing the self to preserve it." Dewey maintains that Kate, hurt badly by abandonment, closes out her emotional life at eighteen, choosing instead to imitate the desperate strategy of a suicide: "the joyless withdrawal from experience." If she is loved, "she will withhold her heart; approached, she will bolt" (Dewey). Nonetheless, for this reader Kate's joyless withdrawal from motherhood remains a mystery.

Price begins the novel by negating the significance of bridal virginity and the condemning moral identity of nonmarital sex. Kate is a willing sexual partner with Gaston and with Douglas Lee, and with deadpan forthrightness makes it clear that when it comes to sex, she enjoys herself. Remarkable for a girl of the early 1940s, she feels no sexual shame, even though she knows she should. She realizes that no matter "how awful [she's] been . . . in the world in general . . . one main trait would set [her] apart from here on out and make [her] an outlaw of sorts forever—[she] could seldom feel shame" (150). Such a claim seems dubious, especially when I recall my own experience in 1965: the waves of shame I felt for my sexual desire, the mortifying act of sexual intercourse itself, and the trepidation my Florence Crittenton sisters and I felt about our loss of virginity. I would like to believe in Kate's lack of remorse. I've always been impressed by women who claim to have casual sex without feelings of shame or exploitation, but I've only met two such women in my lifetime, which has spanned the sexual revolution. Thus, when I hear Kate's claim, I wonder if the assertion has more to do with Reynolds Price, the novel's male author, than authentic female experience. I'm not alone in my skepticism. In her essay "Reading as a Woman: Reynolds Price and Creative Androgyny in Kate Vaiden," critic Edith Hartin argues that Kate is an impersonation. The novel frequently and "jarringly" reminds Hartin, who identifies herself as a "feminist, resisting reader" in the vein of Judith Fetterly, that she is "witnessing a man attempting to pass off the product of his imagination as an imitation of her own." In other words, when Kate insists that she feels no sexual shame, female readers like Hartin and me are being asked "to identify with a character whose impulses have originated in a male mind, a stretch that at many points requires [us], in Judith Fetterly's words, 'to identify against [ourselves]'"(37). While Price might be attempting to create a more androgynous female character and sidestep limiting sexual norms for women, he risks Kate becoming more an extension of his own masculinity than a genuine female character.

Nonetheless, there is no questioning Kate's authentic response when she realizes that at sixteen, she's pregnant and unwed: "The whole dark world fell on me . . . so I could barely breathe" (154). Here Price gets it right. I too felt that crushing sensation of awful helplessness descending on me as I lay wrapped in inadequate tissue paper on a narrow table in our family doctor's office, my feet in the stirrups, my knees bent, my legs spread. When he said those five words, "You are three months pregnant," I began to drown. Today I know that I was having a panic attack, but at the time, as I surged up, gasping and gulping, it felt like all the air in the world was beyond me, denied me. Like Kate, I was unable to help myself, but unlike me, Kate is offered the kind of support I could not even dream of, not then. It's the kind of support that I still wistfully wish had been an option for me so long ago. Kate's discretely gay Uncle Walter offers her "The chance to make something last" (171). He will not only to take her into his home for her pregnancy; he wants her and her baby to stay. He will keep house, support her while she gets her diploma, and make a home for them with or without the baby's father, Douglas Lee. What I would have given for an Uncle Walter with such an offer! But Kate inexplicably refuses the proposal, along with all offers of support from a steady stream of good people who offer her their homes without devious motives. There's the cab driver, Tim Slaughter, who kindly takes her in only to have her bolt even as she admits to herself that she is strewing more pain behind her (179). And there's her aunt and uncle, who with "quiet baffled trust" (201) take her back without hesitating more than once and then, even though they are aging and worn out, raise the son she abandons.

I assume Price wants us to see Kate's inability to forge a permanent bond with her baby, Lee, as a consequence of the string of suicides that have left her so afraid of personal or domestic commitment that she has to flee, but her steely determination to hit the road makes her status as female victim more than questionable. In many ways I want to applaud Kate's resistance to the master narrative of the fallen woman. She is not forced by anyone into exile; rather she aspires to what Nina Baym maintains is the central myth of the American novel: the male flight into the wilderness (131). Her flight clearly goes against gender expectations. Although she enjoys her baby's company after he's born, especially his "peaceful knowing nature," she shows early signs of maternal ambivalence. For example, when her son gets colic and she gets a cold, she is grateful that her aunt takes over, moving his crib outside her room so that Kate can rest. And she can't adjust to the baby's daily routine. She prepares to leave, observing:

Maybe it was lonesomeness, the reason I failed. I didn't have anybody my age near me. I'd got used to fun at Walter's and Tim's. Most of all though—and worst of all—I'd started to worry that no man would want me, no decent man with a regular job. A teenaged mother with a needy bastard-boy and no big skills, no big nest egg or moviestar looks ... Also I was hungry, not for food or love. (210)

Kate's reasons for abandoning Lee are plausible. Certainly there are mothers who resist the ideological and biological imperative to bond with their infants especially when their first months of motherhood are complicated by postpartum depression, but studies show that resistance like Kate's is highly unusual. Solinger gives several examples of maternity homes in the 1930s and 1940s, when the goal was still to ensure a mother would not abandon her infant, where regulations required that a mother "nurse the baby and care for it for six weeks even if she [planned] to place it for adoption." The practice ensured that young women who had wanted to give up their child would no longer think of doing so after caring for them for several weeks or months (150). Based on my own experience, I am certain this sealing of maternal affection occurs. My affections for my daughter were inextricably sealed in just the one minute I was allowed to see her after her birth. I never completely recovered when that permanent bond was severed. It's no wonder that adoption activists want to change adoption laws and require that a "mother and her baby should have a minimum of 90 days together before an adoption plan is considered and a consent form is signed" (Walton). And it is telling that recent landmark legislation in South Korea takes concrete steps to stem the overseas adoption of Korean children by requiring single mothers to live with their babies for a week before they relinquish custody (Sang-Hun). Such practices are meant to protect birthmothers like me from being pressured to hastily sign surrender papers they will forever regret. Kate's decision to leave Lee after caring for him for several months because she can't "just maim that much of [herself] by bolting doors on the wide green world and camping down forever in a house with no man near me under sixty years old" (211) remains, for me, improbable and problematic.

If it is the masculine myth of flight into the wilderness to achieve "complete self-definition" that propels Kate, it is never realized. Once she goes, she is far from autonomous. People continue to help her on journey, including Whitfield Eller, who proposes marriage, a former teacher, Miss Limer, who helps her get her high school diploma and employment, and a woman she meets on a train, Daphne, who helps her relocate. But the journey never seems to have a point, or Kate never sufficiently articulates one. She suffers pangs of guilt when she faces up to her own moral choices and is "pressed raw against one sure certainty," that she had abandoned her child. She rationalizes her reasons: "I didn't think I'd be a worse mother than many . . . I didn't think his presence—a baby bastard—would scare men off me or cost too much . . . All I could think . . . was *I did not want him*. I never once doubted that those four words were awful as any person can say. But I knew they were true" (264). There are moments when she waivers as she imagines what Lee's face would look like and realizes that she would like him, that she "wanted to see him and help him grow" (264). She even dreams of finding a letter in her mailbox with the return address, "Lee Vaiden, Box 68, Macon, N.C." (283). But she remains alone—for almost forty years—living in Raleigh, only sixty-five miles away from her son. She sends no support, no letters of inquiry, no missives of concern. When she meets new men, she still enjoys sex without shame, admitting, "I have touched more than my share of boys" (285), but she is not without guilt. She when she thinks of falling in love, she balks at such intimacy because she can't tell her story; she knows "it was just the one tale men couldn't believe or, worse, couldn't bear . . . An outlaw mother is the black last nightmare any man can face" (282). Although she convinces herself, as so many women who surrender children try to do, that Lee is better off without her, she also knows she may be harming him every instant that she stays away, and she flings that wounding likelihood "at [her] own eyes and teeth [for] a billion nights" (282). She forms no lasting bonds with anyone; her "mind [stays] clenched [her] whole adult life" (285); her loneliness is continuous.

Kate does not live a life of chastity, unlike many of the other unwed mothers we have encountered, but like Hester, she remains on the margins, excluding herself from the feast of life. Presumably with a nod to Hawthorne and Hester, Price adds another unusual link; Kate also develops a preternatural sixth sense that lets her distinguish between truth and lies. Since she works for a firm of lawyers that deal in criminal cases, she claims to have saved some lives, but this skill is mentioned only in passing and is hardly a justification for a life of isolation (285). Although she is a great reader, Kate never overtly mentions Hester Prynne, so we can't assume she is consciously trying to make Hester her role model, as I once did. But Hester's stoic example has always eluded me. I had to learn that her circumstances were nothing like my own and that I couldn't begin to approximate her opportunities or her behavior given the different intricacies of my life. I find Kate to be even more wanting as a model of behavior for the unwed mother. Her choices would not be mine, nor would I suggest them to anyone facing unwed motherhood. Perhaps Hester and Kate both fail as viable models because they are both products of masculine imaginations. Ultimately, both characters leave me in an uncomfortable position. I respect their independent, rugged individualism, but at the same time, I find them distortions of female experience. To identify with Hester is difficult; with Kate it's impossible.

When Kate is diagnosed with cervical cancer, she believes she is being "punished at last in the place where [she'd] failed, the scene of the crime" (290), but as she imagines standing up at Judgment "before [she's] fried," she realizes she needs to see her child. She can't die "never knowing the one good thing [she] made" (291–92). She begins the search and although Price ends the novel before a reunion, Kate learns where to find Lee, now a navy commander who, when he's not at sea, lives in her uncle Walter's house. A relative she tracks down tells her enigmatically that Lee "needs more help than he knows" (302), but this need is never explained and the comment doesn't worry Kate much. It's not an impetus to send her flying to his door. She does pick up the phone late one night and calls him, but when she gets his answering machine, she leaves a dumfounding message, the kind of message a crank-calling teenager would leave: "I'm the burglar and will be right over" (306). This makes no sense. Does Price want us to think Kate's finally in some warped way fessing up to stealing away in the night? Who knows? We're never told Lee's response to the message, which feels to me cruel and harmful, because Kate is not going to "be right over." Instead she decides she'll first write a book that will serve as an introduction for Lee so that when she does finally does really contact him, he will "have all the facts" and "be free to choose" (306).

I understand wanting to give an abandoned child the chance to choose. I've been there. I've written that letter. I spent days finding just the right words to give my daughter the choice to get to know me or not. My mental health rested on her decision. I knew my first words were critical. So I find myself incensed by Kate's flippant, enigmatic message. It doesn't ring true. It's the last thing a birthmother would say once she located her lost child. Whether she abandoned, or lost, or gave up, or surrendered that child, she would return with seriousness, care, and fear. And who would stop to write a book? I have also needed to write to explain, to expound, and to atone, but books can be written later. Kate simply doesn't have time. At the most her doctors have given her four years. The novel ends not with Kate's firm decision to start the book tomorrow and get it done quickly so she can see Lee soon. Rather Kate muses, "I could start tomorrow. I could finish by fall" (306). Of course, given that we're reading *Kate Vaiden*, perhaps we are to assume that she does finish her book and, in so doing, achieves an androgynous version of what Baym calls a "melodrama of beset manhood," a narrative in which "a person will be able to achieve complete self-definition." But that's cold comfort to this reader, who keeps her own experience in the forefront and refuses dubious masculine myths of rugged individualism and "complete self-definition."

Finally *Kate Vaiden* fails to live up to my hopes for a revision of the fallen woman's master narrative. Like unwed mothers before her, Kate falls, gives birth, and departs for a life of separation from her extended family and her son until she must confront her apparently predestined punishment, death from cancer. Price's narrative swerve, that this birthmother willingly chooses her lonely exile and finds it satisfying, is reminiscent of Hester Prynne, who returns to Boston after raising Pearl, restores the scarlet *A* to her breast, and resumes her life of good deeds in solitary martyrdom. Hester's self-imposed exile remains illogical and unrealistic until we read it against the backdrop of the fallen woman's master narrative in which such a woman must pay not just for a while but for a lifetime. Persephone doesn't have to return to Hades only once for eating that pomegranate; she has to return once a year forever. Price can't resist that narrative arc, and Kate must atone alone for her fall year after year. But her decision to abandon Lee is more problematic than Hester's refusal to surrender Pearl. Hester only returns to exile after Pearl is grown and married. Kate's decision to leave her son behind may not be morally wrong, but it is disappointing and improbable. Birthmothers sometimes walk willingly away from their babies, but rarely when they're offered generous and loving family support for them and their babies. That Kate would abandon her son, stay away for decades, and not be eager to reunite with him when she knows she's dying is mind-boggling. I don't say this because I buy into what Dewey calls "biological totalitarianism," the belief that all women want to nurture their offspring and provide an "appropriate nest." The desire to mother is not automatic or universal. Like most of my contemporaries, I know the importance of developing an autonomous selfhood. As a women's studies teacher and feminist, I try to demonstrate ways that my students might resist oppressive "feminine" expectations. And women certainly need to be relieved of the unequal burdens of childcare.

But I know myself, and I know many other birthmothers like me who were forced by controlling people and institutions to surrender our newborns. We did so unwillingly and with lasting regret. For Reynolds Price to suggest otherwise seems wrong.

LOVE MEDICINE

My second attempt to find a novel that forged a new moral identity with more permissive sexual norms, a committed extended family, a well-loved illegitimate child, and a birthmother who is not forced into exile led me back to Erdrich's *Love Medicine*. It had been years since I had first read the novel, but I recalled lingering over its last, elegiac pages and closing it with a sigh and deep appreciation. Later it was joined on my shelf by each of the eagerly anticipated interconnected novels that followed. Readers often remember what they want or need. Our memories imaginatively revise plots and outcomes according to our own narrative desires at the moment. This was definitely the case for me. What I remembered had more to do with my own psychology, my anxieties, and my emotional needs than with the actual novel. It will come as no surprise that while I vaguely recalled that the novel was about a mother who left her child, my memory was narrowly selective and flawed. I remembered the child, Lipsha, as a clever whiz kid raised on the reservation in a large, loving clan that shared parenting and was headed by wise and committed elders. I remembered his mother, June, as a tragic beauty who died trying to get home to him. My memories completely whitewashed the hard realities of Lipsha's life, the desperate actualities of June's life, and the pitiful details of her death.

As I reread the novel I had much to discover about my own narrative desires and much to correct about the "true" story. I was surprised to find that June and Lipsha are not the only birthmother and illegitimate child in the novel. In fact, Elaine Tuttle Hansen observes that in Erdrich's fiction in general, "women who lose or surrender their children abound" (116). In *Love Medicine* that is surely the case. Erdrich introduces us to several unwed mothers and their illegitimate children: Sister Leopolda (Pauline Puyat), whose secret daughter is Marie Lazarre Kashpaw; Fleur, whose daughter is Lulu Nanapush Lamartine; Lucille Lazarre, whose daughter is June Morrissey; and June herself, whose illegitimate son is Lipsha Morrissey. Their stories intertwine as the six different first-person narrators of the novel weave, break, and restore connections. In her essay "File It Under 'L' for Love Child," Jill R. Deans notes that Erdrich writes from experience: "[Her] own family appears as complicated as her fictional families," which gives her "a remarkable, if complicated, sensitivity to . . . individuals who may have fallen between the cracks of conventional family structures" (232–33). Erdrich demonstrates the intricately convoluted consequences of unwed motherhood for all these characters, but the penalties are most painful for June, whose disastrous decisions inevitably haunt her son, Lipsha, who is actually a melancholy misfit, not, as I remembered, a clever whiz kid.

We first meet June on Easter Eve, the night she walks to her death. After a long absence, she is planning to return to the reservation when she is picked up by a mud engineer in a bar in Williston. June has always been haunted by a story about a mud engineer who was killed by a pressurized hose that shot up out of the ground into his stomach and took out his insides. When she's alone in her dark room at night, she often thinks about that man and "that one moment, of realizing you were totally empty. He must have felt that" (3). Teetering on the edge of psychological disintegration, June knows what it's like to be empty. On this day, she feels so hard and brittle that she is afraid to bump against anything, for fear that she "could fall apart at the slightest touch" (4). She doesn't wear a beautiful mantle like Hester's embroidered with a scarlet *A*; instead, she wears a sweaty pink shell that she keeps hidden under her white leather jacket because it is "ripped across the stomach" (4), an ugly reiteration of the gutted mud engineer. She fills the empty hole of restless destitution with alcohol, cigarettes, and men. On the day she dies, she can't remember the last time she's eaten. After she and the engineer get totally smashed, he drives her out beyond town, tries to have sex with her, and passes out. June lets herself out of the warm truck, thinking she can make it across the miles and miles of ice-covered fields all the way to the reservation. Drunk and broken, she walks into the drifting snow that "fell deeper that Easter than it had in forty years, but June walked over it like water and came home" (7). The liquor and sex she has used for years to hide from a terrible emptiness have now led her too far astray.

In flashbacks we learn that June is not technically an unwed mother when she gives birth to Lipsha. She is married to Gordie Kashpaw and they have a son, King Kashpaw, but their marriage is doomed by brawling and alcoholism. June tries to save herself and leaves Gordie and King several times, trying to make it somewhere as a beautician, or a secretary, or a waitress, but she always returns defeated. During one separation, she falls in love with

Gerry Nanapush and has his son, Lipsha. When her Gordie can't "handle another man's son" (337), she gives Lipsha to her aunt, Marie Lazarre Kashpaw. Although Lipsha grows up knowing his Aunt June and admiring Gerry, the fact that they are his biological parents is kept from him even when everyone else, including his half brother King, knows the truth.

June's cousins, Zelda and Aurelia, come to the conclusion that June walked out into the snow because she had nothing to come home to. Zelda faults her for treating Gordie so poorly. He should have "just let her go to ruin," she maintains. But Aurelia notes, "she couldn't get much more ruined than dead" (14). Of course she dies from hypothermia brought on by an alcoholic binge, but behind that medical cause, there remains the suggestion that her death is a result of her psychological ruin. She is at the end of the day overcome by the consequences of her past, seeking escape from pain caused by abandoning King and relinquishing Lipsha to Marie, by the shame that has driven her to deny him, by the onus of a secret that has left her so unfulfilled that she knows how the disemboweled engineer must have felt. Her niece Albertine believes that June was conquered by her past, yet as she looks at the Northern Lights one night shortly after June's death, she also knows that her aunt was "one of the world's wandering souls." Albertine wants to think that June is dancing a two-step in "the dance hall in space," amused by "both the bad and the good," by both her defeat and "her reckless victory. Her sons" (37). Although June's victory may have been her two sons, Lipsha is her defeat. She is vanquished by the shame that came with him, the shame that accompanies adultery and abandonment, the shame that marks the biological mother who voluntarily surrenders her son and then pays and pays, ultimately with her life, for doing so.

Lipsha is regarded as odd. He has never done well in school and often doesn't make sense. His adoptive mother, who he calls Grandma Kashpaw, calls him "the biggest waste on the reservation," and he himself admits, "I never really done much with my life" (230). The only thing he thinks he knows about his mother is that she tried to drown him when he was an infant by tying him in a potato sack and throwing him in a slough. When Albertine tries to correct this myth, saying "She didn't do that . . . She wanted you," he remains unforgiving. Even if she came to him, "got down on her knees and said 'Son, I am sorry for what I done to you,'" he would not relent (39). On the same night that Lipsha and Albertine watch the Northern Lights, his half brother King fights with his wife and ruins the pies that Zelda and Aurelia had spent the day baking. As Albertine attempts unsuccessfully to put the pies back together, she observes, "once they smash there is no way to put them right" (42). On the surface, her words are about the ruined pies, but she is also describing June and Lipsha. With June's death, any possibility of repairing the metaphorical smashed pies that separated her from her son is gone. There is no way to put it right.

As we have seen in *Bastard out of Carolina*, the consequences of illegitimacy can be extreme, and although Lipsha doesn't suffer like Bone, he is afflicted by aimlessness. However, although he has no profession and no desire for one, he does have "the touch," a shamanic power that he has unknowingly inherited from his birthfather's side of the family. He has "secrets in [his] hands" and when "the medicine flows out of [him]," he can make people feel better by running his hands over painful "clumps of blue snails" (varicose veins), or by knocking gently above hearts, or by making circling motions on stomachs (231). But when Lipsha tries to work some love medicine on his grandfather only to have him choke to death on a turkey heart, his grandmother decides to give him a more potent totem, June's black beads. Finding himself curiously moved by the gift, Lipsha goes out to dig dandelions:

> With every root I prized up there was return, as if *I was kin* to its secret lesson. The touch got stronger as I worked through the grassy afternoon. Uncurling from me *like a seed* out of the blackness *where I was lost*, the touch spread. The spiked leaves *full of bitter mother's milk. A buried root. A* nuisance people dig up and throw in the sun to wither. A globe of *frail seeds that are indestructible.* (258; emphasis added)

Although Lipsha may literally be describing nothing more than irritatingly robust dandelions, he is, in fact, providing a metaphor for the "indestructible" bond that "uncurls" from the "blackness" of his unknown past, a connection that links him to his mother and her mysterious black beads, to his father, who can work strong magic and disappear into thin air, and to the "buried root," his father's father, a powerful healer and hermit, Moses Pillager. The Pillagers have always been "practitioners of medicines so dark and helpful that the more devout Catholic Indians crossed their breasts when a Pillager happened to look straight at them" (312). The Pillager touch cannot be repudiated; it has the resiliency of genetics, and although Lipsha may feel illegitimate, "like a nuisance people . . . throw away," he bears his ancestors' potent and irrepressible magical ability.

However, because he is kept in the dark about his ancestry, he drifts, confused and resentful. The consequences of illegitimacy are practical as well as emotional. As a bastard, he is not incorporated into the tribe. Unaware of his rights as a member of the Pillager clan, he can do nothing to protect sacred places on the reservation like Matchimanito Lake, where some tribe members want to build a casino. Lipsha is "the hinge of blood" between two powerful clans: the Pillagers and the Nanapushes (318), but he can do nothing until he learns who is parents are and his tribal status is validated. Finally, Gerry's mother, his biological grandmother Lulu, tells Lipsha the truth—that he is the "bastard son of June" and Gerry Nanapush (332–35). "Seeing as [his] blood mother wanted to tie a rock around [his] neck and throw [him] in the slough" (335), he insists he would rather not think of June as his mother, that his "real mother's Grandma Kashpaw," Marie. Marie has been a good mother to Lipsha—I remembered that part right. Hansen observes, "Marie is . . . the more fully and realistically evoked figure of the loving hardworking Native American mother," the mother who does not abandon her children; instead, she finds "strength in mundane and fragile acts of independent maternal work" (131). Lipsha is loyal to Marie for good reason. She is down-to-earth and nurturing, and she has always taken "action against lurking danger to the child" (Hansen 31).

But Lulu makes a persuasive argument for why Lipsha should know the truth: "They all know it . . . all of them Kashpaws. What the heck is it anyway? Do you like being the only one that's ignorant?" His only reply is "No" (365). And indeed, what is the point of remaining in the dark? I've met adoptees like Lipsha who don't want to know anything about their birthparents out of loyalty to their adoptive parents and out of fear of complicating their lives with a new, unwanted, unneeded, and possibly needy birthmother. Still, choosing this kind of ignorance always dumbfounds me. In the ongoing disagreements over opening birth records, there are many who think birthmothers need be protected from such disclosures and that the anonymity they were once promised must be honored. Clearly the incriminating shame lurking behind unwed motherhood has not been relegated to history, and until Lulu steps in, Lipsha and June have been "protected" from one another with damaging consequences for both.

In *The Sacred Hoop*, Paula Gunn Allen articulates the drawbacks for adoptees of not knowing their biological mothers. Her words are especially applicable to the dilemma that Lipsha has faced growing up:

Failure to know your mother, that is, your position and its attendant traditions, history, and place in the scheme of things, is failure to remember your significance, your reality, your right relationship to earth and society. It is the same as being lost, isolated, abandoned, self-estranged, and alienated from your own life. (209–10)

Lipsha is fortunate. Lulu doesn't just fling the truth at him; she patiently tries to help him understand his significance, his position in "the scheme of things," by answering his questions: that June had not tried "to sling [him] in the marsh"; that she was "real upset about the whole thing"; that she had always "watched [him] from a distance, and hoped [he] would forgive her one day"; that she had wondered why he "turned out odd" (337). Is the truth liberating for Lipsha? Not immediately. It is necessary but unsettling, and like most illegitimate children and adoptees who have not been told the truth about their biological roots, he finds himself even more confused, admitting, "It was the taxingest problem my brain had ever had to work with" (338). Feeling even more "alienated from [his] own life, he decides to steal Lulu's savings and run away:

I justified my criminal act by being so unhappy I could die . . . It was a bleak sadness sweeping through my brain. Sirens blowing. Random anger, which had never been my style before. More than anything I resented how they all had known . . . and then shame hit but good. Shame rolled over me in waves and a tidal wash. I was buried in it like a sinkhole. Shame had me by the neck. (338–39)

Lipsha is awash with emotion: sadness, anger, resentment, and most of all, crippling, shame. His childhood ordeals begin to make new sense to him, such as the way his cruel half brother King would call him "little orphant" and steal his food, taunting, "Only the *real* children get that." Lipsha now understands why King "did his best to make [him] feel like a beggar at the table of life" (341); King has always known they have the same mother and has been so emotionally threatened by Lipsha that he has even taken a potshot at him while they are hunting. Bitter sibling rivalry has reigned, even though Lipsha hasn't known there is a battle going on. No matter how carefully June, Gerry, and others have hidden the secret of Lipsha's illegitimacy, it has still followed him and marked him as a target for deadly bullying.

Scrambling for a way to redefine himself and to feel less like a beggar at "the table of life," Lipsha impulsively enlists in the army, realizing within minutes that he has made a disastrous mistake. He decides to keep running, but where to? He does not want to return "to the rez where every damn

Kashpaw cousin knew the secret of [his] background all those years. [He] was too galled" (340). Without a clear direction, he finally takes the opportunity to ask himself "point-blank what exactly [he wants]," and his answer comes "quick and surprising." Like so many adoptees that grow up feeling alien in their adoptive families and want to meet their biological parents so they can know themselves better, Lipsha wants to meet his father.

He accomplishes his quest by tracking down King in Minneapolis, only to find the legendary Gerry Nanapush, his father, on the run from prison. Lipsha has inherited another Pillager "touch" from him—clever fingers adept at "understanding" a deck of cards (354). Fittingly, he wins King's car in a poker game, the car King bought with June's life insurance money, and helps Gerry escape to Canada in it. As they drive toward the border, he asks Gerry about June, and Gerry speaks of her with love and tender admiration. Longing for some kind of sign of paternal recognition, Lipsha tells his dad about his ill-fated enlistment. And finally he receives the acknowledgment he so needs and deserves. Gerry tells him he won't be able to pass the army physical because he's "a Nanapush man," and that Nanapush men have this "odd thing with their hearts"; they go "something like *ti-rum-ti* instead of *ta-dum*" (365–66). When Lipsha lets his dad out of the car at the border, darkness instantly swallows him up, but not before they "[hold] each other's arms, tight and manly," not before Lipsha knows he is "a son of a father" and feels an "expansion, as if the world was branching out in shoots . . . [He feels] the stars . . . [feels] them roosting on [his] shoulders with [Gerry's] hand" (366). Knowing his Pillager-Nanapush heritage of energy and spirit is revitalizing for Lipsha. He has escaped the illegitimacy curse, June's curse.

As he approaches the reservation and home, Lipsha stops at a bridge over the boundary river. Finally he can think of his father and his mother with reverence; he can think of June and her great loneliness. He knows now that "there was good in what she did for me . . . The son that she acknowledged suffered more than Lipsha Morrissey did." In this new version of the fallen woman's narrative, forgiveness is possible for the abandoning mother even though we never hear her version or understand her choices. Hansen maintains that we can arrive at forgiveness because we accept that "the mother herself is constructed as a victim who made the best choice she could for her child, and in part because the community has a well-established tradition of providing alternatives when the biological mother cannot or will not care for her child" (134). This is nothing new. Birthmothers who surrender their babies have been fed this rationalization forever: do what's best for your child; give him to those who can better provide. Clearly this unfounded reasoning continues to work on the consciences of birthmothers who do want to do what's "best" and ingenuously believe this enduring justification for separation and sorrow. June apparently believed it and so does her son. Even though he never gets to hear his mother's full story, Lipsha accepts the standard rationalization for surrender, concluding that he is glad his mother turned him over to Grandma Kashpaw.

The fallen woman narrative may be revised to allow for forgiveness, but the abandoning mother still has to die. We never do know the cause of June's precarious mental health. Did she turn to alcohol after surrendering Lipsha? Did the separation push her into exile and self-destructive addiction? Was her death an accident or a suicide? As critic Robert Silberman notes, "June's presence, that is, her absence, haunts the book" (104); she won't let go. The thought of her "grabs [Lipsha] by the heart" (367). But it's significant to this revision of the master narrative that he, the illegitimate child, is not marked by the ruinous anguish that pushed his mother to abandonment, addiction, and alcoholism. Lipsha is not June, who if she didn't commit suicide, died because she was so addled by the puzzle of shame and sorrow that was woven into her psyche that she tried to walk home in a blizzard. As Lipsha drives home in King's car, which now feels more like a holy reification of his mother than a car, he rejects suicide, and we can trust he will not be consumed by loss and self-destruction.

But Erdrich resists the "homing" plot. Now that Lipsha knows with certainty his birthparents, he can construct a more informed and psychologically healthier identity for himself, one that includes the traits and powers that he has inherited from his biological family. However, he is not returning to a reservation where communal identity and harmony await him. As critic Louise Flavin points out, the sacred ceremonies have disappeared; the men that knew the ways of the woods are old and dying; much of the reservation land has been sold to whites and lost forever (64). Lipsha's problems with identity, which is always contingent, and with June, whose ghost will continue to haunt him, will persist in *The Bingo Palace*. As critic Patrick Houlihan points out, even in *The Bingo Palace*, "Erdrich leaves [him] . . . nascent, emerging, in the process of becoming whole" (203). Nonetheless, at the close of *Love Medicine*, we find Lipsha reconciled to June, the forever absent mother, and to Gerry, the gentle criminal father. He has arrived at clarity, for awhile at least: "The morning was clear. A good road led on. So there was nothing to do but cross the water, and bring her home" (367).

Having confronted at least some of his mother's ravaged past and her heartbreaking secret, he can begin to re-embroider her dangerously metastasizing shame into something sacred, an emblem of June's beauty, of their ancestors' power—an achievable goodness that he can carry on.

Kate Vaiden and June Morrissey in their own ways become convincing portraits of fallen women, characters who within their unique cultures have had to bear the consequences of unplanned pregnancy and the consequent shame and exile. Like so many fallen women and unwed mothers before them, they too receive a death sentence, one by cervical cancer, the other by suicide/accident. They have become part of an ongoing novelistic lineage, and their creators—Price and Erdrich—have added to the narrative's intricate embroidery, bringing it to new places, infusing it with new possibilities for meaning and interpretation in the capacious American tradition. The narrative of the fallen woman is in a state of constant transformation. It is copious, fluid, and too complexly lived to be contained. It encompasses desire, punishment, liberation, sin, alienation, allure, shame, secrecy, and this is only a few of the social and cultural implications it carries. It acts upon the lives of characters in countless ways; it alludes to other texts; it plays intertextually with texts; it invades other cultures; it bridges diversity. It lives as means of defining experience and as a myth to explain behavior. It is as entrenched as patriarchy, but it is not stable. It is always open to revision, artistically open to re-embroidery, culturally open to change, and, therefore, potentially open for escape from a vexed and fraught history.

But my search for narratives that do not represent unwed mothers as ruined, that do not punish, that do not exile, that do not force a painful separation between mother and child is once again frustrated. June and Kate fall, and once fallen, they are destined to be solitary, alienated, disaffected women in exile. They are not powerless victims, but the decision to abandon their sons and become sexually and socially self-determining women somehow doesn't erase their isolation or desperation. Neither novel permits recovery, reunion, or repair. Maybe Albertine is right when she says that, once some things are smashed, "there is no way to put them right" (42). When the connection between a mother and a child is severed for decades, there may be no way to put it right. The cracks in my own damaged psyche have healed significantly since my reunion with my daughter, but it is a patched-up job with scars that fester and foundations that falter. Nonetheless, unlike Kate and June, I have recovered from a great loss; a piece of me that was torn away by heartless standards of morality and tradition has been partially restored.

I am not Kate. I don't have to live the lonely life of an isolate. Nor am I June. I don't have to sleep with strange men to feed my addiction. But I am like them in one important way: I have been forgiven, yet I cannot forgive. Lipsha forgives June for abandoning him, and we can surmise that Lee would forgive Kate if they were to reunite. My daughter, Merideth, has forgiven me. But can we forgive ourselves? Can we forge new, more forgiving moral identities for birthmothers? Not me. Not yet. I remain unforgiving of those who judged me, and unforgivable for surrendering my first child.

CHAPTER EIGHT

Fathering Illegitimacy

What to say about the birthfathers of illegitimate children? How not to be negative, dismissive, angry? I know there are committed birthfathers out there. I've met a few—well, two—at CUB (Concerned United Birthparents) retreats and have been touched by the pain they have experienced; their hurt and sincerity was clear. But I also know they are the exception. Birthfathers, notes Ellen Herman, have been "shadowy figures." If they are acknowledged at all, it has been as "targets of quasi-criminal legal proceedings designed to extract financial support and pressure them into marriage." Social agencies from the 1930s on have pronounced them maladjusted, immature, "neurotic" and "as driven by unconscious needs as their female counterparts" (107). Agencies in the mid-1960s, when I surrendered my daughter, preferred to ignore "putative" birthfathers as legally irrelevant (Ellen Herman 201). That certainly was the practice in my case. But my own relationship with Merideth's birthfather, Alec, was so intense that I could neither ignore nor dismiss his relevance. Without an inkling of uncertainty or caution, I had given him my unprotected and apparently extraordinarily fertile body in passionate delight and with it, my tender ingenuousness. Like the narrator of "One Holy Night," I believed in all the illusions of first love, one love, endless love.

After one sexual encounter, I became pregnant in late June, just as he was graduating from high school and summer was setting in. But I didn't stay home that summer. I went off to my beloved summer camp for a month. That year we backpacked into the soaring granite splendor of the Sierra wilderness. I had carefully packed my tampons in a special pocket of my pack, but there was never a need for them. I didn't let myself think too much about this; it had to be the altitude. When I returned to San Marino, my parents sent me to stay with my grandparents in Laguna Beach, and I lolled away the rest of the summer, swimming and tanning. On some days my grandfather would drive me up the coast to my girlfriend's family beach house on Balboa Island, and she and I would take the little ferry over to Newport and back. It was a blissful summer as long as I didn't let myself worry about missing my period. I was in complete denial about anything that was different about my body. I didn't see much of Alec, though I would have liked to. While I was away at camp, I heard he had taken up with a new girl whose name was Candy, of all things. I saw them together one night late that summer. I was with my parents on our way out to dinner and my dad's headlights illuminated Alec's face as his car passed ours. Candy was right next to him, the way kids used to sit close when cars didn't have center consoles and seat belts weren't de rigueur. Seeing him with her was sad but not heartbreaking. Rather than jealous, I was wistful. He had often told me, "You're the love of my life," but that ingenuous singularity was over for him now. Not for me. I also remember feeling relieved that I was in safe hands with my parents, that I was still their good girl and didn't have to grapple with the sexual pressure that Candy would surely have to face that night. But goodness and safety were soon to be demolished.

When my mother finally confronted me about not having a period, and the doctor confirmed that I was pregnant, Alec was already on his way to college, and immediately thereafter, I was on my way to Cleveland with no chance to tell him anything. His parents were not told; my sisters were not told; my school was not told. My aunt forbade me to write him, so all he knew was the official story: I had fallen in with a fast crowd and needed to improve my grades for college, so my parents sent me to Ohio to attend school while living with my aunt. He didn't know that I went to Florence Crittenton in January; he didn't know that I went into labor on the night of a surprise blizzard, that I had to wait alone, that I was terrified by excruciating pain for hours until the on-call nurse could get across town to fetch me. He didn't know that in the back of the taxicab, in a moment of unfathomable heartlessness, the nurse slapped me because I wouldn't stop wailing, grunting, pushing; he didn't know that I gave birth to our baby less than an hour after finally getting to the hospital; he didn't know that two weeks later I was told that I had no choice but to sign the papers to surrender our daughter to adoption. He knew nothing.

In the conservative community of my adolescence, the shame that accompanied my pregnancy was so extreme that absolute secrecy was mandatory. And secrecy meant he never had to know the consequences of our sexual foray nine months earlier. Secrecy meant he never had to feel shame or fear or exile. Secrecy meant that on a March night when a massive blizzard hit Akron, Ohio, he could be thousands of miles away, pursuing his dreams in a tropical paradise while the last warming rays of my childhood idyll went out for good. Secrecy and shame and gender kept him in his own protective bubble. I was the only offender in this narrative; he got to stay safe and good.

Can I blame him for the pregnancy? Can I hold him responsible for being an eighteen-year-old honor student and not knowing enough to use a condom? Is he to blame that his parents were never informed of my pregnancy? Is it his fault that my parents and my aunt chose to manage the arrangements for my year "away" and bear the financial costs on their own? Is he to blame for escaping the exigencies of pregnancy and childbirth? Can I fault him for dodging the lifelong pain of parent/child separation? I could, but I don't. It was a time and place where secrecy trumped accountability. He got away with it—our one night of confused passion. And the manifold, intricate plot twists that I've followed since that one night. He's missed it all.

My attachment to Alec was magnified by my daughter's birth. So there were two losses for me: the loss of my baby, from which I've never fully recovered, and the loss of Alec, from which I have fully recovered, even if it took a long time. Perhaps my steadfastness was noble but it was entirely misplaced and undeserved. Years after he had moved on to many other relationships, I was still irrationally hopeful that he would return to me lovingly and completely, and we would put right what had gone so wrong. One night, I decided maybe the truth would make the difference. I knew where he lived; I showed up at his door: I told him my story, our story: I had given birth to his daughter; she lived in Ohio; I gave away a part of ourselves. His response still staggers me. He didn't believe me.

Three culturally astute and award-winning writers, Anita Shreve, T. C. Boyle, and Sherman Alexie have approached the subject of young, unprepared birthfathers, boys that are a lot like Alec was at eighteen. Each tells the story of an intelligent young man in college, a young man full of promise and ambition who falls in love. But unlike Alec, these birthfathers are not immune to the consequences of sexual intercourse. Each must face the unexpected and serious responsibilities of his girlfriend's unplanned pregnancy.

"THE LOVE OF MY LIFE"

T. C. Boyle's "The Love of My Life" is influenced by a sensational 1996 news event involving two college freshmen from an affluent suburb in New Jersey,

Amy Grossberg and Brian Peterson. Amy managed to hide her unplanned pregnancy from everyone except Brian. When she went into labor, rather than going to a hospital, they checked into a Comfort Inn. Amy gave birth to their son and immediately afterward, Brian threw the infant into a Dumpster. Though both Amy and Brian insisted the baby was stillborn, forensic doctors concluded that the baby was alive when Brian disposed of him. Amy and Brian ultimately testified against one another, and both served a brief time in prison for manslaughter.

Fascinated and perplexed by the newspaper accounts of the tragedy, T. C. Boyle wrote the short story "The Love of My Life" in hopes that a fictional rendition of the scandal would help his readers and himself understand how two smart, well-loved, and well-off kids could do such a thing. In an interview regarding the collection of short stories it appeared with, he says the following about his motivation:

> I had heard of the case in passing, as well as another similar case (the Prom Mom) that occurred around that time. As often happens in my stories I began with the why—why might this have happened and what does it mean? I was fortunate with the story, in that it turned out to be one of the gems of the collection, passionate and heartbreaking. We've all been in love. We've all been in that motel room. And we've all made our choices.

I always find Boyle's words in this interview unnerving, given what happened to Amy and Brian and their newborn son. I'm never quite sure what he means when he says, "We've all been in that motel room." Maybe this is because on that terrifying night in Akron, Alec was nowhere near the hospital delivery room where our daughter was born, although he has, since then, made his choice. Nonetheless, I teach this story often and students always seem to think they know what Boyle means. They focus on the "We've all been in love" part, and most of them have been in love by the time they arrive in my college classroom. Those who have been sexually intimate have made choices about birth control and the consequences of their actions. But whether they are sexually experienced or not, whether they're parents, or plan to be parents, or never want children at all, they almost always condemn with little mercy the story's protagonists, Jeremy and China, Boyle's fictional stand-ins for Brian and Amy.

Like their real counterparts, Jeremy and China are outstanding high school graduates as well woefully unprepared, unwed parents. They are passionately in love and sexually intimate, but they have great distain for the teen mothers at their school, girls China refers to as *"breeders that bring their puffed-up squalling little red-faced babies to class"* (580), so they have been very careful, using birth control responsibly. But on a summer backpacking trip, China forgets to pack her pills. When they realize she's pregnant, Jeremy urges her to "go to a clinic," to "get rid of it," but she is paralyzed. It's not because she wants the baby; she simply refuses to acknowledge it. She starts her freshman year at Binghamton wearing "huge sweats, sweats that drowned and engulfed her ... [So] what if she was putting on weight? Everybody did" (581). Her denial seems implausible, but I understand it completely. I don't think I would have ever admitted my pregnancy to my parents or myself if I could have continued to hide it, if my mother hadn't confronted me and our doctor confirmed her terrible suspicion. Even after I knew the truth and was whisked off to Ohio, I was happy to wear the tight girdle and baggy sweaters my aunt bought me, to pay no heed to the initial flutters and subsequent sturdy kicks from within, and to think of Florence Crittenton as a boarding school rather than a maternity home. I don't think I completely realized I was having a baby, a real baby, until I felt my body push her out, until I saw the cord linking us, until I saw her there in the nurse's arms so perfect, so utterly real, so alive. Then, of course, I wanted her terribly, but as we know, that is not always the case.

As we discuss Boyle's story, once in awhile someone other than me will have some compassion for China. It's always a female student and usually she has known a girl like China, a desperate adolescent overwhelmed by fear and shame who manages to hide her pregnancies from her parents, her friends, even herself. But all sympathy fades for these girls if the denial goes too far. Students may not have heard of Amy and Brian specifically, but they've almost all heard of the "Prom Mom," the infamous teenager Boyle mentions in his interview. He's referring to Melissa Drexler, the girl who kept her pregnancy a secret from her parents, her friends, and her boyfriend and delivered her baby in a toilet stall during her high school prom. She cut the cord on the edge of a sanitary napkin dispenser, wrapped the baby in garbage bags, placed it in a trash can, and returned to the dance. Like Amy and Brian, Melissa was convicted of manslaughter, spent more than three years in jail, and has presumably resumed a nondescript life in private (Smothers), but the "Prom Mom" has become legendary, even inspiring a musical number on *Family Guy* called "Prom Night Dumpster Baby" and a song by Nickelback, "Throw Yourself Away."

We begin to see the perilous consequences of China's steadfast denial as childbirth approaches. She tells Jeremy that rather than go to a hospital, "she would die, creep out into the woods like some animal and bleed to death" (582). Instead they meet in a motel room and as China thrashes through labor without information, training, or assistance she cries, "It's like *Alien . . .* like that thing in *Alien* when it, it—." At that point any remaining sympathy my students might still harbor for China vanishes, but they condemn her irrevocably when, after hours of crushing contractions that feel "like a knife blade thrust into her spine," she delivers her baby only to mutter to Jeremy, "Get rid of it. Just get rid of it" (583). And he does. Later that night after taking China back to her dorm room, Jeremy cleans up the motel room without "a thought to what lay discarded in the Dumpster out back, itself wrapped in plastic, so much meat, so much cold meat" (583).

Jeremy and China witness birth from the shattering perspective of not just unwed parents in deep denial but of terrified children alone in a dark wood. Even for well-prepared wedded parents with attendant doctors or practiced midwives, childbirth can be fearsome and agonizing, but once their baby is born, fear is transformed into much-anticipated, unsurpassable joy as nurses rush to stimulate, measure, and warm the long-awaited newborn. But for Jeremy and China, birth is the worst outcome of a horrifying nightmare. Rather than a roseate, squirming, squalling cherub, they see this "baby girl all slick with blood and mucus and the lumped white stuff that was like something spilled at the bottom of a garbage can" (583). Jeremy never shows remorse. To him, it was a "thing" that came out of China and that he put in the Dumpster: "he refused to call it human, let alone a baby . . . There was no baby. There was nothing but a mistake, a mistake clothed in blood and mucus" (586). But he knows the baby was alive. He remembers "the shuddering long gasping rattle of a breath he could feel ringing inside her even as the black plastic bag closed over her face and the lid of the Dumpster opened like a mouth." Still no remorse, no guilt; in fact, he maintains he did the world a service by ridding it of another unwanted child: "They should have given him a medal," he thinks (587).

Despite Boyle's perceptive fictional renditions of China and Jeremy and a clearer picture of how two kids could resort to infanticide, it's almost impossible to forgive them. Not surprisingly, it's the birthmother, China, who feels remorse and mourns, though we are not sure if her mourning is for the baby or Jeremy. She is willing to face the severe punishment she believes she deserves. She even imagines a verdict that echoes Hester Prynne's and her scarlet *A*, though modified to fit China's crime: "She didn't care what they did to her, beat her, torture her, drag her weeping through the streets in a dirty white dress with 'Baby Killer' stitched over her breast in scarlet letters" (585). She would like to visit her "daughter's grave" (587), but we leave her living impassively under house arrest, gorging on M&M's and sunflower seeds and dreaming of Jeremy, "the love of her life" (588). We know that her counterpart, Amy Grossberg, didn't get dragged through the streets or have to wear bright, scarlet letters on her breast, but she did go to jail for thirty months, while Brian Peterson struck a deal and only had to serve twenty-four (Smothers).

Ultimately Boyle decides to make the birthfather his most insidious villain. After being found guilty of aggravated manslaughter, Jeremy remains unrepentant, even while serving out his sentence at Drum Hill Prison "with eight and a half thousand terminally angry sociopaths" (586). It's not clear if Boyle includes Jeremy in that count of sociopaths or not, but Jeremy's deluded, self-serving rationalization for his actions makes him sound like a killer, a birthfather with little sense and less heart.

LIGHT ON SNOW

The creative spark that inspired Boyle's muse after he read about Melissa Drexler, Amy Grossberg, and Brian Peterson seems to have also caught the imagination of novelist Anita Shreve. In *Light on Snow*, Shreve gives us another rendition of a birthfather/villain. Shreve rocketed to fame in 1999 when Oprah chose her novel *The Pilot's Wife* as her book club pick. Since then, she has continued to be productive and popular. She began her career as a journalist, writing an influential piece for the *New York Times Magazine*, "The Group, 12 Years Later," which in retrospect, helps explain her rote characterization of men and women in *Light on Snow*. In the article, Shreve reports on the reunion of five women who had participated in a consciousness-raising group in the seventies and concludes, "consciousness-raising appears to have been a mixed blessing." Shreve maintains that the women are too hard on themselves for not achieving the lofty goals feminism set for them. She reveals her more conventional values when she concludes that the women have had to learn that "a feminist perspective has a way of sabotaging relationships with men whose expectations are rooted in traditional roles" (2). And in *Light on Snow*, Shreve does little to interrogate or subvert traditional roles. There is still a helpless fallen woman / birth-mother completely undone by her snaky seducer/birthfather.

The novel begins with the discovery of an abandoned newborn that has been left to die on an icy night in the woods behind a motel, wrapped in a cheap sleeping bag. The baby girl serves as a plot device for the redemption of another father, Robert, who has emotionally abandoned his surviving child since his wife and baby were killed in a car crash two years prior. Having dumped his Manhattan career, Robert has moved to an isolated house in New Hampshire where he wallows in grief and ignores his daughter, twelve-year-old Nicky. When they find the baby, her lips are blue from exposure. Robert zips her up in his coat and gets her to a hospital. When it's clear she'll live, he asks what will happen next. The doctor replies, "Foster care. Adoption if she's lucky" (29). The baby's birthparents, whoever they might be, are already erased from her future.

Shreve is not content with just one story of a discarded infant. She capitalizes on the sensational nature of the crime by finding a way to narrate even more grisly examples. As an unsympathetic detective examines the motel room where the baby was born, he provides a litany of other gruesome cases: a baby thrown out of a second-story window; a newborn left on a shelf at Ames; another discarded in a trash bin outside a college dorm; another abandoned in a park to be found by ten-year-olds. Shreve's methods are unnecessarily heavy-handed as she gratuitously provides each case with more and more appalling details that stoke her readers' horror. As the investigation escalates, Nicky and Robert return to their reclusive life in the forest only to be interrupted ten days later by an unexpected visitor, Charlotte, the birthmother who is now wanted by the law. A pasty-faced girl with blue half-moons under her eyes, Charlotte has come to thank Robert for saving the baby, that is until she vomits, pleads for a sanitary pad (not mercy), and faints.

Charlotte's situation is not unlike the scenario Boyle creates for China and Jeremy. She is a nineteen-year-old college dropout desperate to keep her Catholic parents from knowing what has happened. Her boyfriend, James, is also in college. He doesn't want anyone to know of the pregnancy for fear of losing his hockey scholarship. Like Boyle, Shreve gives a more sympathetic characterization of the birthmother than the birthfather. Charlotte bears a devastating guilt for abandoning the baby, one that has led her back to the scene of the crime. When Nicky takes her to the lonely place in the woods where they had found the baby, Charlotte administers a brutal form of self-punishment: "Hurtling [with] grief" she plunges her face into the

snow, cuffing and slapping it while screaming phrases like "[how] *could I*,"
"*stupid*," and "*God, God, God*" until she seems to lose consciousness. When
Nicky manages to revive her, Charlotte's hands are cut, her face is scratched,
and "she looks as though she's been beaten up." Charlotte may at first seem
reprehensible; indeed book critic John Hartl calls her a "disarmingly soft-
spoken monster," but Shreve gives her the opportunity to make her confession as she, Nicky, and Robert wait out a snowstorm:

She had wanted the baby, and still under the thrall of naive romance
narratives, had convinced herself that James planned to marry her, that she
would have the baby, that they would live in his apartment and he would go
to medical school, but the nefarious James had a very different plan. When
her labor pains began, James, who had supplied himself with several doses of
Demerol, drove her as far away from Burlington as he could to the remote,
New Hampshire motel. Completely unprepared for childbirth, in unimagi-
nable pain, and with contractions coming one after the other, Charlotte willingly took all the Demerol James had. After the baby was finally born, she
passed out. Later, when James moved her back into the car, he reassured her
that the baby was asleep in the backseat. She fell back asleep. Only when
they got back to their apartment had he confessed that the baby had died
and that he had left its body in a sleeping bag behind the motel. Expected
home for Christmas, James makes a quick getaway, abandoning Charlotte in
her apartment to recover alone.

By creating such a wicked birthfather, one who actually plans to trick
the helpless birthmother and abandon the baby, Shreve manages to inspire
some sympathy for hoodwinked Charlotte, but Charlotte's unconsciousness
seems contrived and James's villainy is too thorough. When Charlotte hears
on the radio that the baby is not dead and realizes that James had left the
baby to die, she tries to call him at the home of his affluent parents, but he's
not there; the blackguard has gone skiing in Switzerland. Scared, penniless, and friendless, Charlotte finds Robert's name and drives to his home.
Now, when he asks her, "Why?" she ends her story inexplicably, remarking,
"What was my life worth if I didn't thank you?" (237), which disappointingly
explains nothing. Are we to think that Charlotte's effort to thank Robert is
her attempt to atone? Had she planned to commit suicide at the scene of the
crime? Does she harbor irrational hope that Robert will help her retrieve
her baby? Book reviewer Jane Torrance Kelly observes, "Ms. Shreve draws
the outlines . . . [but] doesn't fill in those outlines with depth and light. We
never really know Charlotte . . . How did she fall in love with a man who

could leave his newborn baby out in the snow? [She] doesn't even offer us a glimpse of the answer, except to note that he was rather good looking." Shreve fails to deliver what could have been two multidimensional character studies of birthparents.

Charlotte does not escape. Although they try, Robert and Nicky can't protect her. After she is arrested, Robert tells the detective why he didn't turn her in: *"I wasn't willing to just walk away from her . . . To leave her to you, if you want to know the truth. Every time I thought about picking up that phone, a bad taste would rise in my throat"* (282). By letting Charlotte tell her story, Shreve gives Robert, if not her readers, a way to understand the desperate plight of at-risk birthmothers. In the denouement, we learn that Charlotte may serve time—worst case, fifteen months. James, on the other hand, will be in for "ten, twelve years. Might get out in six" (302). The detective takes Nicky and Robert to see the baby at her temporary foster home. As they watch the family gathering, Nicky sees there is "a kind of healing" going on in her father, "the equivalent of a sigh released" (305). James is irredeemable, but the widowed father, Robert, has found some measure of emotional recovery.

Ultimately, Shreve's primary focus in *Light on Snow* is Robert's redemption, but she also gives us a fuller rendition of a birthmother by allowing Charlotte opportunities to demonstrate her youth, confusion, misplaced trust, and helplessness. James, however, remains uncomplicated and flat, a convenient villain who comes from wealth and opportunity but self-interestedly hides Charlotte from all the adults who could have helped her, and then premeditatedly leaves the baby for dead rather than face the responsibilities of fatherhood. In revising the fallen woman's master narrative, Shreve creates another birthmother as victim, one who falls under the spell of a scoundrel on a par with Hawthorne's Chillingworth. If not innocent, Charlotte seems guilty of no more than weakness and gullibility. Still, as I rethink the novel, I remain frustrated with Shreve's characterization of Charlotte, who is completely disempowered by unwed motherhood. She cannot and will not be her own advocate. With no backbone, she is at the mercy of James, then of Robert, then of the legal system. When Nicky suggests that she might get her baby back, that she deserves to be her baby's mother, it is clear that Charlotte believes that she has forfeited all such rights. She repeats several times our culture's line of reasoning that insists young, unwed mothers are neurotic and inadequate, that they must surrender their babies for the baby's own good. I don't find Charlotte a monster, but she has accepted society's rendition of her as incapable when she says: "I couldn't take care of her. I had no money. I would have to leave James's apartment. I couldn't go home to my family with a baby" (236). She consents to society's estimation of her unworthiness and erases herself from her baby's future. Nicky, Robert, and the reader are expected to agree automatically to that necessity. Charlotte, like many seduced women and female victims in general, must pay for her victimization, for getting "in trouble," for giving herself over to James, and for her helplessness. Charlotte may serve some jail time, but her real hard time will last a lifetime. The baby she wanted is gone forever. The guilt she bears will be everlasting.

"JUNIOR POLATKIN'S WILD WEST SHOW"

Sherman Alexie provides my final example of a birthfather in his short story "Junior Polatkin's Wild West Show," published in the collection *The Lone Ranger and Tonto Fist Fight in Heaven*. Alexie recasts the master narrative of the helpless fallen woman who falls prey to a wicked seducer in significant ways, especially given that the birthfather in this story is not the dangerously callous, self-centered antagonists we saw in Shreve's and Boyle's renditions, but the sympathetic, good-intentioned main character of the story.

In the *American Indian Quarterly*, critic Denise Low remarks that Sherman Alexie's short stories in *The Lone Ranger and Tonto Fistfight in Heaven* "range across all of Indian country. Along the way [Alexie] does not leave out television, Seven-Eleven stores, or other institutions of contemporary pan-Indian life . . . that add up to a new kind of written storytelling that comes-often-too close to the truth." His characters, maintains Jerome De Nuccio, "confront the dilemma of how to be 'real Indians,' of how to find . . . a warrior dignity and courage when it is 'too late to be warriors in the old way' . . . of how to amend what Adrian C. Louis has termed 'the ghost-pain of history'—that haunting sense of personal and cultural loss that generates a paralyzing sense of ineffectuality" (86). The families that populate the stories face serious challenges, and children are especially vulnerable to parental neglect brought on by alcoholism, but even the most dysfunctional families are for the most part intact, two-parent families. In the story "Because My Father Always Said He Was the Only Indian Who Saw Jimi Hendrix Play 'The Star-Spangled Banner' at Woodstock," one character gives an ironic explanation for this: "On a reservation, Indian men who abandon their children are treated worse than white fathers who do the same thing. It's because white men have been doing that forever and Indian men have just learned how. That's how assimilation can work" (34). "Junior Polatkin's Wild West Show" is the final story of the award-winning collection. Here Alexie provides us with another promising young man, but this young man doesn't have the sense of entitlement that our first two birthfathers, Jeremy and James, inherited with the privileges that came with their race, class, and academic aptitude. Rather than a sense of entitlement, Alexie's birthfather, Junior Polatkin, is faced with a sense of ineffectuality and inadequacy, inherited along with the disadvantages that come with his race and poverty. As we will see, Alexie reverses the master narrative when Junior, despite his academic aptitude, is undone by the out-of-wedlock birth of his son, while the birthmother manages quite well. In that sense, the master narrative does not shift completely. Someone still has to pay, but in this situation, we witness the possibilities and promise that a caring but confused young man must forfeit.

As we get to know Junior Polatkin, we see he has been influenced by romantic illusions quite different from those Cinderella fantasies that hoodwinked China and Charlotte but myths that are no less powerful. Alexie refers to them as "the colonial forces of Hollywood" (qtd. in Nelson 140). Junior likes to dream that he is Sonny Six-Gun, an Indian gunfighter with braids and a ribbon shirt who guns down Wild Bill Hickok, Bat Masterson, even Billy the Kid. As Sonny Six-Gun, he doesn't speak English, only Spokane. He is a "real Indian" (20), a "warrior in the old way" (63), and both white and Indian people sing ballads about him (232). In fact, Junior is the only Indian student at Gonzaga University in Spokane, a Jesuit school that was "originally founded to educate the local tribes" but now caters to "upper-middle class white kids running away from their parents" (232–33). Junior doesn't feel like he fits in there, but he also doesn't fit in at home. On the reservation, he has been labeled an assimilationist. At school, Junior has an unrequited crush on his fellow history student Lynn Casey, a beautiful Irish blond whom he greatly admires for the way she boldly challenges their history professor. When Junior decides to stay in his dorm for the Christmas holidays rather than go home and "endure the insults that would be continually hurled at him" there (234), he and Lynn have a chance sexual encounter that Lynn initiates because "she just [wants] some company" (239).

Junior puts a sheen of romance over their one night together, imagining them starring in a western with Mel Gibson playing him and Kim Basinger playing Lynn (237). He pictures the camera fading out, "just as they [fall] into each other's arms" (238). Afterward, Lynn rubs her belly, wondering "what their imaginary baby would look like." She is dismayed by how much Junior fits the sexual stereotypes about Indians, even when she realizes "there [are] no sexual stereotypes about Indians." Lynn plays the typically masculine role. Junior has been a kind of sexual experiment for her, a momentary distraction for her loneliness, a "Santa Claus with braids" (239). Besides, he does live up to some of her negative Indian stereotypes: he is quiet; he drinks a lot; he is always late.

When Lynn tells Junior she is pregnant, his first response is that they should get married, but Lynn dismisses that option immediately, declaring bluntly, "No . . . I don't love you. It was just one night." She also rejects an abortion (she's Catholic) and adoption, declaring, "I couldn't give my baby away" to which Junior responds, "Our baby . . . *Our* baby" (239). But Lynn has no intention of including Junior in any significant way in her future. The baby is *her* baby, never *their* baby. The healthy boy, Sean Casey, has Junior's dark skin and Lynn's blue eyes, but he is defined by Lynn's Irish heritage almost from the moment of conception. Lynn's parents refuse to acknowledge Sean's Indian blood, exhibiting "a kind of denial that was nearly pathological in its intensity" (240). If their racism means they must ignore Sean's racial mix if he is to be *their* grandson, then they must deny his Indian father absolutely.

Although Junior would like to help raise his son, he has almost no access to Sean and only learns the details of his life through random phone calls and irregularly timed visits. Lynn is dependent upon her parents, but she is never characterized as a helpless or needy unwed mother, nor does she appear to have to shoulder any shame. But in this narrative someone still must be exiled. The burden of shame has been historically placed on the more powerless of the two birthparents, which heretofore has always been the birthmother, but in Alexie's story, it is Junior. As a victim of denigrating racial stereotyping, Junior's sense of masculinity and self-worth has always been shaky. When Lynn and her parents banish him emotionally and ultimately physically from Sean, he is unequipped to assert his paternal rights, Instead he acquiesces, accepting that it's futile to press for anything more than minimal visitation rights (240).

The disenfranchised, stereotyped birthfather is driven out; the sacrifice is his to make; the exile is his to suffer. Although he can imagine a detailed, happy-ending movie for Lynn, Sean, and himself, one in which Lynn completes her master's degree and publishes a thesis that interrogates American

Indian stereotypes, his script is an unrealizable pipe dream. At Gonzaga he tries to establish a more confident, respected identity by challenging his history teacher "just like Lynn had done" (241), but he only succeeds in rankling the professor, who takes the opportunity to humiliate him rather than encourage his intellectual foray. Embarrassed and frustrated, Junior abandons Gonzaga and hitchhikes back to the reservation, only stopping at a pay phone to call Lynn collect. Believing the reservation will be his ruin, Lynn warns Junior, "You'll die out there" (241), but Junior can imagine no other options. "I'm dying at school too," he responds. Defeated by racism, shame, and rejection, his only alternative is retreat, or as he puts it, "[choosing] his own grave" (242). When Lynn puts Sean on the phone and Junior hears him say the Spokane word for love—*Quen comanche*—over the phone, it is too little and too late, and Junior's acquiescence shifts to abandonment.

It is important to resist romanticizing Junior's return to the reservation as a return of a prodigal son to his truer, more sustaining roots. His acquiescence will not magically transform into affirmation. Given what Alexie has said in interviews about the anti-intellectualism of reservation life (Alexie "Humor is My Green Card" 141), Junior's return may not be as Lynn sees it, a death sentence, but it will probably be self-defeating. Alexie has been criticized for not writing fiction that serves to "strengthen tribal political sovereignty" and for not endowing his characters with appropriate volition, agency, or self-determination (Alexie "Humor is My Green Card" 140–41). In fact, in a 2010 interview for *World Literature Today*, he acknowledges that he has moved off the Spokane reservation, bitterly adding that his "tribe is run by Sarah Palins," and that he had to leave in order to escape religious persecution in what amounted to a "Third World banana republic" (qtd. in Alexie "Humor is My Green Card" 141–42). Alexie insists, "The only way to improve our life and the life of our people is through our own individual efforts to educate ourselves and get better jobs" (143). When Junior abandons his efforts to gain a college education, it is safe to assume that he also destroying an opportunity, fraught as it may be, for agency and self-determination. Nor by returning to the reservation will Junior claim an Indian legitimacy by assuming traditional masculine roles. Alexie maintains, "Those . . . roles—you know, hunter warrior—they're all gone. I mean driving a truck for the BIA is simply not going to fulfill your spiritual needs, like fishing for salmon or hunting deer once did, so in some sense Indian men are much more lost and much more clueless than Indian women" (qtd. in Alexie "Sending Cinematic 'Smoke Signals'"). Rather than providing direction, Alexie suggests the reservation leaves young men like Junior even more purposeless, uninformed, and disempowered.

The defenselessness of the unwed parent, this time made even more precarious by racism and alienation, leads Junior to relinquish his education and abandon his son. Without ambition or purpose, he returns to an unwelcoming reservation. Alexie has never been interested in "formulas for successful screenplays" (qtd. in Alexie "Sending Cinematic 'Smoke Signals'"), and in this short story, he rejects the kind of ameliorating closure that William Bevis refers to as the "homing" plot (584). In the more typical Native American story, the hero finds fulfillment, personal growth, and value in returning to his "cultural past and his inherited place" (586). Although Junior wishes he could write a different movie script for his life, the one he has imagined in which "he [is] walking off into the sunset, into a happy ending," he concedes that he has known "all along [that] on the road he [travels]" there will be nothing more than "reservation drive-ins, each showing a new and painful sequel to the first act of his life" (242). Rather than affirmation, Alexie's birthfather succumbs to a debilitating aimlessness. This Wild West show will not have a happy ending.

And my baby's birthfather? Like many birthmothers and birthfathers, Alec also chose denial. He denied the consequences of our sexual initiation. He conveniently, though I believe without malice, ended our relationship right when those consequences became painfully complicated. When finally confronted with the truth, he denied our daughter had ever been born. His disbelief was hurtful, but I have come to understand how such denial was possible. Had he known from the beginning that I was pregnant with his baby, I am certain he would also have resisted any involvement. He is not a Brian Peterson, or a Jeremy, or James, but he's also no well-intentioned Junior Polatkin. His role as birthfather was and has remained negligible. He supplied one microscopic sperm—nothing more. Although Merideth approached him a while back to let him know that she's living happily in New Jersey, he does not want to meet her or her family. Unlike her birth and adoption, when he was kept ignorant and never had to make a choice about paternal involvement, this time my daughter gave her birthfather a choice— to welcome her or reject her. He chose the latter. I am not surprised. But the bubble-like ignorance he was allowed in the past and the wounding rejection he has dealt out in the present are unfortunately more typical than not. The responsibilities of unwed parenthood will continue to involve more and more birthfathers, but so far they are nobody's hero.

CHAPTER NINE

The Legacy of Secrets

I grew up under the shadow of a family secret. I did not learn there even was a secret until late in my adolescence, but its ramifications of the secret had tremendous implications for my family's cosmology, the atmosphere my parents cultivated through their actions and reactions to the daily events of our lives. My two sisters and I were raised under an imposing aura of control that privileged concealment and routine. No matter what the turmoil, the ebullience, or the injury that might befall us, we were expected to keep our most spontaneous, our truest emotions, whether they were fear, elation, or sorrow, carefully restrained. We learned early on that our only acceptable performance was courteous containment, and we respectfully complied. We were groomed to be the angel of the house. Being quiet was superior to being truthful. Deferring to authority was preferred over autonomy. Acquiescence and submission were golden. But I took that submission too far by yielding to my boyfriend's sexual demands, and on the night I admitted to my parents that I might be pregnant, I completely demolished all the carefully constructed containment they had cultivated. Still, the emotional uproar lasted only a matter of hours. By morning, it had been replaced by seemingly seamless control and step-by-step suppression. I couldn't quite believe how quickly my pregnancy became an efficiently managed secret. Within twenty-four hours my parents had made all the necessary arrangements to spirit me away without telling anyone except my colluding aunt and uncle why such orchestrated subterfuge had become so expediently necessary. Only later would I learn how my parents had become such resourceful experts in secrecy. It turns out that they had been efficiently hiding a family scandal for years.

And to them I was a scandal. That I could possibly stay home through-out my pregnancy, give birth with them standing by, and raise my child under their roof was never even a consideration. It's no wonder. When they were growing up in the late 1920s in America, illegitimate pregnancy was believed to be caused not only by moral degeneracy but also by the unwed mother's "biological incapacity to resist seduction," or as my mother put it, "hot pants." Solinger discusses one investigation of that era that found unwed mothers to be "excessively equipped sexually, but lack[ing] ordinary normal inhibitions." Here we can see the origins of the descriptive my mother used to explain my adolescent pregnancy in 1965. But the assumptions made about unwed mothers went beyond accusations of hypersexuality. In a 1927 assessment of eighty-four unwed mothers, Henry C. Schumacher, MD, found "a definite causal relationship between [the girl's] weak inhibitions and her intellectual level." He goes on to refer to the unwed mother as "a young moron" (qtd. in Solinger 15–16). Perhaps most insidious of these damning appraisals was the conclusion that an unwed mother's hypersexuality and low mentality were untreatable and inheritable. Not only was the unwed mother unalterably deficient, her illegitimate child was doomed as well. Given the ruinous power of such bogus genetics, is it any wonder that families went to great lengths to hide unwed mothers from view and keep illegitimacy a secret?

Thankfully, the rigid biological determinism endorsed by psychiatrists and sociologists in the early decades of the twentieth century is now disdained. Unwed mothers and their illegitimate children are no longer regarded by professionals as biologically deficient. Nevertheless, biological determinism was replaced with psychological diagnoses, and until recently, unmarried mothers have been identified as maladjusted, neurotic, or "anormative" because of their inability "to form a sanctioned relationship to a man" (Solinger 16). This was definitely the diagnosis I faced in 1965: a troubled, confused, overly affectionate, problem girl with "hot pants." But I was offered a "cure"—a return to adolescent ordinariness—but, of course, I had to pay for my sins. I was offered what Solinger refers to as a "neo-Faustian deal" (17), a trade-off that comes right out of ancient mythologies: by sacrificing my first child, I could reenter a "normative" life. I could even anticipate a happy "marriageable" future, but only if I kept the secret.

It would be nice to think that the characterizations of unwed mothers as feebleminded, hypersexual, maladjusted, and neurotic have vanished, but such stereotypes are durable and they make shame and secrecy almost impossible to eradicate. Whether such secrecy conceals illegitimacy, suicide, incarceration, incest, madness, or any other shame-laden calamity, it moves surreptitiously from one family generation to the next. Family secrets remain illicit, only to be repeated in sub rosa conversations on the margins of family gatherings, but they endure and their ghostly presence is never benign. Skeletons in the closet are always waiting to be revealed. Secrets are always ripe for the telling. In the master narrative of the fallen woman, especially when it involves an unwed mother and an illegitimate child, secrecy abounds. Families agree to keep the secrets of their unwed daughters and their illegitimate children to avoid disgrace, but the consequences of their secrecy never abate. They live on, indistinctly, mysteriously, powerfully resurfacing to test and stretch family ties, sometimes to the breaking point.

THE BONESETTER'S DAUGHTER

The Bonesetter's Daughter (2001) provides a riveting demonstration of how the disposition for shame and secrecy can be set in the bone, so engrained that, like DNA, it passes down through generations and across continents and cultures. The novel, which has also been made into an opera by Stewart Wallace with libretto by Amy Tan, mirrors the journey Tan herself took to uncover her own family secrets. She began the writing process while she was caring for her mother, Daisy Tan, who was suffering from Alzheimer's disease. On the day her mother died, Tan learned her mother's true birth name, Li Bingzi (Snow White or more literally "little ice cube"). The discovery was astounding, and its many implications meant that she had to start writing all over again, almost from scratch, in order to tell not only the story of her mother's early life in China but also the haunting secret story of her grandmother, an unwed mother.

The Bonesetter's Daughter becomes a compelling blend of genres, spanning three generations of Chinese and Chinese American women. The fictionalized writer, Ruth Young, makes her living as a ghostwriter, but her career is interrupted when she must care for her failing mother, LuLing Liu Young, a Chinese immigrant. In the process, Ruth comes to understand her damaging inheritance of shame as she uncovers the story of Precious Auntie, the bonesetter's daughter. The novel brings to light Tan's interest in the traditional Chinese belief in destiny and inevitability, particularly when it conflicts with American ideology and its emphasis on autonomy and free-will. Tan's novel is a search for what in Chinese culture are the roots of a fate that bind us to an inevitable future. In American culture, most of us think less deterministically and more therapeutically. And so we optimistically undertake narrative quests in writing or in therapy with the belief that once unraveled and understood, the lingering effects of a tightly woven, secretive past, even one that hides illegitimacy, will abate and allow us to live more freely and contentedly in the present.

Ruth has grown up in San Francisco under the shadow of her mother's depression. LuLing, her mother, has always been "immersed . . . in a climate of unsolvable despair" (16), unsolvable because it emanates from an ineradicable curse. According to LuLing's cosmology, "the world was against her and no one could change this, because this was a curse" (46), and the "curse" has been passed on to Ruth, an exceedingly capable woman who is, nonetheless, weighed down by inexplicable shame and anxiety that keep her from genuinely loving relationships with her partner, Art, and her mother. Ruth understands intellectually how the effects of a "curse," be it diabetes or a propensity for depression or anxiety, can be multigenerational: "Parent[s] intentionally or not, [impose] a cosmology . . . through their behaviors, their reactions to daily events . . . [Their] child might grow up thinking either that day and night are predictable . . . or that the world is chaotic, frantic, or freely evolving" (45–46). But as we know, intellectual awareness is not necessarily curative and Ruth has not vanquished her emotional tribulations. Sometimes, as I well know, we can only begin to revise detrimental emotional patterns if we confront long-held secrets, but Ruth has been avoiding the past for years. Only when LuLing begins to descend into serious dementia does Ruth delve into the life story LuLing had written years earlier about her life in China during the early decades of the twentieth century. Finally the manuscript reveals a series of painful, guilt-ridden secrets, secrets that have tormented LuLing and have made Ruth's childhood so fraught. With Ruth, we learn the following:

Until LuLing is fourteen, she believes that her horribly disfigured nursemaid is her aunt, but in fact, Precious Auntie is her mother. When Precious Auntie's fiancé was murdered on his way to their wedding, Precious Auntie tried to commit suicide by swallowing boiling resin. She lived, but her scars left her mute and unrecognizable and serve as a gruesome badge of shame. She is kept as a nursemaid for her illegitimate baby, and her sister-in-law "adopts" the child. For years Precious Auntie devotes herself to LuLing but doesn't tell her she is her true mother. LuLing, who both appreciates and resents her, is left to wonder why she can never please her "mother" (i.e., her aunt) or fit in like her "siblings." Tan gives us a fitting metaphor for the adopted child who cannot adapt to his or her adoptive family: LuLing feels like "a turtle lying on its back, struggling to know why the world [is] upside down" (188). Only when LuLing's "parents" arrange for LuLing to marry an unscrupulous bully (the son of her biological father's murderer) does Precious Auntie write down the true story for LuLing. But like Ruth, who postpones reading LuLing's memoir, LuLing refuses to read Precious Auntie's missive, insisting instead, "[Precious Auntie] doesn't care about my future happiness. Only Mother does. That is the difference between a nursemaid and a mother" (220). LuLing's illegitimacy and Precious Auntie's shame have worked themselves insidiously into the family, twisting motives, loyalties, and trust until LuLing turns against her true mother, the only family member who has actually cared for her well-being and now wants to protect her.

But Precious Auntie, the ruined woman cursed by disgrace and trapped in silence, has no freedom, no strength, and no way to maneuver in her oppressive situation. Her only tactical weapon is her body, and she uses it to stop the wedding by attempting suicide. This time she succeeds, and her shameful death halts all wedding plans. Only then does LuLing finally read the story: "*Your mother, your mother, I am your mother*" (222). Precious Auntie's body is thrown into the town dump and all efforts to pass LuLing off as a legitimate child end. Renamed "bastard daughter" (222), she is sent off to an orphanage. Precious Auntie's curse, the curse of sexual ruin and suicide, descends on LuLing and shame of illegitimacy sweeps through her with such intensity that she feels "as if blood [is] going to pour out of [her] ears" (232).

In the present, after fifty years in San Francisco, LuLing still believes Precious Auntie's suicide was her fault and that the curse still stalks her and her daughter. The trauma, which had left horrifying physical scars on Precious Auntie and deep psychological scars on LuLing, has left its scars on Ruth as well. She is plagued by inexplicable anxiety and a habit of secrecy. The unyielding "curse" has crossed from East to West, and in this instance, has colored three generations with scandal, distrust, and above all, guilt. Its capacity for harm seems unending.

Nonetheless, learning the truth does make a difference. By unlocking her mother's secrets, Ruth can finally appreciate the family cosmology and its effects on her own psyche. She can, in effect, begin to revise the family secret that had doomed Precious Auntie. The curse that her mother believed haunted them was the specter of shame that had originated in unwed motherhood and illegitimacy only to grow into a powerful, prevailing sense of guilt caused by suffering, betrayal, and suicide. Poignantly Ruth realizes, "she was her mother's child" (315), that like LuLing, she too was suffering because of a secret. But knowledge can be liberating. Understanding can be salubrious. "After years of doctoring other people's stories, Ruth has finally found her own" (Willard). As she re-embroiders the story, or more metaphorically, resets the broken bones, she identifies with her grandmother as a young woman and her mother as a little girl. She understands and respects the women "who shaped her life, who are in her bones" (367).

When Ruth asks LuLing's "adopted" sister why LuLing had felt it necessary to keep her secrets for so many decades, GaoLing explains:

> Your mommy was afraid of so many things—oh, she said the authorities would send her back to China if they knew she wasn't my real sister. And maybe Edwin wouldn't marry her . . . Then later you might be ashamed if you knew who your real grandmother was, unmarried, her face ruined, treated like a servant. Me? Over the years, I've become more modern-thinking. Old secrets? Here nobody cares! Mother not married? Oh, just like Madonna. But still your mommy said, No, don't tell, promise. (341)

In many ways, GaoLing is right. The curse of unwed motherhood has dissipated; we think differently about out-of-wedlock births and illegitimate children. We might almost be tempted to conclude that the stigma is gone, especially given the latest statistic that 40.6% of U.S. births are to unmarried women (Carey).

We may, as GaoLing claims, be more modern thinkers when it comes to the "curse" of illegitimacy, but the habit of secrecy is resilient. Having been born into Precious Auntie's and LuLing's cosmology of secrecy, Ruth has grown up to believe that that is what women do, they keep secrets, and she finds it natural to keep her own. But her habit of secrecy has kept her emotionally estranged from her partner, Art. After a trial separation, Art asks her to return home, but he wants her to come back on new, more intimate terms: "I don't think I know an important part of you. You keep secrets inside you. You hide. It's as though I've never seen you naked, and I've had to imagine what you look like behind the drapes" (354). Ruth maintains that she has not "consciously" hidden anything from him, but she admits that she has never revealed what she calls "that intimate-soul stuff." With a newfound understanding of the cosmology of the ominous "curse," a "curse" imposed on fallen women in both Eastern and Western cultures for threatening patriarchal lineage, Ruth understands why she grew up "like those kids who live with gunfire going off around them," just trying to stay safe and make sense of what's happening. Despite Ruth's generational and continental distance from Precious Auntie, the fiercely potent "curse" managed to overshadow all hope for a carefree childhood for Ruth. Instead she grew up unaccountably fearful and ashamed of something; she just wasn't sure what. She hid the damning specter behind "drapery" even though she had no clue of the actual roots of the curse and its historical significance. But she felt its generational persistence. Only when she steps out of ignorance and sees the truth and all its unjust, outmoded, but consequential ramifications can she begin to rework the story that she has unknowingly born into her American life. Only now can she unravel layers of shame and fear and replace them with the rich new hues of understanding, compassion, and honor.

The family secret that was passed down in my bones was my uncle's suicide. But it wasn't just a suicide. It was much, much worse. After World War II, my father and his brother both relocated their young families from Detroit to the San Gabriel Valley, a short commute into Los Angeles. My father succeeded splendidly, passing the California bar exam and landing a job as an attorney, but my uncle floundered. It seems that he had an affair, though that part of the secret has been difficult to unravel. He definitely lost all his money, and my father bought the family train tickets to go back to Michigan to their parents, who were willing to take them in. But my uncle never showed up that day to catch the train. Instead, he took his wife and children to a gully near the Rose Bowl where he shot them and then committed suicide. His wife lived, though she was blinded for life, but the children and my uncle all died.

It's a horrifying family secret. Although I regret that my uncle was excised from the family, I can understand why my parents and grandparents did so. I never saw a picture of him until I found the newspaper story about the suicide/murders on microfiche. I was stunned by how much he resembles my father and his daughter, my cousin, looks uncannily like me. But there are no pictures of him or of his family in our family albums. Those pages were easily torn out and destroyed. But that didn't vanquish him or his deeds. Instead, he became a mystery, a specter whose shadowy example remained a threat to the light-filled finery of our California home. The shadowy residue manifested itself in my father's heavy drinking, my mother's bouts with depression, my older sisters' eagerness to flee, my own inexplicable fears and loneliness. Always there was the firmly imposed insistence on control, the required dissembling, and the ensuing shame that followed any demonstration of unbridled emotion. The habit of secrecy was integral to our family modus operandi. I had been conceived, as babies often are, in an effort to heal. I was the new life, the clean slate, the newborn possibility for repairing a demolished past. And although I tried to live up to all that promise, my uncle's fervent and destructive responses to the world were part of my legacy. I've never attempted suicide, but like him, I have let my passions get the best of me. And as my parents taught me to do so well, I knew how to keep my secrets for a long, long time.

The time came when I was able to reveal my secrets and my uncle's secrets and in doing so, like Ruth, gain a better understanding of myself and my emotional inheritance of secrecy and shame that kept me from the intimacy that comes with honesty. My parents were so ashamed of my uncle that they couldn't acknowledge that he had even lived. They were so ashamed of my pregnancy that they made it a requirement that I never acknowledge that my daughter, their granddaughter, existed. They had, after all, thoroughly vanquished four people from family lore, much like the ancient tribes that, anthropologists tell us, performed rituals to expunge all memories of the dead. Surely it would be best to erase my daughter, to forget that she was living out her anonymous life. They never asked me about the night of her birth. We never talked over the circumstances of her adoption. And although they witnessed my decades of emotional instability and ongoing sorrow, although they knew their source, they never brought her up; they never came to me and said, "Let's get to the bottom of this." And I was so ashamed of myself that I obeyed their dictum to hide the truth for more than thirty years.

Given our contemporary, more forgiving, less shame-laden attitudes toward unwed mothers, we might assume that the sacrifices and silence demanded of me and other post-World War II unwed mothers might have abated, and in some ways, they have. Young women no longer have to pay with their lives for having a child out of wedlock, and their babies are no longer expected to wear the mantle of shame that once was standard for illegitimate children. No one has to keep a scarlet A affixed to her breast. Single women give birth without much social stigma or the deprecating labels of the past. Does this mean that the scarlet A has finally vanished from American culture? Can girls have sex outside of marriage without risking social disapproval? Perhaps, but as we know all too well, the label "slut" is still readily applied and young, unwed mothers are still cast as a social "problem." Bristol Palin and Jamie Lynn Spears are the exception. Rather than making a career out of advocating celibacy or performing on *Dancing with the Stars,* most young, unmarried mothers are faced with daunting responsibility and uncertain relationships. They may not be pilloried, branded, and banished like Hester to the outskirts of town like Hawthorne's Hester Prynne. But their youth and lack of resources leave them vulnerable and reliant. Rarely are they seen as worthy of sympathy. Instead, their neediness is greeted with resentment and frustration, if not outright antagonism. Although surrendering their babies may no longer be de rigueur, the onus of unwed motherhood prompts some to choose adoption, or to submit to a coerced relinquishment, or to abandon their babies in shocking circumstances. But no matter what the circumstances, fictional representations of unwed mothers who surrender their babies are consistently problematic, and surprisingly, their hypothetical need for secrecy persists.

BLESSINGS

An immensely popular, culturally astute, progressive columnist, novelist, and pundit, Pulitzer Prize–winning Anna Quindlen, has approached the subject of a young and desperate birthmother in a national bestseller, *Blessings* (2002). In much of her fiction and nonfiction, Quindlen has demonstrated her commitment to writing about oppressed women. Critic Karen Lehrman describes her as the "literary and journalistic conduit for unsung Americans." According to Lehrman, Quindlen's "journalistic career has been based on the belief that the woman's voice—the voice of compassion, humanity, softness—is missing"; hence, Quindlen attempts to provide that voice by reflecting on her own life and the lives of other women. In her review of *Blessings,* Patricia Volk maintains that Quindlen is "America's Resident Sane Person," the one who can cast a critical eye on ideology and "speak to many people about what's on their minds before they have the vaguest idea what's on their minds." In this novel, Quindlen's fourth, Quindlen puts into words our unarticulated cultural anxieties about "Babies in bathrooms. Babies in shopping bags. Babies in bulrushes" (Volk). If it's true, it's an impressive opportunity, but one that ultimately falls short. In *Blessings,* Quindlen fails to go beyond cultural group-think to seriously contest conceived, stereotypical representations of birthmothers.

Quindlen knows a lot about teen birthrates and has written critically about abstinence-only sex education and "junk virginity pedagogy" ("The Last Word"). She makes a point of being an informed cultural critic by getting firsthand accounts rather than relying on the say-so of others. For example, in order to write a column about the Baby M case,[1] she visited Mary Beth Whitehead-Gould, the vilified biological mother who reneged on a surrogacy agreement only to be denied custody of her daughter. After her visit, Quindlen observes: "It would be good for everyone in the business of passing judgment . . . to see her . . . staring out into a backyard full of toys, wondering whether her [other] children will have to give up someone they love because once, in the white glare of the world court, their mother refused to do the same" ("Public"). Quindlen's sympathy for Mary Beth Whitehead-Gould seems sincere. And in this case, she clearly understands how public opinion works against birthmothers, particularly those who won't compliantly disappear into anonymity. So it is especially disappointing that Quindlen does not look past public opinion when it comes to characterizing two unwed mothers, young and old, in *Blessings*. Rather than use her knowledge and her compassionate "women's voice" to craft a realistically frightened, confused, desperate girl, she offers an unoriginal, condemning caricature that perpetuates the traditional controlling stereotype of the teenage birthmother as unfeeling and unthinking. Also unsympathetically characterized, the elderly unwed mother is no Hester Prynne dispensing wisdom to girls in need from her rural cottage; rather, she lives so buried in her secrets that any sort of effectiveness, which would win a reader's respect, is beyond her.

The novel opens with two teenagers, "poised between the raw uncertain beauty of adolescence and the duller settled contours of adulthood" (5). They have chosen Blessings, an idyllic if dilapidated country home inhabited by elderly Lydia Blessing and her caretaker, Skip Cuddy, as the place to abandon their just-born infant in a cardboard box that says "Drink Coke" (9). Quindlen provides brief but thoroughly disparaging images for these two. The hard, determined boy deposits the box by the garage and wipes his hands on his pants before driving off; the girl beside him weeps, "wipe[s] her eyes with a tissue," and then in a gesture that underscores her adolescent narcissism, "put[s] gloss on her lips with the end of her little finger from a plastic pot she took from her purse" (9). Both are ignorant of the crime they have just committed. When the girl halfheartedly worries that they left the box by the wrong door, the boy demonstrates his denial by replying,

"Somebody'll find it." To him, the box contains an object, not a baby. Still a child herself, the girl can only whimper, "I want to go home" (10).

Recently released from jail, Skip finds the abandoned baby girl, decides to keep her, and tries to keep her presence at Blessings a secret. As he figures out how to care for her, his devotion becomes the means of his redemption and the novel becomes a romanticized variation of what Novy refers to as the adoption myth (*Imagining Adoption* 1–2). In Quindlen's version, these birthparents are immature, self-absorbed adolescents, while the adopting parent is a self-sacrificing, honorable knight in shining armor. Though Skip lacks parenting skills, has little education and no dependable support system, he is surprisingly resourceful. With a generous heart and a single-minded resiliency, he learns how to care for the baby, whom he names Faith, and in the process of saving her, he saves himself. Furthermore, he quickly resolves that Faith rightfully belongs to him. When she smiles at him, tightening her fist around his finger, Skip knows "she [is] his" (40). Even though Quindlen once sympathized with Mary Beth Whitehead-Gould, in this narrative nurture must trump nature once again.

The narrative is complicated when Lydia Blessing discovers the baby. Sixty years prior, Lydia was unwed and pregnant. Desperate, she married the first available man, Benny, who was killed shortly after the baby girl was born. Lydia has never told anyone, including her daughter, that Benny was not her biological father. Although Lydia had once anticipated a dynamic career for herself, after the baby's birth and Benny's death, she incarcerates herself at Blessings and is living out her life following a rigid, parsimonious, nun-like routine. Although she chooses to live much like Hester and Jennie Gearhart did on the outskirts of their communities, Lydia is not saintly; the secret she bears demands solitary confinement. She pays for her "fall" with a lifetime of lonely celibacy, rectitude, and regret, maintaining a bitter, self-imposed silence (201). That silence is disrupted the day she discovers Faith, and Skip, expecting to be fired, is taken aback when she decides to help him. The reader better understands her ongoing need to atone for the secrets she hides.

Even though Lydia was once unwed and pregnant, she cannot oppose controlling assumptions. For example, Skip offers the following conjectures about Faith's birthmother:

So let's say some girl has a baby and she figures she has zero money or no good place to live or whatever. Maybe she's one of those big fat girls you hear about on the news who gets pregnant and no one even figures it out, just thinks it's too many Quarter Pounders or something. She might think if she has the baby in the bathroom and then leaves it there it will have this great life. (69)

Lydia does not dispute Skip's typecasting (and Quindlen's unnecessary rep-etition of popular culture's sensationally villainous "Prom Mom"). Instead, we are left to think that Lydia's long-standing guilt keeps her silent. When she feebly suggests that Faith's birthmother "is her mother, after all" (110), Skip responds vehemently: "No, that's where . . . you're wrong . . . that's not how you get to be the mother . . . You get to be the mother by changing her and giving her a bath and walking her around in the middle of the night and loving her and making her feel like everything's all right . . . That means I'm the mother, more or less" (111). Quindlen repeats the ongoing argument of what constitutes motherhood, or in this case parenthood, and once again the argument is made with only two sides represented—the adoptive parent(s) and the well-cared-for baby. The birthmother's parental rights, in the ethos of this novel, are relinquished as soon as she abandons the baby. The healthy baby and the exultant adoptive parent take automatic precedence.

The rosy picture is made even more idyllic by Faith herself: "[She] had brought out the rectitude and responsibility in [Lydia] . . . and the capability in [Skip], so that she had made him think well of himself" (119). Skip uses his newfound redemption to further rationalize his right to parenthood. He is convinced he is doing the "right thing" not only for Faith but also for her birthparents, who, he readily assumes, must be poor and unprepared to give a child the care it needs. He maintains, "Having a baby [makes] all those people who [are] piss-poor humans more piss-poor than ever" (119). Despite his own poverty, inexperience, unlawful friends, and unstable subsistence, Skip resolves that he is meant to be this baby's parent, that he is the bet-ter parent, and that he is solving a social problem by keeping her. These rationalizations are nothing new. He is simply repeating in his own way the cultural mantra that has always buttressed adoption.

His resolution may be well intentioned, but keeping Faith depends not just on his determination but on the secrets and lies he and Lydia agree upon (178). However, as we know, the past will not be renounced; no matter how carefully we weave them, our secrets will unravel. Skip's past catches up with him when his ex-cohorts show up to rob Blessings. Lydia mistakenly assumes Skip is involved, has him arrested, and then watches helplessly as a social worker takes Faith away. After Skip is cleared and released, Lydia tries to persuade him that her lawyer can fight for Faith, but he bitterly replies: "She has a mother. The mother always wins. That's the way it is" (186). Of course, we know this is *not* always the way it is, but if it were so, the novel fails to help us see why and how it might be reasonable that "mothers always win." Instead readers are meant to sympathize with Skip, see the baby's removal as unjustified, and Lydia as a frustrated, powerless crone, made petty and weak by her fidelity to her secrets.

Only at the end of the novel do we learn more about the Faith's birthmother. She is Paula Benichek, age nineteen, a sophomore at the state university and the daughter of an insurance agent and a middle-school English teacher. When her secret is uncovered and she is reunited with her baby, Quindlen does nothing to redeem her. Instead, Paula sits "with her arms crossed and her face truculent . . . with a broken terrified expression in her eyes" (195). Rather than take the opportunity to explore Paula with at least curiosity if not sympathy, Quindlen instead represents her as the pathetic ne'er-do-well that negatively colors our cultural baggage.

Skip leaves Blessings. Lydia, whose guilt for her secret is heightened by her part in losing Faith, dies alone. She never reveals the truth, but in an effort to right some of the harm she has done, she leaves Skip a secret stash of $70,000, enough money for him to buy a house and start a business. Skip can imagine a new, better life for himself even without the baby. But, when he thinks of Faith's mother, it's as "that bitch, that witch, that things-so-bad-I-can't-put-them-into-words girl, that girl Paula . . . [He] swore he would never call [her] a mother in his mind." When Paula visits him unexpectedly, perhaps looking for some kind of understanding if not exoneration, he finally does see her as "just a girl, aimless, quiet, a little lost" (217), but Quindlen can't help but throw in negative details—her ragged nails and a bad hair dye job. When she complains to Skip about how much work it is taking care of a baby, about how she can't go wherever she wants to anymore, her grumblings reinforce assumptions about the immaturity of teenage mothers.

When she asks Skip if he would like to see the baby from time to time, he declines, making the argument that still encourages closed adoptions and echoing Lydia's rationalization for never telling her daughter the truth about her biological father: "I don't think that's a good idea," Skip maintains. "It might confuse her. Kids need to understand who's who, you know?" (219). But he can't help but give Paula some sanctimonious parenting tips, advising her to "look at [the baby] like she's not [hers] . . . [because] she does all these amazing things." When Paula asks him why he gave the baby up if he cared about her so much, Quindlen gives her hero the last reproving words: "I didn't give her up. You gave her up. I gave her back" (320). Quindlen forbids Paula a reply, and the novel ends with both birthmothers, Lydia and Paula, silent, unredeemed, and evidently unredeemable. Paula will live, but she is branded by the unhelpful stereotype of the contemptible, undeserving teenage mother. Lydia dies alone, cut off from the world by the secret she never tells. Her life of isolation, celibacy, and rectitude are insufficient recompense for her transgressions. Like so many birthmothers in literary history, she has to die.

Quindlen's novel makes me think of possibility, of what might have been had Quindlen refused conventional typecasting and allowed Lydia the occasion to tell her secret. When will the narrative paradigm shift? Amy Tan demonstrates that it can, that it must; however, she learns this lesson from her own life experience, from having to wait until the day her mother died in order to finally know that her mother wasn't only Daisy Tan, that her true birth name was Li Bingzi. She tells Precious Auntie's tragic story because she experiences firsthand the damage keeping secrets can do, not only to those directly involved but to generations that follow. Secrets are harmful. They are rarely necessary. Perhaps it is in our desire to belong, to be part of the village, to be on the inside that we agree to keep our secrets in the first place. Certainly that is what motivated my parents and grandparents to keep my uncle and his family's tragic demise a secret. How could they find acceptance in their new Southern California communities if "people" knew the truth? And so they became secret-keepers, not just about my uncle but about all the things that made us unique and extraordinary. What a price to pay for "normalcy"!

Ultimately, secrecy failed. I couldn't keep the family secrets and live a whole and healthy life. I did not want to live with my legacy of shame. I did not want to end up like Quindlen's Lydia in my own version of solitary confinement. But the only way to escape that imprisonment was truthfulness. Telling the truth is scary for birthmothers. Letting go of secrets is risky for everyone. But without doing so, we risk Lydia's fate. Ironically, in an effort to "save face," we put on dissembling masks. We forfeit the opportunity for unqualified self-acceptance and the possibility for unreserved mutual love that must be based on veracity and authenticity. Telling secrets isn't magic. The legacy of shame may not completely disappear; it hasn't for me. I still stumble on shame. But I know firsthand that its stultifying grip can be loosened by narratives that reject the implacability of fate and embrace the optimistic prospect of transformation that comes with a legacy of truth.

Birthmothers in the Adoption Triangle

Because Hester Prynne does not have to surrender Pearl to adoption, she is not technically a birthmother. In fact, she is actually not even an unwed mother. Although neither she nor Chillingworth reveals that he is her husband, he obviously is very much alive and could have revealed himself to the people of Boston and resumed his place as master of the Prynne household had he not been so ashamed of being cuckolded. Finally the only epithet that correctly applies to Hester is "adulteress," and yet she stands for me as my shining star—the heroic birthmother that I could never be. I lacked her maturity, her vocation, her courage, and her resilience. I was defeated, banished from my daughter's life for thirty-five years by a closed adoption. The truth about those years? They were full of happy events, exciting arrivals, optimistic promises, and satisfying accomplishments, but ultimately, every-thing new thing I tried—marriage, motherhood, scholarship, adventure—failed to fill the empty chamber in my heart, that dark space deep within me of lack, need, and desire. How could I have been so undone by that early loss? So damaged that despite herculean attempts to forget, replace, and re-vise, I inevitably found myself wandering around that empty chamber, for-lorn, bitter, and emotionally destitute.

Because I couldn't talk about my loss, I didn't completely understand the ways that loss had damaged me. Had I spent time in therapy, I would have undoubtedly come to understand the roots of my sorrow, but I was so busy running away from unhappiness and shame that I rarely took the time to be retrospective. I carried on in my own version of frenzied activity, keeping all the lights in my precarious psyche ablaze. Hard work helped me avoid the dark spaces. Overwhelming responsibility kept those scary descents into uselessness, grief, and regret at bay. I was a puzzle to myself. Looking back, I now know what could have helped. If I had known other birthmothers, if I had had the opportunity to read about the experience of others like me, I might have been different. But we birthmothers have been too ashamed to tell our stories. Only now are we finding our voices, are we expressing our grief, even our outrage over the way we were used, the way we were humiliated and isolated, the shame and secrecy we were expected to bear willingly, even gratefully. Hester Prynne set an unreasonable example for me. I couldn't be her. I had surrendered my daughter irrevocably, I thought. I needed the stories of girls like me, the unwed mothers who couldn't stand up to authority and insist, "She is mine. You shall not take her!"

Had I been able to read novels or memoirs about experiences like mine or to see films that told stories about girls like me, it might not have taken me so long to get my bearings, hold my own head up, and tell my story of coercion, pain, and loss. There are many nonfiction books that could have guided me had they arrived earlier in my reading life, books like Margaret Moorman's *Waiting to Forget*, Ann Fessler's *The Girls Who Went Away*, and Meredith Hall's *Without a Map*. They have helped me immeasurably, as have the many memoirs by brave writers who finally decide to tell the destructive secrets that do invidious harm to our psyches and hearts. Had I found them when I was sixteen, eighteen, twenty-five, even thirty-five, I would have found comfort, the solace that comes when we hear the stories of others, women so much like us. We aren't alone in our shame and bitter regret. We have sisters.

GIRLS IN TROUBLE

Girls in Trouble by Caroline Leavitt is the novel I needed to read decades ago. Published in 2004, forty years after I surrendered my daughter, Leavitt breaks new narrative ground by creating a fully realized, complicated, and conflicted young birthmother as her protagonist. Throughout the narrative, Leavitt challenges social convention by demonstrating that adoption may not always be the best option for all unwed teenage mothers and their illegitimate babies. As the novel opens, there are no lurid tales of abandoned babies or disgraced birthmothers. Instead we begin with an all-too-common and much less sensational event: a frightened, unprepared sixteen-year-old, Sara, is about to give birth. Sara's mother and father have made all the legal arrangements for an open adoption, and the adoptive parents, Eva and George, are in the delivery room for the birth. It's 1987.

Gone are the days when pregnant girls were sent away to homes for wayward girls and not "given any pain medication because the nuns felt [they] should suffer for [their] sins" (31). Sara's parents don't pillory her, nor do they put her in hiding, but they do, in a sense, drive home that her body will be marked from here on out. Her mother laments, "Oh God . . . When I think of that young unspoiled body getting all blown out of shape" (79). After giving birth, Sara does not face the stigmatizing labels of "unwed mother" or "ruined woman," but she does not get the "fresh start" her mother promised. Instead she finds herself weighed down by debilitating sorrow. She is unhinged by grief; she cannot relocate her academic, goal-oriented drive; she desperately misses her baby and the baby's birthfather Danny, the "black sheep" who skipped town. Her parents try to intervene; they encourage counseling; they say things like "We just want you to move on with your life" (84). But Sara cannot be consoled. She wants nothing more than to be with Eva and George, the couple who agreed to an open adoption, and the baby they have named Anne.

Leavitt has had some personal experience with open adoption, having sought one herself unsuccessfully. In an article she recalls trying "to court" birthmothers. She did not get far in the process, but she found that as she talked to young birthmothers, "they wanted to talk about teenage stuff . . . They wanted almost to be part of my family. They wanted me to adopt them" (qtd. in Galant). So it is with Sara, who has fallen in love not only with Anne but also with Eva and George, and they welcome her daily visits. Sara seems to be living out my birthmother fantasy. Rather than surrender her daughter, all she has to do is share her with a new extended family.

Sara has an intuitive knack with Anne and can calm her when Eva can't, but she oversteps a maternal boundary line while bathing Anne one warm afternoon. Slipping off her dress and sliding into the inviting tub, she lifts the baby out of the nonskid baby seat and pulls her close, their naked, bodies nestling comfortably together. It's a deeply intimate moment, but when Eva finds them, she is both furious and envious. This is just the kind of dangerous, impulsive thing that an imprudent teenage mother would do. And Eva wants and resents the relaxed, sensual connection that Sara has with Anne. Like Sara's parents, Eva and George had anticipated that Sara would "go on and have [her] own life," but the bath scene convinces them the open adoption is "too open" (117). It's not surprising that when they insist on a new, restricted visitation plan, Sara objects, trying to justify her intrusiveness with the words, "I just like to spend time . . . with *my* baby" (117; emphasis added). Sara's confusion over "my baby" and "your baby" is for me, a birthmother, understandable. I've never stopped referring to Merideth as *my* baby and *my* daughter, but for Eva, the adopting mother, Sara has gone too far, and she lashes back: "*My* baby . . . It's *my* baby" (124; emphasis added).

Leavitt understands what so many in our culture do not: for birthmothers there is no turning back to ordinariness. Sara neither will be nor can be a "normal" high school student again. Instead, observes critic Carrie Brown, she is "desperate to discover a role for herself in the altered universe of being a teenage mother." But her maternal longing only leads her to another life-altering mistake. Unwilling to abide by Eva and George's new rules, she kidnaps Anne, only to be quickly apprehended by the police. Anne is returned safely to Eva and George, and Sara is traumatized and suicidal. Faced with going to jail if Eva and George press charges, she is stunned into obedience and lets the now-closed adoption be finalized. She finishes her senior year of high school as if she is "sleepwalking" (157).

Leavitt demonstrates what I learned all too well: the promises made to mollify birthmothers' uncertainties about relinquishing their babies—that it will all be over then; that their mistakes are behind them; that they will have a fresh start—are empty and misleading. As Sara tries to cope with her new, empty life, she recalls a story Abbey told her about a home for birthmothers. When one of the girls decided to keep her baby, she was immediately turned out. "We didn't want her decision infecting the other mothers," the house mother said. "*Infecting*," Sara thinks, "that was the word . . . As if the girl herself were a disease for wanting her own baby. A disease that had to be knocked out" (161). Many birthmothers like Sara and like me discover that "the disease" of wanting one's baby is incurable. "It" will never be over.

Sara pushes herself through high school and depression and does well at Columbia, working tenaciously to earn "A" grades. Each one stands as a "badge of honor rather than shame" (185). She tells no one about Anne and begins graduate school in clinical psychology, only to break down after hearing a client's story about losing her baby to SIDS. When she must admit the truth and explain her collapse in her mandatory therapy session, her sympathetic and well-meaning therapist tries to help, but does so by trotting out the same clichés birthmothers have been told over and over again: Sara had done the right thing by surrendering Anne; she "never would have come this far"; she "wouldn't have been able to go to school, to have a life" (193). But Sara's reopened wounds cannot be staunched by these platitudes. Rather than continue graduate work, obligatory therapy, and the introspection that it would require, Sara drops out of school altogether. Once again she has to apologize to her parents for disappointing them. Her father admonishes her: "[You're] not living your real life. The life you were meant to have." He doesn't want her "waking up at forty finding [she] missed [her] chances" (203). But Sara has learned too well that time does not heal:

> That was the big lie. Time stretched so that some days pain was far from you, and other days it was close as your own heartbeat. The best you could hope for when it came to pain were scars, healing so you could get used to them. And even then you had to do everything you possibly could not to reopen the scars, not to make them fresh again, because then you might bleed and bleed and never stop. (205)

Nonetheless, she succeeds at her low-paying job; she has a serious boyfriend; she even has a pregnancy scare, though when she starts her period, she's shocked by the intensity of her grief. As her relieved boyfriend wraps her in his arms, she silently mourns her loss, wondering "how anybody could ever feel this empty, this absolutely alone" (228). This fresh sorrow pushes her to action, and she tracks down Anne's birthfather, Danny, who is happily married with a child of his own. He gives her new information, the details of the machinations her parents and his mother had set in motion years ago to keep them separated. Sara's father had threatened to have Danny arrested; his mother had sent him away and gotten his brother to forge the adoption papers. Furious, Sara confronts her father, who defends his actions by pleading, "Let it go . . . You would have ruined your life! . . . I didn't want you married and with a baby at sixteen and no future at all" (241–42). But Sara understands what I understand and what most birthmothers know: "good intentions can produce disastrous outcomes" (Harrison). Adults had assumed they knew what was best for Danny, for Sara, and for Anne, and they used their money and power to separate them from one another. By their standards, they had saved Sara from a bankrupt life. Even after witnessing Sara's years of suffering, depression, and turmoil, Sara's father remains blinded by the prevailing cultural assumptions about teenage parents. He did what he did, he says, because he loved her with "the love that counts . . . the love for your child." When Sara counters, "Did you hear what you just said?" he still doesn't get it (241–42). But Leavitt does, and in so doing, she bucks social convention by suggesting that adoption is not always the best option for unwed teenage mothers. Sara knows and I know and Leavitt suspects that not all young birthmothers should be coerced into surrendering their babies.

Eva and George, we learn, have also manipulated Anne's life in untruthful ways. Most importantly, they have never told her she is adopted until Sara, galvanized by the parental trickery that had deprived her of her daughter, tracks them down in Florida and shows up on their doorstep. They have rationalized withholding the truth in a time-honored way: "*What did it matter?* Eva thought. The fact was that the people who raised and loved a child were the parents. The rest was just biology" (273). Again, the nurture trumps nature argument. Eva and George are not unique in their decision not to tell; even though most professionals from the 1930s on agreed that the shock of revelation would be more harmful to children than the fact of adoption itself, many parents like Eva and George postponed telling for years. Their reluctance is understandable. Ellen Herman notes that adoptive parents were "encouraged to believe that their family was as real as real could be," but telling reminded them that their "particular kinship was . . . something less than completely natural and equal" (270). By the 1970s, telling emerged as the leading therapeutic issue in adoption (Herman 273), and detailed instruction with the exact words to use or avoid in telling were available to adoptive parents. Interestingly, while most parents did tell their children they were adopted, they were often not candid about the reasons for their adoption, particularly if the child was illegitimate. "Many parents lie to their children, 'killing off' birth parents rather than saying they had been unmarried" (Herman 277). Eva and George can't "kill off" Sara, but they offer Anne the same arguments we've heard over and over again to justify her necessary adoption: Danny and Sara were too young; they were just babies themselves; they had no money; they had no education. "What kind of life would you have had?" they ask Anne, who quickly fires back, "*My* life?!" (208). Anne feels robbed; Sarah feels robbed; Eva and George feel unjustly accused and unappreciated; and Leavitt deftly demonstrates the hazards and disingenuousness inherent to the adoption process.

Like her birthmother, Anne will not be appeased. As she tries to process everything her parents have and have not told her, she thinks:

Liars . . . *Liars.* . . . All those stupid made-for-TV movies about kids finding their birth mothers, about birth mothers finding them, everyone dissolving into tears of happiness as if they had finally been completed. "*I didn't grow under your heart, I grew in it.*" What a bunch of treacly shit. (280)

She's right. Popular culture has made a spectacle of adoptee/birthparent reunions, sentimentalizing away their complexity and the challenges that follow. Leavitt avoids overromanticizing the situation. Instead, she realistically represents Anne's anger at her parents for lying to her and at Sara for surrendering her.

Eventually, after much adolescent Sturm und Drang, Anne does come to a harmonious if provisional resolution concerning Eva, George, Sara, and Danny. "We all always loved you," Sara explains. The words are inadequate but accurate. Everyone involved acted out of love, and Leavitt has captured love's inevitable imperfections. Anne can be assured that she will always have a doting family, a differently configured but devoted group of adults eager to vanquish any lingering feelings of betrayal or abandonment. Illegitimacy has little negative effects these days, especially for much-desired babies like Anne. Hundreds, if not thousands, of childless couples, like Leavitt and her husband, would be ecstatic to claim a baby like her as their own.

It's Sara for whom the novel ends sadly, though perhaps my own lingering sorrow as a birthmother makes me read the ending pessimistically. Sara returns to graduate school, emotionally stable enough after the reunion to realize her dream of becoming a psychologist, but she is very much alone. There's no Prince Charming waiting in the wings, no pretty baby to help her heal, no happily-ever-after. Instead, she has no boyfriend and few friends and is far removed from her parents. When she is invited to attend Anne's high school graduation, she finds herself on the sidelines, everyone passing her "as if she were a ghost" (353). Finally Eva, radiant and exultant, spots her in the crowd and welcomes her. Anne is the happy center of attention. Danny is there with his adorable son and his beautiful wife, who is holding their newborn. George is there, officious and proud, making a show of seating them all, Sara included, at the family table. Nonetheless, Sara remains isolated. There is something inconsolable in her, an irremovable scar that keeps birthmothers relegated to the margins. Sara remains, like Hester, Jennie, Charlotte, and Kate, excluded from the feast of life. As she takes her seat, she tries to console herself, thinking, "For another moment . . . all of them [are] here, together," but the knot of sorrow, of the life she was denied overwhelms her, and she has to pause until she can "lift her head again" (355).

My gratitude to Carolyn Leavitt is immense. Finally a novelist creates a sympathetic rendition of a contemporary birthmother, a girl who tries hard to be heroic, independent, and capable of mothering her child. That she is defeated in doing so by the people who think they know best is entirely plausible. It does not surprise me that since its publication, "adoption agencies have become more critical [of the novel but] birthmothers have embraced [it]" (Galant). In *Adoption Quarterly*, a woman, who read the book while waiting to adopt, reports that the novel "disturbed and frightened her" (Johnston), and I can understand why. Leavitt disrupts the adoption myth of happily-ever-after by focusing not on the jubilant adopting parents, but on the birthmother's story of coercion, heartbreak, and regret. And she is doesn't sugarcoat Sara's loss by a treacly mother-child reunion. Like Sara, I have been reunited with my daughter, and that is a good and necessary thing, but Leavitt has it right; she realistically represents a reunion between birthparent and adopted child as confusing, clarifying but conflicted.

When Sara sits down at that family table at Anne's graduation, I know how she's feeling. Since opening the secrets of my daughter's closed adoption and finding her living happily in the midst of a large, boisterous New Jersey family, I've been graciously invited to comparable family celebrations and sat at similar tables. Yet after taking my seat, I too have remained self-consciously separate, unable to shake my sense of intrusiveness, hyper-alert to both the welcoming and the wary glances around me. There's an awkwardness I can't quite overcome, a repose I can't quite achieve. These lovely evenings in which I am so fortunate to be included inevitably leave me with my stomach in knots, my insomnia in full gear, and my emotions—gratitude, fear, sorrow, regret, and love—too close to the surface for any hope for a night of rest.

Birthmothers know that even though reunions bring about welcomed healing, they can never restore the babies we surrendered; they cannot expunge years of unhappiness and uncertainty. As Sara herself observes, the scars remain. Our wounds heal enough so that we can live with them, but they are never erased and never forgotten.

LOGGERHEADS

Leavitt takes us sixteen years post-adoption to see the difficulties that can linger for all members of the adoption triad, especially the emotional risks for the birthmother even in the most carefully crafted and optimistically progressive adoption plan. In his tragically realistic film *Loggerheads*, Tim Kirkman intertwines three deceptively incongruent narratives of the members of the adoption triad twenty-five years after a teenage unwed mother surrenders her infant son to adoption. The first narrative thread is Grace's, the birthmother who has never emotionally recovered from relinquishing her son when she was seventeen. After a suicide attempt at age forty-three, she ends up back home in Asheville, North Carolina, living with her mother, her only family. Still debilitated by grief, regret, and uncertainty, Grace realizes that if she is ever going to gain a measure of psychological stability, she needs to find her son. The next narrative thread is Mark's, Grace's relinquished son, a gay drifter suffering from AIDS and alienated from his adoptive parents. He has come to Kure Beach on the North Carolina coast not far from my Wilmington home to save as many baby loggerheads as he can. The third thread is the story of Mark's prim, traditional, and repressed adoptive mother Elizabeth. For years, she has obeyed her strictly religious husband Robert, a conservative preacher who has forbidden her to speak of their runaway, gay, adopted son. But when Elizabeth learns Mark is dying, she takes steps to find him in spite of her husband's dictum.

Kirkman's metaphorical conceit, of course, is the endangered loggerhead turtle that with uncanny precision steadfastly returns year after year to the same beach to lay her eggs, only to abandon them. The tiny female loggerheads that hatch and survive their dangerous trek across the sand and into the ocean will likewise take up the endless return to the very beach where they were hatched. Mark identifies with them, and we can't help but connect Grace with them as well, especially because she has been unable to halt the psychological return of the repressed, the scene of abandonment, Mark's adoption. As film critic Stephen Holden notes, Grace embodies the "agonizing sense of personal incompleteness compounded by years of pent-up shame" ("An Adopted Gay Son"). She cannot cast off the psychological straitjacket that keeps her locked in a kind of Nietzschean eternal return, unable to "move on" to all the things she was expected to accomplish.

Finally, in search of information about Mark, she returns to the "home" she lived in while waiting for his birth. There, the frosty, righteous administrator of the still-operating Christian adoption agency unsympathetically admonishes Grace for her desire to reconnect with her son, pitilessly reminding her that the adoption had been her, Grace's, decision. Grace immediately and adamantly fires back: "It wasn't *my* decision!" And she's right;

it was not her decision. Well-intentioned parents like Grace's, like Sara's, and like mine did not give us the opportunity to choose adoption or not. When Grace confronts her mother, contending, "We could have kept him," her mother defends the choice *she* made for Grace, saying that she "thought it was best for everybody"; she claims that she had to relinquish the infant if she was going to keep Grace from ruining her life. But she is silenced when Grace points out the obvious truth: her mother's decision to relinquish the baby ruined Grace's life. She has not achieved much, she notes, other than swallowing a bottle of pills. By refusing to whitewash adoption, by peeling away the stereotypes that too often characterize the triad, and by honestly representing people made deeply unhappy by adoption, the film asks us to ask the question: "Is adoption the best for everybody?"

Before a private investigator, who conducts "a kind of modern day underground railroad" that links birthmothers and their surrendered children, can locate Mark for Grace, he dies. Devastated, Grace visits the only person she can, Elizabeth, who, we learn, was able to reunite with Mark before he died. Elizabeth tries to console Grace, telling her they were both Mark's mothers and that their meeting is a way for Elizabeth to "give him back" to Grace. But Grace will never get Mark back and we imagine she will never entirely recover. Film critic Owen Gleiberman calls her "a middle-class wreck," but that is unfair. She is a mother who lost her child. As she stands on the beach where the loggerheads return and where Mark lived out his last days, she has every reason to be bereft. She may return year after year, but she will be forever denied the child that she will never be able to emotionally relinquish.

Grace and Sarah, damaged, deprived, and alone. We might write them off as nothing more than self-pitying wreckage. Our popular culture is currently foregrounding empowered women who can jump into all kinds of precarious situations, seize control, slay the baddies, save the babies, claim the son and the daughter, and still look beautiful doing so. Apparently we have little patience with pitifully tragic heroines who can't beat the odds and turn helplessness into brute force, weakness into command. Sarah and Grace may move toward their goals, and, indeed, even accomplish their quests and find the lost children, but they are still bound to disappointment. There is no reward, no transcendence. They remain trapped by the constraints of their gender-determined lives, by nine months of unwed pregnancy and childbirth that ironically defines them as birthmothers yet leaves them forever pining for motherhood. Leavitt and Kirkman create characters that make closure problematic, especially for readers and moviegoers who still want to hear at the narrative's end the classic, "Reader, I married him."

If, as Brownstein suggests, "A heroine, unlike other women, controls her life, shapes her self, makes her happiness" (134), Grace and Sara fall short. They may gain some self-control, but they cannot reshape themselves into happy heroines. Nonetheless, they have much to teach us about the dangers of coercion and much comfort to bequeath to those of us who were unknowingly coerced into joining the adoption triangle. Hearing their stories that in so many ways repeat my own is consoling and, yes, even empowering. Unlike Hester's courageous example that I could never measure up to, their plaintive stories confirm my own. I jump at the repetition. I'm not alone, and my outrage is not unwarranted. Grace and Sara give me more reason to insist that we control our bodies and our lives, that we shape our futures ourselves, that we make our happiness by trusting ourselves, by refusing exploitation, and by choosing, if we so desire, to be mothers even if a politician, or a social worker, or a priest, or a parent says we're not old enough, educated enough, independent enough, or capable enough. Leavitt and Kirkman push us to think beyond the traditional family paradigm that insists two-parent homes are always best, no matter what, and that adoption is always the better choice for the unwed teenage mother and her child. Surely motherhood does not automatically rule out education, ambition, and independence. And certainly we must acknowledge that adoption does not assure happiness, especially if we really consider all the members of the adoption triangle.

CHAPTER II

Comedy and the Unwed Mother

There is so much sort of unplanned pregnancy material circulating this year. It's just—it's in the zeitgeist for some reason.

DIABLO CODY ON *FRESH AIR*, DECEMBER 6, 2007

I've always been wary of the dark. At home I keep nightlights on in several rooms, upstairs and downstairs. The gentle penumbra they offer me is a comfort if I'm not sleeping. But it's not just those small hours of the night that unnerve me. Evenings are hard too, if I'm alone. The dwindling light and encroaching shades of gray can cast a pall of despair over my normally bright outlook. Though most people savor twilight, it can make me antsy, anxious for home. If you meet me for a late afternoon coffee, you'll find that I'm not one to linger. No, I want to be home to turn on our cheery yellow porch lights, pull the shades, to retreat to my warm, comfy kitchen, to feel enclosed and secure. Much of this is due to that dark, howling night in Akron, Ohio and the taxi barreling through that sinister blizzard to get me to a lighted room, qualified people, safety. I never want to be caught out in such perilous darkness again, and I always take steps to make sure I'm not. Still, it can't always be helped, and if my day stretches past my witching hour, I find comfort where I can.

Such a night came about when my thoughts about this book were just beginning to percolate. I was teaching a late afternoon class and we didn't end until 6:30, well past dark in Wilmington in December. Driving home from campus, I turned to a familiar voice to lighten my way and keep me company—Terry Gross on NPR's *Fresh Air*. I was not disappointed. In fact, the drive was transformed from dismal into an enlightening jaunt. It felt like kismet. Terry was talking to Hollywood screenwriter Diablo Cody and director Jason Reitman about their new film, *Juno*, a comedy about an adolescent unwed mother. Such an idea seemed like an oxymoron to me. What could possibly be comical about unwed motherhood? There had been absolutely nothing funny about my teenage pregnancy; giving birth to my daughter had been so frightening that I had spent most of my life dreading the onset of night, and surrendering her had been so tragic that I had a diminished sense of humor for decades. But that night, in spite of my after-dark anxiety and hard-earned skepticism, I found myself laughing all the way home. Reitman and Cody were engaging and my curiosity was peaked, especially when Diablo Cody informed Terry Gross that unplanned pregnancy was in the zeitgeist (Cody). Could it be that my shameful and traumatic secret had become the raw material for a funny movie? I had to find out.

Anyone who enjoys the movies can bear witness to the significant increase of sex, profanity, and violence in films released since the mid-1990s; it is no surprise that the Motion Picture Association of America has been accused of a "ratings creep." Given the greater latitude toward sexual content, what was once "X" is now "R" and "R" has morphed into "PG-13." It is also not surprising fallen women and their illegitimate children make good material for contemporary films. The passionate sex is there; the conflict between baby mama and baby daddy is there; the tragedy, whether it be abandonment, betrayal, or murder, is there; and the moral thread is there to be challenged, subverted, or extolled. Fallen women supply sexual stories from tragic cinematic representations of unwed mothers and their unhappy surrendered children, like Grace and her ill-fated son in *Loggerheads*, to comic renditions of fallen women, à la Olive in *Easy A*.

We might say that *Easy A* doesn't quite qualify since even though Olive is seductive and racy, she never gets pregnant. In fact, she never actually has sex. She dons the scarlet *A* of her own accord, which helps explain why audiences find this "fallen" girl hilarious rather than tragic: she's playing a game—a sexual one, yes—but ultimately, a game whose denouement lets Olive take the higher moral ground. *Easy A* may not strictly qualify as a comedy about an unwed mother, but there is no dearth of ones that do. In 2007 alone, there were three comedies released in which unwed mothers play major roles. But how could such a painful moment in a young woman's life be humorous? If I was going to answer that question, I had to see all three: Judd Apatow's *Knocked Up*, Helen Hunt's *Then She Found Me,* and Jason Reitman's *Juno*. I was prepared to be uncomfortable, dismissive, even censorious as I watched each film, and although there was discomfort, I also found myself laughing in the dark. When it comes to the movies, women still fall, but now they can be funny and resilient when they do so.

KNOCKED UP

Apatow's rowdy, obscene *Knocked Up* is a good place to begin because as a commentary on the cultural climate of unplanned, out-of-wedlock parenthood, it is a revealing snapshot. With a "barrage of gynecology-inspired jokes [that] would have driven the prudes at the old Hays Office mad," Apatow captures what film critic A. O. Scott identifies as "the sexual confusion and moral ambivalence of our moment" (Scott "Bye-Bye Bong"). The film focuses on Alison, a newly promoted, career-driven, attractive, young blond, and Ben, a pudgy, pot-smoking, unemployed and unkempt slacker. They meet, get drunk, and have a one-night stand during which there is a misunderstanding over a condom. Afterward, Alison has no intention of ever seeing Ben again, but eight weeks later she realizes she is pregnant. The time comes when she has to tell her mother—a scene I'm predicting will be, rather than funny, full of dread, fury, and disappointment. Instead, Alison's puffed-up, admonitory mother gets a laugh even when she insists: "Take care of it. This is a big mistake. This is not the time. Think about your career." Here we get an accurate indication of the acceptability of abortion these days as a reasonable option. But that's not the "choice" Alison will make. Abortions are still far from funny and since Apatow is writing comedy, that alternative is quickly nixed. Critic Joe Morgenstern notes that the "subject of abortion no longer lends itself readily to dramatic surprises, [but] keeping a baby means new problems and complexity, both of which are indispensable to an interesting plot." Thus, according to the narrative parameters of the contemporary zeitgeist that demand dramatic surprise, Alison must emphatically declare, which she does: "I'm keeping it!" With such a plot device, the director now has the opportunity to confront the many challenges of unplanned pregnancy. But by turning them into ticklish, tickling problems and droll complexities, he also turns the film into an appealing but implausible, feel-good fantasy.

For example, when Alison tells Ben, whose ambition is limited to cataloging movie scenes of naked actresses, that she is keeping the baby, he responds with feigned delight:

That's good. That's what I was hoping you'd do. Awesome! I know we didn't plan this, but life is like that, you can't plan for it. Life doesn't care about your plans, necessarily, and you just kind of have to go with the flow. I know my job is to just support you in whatever it is you wanna do and I'm in. I'm on board. Yay!

His quixotic reaction is sweet but highly improbable for a twenty-three-year-old, puerile ne'er-do-well who has an impressive collection of bongs but only $117 to his name.

As Alison's pregnancy progresses, she is never in danger of being branded as a fallen woman, but she knows some collective disapproval is shadowing her, and she is aware of potential penalties even in modern-day, au courant California. Although she insists, "Just because I'm pregnant doesn't mean I'm some ruined woman," she finds it imperative to hide her pregnancy from her employers for fear of losing her job. Anxious and confused, she knows "her body and her future are on the line" (Scott "Bye-Bye, Bong"). But it's not just in the workplace that Alison feels in the wrong and exposed. At home, when her niece asks her, "Aren't you supposed to be married to have a baby?" she is so embarrassed and befuddled by the question that she can't even respond. Instead, her older sister, Debbie, steps in to spout the morally appropriate order of events that still stands when it comes to pregnancy: "They [Alison and Ben] *should* be [married] because they love each other and people who love each other get married and have babies." Still perplexed and unsatisfied, the child persists, asking Alison and Ben point blank," Do you love each other?" Ashamed to admit that they barely know each other, they sit in awkward silence. Not only did they conceive a baby out of wedlock, they were no more than passing acquaintances, which puts them well beyond the borders of conventional heterosexual, monogamous propriety. But Apatow is not interested in reasserting traditional "family values." Rather he wants to contest the contemporary mores Debbie unyieldingly upholds, for we find out in the course of the film that following the rules has not worked well for Debbie, who is mired in a nightmare of genteel domesticity that is exacerbated by her cynical, duplicitous husband. Nonetheless, Debbie espouses the status quo and reiterates present-day cultural expectations of respectability: "Yes," she insists. "They love each other. Because that's what you do. When you love each other, you get married, and you have a baby." Debbie paints a false tableau of Alison and Ben, one that is obviously counterfeit but is, nonetheless, the obligatory explanation for a precocious six-year-old.

Despite, what Lisa Schwarzbaum calls Ben's "shlubby," "hapless meatball," juvenile behavior—which is, in fact, a highly socialized and not atypical role of delayed adolescence—he demonstrates that he too has been inculcated by cultural expectations of propriety. As he tries to come to terms with Alison's embarrassment over her pregnancy, he assumes: "I really think it's cuz, like, I haven't made an honest woman out of her. She's carrying my bastard child. No one wants that." When he says "bastard child," he gets a big laugh. What was once a damning label has been so thoroughly reinscribed that it is cause for low humor rather than opprobrium. But the perception that the only way he can help Alison is by making her "an honest woman" goes unquestioned. Eventually Ben's goofball solipsism is too much for Alison and she breaks off their stumbling relationship. The story then turns to Ben's redemption, not an unusual offshoot for illegitimacy narratives. In due course, the frog turns into a prince, gets a job, rents his own apartment, gets Alison to the hospital when she goes into labor, and advocates effectively for her by maturely and reasonably negotiating with a ludicrously unsympathetic doctor.

The film ends as all comedies must, by restoring conventional order and re-establishing dominant social codes. Ben overcomes his delayed adolescence; he and Alison declare their love for one another, and a redeemed Ben, imbued with integrity and gratitude, takes his family home from the hospital to the "castle" he has prepared for them. To be certain that the fairy-tale ending is made indisputable, we are given closing images of the family one year later—Alison, Ben, and their baby as well as the picture-perfect extended family of friends, aunts, uncles, and grandparents—all blissfully bobbling the baby into "happily ever after." Traces of the fallen woman and the lingering years of alienation, guilt, and atonement she was once compelled to endure are nowhere to be found in this dangerously naive version of unplanned pregnancy and its consequences.

Nonetheless, even though I know too well that the situation this film so cavalierly refers to as "knocked up" never leads to unqualified happy endings, I cannot help but appreciate the utter joy Ben and Alison find in their baby girl—the baby they choose to keep, the baby they take home. Earlier in the film, when Ben is looking for advice and guidance, he asks his father, "If I had not existed, wouldn't you have saved yourself a whole massive heap of trouble?" His father replies without hesitation, "I love you totally and completely. You're the best thing that ever happened to me." In this silly, impractical, overly romanticized film, that is a line to be taken seriously.

THEN SHE FOUND ME

Helen Hunt's more serious comedy, *Then She Found Me*, which is based on the novel of the same name by Elinor Lipman, takes on not only unplanned, out-of-wedlock motherhood, but also the precarious reunion of good-girl adoptee April and her histrionic birthmother Bernice, not to mention April's quest to have a baby that is, as she puts it, "really hers." Why a "serious comedy"? There's heartbreak underneath all the jokes. *Then She Found Me* is like an old, tattered, gloomy house that's been "flipped," transformed into a new, jazzy, sprightly abode. But the dark old house is still there under the layers of fresh, cheerful paint.

April, our protagonist, is a deglamorized elementary school teacher; Bernice is the other extreme: a garrulous daytime TV talk show host who will not be dissuaded from anything she puts her mind to. When she learns that April's adopted mother has died, she arranges to be reunited with April whether April wants it or not. This is a significant departure from the culturally historical view of birthmothers, whose nonexistence has been a legal, social, and narrative requirement. As Margaret Homans points out, "the birthmother is not meant to survive, much less speak" (35), so when Bernice audaciously decides to make herself known, she is immediately on treacherous ground. It's not surprising that Philip French refers to Bernice as "the birthmother from hell" in his review for the *Observer*; in the *New York Times*, Stephen Holden is more restrained, describing her as a "narcissistic drama queen with a good heart." Not only is she persona non grata, she is overly assertive and indelicately inquisitive—qualities that make for a good talk show host but not a cautious, sensitive birthmother who dares to speak. Her many missteps begin when she presumptuously signs her letter of introduction to April with "Your mother, Bernice." Even I flinched at her unearned use of the moniker. Although there is some controversy over what women who have lost their children to adoption should be called and although some do call themselves mother without qualification, most are conscientiously respectful of their surrendered child's adoptive parents and identify themselves as birthmothers, first mothers, biological mothers, or natural mothers. Cast as a bumbling, brash harridan, Bernice both horrifies and entertains us. More importantly, rather than sympathize with her, we laugh at her slapstick ineptitude.

Their first meeting is a disaster. Bernice insists on calling April "Gabrielle," the name she gave her thirty-nine years ago; she imprudently asks April if she's married, or if not, does she have someone to hold her at night. Without giving April a chance to get her bearings, she pushes on with smothering declarations like, "I feel like you are the reward for everything I ever did right in my entire life," and "You are the most important thing on earth to me," followed by "My family is me and you." When she finally gives April an opening, April asks an awkward but legitimate question: "Why did you give me up?" With surprising gusto, Bernice explains: April's father is the actor Steve McQueen; April was conceived during a feverishly impassioned one-night-stand; she was taken from Bernice when she was three days old. In spinning a highly romantic if far-fetched plot for her birthmother story, Bernice turns to fairy-tale imbrications to entice her daughter into her the web of her life. And for a moment, it works. April is quite naturally intrigued. Isn't it every adopted child's secret fantasy that they are the love child of a famously handsome actor or actress, stolen at birth by an evil witch? April may be sensible but she can't resist such star-struck news.

It doesn't take her long to figure out that Steve McQueen could not have possibly have been her birthfather. Caught in a lie, Bernice must admit that April was actually conceived at the drive-in under circumstances Bernice finds "ugly and ordinary." She had wanted to make the tacky truth into something beautiful, but no matter how creatively she embroiders April's beginnings, they cannot be beautified. Reviewer Christopher Kulick finds Bernice "full of inner conflict, confusing real life with the exaggerated discussion on her televisions show." Indeed, she is very conflicted. Although seemingly confident and self-aggrandizing, Bernice is actually so burdened with shame and fear that she believes she must invent a romantic seduction with a dreamy movie star in order to claim legitimacy.

Exasperated, April tries to "break off" the reunion. In a public park, Bernice, desperate and pitifully obsequious, begs April to forgive her lying and to give her another chance. The memorable shot, with Bernice on her knees in supplication and April standing above her in judgment, is used for much of the advertising for the film and for the cover of the reissued 2008 edition of Lipman's novel. It's a telling choice, an image that resonates with the general idea that birthmothers need to apologize for the relinquishment. The repentant, remorseful, and blameworthy birthmother obsequiously begs for mercy. Bernice may not be pilloried and there is no emblazoned A on her breast, but she is unmistakably in need of forgiveness, and April forgives her because she needs her. Yet despite all of Bernice's promises of honesty, she still hasn't come clean. When April learns that she was not "taken away" from Bernice, that, in fact, Bernice did not relinquish her until she was a year old, she is again infuriated by her birthmother's ongoing deceit. Bernice tries to explain:

I was fifteen years old. Your father completely disappeared. My father completely turned his back on me. My mother said I had ruined my life. They threw me out. I had a bag of clothes and $48. I didn't know how to open a fucking can of soup. You wouldn't stop crying. Like an idiot, I thought it was for the best and then it was too late.

Unmoved, April coldly replies, "Just say you wanted a life more than you wanted me," and miserably, Bernice says just that: "I wanted a life more than you." It's a dreadful moment, a searing admission for Bernice to have to make and for April to have to hear. And it is not a fair or true summation.

Bernice surrendered April for the same reasons most birthmothers "choose" adoption: she had no support system, no means of sustenance, no partner with whom to share the responsibility of an inconsolable infant who got sick a lot, and nothing more than a prognosis of ruin from those who could have helped her. Is it any wonder Bernice momentarily thought relinquishing April was for the best? And given her entrenched shame and enduring regret, is it any wonder Bernice felt it was necessary to lie? The permanent psychological damage that birthmothers live with after surrendering their babies is not addressed. Bernice is never seen as an unfortunate victim of a social system that did not assist her, that , in fact, readily took advantage of her desperation. April thinks of Bernice as guilty; Bernice thinks of herself as guilty; and with that established, the film can end happily. April forgives Bernice, finds Mr. Right, and taking Bernice's advice as well as her adoptive mother's, she cheerfully and unself-consciously adopts a little girl from China. The film never questions the assumption that kids are better off adopted, despite the fact that "the Donaldson Adoption Institute, the Child Welfare League of America, and numerous other experts on child welfare tell us that the vast majority of children are in fact *better off with their biological families*" (Edwards). We are to accept without question that April was better off in an "intact" family with money than with her struggling biological mother, even though April's adoptive mother is depicted as difficult, even obnoxious. April and Mr. Right's international adoption is automatically accepted as good for everyone. The assumption that children rescued from foreign orphanages are always better off in America goes unquestioned, despite ongoing revelations of kidnapping and corruption. In the demarcation of good guys / bad guys in this film, only Bernice, the birthmother, is made to wear the black hat, whether she deserves it or not, while two sets of adoptive parents' don white hats with unexamined entitlement.

Happy ending? Yes, happy for April and Mr. Right and as happy as it can be for Bernice, but in the closing scenes of the film, the birthmother still must pay. Although in Lipman's novel, April and Bernice accommodate somewhat to each other, the film depicts Bernice as doing all the accommodating. Rather than show an irrepressible, still uproariously inappropriate Bernice invited to sit at the family table with warm acceptance, warts and all, we are given a chastised, chastened, humbled Bernice. And she's not seated at the table. Rather, she is obediently clearing the table. No matter how flamboyantly capable and admired Bernice has been for most of her life, she cannot be allowed to creatively reestablish a relationship with April with her own dramatic flourishes; rather she must acquiesce to April's punitive version of abandonment and selfishness and accept April's restrictive terms of control. Is Bernice really going to totally change her personality and become humble? I don't believe it, but in Hunt's version, it's her only option. If the relationship is going to continue at all, Bernice must confine her ebullience and agree to restraint. Only then can she clear the table. She has been invited in to the feast of life, but only if she cleans up afterward.

JUNO

Under the thrall of the "zeitgeist," *Juno*'s screenwriter Diablo Cody and director Jason Reitman joined the ranks of what Ty Burr of the *Boston Globe* calls a "peculiar mini-genre," "the coming-to-term pregnancy comedy." The popularity of *Juno* attests to its winning depiction of a savvy, smart-mouthed sixteen-year-old facing pregnancy with courage and humor. But unlike Helen Hunt, who makes an effort to represent the painful consequences of adoption, Cody and Reitman unself-consciously represent Juno's adoption arrangements as complicated yet ultimately the most responsible, best option for all concerned. In so doing, they ignore another evolving part of the unplanned pregnancy zeitgeist: the growing corpus of music, memoirs, films, and novels that detail a birthmother's anguish. More and more popular authors, musicians, and filmmakers are telling these stories, going back to Joni

Mitchell's popular song "Little Green" (1967), to important nonfiction like Moorman's *Waiting to Forget* (1998) and Fessler's *The Girls Who Went Away* (2006), to award-winning films like Mike Leigh's *Secrets and Lies* (1997) and Kirkman's *Loggerheads*, to novels like Leavitt's *Girls in Trouble* and Lipman's *Then She Found Me*—to name only a few representative examples.

I watched *Juno* in a theater packed with teenage girls and middle-aged women. The teenagers laughed uproariously throughout, especially when Juno MacGuff recalls having sex with Paulie Bleeker in a basement barco-lounger. Everyone hooted with delight when Juno visits the Women's Choice Clinic and encounters the punk receptionist whose partner's balls smell like pie. And everyone chuckled, well, everyone but me, when Juno tells her baby's prospective adoptive parents to "kick it old school" when their lawyer raises the possibility of an open adoption. Juno replies:

> Whoah. I don't want to see pictures. I don't need to be notified of any-thing . . . I could just put the baby in a basket and send it your way. You know, like Moses in the reeds . . . The way people used to do it. Quick and dirty, like ripping off a Band-Aid . . . Shit, yeah. Close it up. (Cody 35.53)

When the film ends happily (ostensibly), I made myself pause to note the teary smiles and wistful sighs on those around me, as Juno and Paulie, with-out a care in the world, sing the Moldy Peaches' "Anyone Else But You" on Paulie's stoop before the camera pulls "out to reveal the surrounding green suburbs buzzing with life and summer activity" (101.121). For this represen-tative audience, the film was, as Cody anticipated, "a funky little movie that wears its heart on both sleeves" (ix). It fits the "happy adoption" myth that, according to Novy, acts as a pervasive paradigm that shapes our "feeling, thoughts, language, and even laws about adoption" (1). But for me, *Juno*'s end-ing was something quite different. Slammed with emotion, I blundered out of the theater, stumbling to my car so that I could cry, hard and unobserved.

Given Cody and Reitman's remarks on *Fresh Air*, I had anticipated that the film might be disconcerting rather than enjoyable for me, so I prepared myself for it by rereading *The Scarlet Letter*. I wanted to steel myself, as I had tried to do in 1965 at the Florence Crittenton Home, with Hester's courage. I wanted to remember her dignity after the birth of her illegitimate child be-fore I took on Juno's casually sardonic account of unwed motherhood. After seeing the film, my purpose became clear: to demythologize *Juno*'s "happy ending" representation of adoption, especially its embedded endorsement of closed adoption. To do so, I again draw comparisons between a fictional romance and my own experience with unplanned pregnancy in the 1960s. At first glance, *Juno* stands as part of a larger, continuous narrative, one in which unwed mothers have been for the most part heretofore excluded, in which a mercurial hero, beset by seemingly insurmountable adversity, triumphs and is rewarded (McPherson 3, 5). Though *Juno* may seem at first to fit this mythical paradigm, I challenge the assumption that it does so. As someone who suffered for decades after relinquishing my daughter to a closed adoption—"the standard operating procedure [in the sixties] . . . when all identifying data about birth and adoptive parents were guarded like nuclear secrets" (Pertman 12)—*Juno*'s version of coping with an unplanned pregnancy by choosing a closed adoption gives me and, I would hope, our culture pause. Based on my experience and the experience of birthmothers like me, I maintain that *Juno* is far from a triumph at the story's end. Rather, the film's conclusion, although seemingly benign, portends tragedy rather than reward.

It is no wonder that Cody and Reitman were drawn to a plot similar to *The Scarlet Letter*. The same young and impressionable people who were gobbling up *Juno* in movie theaters would most likely have either read *The Scarlet Letter* or encountered its cultural representations in high school (à la Olive Penderghast of *Easy A*). Cody and Reitman cleverly re-embroider Hester's scarlet story, weaving into it the contemporary intricacies of the cultural response to pregnancy outside of marriage, a response that has shifted from opprobrium to tolerance. *Juno* marks yet another phase in the interpretations of Hester's plight and punishment, but now, rather than shameful, sex outside of marriage has become fashionable, and so, it seems, has teen pregnancy. In her *Slate* review of the film, Dana Stevens quips, "Let's hope that the teenage girls of America don't cast their condoms to the wind in hopes of becoming as cool as 16-year-old Juno," and *New York Times* reviewer Ginia Bellafante observes that pop culture is enamored by teen pregnancy but "displays an almost aggressive aversion to moralizing about [it] . . . refusing to lay out the grim consequences of premature motherhood" (B8). Rather than a symbol full of cautionary portent, Cody has re-embroidered Hester's story and her scarlet *A* to stand as a symbol of teenage autonomy and choice.

Nonetheless, if we look closely, we can find that the ethical implications of Cody's version of the punishing *A* are all too evident in the moral code of

Juno and its characters, all of whom would seem to be safely outside of any absolutist moral codification. No one calls Juno a "fallen woman"; she has no literal *A* to bear. In fact, as Ellen Page, the actor who plays Juno, notes, "She dresses like she wants, says what she wants, and doesn't apologize for it" (qtd. by Spines 26). She is not ostracized from her family; she attends high school throughout her pregnancy; her greatest punishment is having to forgo the prom. The words "immoral" and "illegitimate" are never mentioned in regard to Juno, her accidental pregnancy, or her child. The film thus stands as a revised cultural touchstone, one that represents the amoralization of illegitimacy.

However, although pregnancy outside of marriage may no longer be branded immoral, in every advertisement for the film, in every photograph accompanying its reviews, and on every DVD cover, a profile shot of Juno's hugely pregnant belly is the predominant image/fetish. Clad in classic teen garb—a hoodie, tattered jeans, sneakers, and a stretched-to-the-limit tee—she does not have to wear the literal *A*; her flagrantly jutting stomach takes its place. She simply embodies its latest attenuation. Serving as the damning symbol of the still-stigmatized birthmother, her belly literally stands out in contrast to the flat, toned tummies of her adolescent peers. It becomes the connection between biology and culture; it is the site where social values are emblazoned. Rather than being abolished, the *A*'s meanings have divided, shifted. Dispersed but never dissolved. Our fascination with female desire has not been quelled just because it has been supposedly liberated. It still conveys problematical penalties. Juno may think her greatest humiliation is being called "the Cautionary Whale" (68.84), but in fact she is judged automatically and harshly by a cultural authority as unforgiving as Puritan New England—not one that finds her necessarily immoral, but one that does find her, like Hester, unfit to raise her child. And Juno has no Dimmesdale to argue her case. Unlike highly capable Alison of *Knocked Up*, Juno's youth and financial dependence provide her no recourse or means of rebuttal. With no judge in sight, she, like Bernice, is automatically found guilty of being an unqualified mother. The film repeats the long tradition of punishing female sexual desire by forbidding, if not ultimately repressing, Juno's maternal desire. She herself may no longer be branded a banned object, but her baby is. Her child will be forbidden her.

Juno has a sense of right and wrong, but enmeshed within her community and its reigning ideologies, she cannot gain the critical perspective that would allow her to interrogate the class and age biases that brand her as unworthy of motherhood. Still, we can applaud her for her pluck. When she finally must acknowledge that three pink plus signs on three Teenwave Discount Pregnancy Tests confirm that she is, as she puts it, "definitely up the spout" (5.17), she does not fold into a morass of despair and helplessness. Not Juno. Her only hint of dejection is a halfhearted, absurd attempt to fashion a noose out of a giant licorice Super Rope. With Bleeker's blessing to "do what you think is right" (10.28) and her best friend Leah's automatic response to avoid the Havenbrooke clinic since "you need a note from your parents for Havenbrooke" (6.17), Juno takes steps to, as she says, "procure a hasty abortion" (14.32). Inculcated by the "right to choose" mind-set that *Roe v. Wade* has allowed to flourish, abortion for Juno is at first unquestionably amoralized, and so she trudges to the Women's Choice Clinic.

Once there she encounters one lone protester, her classmate Su-Chin, and it is here that the film takes what many have seen as a moralistic swerve when Juno must confront the morality/immorality of her next step. Su-Chen tells Juno, "Your baby probably has a beating heart, you know . . . And it has fingernails" (19.41), and it's those fingernails that tear away Juno's protective veil of sardonic casualness. "Terror-stricken," she flees, "tear[ing] down the street, running as fast as she can" (20.42). Though worrisome to pro-choice proponents, Juno's change of mind has more to do with her capacity for empathy than with any rigid right-to-life ideology. She practices her own form of the Golden Rule by identifying with the fetus. Its potentiality trumps the inconvenience of carrying it to term. One could argue Juno's unselfish concern for another sentient being—Su-chin also tells her, "It can feel pain" (19.41)—outweighs her earlier decision to terminate the pregnancy, or in her words, "nip it in the bud before it gets worse" (10.28). But her seemingly self-sacrificing application of the Golden Rule is followed by an even more seemingly magnanimous resolution.

Not only will Juno "stay pregnant," she tells Leah, she will also "give the baby to somebody who actually likes that kind of thing . . . like a woman with a bum ovary or something. Or some nice lesbos" (21.43). Juno, like Alison of *Knocked Up*, can make this choice because of our particular cultural context in a fractured ideological America. The issue of reproductive choice is constantly being contested publicly in the media, on our street corners, and in our homes. Gathered outside abortion clinics across the country to bully would-be patients, "pro-life" protestors—like Su-chin—have a powerful influence as do, in different venues, pro-choice and adoption advocates. However, there is one group that has only begun to speak out, one that is completely and, I maintain, perilously ignored by the film: the voices of the birthmothers, like me, who have relinquished their babies to closed adoptions and have never stopped regretting that decision.

Juno has no conception of the perilous emotional ramifications of her choice. Her automatic and unexamined generosity is an example of innocence and ignorance, a cultural unawareness that she and the huge audience that loves her share. In Juno's fictional and in our real world, the issue of relinquishing a child to adoption is almost always accepted as morally good, so much so that Juno can blithely joke about possible sainthood—"Maybe they'll canonize me for being so selfless" (21.43)—without any knowledge of the abiding consequences she is inviting into her life. Juno has been absolutely acclimatized to a culture that automatically approves of adoption as prudent, morally upright, and an unselfish answer to unplanned pregnancy.

In her op-ed piece "Sex and the Teenage Girl," Caitlin Flanagan insists that *Juno* is a fairy tale. To believe that a young girl like Juno can emerge unscathed from an unwanted pregnancy, "completely her old self again," is magical thinking, says Flanagan. "As any woman who has ever chosen (or been forced) to kick it old school can tell you, surrendering a baby whom you will never know comes with a steep and lifelong cost" (13). Still, it is not fair to condemn the sixteen-year-old Juno, who readily and honestly admits, "I have no idea what kind of girl I am" (Cody 29.47), and about this, she is absolutely right. She is clueless about the punishing implications of her choice. But it is reasonable and necessary to criticize the film's screenwriter, Cody, and its director, Reitman (both obviously socially informed and critically aware adults) for the film's psychological obliviousness.

As we have intimately learned, the sorrow of bearing a child outside of marriage is not new. Had Cody and Reitman been more responsibly committed to realistically representing Juno's dilemma than to making a feel-good, commercially successful comedy, they would have paid heed to the sorrowfully accurate big-screen representations of young unwed mothers who lose their babies, like Tess in Roman Polanski's award-winning adaptation of *Tess of the D'Urbervilles* and Celie in Steven Spielberg's *The Color Purple*. They would have done well to remember Hester, who knows that losing her child will be more punishment than even she can bear and so demands that Pearl not be taken from her. Instead Cody and Reitman create a romantic fable, one that can be promoted as a "funny, savvy feel-good comedy" (Kirk Honeycutt, *Hollywood Reporter*), "a sheer joy from beginning to end" (Dennis Dermody, *Paper*), one that almost entirely represses the separation of mother and child into the cultural unconscious and depicts Juno, returned to her girlhood without a scratch, toodling through her carefree Eden, strumming her guitar with Bleeker, the love of her life: "Here is the church and here is the / steeple. We sure are cute for two / ugly people." But what's wrong with this happily-ever-after ending, you might ask?

If, as Janet Todd maintains, "in all forms of sentimental literature [film included], there is an assumption that life and literature are directly linked, not through any notion of a mimetic depiction of reality but through the belief that the literary experience can intimately affect the living one" (4), then there is much wrong with *Juno's* mythical ending. Whether the film is a fairy tale or a realistic representation is ultimately inconsequential. What does matter is the ways in which Juno's experience can intimately affect the lived experience of young, unwed mothers in today's world of adoption.

The film does offer one moment when Juno's maternal unworthiness is contested by Juno herself. When she goes in for her first ultrasound, the technician is relieved to learn that Juno will be giving the baby up for adoption, remarking: "I just see a lot of teenage mothers come through here. It's obviously a poisonous environment for a baby to be raised in" (47.63). For about a minute, we are on the threshold of questioning the assumption that teenage girls make "poisonous" mothers. Juno replies indignantly, "How do you know I'm so poisonous?" But rather than considering seriously the notion that she could indeed raise this baby responsibly and lovingly, she and her stepmother, Bren, confront the technician's (and our culture's) assumption that the baby's adoptive parents will be better parents. Bren suggests that they might turn out to be "utterly negligent" people who might do "a far shittier job of raising a kid than my dumbass stepdaughter ever would" (47.63). However, her wariness, a skepticism that might lead her and Juno to rethink the adoption plan, is immediately suppressed. Instead Bren berates, demeans, and dismisses the technician and in so doing effectively displaces her (and Juno's) anxieties onto the inconsequential technician and avoids, I would argue, her (and Juno's) potentially valid misgivings about adoptive parents and sidesteps Juno's consideration of herself as the worthy mother.

The film never again pauses to interrogate the assumption that Juno is doing the "right thing." Instead it reinforces the glossed, romanticized, and unrealistic forecast that all adoptions are happy adoptions. Rather than critique the lifestyle of her baby's would-be adoptive parents, Vanessa and Mark, for its conspicuous consumption, or interrogate the rarely contested cultural assumptions that lead almost everyone to believe that they will prove the better parents, Juno instead accepts without question the mainstream values that grant the Vanessas and Marks of our world respectability and worth and write off the Junos as unfit and, therefore, exploitable. Only Bren accurately articulates the gravity of Juno's choice, warning, "Junebug, that is a tough, tough thing to do. Probably tougher than you can understand right now" (28.47). She's right, but rather than help the naive Juno more fully understand the lifelong costs she will incur by giving away her baby or step in to help her raise the baby in a stable if not wealthy home, she too succumbs to the culturally popular rationalization that a young mother's loss can be erased and that adoption is always for the best. "Somebody else," Bren insists, "is going to find a precious blessing from Jesus in this garbage dump of a situation" (30.47). At the movie's conclusion, we find Bren rewarded with her own "precious blessings," the Weimaraners she's been longing for. Perhaps there is a subtle critique here of Mac and Bren, who so easily agree to relinquish their grandchild and adopt puppies instead, but if so, the criticism is too understated, too easily laughed away. In fact, one film critic, David Wiegand of the *San Francisco Chronicle*, applauds Mac and Bren for being "loving, attentive parents" who empower Juno to "[control] her body, her thoughts and her life." I would counter that the benign characterization of Mac and Bren and their easy acceptance of Juno's choice perpetuates the deceptive myth that parents are helping their pregnant daughters when they encourage them to deny their anxiety and surrender their babies to strangers. Rather than take on the responsibility for another child in the family or truly consider the emotional damage Juno will incur, Mac, Bren and the audience are encouraged to believe in Juno's naive "promise [that] this will all be resolved in thirty-odd weeks, and we can pretend it never happened" (26.47).

Bren and Mac may sidestep the long-lasting repercussions of Juno's pregnancy, but they do not step away from her during her pregnancy. They keep her at home, treat her with kindness and a surprising degree of forbearance, and deliver her to the hospital when she goes into labor. Bren and Leah, her best friend, stay by her side, as does Mac, who is there at her bedside when the delivery is over. In so doing, they deservedly earn our admiration. Gone are the mortified parents of the 1950s and 1960s who sent their daughters into exile right when they most needed their emotional guardianship.

In contrast, the responsibility of birthfathers seems to have changed little since Dimmesdale was allowed to keep his paternity a secret. In fact, Bleeker's paternity is even less pertinent than Dimmesdale's, for he feels none of the guilt that obsessed Dimmesdale so mercilessly. Bleeker is very much a birthfather of the 1650s, the 1850s, the 1950s, and so on. It is Juno who is immediately held responsible for their intercourse, and it is Juno alone who must endure the consequences. Like my own daughter's father, Bleeker is not only automatically excused from all material responsibility for Juno and her pregnancy, he is also allowed to remain emotionally disconnected from her and from their child. Bleeker's sense of blamelessness and his utter lack of involvement is the most realistic representation in the film, for even though our culture has traditionally declared teenage mothers disgraceful (if not immoral), such harsh judgment has never been applied to both genders. Boys like Bleeker are never mocked or denigrated if they have sex before marriage; *au contraire*, sexual experience adds to their status.

Juno does inform him early on of her pregnancy, but adds quickly that she's planning "to nip it in the bud." He replies, "Yeah, wizard, I guess. I mean do what you think is right" (10.28). Like my daughter's birthfather and like the Reverend Dimmesdale himself, Bleeker doesn't have to do anything, and it is Juno who protects him. When she visits the abortion clinic, she does so on her own. When she makes arrangements for the private adoption, it's her father who accompanies her. She even convinces Mac and Bren not to "narc [Bleeker] out to [his] folks" (62.7), and it appears that his parents never do learn of his paternity. Although Juno often seems wise beyond her years and culturally savvy, she has been thoroughly indoctrinated by an ideology that makes unplanned pregnancy a woman's or, in this case, a girl's responsibility. As Flanagan observes, "Because Juno let her guard down and had a single sexual experience with a sweet, well-intentioned boy, she alone is left with this ordeal of sorrow and public shame" (Flanagan).

When Bleeker arrives at the hospital after their son is born, he has the luxury of deciding not to see the baby because, Juno explains, "He didn't want to." Bleeker opts out of all responsibility for the pregnancy because he can. He's permitted by Juno, by Juno's parents, by the medical profession, and by the larger community to completely bypass Juno's physical and emotional ordeal. I waited (in vain) for decades for my daughter's birthfather to share with me in even the slightest way the loss of our daughter, but for me, for Juno, and for most pregnant teenagers, there are no fairy-tale princes waiting to stand by our sides and help us claim our babies. There were none for Hester in Puritan New England, none for Bernice in *Then She Found Me*, none for me, and none for Juno in contemporary America.

Even Mark, the creepy, would-be adoptive father, can shamelessly flirt with the very pregnant Juno, and then opt out of fatherhood, leaving Vanessa and their McMansion for a loft in the city shortly before the baby is to be born. Although not quite as venal as Hawthorne's Faustian Chilling-worth, Mark cynically attempts to sexually manipulate the "fallen" Juno in chilling ways. Again the film realistically depicts would-be fathers whose gender protects them from the consequences of their actions and allows them to escape easily the responsibilities of marriage and children. Only Mac accepts his responsibility for his daughter, if not for his grandchild, professing that he'll "always love and support [Juno], no matter what kind of pickle [she's] in" (90.96). He is poignantly if helplessly at her bedside after she gives birth, ready to start up a card game. But he can only offer up oblivious words of comfort: "Someday," he says, "you'll be back here, honey. On your terms" (98.111). Well-meaning but clueless, Mac fails to remember that Juno has taken responsibility for the entire pregnancy and adoption on her own unsuspecting, psychologically uninformed terms.

Bren, Mac, and Bleeker are all able to comfortably deny the reality of Juno's predicament, but it is Juno who is most dangerously in denial. Although she is described by film critics as "not only a smarty-pants but also genuinely smart and self-possessed" (*"Juno"*), a "complex human being [who is] worldly wise [and] can take care of herself" (Wiegand), she is, in fact, excruciatingly young and on treacherous ground as she denies her connection to the baby she carries. Of course, she can't deny her burgeoning stomach, the heartburn that "radiates down to [her] kneecaps" (27.47), the name-calling at school, and she does have some foggy notion that the fetus has fingernails. Nonetheless, when she sees it on the ultrasound for the first time, her response is telling: "It *is* really weird looking," she says. "It's like it's not even real" (46.63). It is unproblematic to give away something that's not "even real," but that unreality is temporary. Like Juno, I too denied the reality of the baby I carried. I anticipated that giving birth would be like having my appendix or my tonsils out and that afterward, I'd simply get well the same way that people got well after surgery. What my body was doing involuntarily seemed to have nothing to do with me.

Tellingly, when Juno shows the ultrasound picture to Vanessa, she remarks, "This is the baby. *Your* baby" (56.70; emphasis added). It's an expedient way to think, and like Juno, I was led to believe that the baby I carried did not belong to me. The babies we carry become very real and heartbreakingly precious, as Juno discovers when the doctor reveals her baby boy, and she remarks with awe, "And then, out of nowhere, there it was . . . There *he* was" (96.108). No longer an "it"; no longer something unreal, something weird, something to be denied. It bears repeating: "There *he* was."

Like Juno, who passes out after seeing her son, I too was granted unconsciousness by a tranquilizing shot, and like Juno, I awoke only to burst into "sudden, ragged sobs" (98.111). But unlike Juno, I can tell you the rest of the story, the story that Cody, Reitman, and the dominant culture repress: the years and years that followed when I would burst into "sudden, ragged sobs" as I recalled with deep, permanent regret the loss of my baby girl. I know what Cody and Reitman don't seem to understand, that when Juno denies her intimate connection to her newborn son by saying that she and Bleeker do not want to see him, that "he didn't feel like ours," her denial is a failed strategy. No matter how hard the Junos of 2008 or 1965 try not to feel and not to recall, the day they relinquish their babies will haunt them. Juno will encounter the memory over and over again: the delivery room, the precise sounds of her baby's cries, her own sobs, the image of her tiny son, so vulnerable, so perfect.

Juno's ostensibly happy, "feel good" ending is dangerously misleading for young women. By depicting Juno as untouched by her ordeal, that it is all now safely behind her, that the baby was "always [Vanessa's]" (99.114), Cody and Reitman add to an ideological environment that allows young women to think that the problem is over when the movie is over. In fact, the movie's conclusion is only the beginning of what will most likely be a life of regret and even psychological harm. *Juno* tells teenage mothers the old, tired, and disproved lie, "If you love your child you must give it up, move on with your life, and forget" (Fessler 2). In a sweeping act of historical and cultural repression, Reitman and Cody ignore the stark fact: birthmothers do not move on; they do not forget; and, especially when they misguidedly agree to closed adoptions, there is no happy ending.

The only cultural assumption that *Juno* ultimately interrogates involves Vanessa, the adoptive mother, and single parenthood. It appears that Vanessa will be an excellent adoptive, single parent. The last shot of her shows her finally able to put her type A perfectionism to rest: "For the first time ever, [she] looks disorganized, unshowered,—and incredibly happy . . . Obviously, she hasn't been away from the baby for a single moment" (99.116). Marc's departure removes any doubt about the sanguinity of this adoption. The good-hearted Vanessa, "glow[ing] with an expression of pure bliss" (99), feeds the baby and remains blind to the deception she has unwittingly been party to by "kicking it old school."

There are no poisonous adoptive parents here; the baby will never be labeled "illegitimate"; Bleeker will never suffer from irredeemable guilt; Juno may miss her prom, but she will never have to don an actual scarlet *A*. Yet the implications of the *A* have not been vanquished, only repressed under layers and layers of cultural embellishment, and Juno will not easily slip out of its embroideries. She believes the shameful lingering remnants of the *A* must be concealed—she from her child and her child from her—but the tension between disclosure and concealment has only begun. Hawthorne wrote to rescue his heroine from the injustices of the *A* (Baym 21); but rather than rescuing Juno by empowering her to embrace the experience of mothering and transmute the stigma of shame into a badge of commitment, ability, and autonomy, her creators forbid her from becoming a prophetess of a new, more enlightened age.

I cannot and will not accept *Juno*'s mythical happy ending lightly. There is (and more importantly, there will be) an unbearable loss and a burden of "life-long sorrow" (Hawthorne 201) behind Juno's carefree facade. A resilient sorrow will live on embroidered into her psyche, as it is in mine, continuing to radiate a never-to-be-fulfilled desire for reunion with the forbidden. Juno will be forever unable to erase or transcend the loss of her child. If we listen carefully to words of the song she sings and imagine her singing them to her lost son and not to Bleeker, we can already hear her sorrow and her regret:

> The pebbles forgive me, the trees
> forgive me. So why can't you
> forgive me? I don't see what anyone
> can see, in anyone else but you. (101.121)

Rather than find comfort in the film's unrealistic and idealized conclusion, we would do well to remember Hester's words when her elders try to take her Pearl away: "She is my happiness! . . . Ye shall not take her!"

There we have it: three ostensible comedies about unwed mothers. Through gutsy fortitude and feisty sense of purpose, Alison, Bernice, and Juno resolve their unwed pregnancies to arrive at "happy" endings. Alison has reformed her baby daddy into a responsible devoted father, a man with integrity, and we're led to believe they will live "happily ever after" with their beautiful bouncing baby girl. It's a nice thought. It's the ending I dreamed of and mourned for. It may actually happen sometimes, but I know it's rare. And then there's Bernice, brought to her knees, repentant and obliging. She gets to clear the table and be in the presence of her daughter and grand-daughter if she continues to behave herself. It is a reward, but it's not moth-erhood. Her place at the table will always be one that comes with conditions.

And finally, Juno. She's carried out her adoption plan. She's surrendered her son. She gets to sit on a sunny suburban porch with her more responsible, more mature, but still lovingly dopey boyfriend. By giving away her son, she gets her reward, the chance to be a teenager for a few more years. I was promised the same.

But what did I really receive by agreeing to adoption? Let's see: one more uncomfortable year in high school where pretending to be "normal" was so deceitful that I came to despise myself; then four lonely years in college when I tried hard to find my purpose, to succeed, to make my parents proud, only to continue to be plagued by my lonely self-loathing and despondency; and then another year adrift, flitting from one man to another, anyone who would show some gentle interest in me, take me out of aloneness, make me feel connected to someone, anyone. Surrendering Merideth gave me six years of unwanted and unappreciated freedom; six years of dejected absence and unappeasable lack. What a waste! What a mistake! What a regret! Then I was pregnant again! The chance to redo the past! How elated I was! How sure I was that this would be the end of my suffering. And when my son was born was something finally returned, something restored? Yes, of course, something was given back, but never her, never my lost daughter.

I wish I had known better. I wish I had been warned, dissuaded, stopped, but the happy ending myth of adoption that informs *Juno* had everyone fooled, even me. Juno thinks she has triumphed. She thinks she will be rewarded for her sacrifice. She thinks she'll be happy, adventurous, young, and free. And dangerously, so does her audience. When will the Diablo Codys and Jason Reitmans of our culture learn that the myth is false? When will they hear our stories, our sorrow, and our regret? Perhaps the myth will only be dismantled when enough of us proclaim loudly and resolutely, "She is my happiness! . . . Ye shall not take her!" Perhaps when enough of us hold tight to our newborns and step into our shadowy, uncertain futures, perhaps only then will the truly happy endings be written.

CHAPTER TWELVE

Bearing Sorrow

And so I come to my final chapter and the most recent renditions of the iconic scarlet woman. Has she changed over three hundred years of representation in the American imagination? Without a doubt. In legal, social, and cultural narratives, her successors are no longer obliged to die for succumbing to sexual desire, nor must they endure the public pillory for pregnancy outside of the patrilineal family. Unwed mothers may still have to cope with disapproval and shame, but their out-of-wedlock children no longer suffer inordinately because of their illegitimacy. Literature has accommodated transformed social practice that no longer marks children born outside of marriage as unwanted, shame-laden "bastards." Given the ideological drift away from overtly enforced punitive codes for regulating extramarital female sexuality and our more forgiving "family values," which no longer indict illegitimate children, the majority of children born out of wedlock are no longer necessary secrets and are much less likely to be surrendered to adoption. Children born out of wedlock will face the same challenges as the legion of children in contemporary America who grow up in single-parent families where the responsibilities of parenthood fall on one overburdened adult and poverty is the norm. As we have seen in the Apatow's fantasy *Knocked Up*, it is now narratively conceivable that a smart, capable, unwed mother can weather an unplanned pregnancy, give birth to a healthy baby, bring her child home with her, and raise it successfully without fear of punishment or even disapprobation. It's nice to think so.

But what happens when adoption does enter the contemporary narrative mix? Are there plotlines available that don't insist on the birthmother's concealment and relinquishment, as in *Loggerheads* and *Juno*? Or are there narratives that don't paint the returning birthmother as a damaged, intrusive outsider, as in *Girls in Trouble*, or the unseemly butt of the joke, as in *Then She Found Me*? Have writers been able to envision new narrative scripts for reconfigured family paradigms in which birthparents, adopted children, and adoptive families might coexist in sustaining and loving partnerships? In the United States, most birthmothers, like Juno and like Sarah in *Girls in Trouble*, opt to meet and choose their child's adoptive parents after reviewing dozens of photo-resumes. Unlike Juno, who thinks she wants a postbirth closed adoption, many birthmothers opt for an open adoption agreement that formalizes at least some regular contact with their child, though what these agreements can guarantee differs from state to state. Given the ongoing uptick in open adoptions, contemporary writers have been slow to create narratives in which birthparents surrender their children without also signing onto years of regret, sorrow, and loss. Likewise, I have not yet found narratives in which birthmothers actually find the freedom and restored youth they were promised after relinquishment in preadoption counseling. Is it magical thinking to anticipate narratives in which adopted children fit seamlessly into their adopted families while maintaining ties of respect, care, even love with their birthparents? Are their narrative examples of adoptive parents inviting the child's birthparents into their families without fear and envy, or must adoption always be a site of angst and conflict in the literary imagination? In this chapter, I discuss three recent narratives that take up my narrative concerns and help me begin to answer these questions. All undertake the important challenge of honestly representing the adoption triangle at the place where *Juno* left off, in the years that follow the birthmother's surrender.

RUN

In her 2007 novel *Run*, Ann Patchett takes us into the middle of a transracial adoption triangle, providing us with compelling if not fully realized characterizations of all the parties that comprise it. The birthmother in this triangle has been living with all the guilt, regret, and longing that surrender so often brings with it. The novel begins with an accident, not an accidental pregnancy but an automobile accident. Patchett uses a heavy New England snowfall to bring a seemingly unconnected cast of characters together. A black woman, Tennessee Moser, is walking through the storm with her eleven-year-old daughter, Kenya, when she sees an oncoming SUV about to hit a young black man, Tip Doyle. By pushing him out of its way, she saves his life, but she is grievously injured. After the accident, Kenya is overlooked in the mayhem. When she is finally noticed, she begs to go home with the biracial Doyle family.

Invoking the nature-versus-nurture opposition in regard to the success of the Doyle family—an adoptive family that has "worked" as it is supposed to—reviewer Janet Maslin settles on nurture, maintaining that this family is "as united by nurture as they are different by nature." Indeed, united they are. Raised by their white adoptive father, the nurturing Bernard Doyle, a widower and former mayor of Boston, Teddy and Tip, adopted biological brothers who are now college-aged, have thrived despite the death of their adoptive mother and the unhappiness of their older, adoptive white brother. In creating such a family, Margaret Homans maintains, "*Run* presents the dream of U.S. transracial adoption: that poor black children can seamlessly join well-off white families to the benefit of the children, the white parents and siblings, and even the racist world they inhabit" (40). Teddy and Tip are close to perfect, and Kenya knows a lot about them, but how? That is "the one thing [she is] never supposed to tell" (70). But with her mother rushed to the hospital and with no one else to turn to, Kenya realizes that only by telling her secret will she convince the Doyles to take her home. And so she tells: Tennessee is Tip and Teddy's birthmother. Kenya knows so much about the Doyles because Tennessee has been watching (stalking?) the Doyles for years with Kenya in tow. Her revelation works: the Doyles take her home.

Tip reacts to Kenya's secret antagonistically. Like many adoptees, he interprets Tennessee's decision to surrender her sons as abandonment. When Teddy insists that they "can't just write [her] off," he retorts: "this is . . . the woman who didn't take you home from the hospital and set me out on the curb at fourteen months, and now she's following us around for whatever reason, jealousy, regret, who knows . . . I don't have to give her a chance . . . I already did . . . I'm not interested" (95). Teddy and Tip are unbending in their loyalty to their adoptive mother, Bernadette, the seemingly requisite "angel of the house" who died when the boys were little. To be drawn to their birthmother would be betrayal. Still, Teddy is interested and concerned, and he and Sullivan decide to visit Tennessee. Heavily sedated, the birthmother is given one meager opportunity to speak for herself in the novel, and like the abject Bernadette in *Then She Found Me*, who must apologize to April on her knees for surrendering her, Tennessee uses this longed-for opportunity to speak to her son to articulate her repentance, murmuring to Teddy, "I'm sorry . . . I wish I had never let you go" (124).

Kenya knows firsthand about the remorse Tennessee has born as she has devotedly watched Teddy and Tip grow up, while Doyle, protected by an impermeable bubble of class privilege, has completely forgotten their birthmother ever existed. This changes, of course, with Kenya's disclosure, and when he takes her back to Tennessee's cramped, dim apartment in a nearby housing project to get some of her things, he shudders when he imagines what it would have been like for Tip and Teddy to grow up there, "sitting on the too soft sofa, their too long legs pressing the edges of the coffee table" (188). For Doyle and for most readers of *Run*, the cultural and educational advantages of their white, affluent upbringing far outweigh the disadvantages we assume they would have faced had they remained with their single, undereducated, working black mother. Doyle recalls when he and Bernadette would watch the little boys sleep, amazed that their "sons who were so unquestionably [theirs] could just as easily have gone to another home, a different fate." But now Doyle recognizes what he and Bernadette never admitted to one another, that Tip and Teddy "had already belonged to someone else, and they could have just as easily stayed where they were" (189). Patchett is subtly but insistently demonstrating what Eva and George of *Girls in Trouble*, Skip Cuddy in *Blessings*, Doyle in *Run*, and the general culture of adoption take for granted: the adoptive parents' rightful claim to their adopted children. Unless the adoption is open, which Leavitt demonstrates is problematic, birthparents are meant to disappear from adoptive parents' lives as thoroughly as they evaporate from their surrendered children's lives. That Tennessee has had a relation to the boys all along, hovering watchfully on the margins of their lives, is unnerving for Doyle and not "right" according to accepted adoption practice.

We are given scant explanation for why Tennessee surrendered her sons. We only know that when she had Teddy, she was eighteen and "could not take him home even though she had been planning to" (205). After relinquishing him to a closed adoption, she sees a picture of the Doyles and their newly adopted baby, her baby, in the newspaper. Now that she knows where he is, she does what she herself calls "unnatural"; she surrenders her older son as well. She explains:

I wasn't feeling so good then, and staying with me didn't sound like anything but a burden this child would have to endure. I started to tell myself that it should be all or nothing, that doing it halfway was a disservice to them both. I had an idea that Tip, he was my big boy, could look after the baby, little as he was himself. They could be together and look after each other. (207)

Her explanation is inadequate for critic Leah Hager Cohen, who is correct to point out that "as portrayed, [Tennessee's] decision . . . carries troubling implications about the maternal instincts and capacities of black women." Had Patchett explored Tennessee's circumstances more thoroughly, she might have elicited deeper respect and compassion for her. As it stands, we can only assume that driven by her own deep-seated sense of unworthiness, which is only exacerbated by the comparison that is so clear now between her circumstances and the Doyles', Tennessee decides to sacrifice both boys for their betterment: "By offering them up, and by the blind good luck of where they landed, she knew she had given them something substantial" (209). She accepts her place à la Hester and Jennie on the outskirts, and consoles herself by maintaining her vigil. Patchett further complicates matters with a contrived and unnecessary plot twist: Kenya is not, in fact, Tennessee's biological daughter. Upon the death of the "real" Tennessee Moser, our Tennessee (actually Beverly) had simply stepped into her friend's identity and taken her name and her baby daughter. As Homans points out, this added bit of information only emphasizes "the disposability of black birthmothers" (42).

Unexplored and silent to the end, Tennessee remains more symbolic than real, serving the plot as protective angel and sacrificing saint with no more depth than the Doyle family heirloom, a statue of the Virgin Mary. Not only does she sacrifice her sons so they might have an ample life, she also puts herself in front of the massive SUV that could "have hit Tip squarely in the back . . . snapping his beautiful and much beloved neck as it pushed him forward" (179). Before she can complicate what critic Janet Maslin calls "an elegant mélange of family ties," she succumbs to an undetected laceration of the spleen. Rather than modify traditional narrative trajectories concerning birthmothers, Patchett bears out cultural notions about the extraneous position and potential threat of birthmothers in the adoption triangle. Having done her part in providing two children to the Doyle household, not only must Tennessee disappear, she must die so that Kenya may also be adopted into the clan where she will not only flourish but also provide the means for Sullivan's reintegration as well.

What's most disturbing is that Tennessee's death does not diminish what is a satisfying conclusion for most readers. In all the book reviews I have consulted, only Homans sees the injustice of Patchett's plot resolution. Maslin praises the novel for its "silken agility"; Leah Cohen for its transporting beauty. Jonathan Yardley maintains, "Patchett has given this [novel] an ending that is just about perfect." John Updike suggests that "Patchett in her own niceness gives us the world as it should be." From the perspective of a birthmother, Updike's and Yardley's assertions seem especially insensitive if not cruel. A happy ending for the adoption triangle requires my demise! Rather than "perfect," Patchett has given us a predictable conclusion, a stock ending that has been employed now for centuries. Once again, for order to be restored, the birthmother must be sacrificed. How else will the Doyle's fit Kenya as seamlessly into their tribe as they did Tip and Teddy? Patchett will not, cannot add Tennessee to the Doyle family paradigm, no matter how far it has been extended. In order to tie the narrative up without the ongoing complications of a vigilant birthmother, Patchett has to stick to the narrative scripts that have paved her way. Once again, ideology confirms that the birthmother is not only the most superfluous part of the adoption triangle, but necessarily expendable if the adoptive family is to live out its happily-ever-after mythological promise.

A GATE AT THE STAIRS

One of the most recent representations of the scarlet woman occurs in *A Gate at the Stairs* by highly respected author Lorrie Moore. When the novel came out in 2009, I thought maybe this time I would find the representation of the birthmother I have been searching for, a birthmother that did not have to be exiled, or live out her life in loneliness, or die. Maybe an inventive, lyrical novelist like Moore would be able to defy the reigning narrative paradigm that damns the fallen woman. Maybe she would be able to subvert the "design paradigm" of family-making through adoption that excises the birthmother from the equation. Maybe Moore would finally do what Patchett could not: imagine a birthmother who is not only worthy of our respect but also worthy of a happy ending.

And indeed, the novel is unusual in some ways, but in its depiction of a birthmother, Moore is disappointingly true to negative stereotypes. The novel's narrator, Tassie Keltjin, a verbally acute university student at "The Athens of the Midwest" (4) who goes to work as a sitter for adopting par-

ents: the fraught but brilliant Sarah Brink and her brainy academic husband, Edward Thornwood. Prior to taking the job, Tassie has thought little
about adoption and not at all about birthmothers, who don't even register in
the adoption process as she imagines it. To her, adoption seems like "a lovely
daydream—a nice way of avoiding the blood and pain of giving birth, or
from a child's perspective, a realized fantasy of your parents not really being
your parents" (16). Tassie is involved in the adoption process from the get-
go. On the first day of her employment, she is introduced to what reviewer
Jonathan Lethem describes as "the Kafka-worthy bureaucracy of adoption
agencies and foster homes" when she accompanies Sarah to a Perkins restaurant in order to meet a prospective birthmother, Amber. Amber is young
and pretty, but she has very few teeth and wears an electronic parole bracelet.
To Tassie, she looks like "a slightly educated hillbilly or an infant freak" (33).
The adoption falls through after Amber, a coke addict and a meth-head and
thus an outrageously inappropriate mother, decides to keep her baby. As
readers, we are surely meant to shake our heads in dismay.

The next adoption opportunity involves Bonnie and her biracial baby,
Mary-Emma. Bonnie, poorly educated, disagreeable, and badly groomed, is
as unlikable as Amber. Tassie remarks, Bonnie is "not bonnie . . . She [is]
heavy . . . Her hair [is] thick and pale, the color of a wax bean, with roots of
darker doorknocker blond . . . her eyebrows [are] shaved into a thin line—
the stubble showing both above and below . . . She [looks] puffy and medi-
cated . . . [and gives] off a whiff of bacon grease and gum" (88). Bonnie agrees
to the adoption, and then, like "good" birthmothers should, she shuffles off
the stage with nothing more than a gold watch from the adopting parents,
"for which" Tassie claims, "she had traded a child" (183). "The large, imposing
dirigible of her . . . just spluttered to nothing. She was something flat and far
and stuck to the wall . . . Where would she go? What home could she possible have?" (96), asks Tassie.

Tassie's prognostications for Bonnie are limited by Moore's debasing
typecasting. When she finds a "bonniegreenbay" on eBay who has put a
gold watch up for sale, our worst assumptions are confirmed. When she
googles "Bonnie J. Crowe," only to find that a woman of that same name was
found murdered in Atlanta, she thinks, "Of course! This would be exactly
the sort thing that would happen to poor doomed Bonnie. Here she was
worried [Bonnie] was suicidal when in fact getting herself murdered would
be more her style" (183). Like Patchett's Tennessee, Bonnie must conform
to the family-making adoption paradigm and disappear. Patchett at least

grants Tennessee dignity; we value her loyalty and her sacrifice. Bonnie, on the other hand, is not only unsalvageable, she's repellent. However, she is not the monster every good narrative seems to need. Edward is.

When Mary-Emma's adoption falls through, Sarah must tell Tassie why. Their secret, what critic Ron Charles calls a "grotesque violation of taboos," makes them unacceptable as adoptive parents. They had a four-year-old son, Gabriel, who was, in Sarah's words, "a difficult child" (233). One day, while Sarah was in the car, Edward punished Gabriel by leaving him on the shoulder of the turnpike. When Gabriel tries to cross the turnpike, he is killed. Edward and Sarah are arrested; they plead guilty; their sentences are suspended; they change their names and move a thousand miles west. This information is withheld in order to adopt Mary-Emma, but when their past is uncovered, Mary-Emma is removed from their home and taken we know not where. Moore may have stayed true to form in characterizing Bonnie, but with Sarah and Edward, she obliterates the adoption myth that portrays adoptive parents as saintly do-gooders. Mary-Emma becomes the victim of Edward's selfishness and Sarah's acceptance of it.

Exploring Tassie's complicated ennui seems to be Moore's primary motivation, so the novel meanders through her unhappy affair, her inadvertent poisoning of her roommate with a puree that Sarah had made and sent home with Tassie (we're not sure why), and the death of her brother in Iraq. The novel ends disappointingly with the repugnant Edward contacting Tassie to tell her that he and Sarah have divorced and then he asks her out. Tassie responds cleverly, rewriting *Jane Eyre*'s famous closing words, "Reader, I married him," with "Reader, I did not even have coffee with him" (321). The would-be adoptive father is confirmed to be a sleazy, unforgiveable reprobate.

Years later, a wistful Tassie, admits that she remains "riveted by little girls who would be [Mary-Emma's] age," doing "a double-take every time [she sees] some dark, lively girl of three or four or five or six." She realizes that Bonnie, if not dead, must be doing the same. She imagines birthmothers, foster mothers, and would-be adoptive mothers "with their hearts seeking and beaming their futile, worthless love through the air . . . all in a line, part search party, part refugee camp." It's a poignant moment of identification.

When Tassie looked at Bonnie, all she could see was "regret—operatic, oceanic, fathomless . . . No matter which path [Bonnie] took, regret would stain her feet and scratch her arms and rain down on her, lightlessly and lifelong" (92). Bonnie is brimming with regret, as is Tennessee, as are all the birthmothers I have encountered so far on this narrative journey. Their regret is realistic; it emanates not just from their mistakes, but from their powerlessness. It represents the authentic remorse too many birthmothers must bear for life-altering decisions we were ill-equipped to make.

MOTHER AND CHILD

I turn then to the most recent rendition of the fallen woman I know, Rodrigo Garcia's film *Mother and Child*. Although some may judge Garcia's narrative as the gushy material of television daytime soap operas, I found the movie an insightfully nuanced representation of the persistent biological and psychological bonds between a mother and child. As Sarah Burns observes in her film review for the *CUB Communicator*, a newsletter published by Concerned United Birthparents, Garcia's film tells "a truth that is rarely reflected in films about adoption"; Garcia "manages to capture the essence of what adoption is all about—the separation of mother and child, and the loss that each must learn to live with" (Burns 3). Burns is a birthmother, so like me, she watched Garcia's film with firsthand empathy.

Garcia, the son of novelist Gabriel Garcia Marquez, is fascinated, observes A. O. Scott, by the "continuities and complexities in the lives and relationships of women" and he is not above the tendency to view them as "sacred and fundamentally tragic ("In a Melancholy Los Angeles"). His credits include HBO's popular *In Treatment* and *Big Love*, and the film *Nine Lives*. And, as Burns points out, Garcia did his homework to learn about adoption by reading "memoirs and stories about young unmarried women who were forced to relinquish their children during what has come to be known as the 'Baby Scoop' era of the 1950s and 1960s" (3), that time in history when 80% of infants born to single mothers were placed for adoption as opposed to 4% in 1983 (Brozinsky 297). Garcia's effort to become knowledgeable about the buried broken hearts that undergird the adoption triangle is evident, but he goes farther than that. He also gives us an accurate account of birthmothers' enduring sorrow that emanates from the calamity called surrender.

When I first read "Mourning and Melancholia," I knew immediately that Freud was describing my own melancholy, my irresolvable, recurring dejection, my enduring devotion to my lost "love object," my first baby girl. And he was right about something else, that alter ego which first descended on me with oppressive wrath when I returned to that gray room at Florence

Crittenton without my baby. Freud distinguishes melancholia from "normal" mourning when grief is accompanied by a fall in self-esteem: "In grief the world becomes poor and empty; in melancholia it is the ego itself [which becomes poor and empty]. The patient . . . expects to be cast out and chastised" (127). Unknowingly practicing my own version of melancholia, I emerged from Florence Crittenton plagued by self-loathing, expecting rejection and chastisement yet desperate to please. In *Mother and Child*, Márquez gives us a birthmother much like me. Karen, a forty-nine-year-old woman, has never fully recovered from her trauma-laden loss after relinquishing her infant daughter many years earlier. The film opens with three flashbacks: a brief glimpse at sexual intimacy between Karen at fourteen and Tom, the birthfather; a quick look at pregnant teenagers sitting around a room that looks eerily like the TV room from my Florence Crittenton; and last, Karen, still a child, giving birth. These are the nightmare scenes that still haunt Karen thirty-seven years later. She has never married and still lives at home, caring for her aging mother. Her past has never been declared resolved and finished. Rather she holds steadfastly to her lost baby girl; her past remains steadfastly alive in her present, harassing her, isolating her, and leaving her angry, resentful and wary.

But rather than pathological and negative, Karen's melancholia might serve as a revealing touchstone for social truth. In their collection *Loss: The Politics of Mourning*, David Eng and David Kazanjian provide a lens for seeing loss from a counterintuitive perspective, and it is through their lens that I want to read the film as deeply political as well as creatively insightful. Karen's loss, my loss, and the losses of millions of unwed mothers and birthmothers can be "melancholically materialized" (Eng 5). Rather than remote and idiosyncratic, their stories of loss can productively enter social, cultural, political, and aesthetic domains. No longer dismissed as pathologically bereft, their stories can bear witness and as such, do real work in the present to bring about social change in supporting unwed mothers, their babies, and reforming adoption practices to eliminate the potentially traumatic catastrophe of surrender. Indeed, Freud himself recognizes that those who suffer from melancholia have a "keener eye for the truth than other people who are not melancholic" (128).

But Garcia's film focuses not only on Karen; it intertwines with Elizabeth, Karen's surrendered daughter, and Lucy, who, unable to conceive, is seeking to adopt a baby through the same Catholic Services office that handled Elizabeth's adoption years earlier. In so doing, Garcia represents the entire adoption triangle: the birthmother (and tangentially, the birth-father), the adopted child, and the adopting parents. Adoption has been no healthier for Elizabeth than it has been for Karen. Like her birthmother, she is isolated, angry, and guarded. A highly capable lawyer, she has recently returned to Los Angeles, where she was surrendered for adoption and where she suspects her birthmother still lives. Elizabeth purposefully ended her relationship with her adopted mother long ago; in fact, she herself picked out the name Elizabeth when she was in high school. But changing her name and eschewing her adoptive family has not soothed her demons. Whether because of a recurring fear of abandonment or an unrelenting need for control, Elizabeth maintains a punishing, adamantine shell that guards her against anything and anyone that might exacerbate her long-standing psychological wounds.

Karen is a more-than-difficult woman. She is cold, suspicious, and often offensively outspoken. She has constructed a prickly shell that keeps her inaccessible, unlikable, and, therefore, friendless as a way of coping with her own war wounds. As Freud predicts for the melancholic, both Karen and Elizabeth have succeeded, "in taking revenge, by the circuitous path of self-punishment" (132). Karen has been writing to her daughter since her birth, and we hear excerpts from the journal when she writes things like "You will forgive me." Karen and Elizabeth have fashioned a kind of emotional armor that keeps them bitter and unfulfilled. Nonetheless, persistent men enter their lives. Paco, a sweet, sensitive, working-class man, manages to get past Karen's armor. On their first date, Karen confesses her scarlet history, telling him about her lost child and her broken life:

> I don't know where she is. I don't know who she is. Everything I do, every thought in my head, takes me back to her. Everywhere I go, I look for her face in the crowd. I write her letters I never send. I buy her birthday gifts. I have a name for her—Rachel. I don't know if she's dead or alive. I have nothing else. That's who I am. I have nothing to give.

Karen's long-lasting melancholia is not that extraordinary. For me, for Sarah Burns, and for thousands of birthmothers like us, Karen's long-standing anguish is validating and true. We never recovered from surrendering our babies; we did not "move on" with our lives. Karen's experience is the more authentic outcome of loss that cannot be recovered.

Many men would say something clumsy and make a quick exit after

Karen's confession, but Paco hears her out, falls in love, and persuades her to marry him. Though Karen's sorrow cannot be assuaged, she follows a path similar to mine in search of at least some measure of redemption. Paco urges Karen to search for her daughter, observing, "Whatever happens when you meet, it will be easier than this thing that's eating away at you." When he asks her what her biggest fear is, Karen, hounded by guilt, expects brutal rebuke: "She will spit in my face." When Paco's grown daughter also urges her to search, noting wisely, "Find her now, before time runs out. After that, only regret remains and regret is a killer," Karen decides to act and takes a letter to the Catholic Services agency that had handled adoption.

Elizabeth, in turn, has an affair with Paul, a black man, and, simultaneously, with Stephen, her married, white neighbor. Even though she had attempted to insure her lifelong isolation by having her tubes tied at seventeen, she finds herself pregnant. Surprisingly, she decides to see the pregnancy through without telling either of the possible fathers. The pregnancy changes Elizabeth. She tells Violet, a young girl who befriends her, that although she used to be angry with her birthmother, "Now that anger just washed out of me." Violet urges Elizabeth to search for her mother, and Elizabeth complies by composing a letter that she delivers to the same Catholic agency. She writes:

> I don't want to impose myself on you. I don't want to be a nuisance. I am pregnant. I'd like my baby to know where she came from. If we were to meet, I think we should look forward—not back—and build something new. My name is Elizabeth. I think of you often.

Elizabeth and Karen are tentative, fearful of imposing on one another, and terrified of rejection, yet the steps they each take toward each other are potential lifesavers. With no access to her family medical history, Elizabeth has entered her pregnancy without knowing she has a deadly bleeding disorder. In this way, Garcia incorporates in his story line not only the psychological damages that occur because of closed adoptions but also the physiological hazards involved.

Lucy, the third member of the adoption triangle, builds a close relationship with a young, pregnant girl, Ray, "a meaner Juno" (Scott "In a Melancholy"), who is planning to relinquish the baby she carries. She has chosen Lucy and her husband, Joseph, to be her baby's adoptive parents. When Joseph bows out of their marriage because he wants his biological child,

Ray has no compunctions about agreeing to Lucy adopting the baby as a single parent. In this story strand we get to see the indifference some young, unmarried girls like Ray have about motherhood. Ray will not listen to her mother when she tries to persuade her to keep her baby. She tells Ray that even though she once thought she didn't want to keep Ray, now, she confesses, "I can't take a breath without thinking of you and wanting the best for you." Ray's mother is not unusual; mothers who call off their adoption plans and keep their babies may find themselves burdened by responsibility, but they are rarely regretful. Rather, the regret descends on the mothers who must surrender. Expecting to escape the shame, guilt, and uncertainties of unwed motherhood, girls like Karen and me find instead that those emotions take up permanent residency in their lives. Ray is spared lifelong regret. Her maternal indifference transforms unexpectedly and ferociously into intense maternal desire once her baby is born. She does not relinquish her motherhood.

Lucy is crushed as this adoption narrative turns into one of "winners and losers," a heartbreaking game in which "winner takes all": a baby. Having already psychologically and emotionally claimed the "winnings," Lucy "loses" in the last inning and not with grace. Security guards have to drag her away from Ray's hospital door as she screams hysterically over and over, "My fucking baby! It's mine!" It's impossible to justify such an unbearable catastrophe. Yet scenarios such as this one play out frequently, and, sadly, when a birthmother changes her mind, her decision is too often regarded as selfish and irresponsible. Lucy does slowly regain her equilibrium after her loss and resignedly tells her mother, "The adoption thing is just so unnatural." In many ways, she is right; it was a mistake for her to think of Ray's baby as already hers, though I have known adoptive parents who have done likewise. I was taken aback when a colleague proudly showed off his soon-to-be baby, an infant girl in a Chinese orphanage, by making her photograph his screensaver. And I was genuinely sorry for him and his wife when that adoption fell through after the baby's birthmother returned to the orphanage to reclaim her daughter. I kept my uncalled-for admiration of the birthmother's bravery a secret when he told me of her return. In this game of "winners and losers," I had been rooting for the wrong side. Still, even though I know that words like "natural" and "unnatural" are indeed problematic in these days of social construction, I also know that relinquishing a baby is unnatural for the body. When I surrendered my daughter, my body was made to do something "unnatural," and it rebelled by producing what felt like buckets of breast milk, despite several injections to "dry it up." There was so much milk that even after I bound my swollen breasts in layers and layers of gauze, it soaked through the gauze, through my nightgown, through the sheets, through the mattress pad, and into the mattress of my narrow bed at Florence Crittenton. I was asking my body to repudiate a bond that it would not refuse. The bond remained, but since my child and I could not be physically rejoined, the link was one-sided, leaving me with swollen breasts, nothing to feed, and a maternal yearning with nothing to satisfy. Like a dangling ghost limb that never stopped throbbing, the unattached link, both body and mind, festered for years, a severance whose pain never receded. Marquez's film reiterates my experience by representing adoption as "a catastrophe—a tear in the fabric of the natural order" (Scott "In a Melancholy).

When Elizabeth's letter for Karen is misfiled and Elizabeth needlessly bleeds out on the delivery table, the injustice done to these women to protect a closed adoption is made undeniable. Not only is Elizabeth dead, there is also no family of record, no one to claim her healthy baby girl. The same Catholic adoption agency that had overseen Elizabeth's adoption now makes arrangements for her baby's adoption. When the nun in charge, Sister Joanne, approaches Lucy, who is still recovering from losing Ray's baby, she tries to allay Lucy's doubts and fears by telling her: "Sometimes there is nobody and this is one of those times. There is no one." But we know there are others. There is Paul, who is unmistakably this baby's father, a kind man who would have wanted his baby girl if Elizabeth's phobic secrecy had not kept him from knowing he had fathered her. And there is Karen, the baby's grandmother, who has been waiting a lifetime for her child and would surely have wanted her grandchild. But Elizabeth's baby goes to Lucy, who we cannot blame. She has the best intentions. She is a responsible, highly capable woman, mature and materially secure. She will be an excellent parent, and yet there is something so sad, so unjust, so haphazard about the paths that were not crossed, the painful links that remained severed.

The narrative moves us one year into the future when Sister Joanne finally finds Elizabeth's misfiled letter and contacts Karen, only to tell her that her daughter is dead. Karen is understandably devastated. The daughter she had been keeping alive in her journal all these years is gone. She will never know her. The same misguided adults who thought it best to take her baby away from her had carelessly misplaced the one link that could have reunited them and possibly have saved Elizabeth's life. There is no way to correct their mistakes, no way to recover what is lost. The only glimmer of hope comes from Lucy, who agrees to let Karen meet her granddaughter, Ella.

When Sister Joanne tells Karen where Lucy and Ella live, all she can do is laugh, for although Karen has been separated from her daughter by decades of guilt and secrecy, her granddaughter lives right down the street. Karen can see Lucy's house from hers. Although a cliché, the notion of "something so close yet so far away" is here poignant and apt.

They meet and Karen is grateful and moved. She tells Paco, "[Ella] has my mother's eyes." There seems to be some measure of redemption here. Karen has been given a future that promises love, perhaps even surcease from the melancholia that has encumbered her for so long even as it has granted her that "keener eye for the truth." I want to take her final words in the film as Eng and Kazanjian suggest, as "insistently creative and deeply political" (23). Their significance is instructive if we are willing to hear and acknowledge them, especially in discourse communities like the one that spawned *Juno* in which surrender and adoption are represented as emotionally benign and socially beneficial. We need a counterdiscourse, and Karen gives us just that when she turns again to her journal and resumes writing to Elizabeth. Hers are words that everyone in the adoption triangle should hear, the words that should have ended *Juno*, the words that our culture must begin to hear if we are going to remedy the unrelenting sorrow that comes with the separation of mother and child. Poignantly and truthfully, Karen makes a compelling case for rethinking surrender, for opening adoptions, and for unsealing adoption records. She writes:

> I never saw you with a new haircut. I never saw you with new shoes. When was your first period? Was someone there to help? Did anyone explain? Did you hear the rain one night when I heard it? What gave you comfort? I've missed it all and I've accepted it. But today I met Ella. Her little face is like a bird that flies high over thirty-eight years that have gone on and on and on like a horrible parade. But now it's past. Only Ella remains. God bless her. Ella is peace.

Perhaps, as she claims, Karen has arrived at acceptance. Elizabeth is lost. That will not change. Her death brings the "horrible parade" to an end, and now there is Ella, Karen's hard-earned gift, her measure of peace at the end of the long and sorrowful journey. We presume that Lucy will consent to a new configuration of extended family, one that will include Karen and Paco, one within which Karen may find a more loving and fortunate path to follow. But a happy ending? Not really.

Karen falls asleep looking longingly at the two pictures Elizabeth included in her letter to her—one of Elizabeth as a child and one taken on the day she wrote the letter. In this scene, Garcia maintains his tragic tone, as he should. Realistically, there can be no unqualified happy ending for a mother who loses her child. Garcia himself observes: "This is a story about two people who missed each other's lives, who were longing for each other, who were trying to connect." But like so many, they are denied that connection. Ella, the welcomed, highly desired, illegitimate child carries no stigma. Instead she is a bird of hope, a gift of redemption, a luminous pearl that marks a new beginning for Lucy and for Karen in a happier, more sustaining future. We can heal. Nonetheless, Karen will never completely shed her punishing grief. Her loss will persist, especially now that it must accommodate her daughter's irrevocable death.

To some extent, Patchett, Moore, and Marquez have liberated their unwed mothers and their illegitimate children from the damning moral implications our Puritan ancestors intended. The scarlet *A* is no longer literally affixed as a humiliating reminder, but has its symbolic presence been eradicated or made innocuous? Not yet. The unwed mother may no longer be cast out or chastised; nonetheless her maternity still carries insistent and painful emotional penalties. In all of these narratives, as in life, Tennessee, Bonnie, Karen, and Elizabeth are defeated by desperation, disgrace, secrecy, and helplessness. They remain unable to intervene effectively in the lives of the children they bear. Perhaps most shockingly, given that these narratives are written in the twenty-first century rather than the eighteenth, unwed motherhood is deadly. That Karen survives, finds love, and is reunited with her granddaughter creates s a hopeful swerve in the narrative trajectory of the fallen woman, but the futures of Tennessee, Elizabeth, and possibly Bonnie are still resolved by death. Has my quest for the empowered unwed mother proved futile? I want her to be capable; I want her to be heroic. But that narrative is yet to be written.

Conclusion

When I began this book, I had an idea of how it would turn out. I anticipated following a red thread through the elaborate and wide-ranging tap-
estry of the American literary tradition, the thread used to embroider the
stories of fallen women from the earliest novels to some of the most recent
novels and film. I would interrogate the past even as I took up an urgent
search for new literary texts that would serve as models, as instruction, and
as inspiration. Confident about the future, I was certain that when I reached
the end of that search, the dark eighteenth-century embroideries of seduced
women would have been supplanted by dazzling re-embroidered heroines.
Rather than fallen and helpless exiles, I would locate confident, capable,
twenty-first-century feministas, flaunting their scarlet, sexual munificence.
The deep-rooted "master narrative," the ancient seduction plot with its pre-
ordained tragic outcome for all "ruined maids," would be banished from the
literary tradition, replaced by transgressive narratives that would subvert the
repressive patterns of the past. In that embroidered space where ideology
meets narrative, where progressive values meet twenty-first-century creativity, the constricting parameters of female sexuality and permissible maternity
would be subverted, replaced by defiant writers and heroic action.

My book has not turned out as I planned. In search of defiant Persephones, no longer sentenced to time in hell, and creative endings, no longer
restricted to exile or death, I came instead to the repetition of the stubbornly
embedded script of the fallen woman. Rather than following the glimmer-
ing red thread to expressive, lustrous possibility and inventive renditions of
scarlet women, unwed mothers, and birthmothers who finally seize their
rightful place as empowered, autonomous heroes, I found the proverbial
plot: fallen women still ensnared in Persephone's narrative trap. According

to Rachel Blau DuPlessis, "narrative may function on a small scale the way that ideology functions on a large scale . . . To compose a work is to negotiate with these questions: What stories can be told? How can plots be resolved? What is felt to be narratable by both literary and social conventions?" (3). The stories and plot resolutions I expected to find in contemporary American fiction are unwritten. In narrative structure, the place where, DuPlessis maintains that "ideology is coiled" (5), sexually transgressive women continue to be feared, condemned, and killed. Apparently, the underpinnings of the old plot have never been seriously threatened.

But I was not only interested in the transformation of the fallen woman's "master narrative" in the literary tradition. This was also a personal undertaking: I was interrogating my own past, my own self-identification as a "ruined maid," and my own scarlet stigma that I had worn for so long. In *A Room of One's Own*, Virginia Woolf had provided me a way to proceed:

> [The mind] can think back through its fathers or through its mothers, as I have said that a woman writing thinks back through her mothers. Again if one is a woman one is often surprised by a sudden splitting off of consciousness . . . when from being the natural inheritor of that civilization, she becomes, on the contrary, outside of it, alien and critical. (97)

If I could think back through my literary sisters, as a woman writing thinks back through her literary mothers, I might find a way to "split off" from the shame and self-reproach I had "naturally" inherited from dominant, patrilineal "civilization." By following the historical literary path of unwed motherhood and illegitimacy, I anticipated reaching a higher psychosexual ground, one that would allow a firmer foothold from which to survey not only the intricate embroideries of my fictional scarlet sisters, but also the entwined crimson threads of my own conflicted narrative of unwed motherhood. My creative practice became what Raymond Williams refers to as an "active struggle for new consciousness . . . a struggle at the roots of the mind—not casting off an ideology . . . but confronting hegemony in the fibres of the self" (Williams 212). My struggle would require that I confront the hegemony of the disgraced girl who had long ago been woven into the fibers of my identity. By engaging in this active struggle, I would finally snip the threads of the obstinate scarlet *A* I bore and repudiate shame and regret forever.

And what of the actual results of this personal, autobiographical quest? By thinking back through my scarlet sisters, have I been able to gain a critical purchase outside ideology and creatively intervene in the narrative of my own life? Well yes, in part.

My qualified "yes" requires explanation and once again, I return to *The Scarlet Letter*, the novel that set me on my journey in the first place. At its conclusion, Hawthorne underscores the always evolving nature of the scarlet *A* with the words on Hester Prynne's tombstone, "on a filed, sable, the letter *A*, gules [*heraldry red*]." Hester has so thoroughly embraced the *A* that she wears it even after death. We might assume from this ending that Hester has not been able to break the established sequence for unwed mothers: fall, exile, death. But I would argue that hers is not the punishing erasure of the irredeemable fallen woman, but simply the inevitable, natural death that awaits us all at the close of a life well lived. Hester has defied ignominy, turned her marginal status to social advantage, and actively achieved heroic status. She does not remove the *A*; she refashions it, embroidering it into an expressive badge of possibility, investing it with courage, resilience, capability, creativity, and compassion, and ultimately transforming its scandalous implications into heraldic dignity.

I know now that I cannot remove the symbolic *A* I donned at sixteen. I was so young when I took it up, so unformed, that it sits, to use Williams's words, "at the roots of my mind." Nonetheless, I have reached a higher ground, a place where Hester, my literary sister/mother, still serves as my guide. At sixteen, I could not be as heroic as she and claim my daughter as she claims Pearl. That defeat can never be set right. But I can follow Hester's example when it comes to the scarlet *A*. I can refashion the *A* I bear by embroidering it with self-awareness, knowledge, and conscientiousness. I can draw from its creative energy rather than allow it—as I know it can—to diminish, stifle, and shame me. Like Karen at the conclusion of *Mother and Child*, I have achieved a peace of a kind.

Culturally, the *A* remains a powerful symbol, but here likewise, its creative potential can be put to good use. By repudiating its destructive power and instead artistically re-embroidering the supple narrative threads it makes available, we can escape the terms of the "master narrative" it has served for so long. As DuPlessis suggests, we can "write beyond the ending." As Hélène Cixous recommends, we can "take pleasure . . . in changing around the furniture, dislocating things and values, breaking them all up, emptying structures, and turning propriety upside down" (1651–52). The indomitable *A* still demands our respect, but it no longer need reiterate or enforce the old laws governing female sexuality. By producing alternative rather than acquiescent narratives, by generating stories of transgressive women who defy the conventional scripts for fallen women, the scarlet *A*, on a field, embroidered, can beckon with passionate promise.

The new narratives and new endings for women who fly in the face of sexual convention are waiting to be told, and they are already being lived. I regularly meet young women who are defying the status quo. They are my students. Take Kristen. She was sixteen when she gave birth to her daughter, Summer, and although her divorced mother and father, who had been on bad terms for years, had joined forces to insist she make an adoption plan, Kristen refused, even after both warned: "Don't expect to come back home with a baby." She admits her refusal wasn't backed by a firm belief that she could raise Summer on her own. Rather, she trusted Summer's birthfather, also sixteen at the time. He promised that as soon as he got a steady job, they would get their own place; they would marry; they would be a family. Kristen says that giving birth to Summer was the hardest thing she has ever done, especially because her mother wouldn't stay in the delivery room with her and went instead to a bar after dropping her off at the hospital. But Kristen loves to tell the following part of the story: "Right after Summer was born, they gave her to me and her eyes were wide open. I was scared because she wasn't crying. She was peaceful, taking it all in. Then she looked up at me. Our eyes met and her tiny fingers curled around one of mine. I could hear her saying 'I'm yours. You're mine. I'm yours. You're mine.' After that, the thought of giving her to anyone else—well that was unthinkable." Promising that it would only be temporary, she went home with Summer to her reluctant, disapproving mother. Five years later she still lives with her mom. Summer's father broke up with her a few weeks after Summer was born, and Kristen says she was surprised how little that mattered to her. She was so head-over-heels in love with Summer that his rejection was beside the point. Although he begrudgingly pays a meager amount of child support, Kristen has to work evenings as a restaurant hostess to make ends meet.

You might very well ask, how is Kristen's story a defiant rewrite of the "master narrative"? Let me try to explain. Kristen has never, not once, regretted her decision to keep Summer. In fact, the mention of an "adoption plan" still makes her shudder and her mother cringe, for it's not just Kristen who loves Summer. Her mother fell in love with her granddaughter and, says Kristen, "Thanks God everyday that I brought Summer home." Summer is part of a large extended family that was once intractably divided. Now doting grandparents, aunts, and uncles gather more peacefully than Kristen can ever remember to celebrate Summer's birthdays, attend her school programs, cheer her on at her swim meets, and smile approvingly as she tears into her Christmas presents. With her mother's and grandmother's help, Kristen graduated from high school, and now she maintains a 4.0 GPA at my university. She plans to be an English teacher. She goes on occasional dates, but she says the men she meets are "either immature, or possessive, or both." She'd like to have another child someday, but she's not sure she'll ever marry. She knows that a marriage license is not a prerequisite to loving and fulfilling motherhood. When she read *The Scarlet Letter* in my class, she identified with Hester, though she insists she has never felt the presence of an oppressive scarlet *A*. She knows other kids at her high school talked about her during her pregnancy and she was embarrassed, but once she had Summer, that all disappeared and now she only feels proud of Summer and of herself. She identifies with Hester because she kept her Pearl. She knows what it's like to stand up to the elders and said, "You shall not take her!"

There are others. Jennie, Rain, Patricia, and Samantha. All are unwed mothers. Jennie's journey has been especially hard because she slipped into postpartum depression after giving birth to her baby girl, Jordan. Her family found the psychological and material support she needed, and gradually she emerged from her depression and, as she puts it, "never looked back." She graduated from UNCW last spring and landed her dream job working for an environmental consortium. Rain will be receiving her university diploma in May with her six-year-old son, Brendan, her family, and her fiancé hooting and hollering in the bleachers. She's planning her wedding—not to Brendan's father—but to the man she knows she can build a stable future for Brendan and the other children she looks forward to having. Samantha graduated a couple of years ago and got a job as a journalist in Raleigh; she recently contacted me to tell me that her son, Gabriel, just turned ten and that she's decided to apply to Ph.D. programs at Duke, Chapel Hill, and Greensboro and hopes I will recommend her. Patricia and her son Julian continue to live with her large family, but it's an arrangement that suits them all. Patricia writes, "There was a time I thought leaving the house that I share with seven other people in my family would be okay. The fact is that my family helps to keep me sane, even if they drive me insane sometimes . . . I know a lot of reality shows right now put a spotlight on all the bad a child brings [to an unwed mother], but in my case it is exactly the opposite . . . When I had my baby, I didn't give up on life. I just had to find a way to change a little." Each of these courageous young women has defied the "master narrative" of the fallen woman. Following their own unique paths, they defied expectations, embraced motherhood and responsibility, and pursued their educations with diligence, curiosity and commitment.

But there is one thing they all have in common, perhaps the necessary ingredient to happy endings for unwed mothers. They were not exiled. Although Kristen's mother threatened not to let her through the door if she came home with a baby, she did take her in and has never been sorry she did. Each of these girls had a safety net, a family that gave them and their babies the very basics—food and shelter—until they could become the independent women they wanted to be. Which leads me to the birthmothers I know, the women who were exiled to the homes of distant relatives or maternity homes and were told they had no option but to surrender their babies.

One of them, Mary Anne, came across a copy of her surrender paper and was surprised, she writes, "by the visceral distaste I still feel towards that paper. I don't like to touch it, read it, or see it . . . I think I lost it for so long because I really hate it, and what it represents, my utter defeat and capitulation that led to the loss of my son whom I should have brought home and raised." Even though Mary Anne has long been reunited with her son and reunion has brought peace and eased much of the pain, she still lives with some defeat and regret. And then there's Stephanie, who knew she couldn't surrender her baby completely and opted for an open adoption, thinking that would soothe the pain of separation. Although she sees her teenage daughter, Elianna, regularly, the relationship is fraught. Elianna has not forgiven Stephanie for relinquishing her, and she resents her half sister, Sophia, the baby girl Stephanie kept. Stephanie can't "see much of a happy ending for [herself]." When she writes about surrendering Elianna, her voice brims with ineluctable remorse: "All I knew is the world didn't think I'd be good enough. Now, I understand more about the importance of that credential that I had, even at seventeen, that nobody else did. I was her mother. We were like one another. I understand her. And my biological imperative was to keep her, hold her to me, care for her . . . I can find no redemption." And there's Connie, who was joyfully reunited with her daughter, Melinda, eighteen months ago, only to find "that the reality of what I lost thirty-six years ago is more painful than ever. When my parents sent me away at seventeen to have Melinda and relinquish her, I became withdrawn and pretty much tried to avoid anything that would make me remember that time in my life. Since finding Melinda, I have had much happiness, but also the sadness with the realization of knowing that I will never get those childhood years back." And then there is Sarah, who, like me, has made a kind of peace with herself after years of "attending lots of meetings about adoption, and learning, learning, learning and reading, reading, reading." Reunited with the son she surrendered, she knows there's no promise of a happy ending, but she and her son try every day for one. They are "very honest and open" with one another. They argue, and fight, and cry, and promise "never to leave each other's lives again." She writes, "I hope we can both keep that promise and I know we try our best."

Long ago, we surrendered our babies forever. We lived for years with regret, uncertainty, shame, and sorrow. We dreamed of them: their first tooth, their first steps, their first day of kindergarten, their first cold, their first love. We cringed when we let ourselves imagine cruel, unloving adoptive parents, or locked hearts we could not soften, or stinging slaps we could not prevent. We rued the childhood hurts we could not mend and the adolescent tragedies we could not ameliorate. We secretly acknowledged each birthday. We gazed surreptitiously at babies, children, teenagers, adults their age. We imagined their graduations and their weddings. We dreamed of the day they would return to us. There would be a tentative knock on the door. We'd run to open it, and there they would stand with their shy, hopeful faces turned up to us. We waited for a long time. We believed that would be our happy ending.

And, in a way, that day came. We gazed lovingly into their beautiful, open faces. We were restored to one another. We were jubilant. We were giddy. We were forgiven. We thought we forgave ourselves. We thought we were healed. We thought the past was vanquished. But we were surprised by our new fears. Did they approve of us? Were they angry with us? Could they love us? Would they reject us? We wooed our children like we would woo a lover. We sent the sentimental cards and over-the-top gifts we had been waiting to send for decades. We redecorated our guest rooms and prepared lavish meals. We overcompensated for years of silence. We couldn't give enough. We asked for too much. We imagined we heard a hint of irritation in their voices. We drew back. We tried not to call too often. We were grateful for small things. We were unappeasable. We were unprepared when our longing resumed. We were frustrated when our regret persisted. We were shocked when our sorrow returned. Our happy endings dissolved. We still wanted the past.

I have come to my conclusion: there can be no unequivocal happy ending for mothers who surrender. The deed cannot be reversed. The baby cannot be restored. The longing cannot be assuaged. The adult child may lovingly return, but the first loss and the deep-seated sorrow at the roots of our being will not be mollified. And yet birthmothers can be and are heroic. We brave-ly, resolutely lead productive lives. We struggle to define ourselves against the demeaning stereotypes of scarlet women and in defiance of the "master narrative" that would brand, punish, or banish. Many of us are adoption activists. We know all too well the coercive forces at play when it comes to "choosing" adoption. We have experienced firsthand the dramatic economic and racial inequalities that continue to compromise adoption practices. We work for a day when young, unprepared girls will never have to surrender their babies. Stephanie speaks for all of us:

> I look towards a future in which culture can collaborate more, live more communally, not just for the benefit of the environment but for us— humans too. "It takes a village," right? Not just one girl or even one woman and one man. I imagine a world in which extended families col-laborate to raise children, to eat, to make money, to contribute to society, to have fun.

Behind Stephanie's utopia stands an argument for family preservation and support rather than adoption, but her vision does not have to be utopian. Her villages exist. They have nurtured the young unwed mothers I know and admire, the girls who kept their babies because they could, because they had a village. Their villages included parents, grandparents, aunts, uncles, social services, churches, educational institutions, and friends who came to-gether to help them raise their children. Their villages recognized maternal rights and encouraged motherly responsibility, but not at the expense of in-dividual aspirations. They provided a home, where everything starts, from which every hero emerges.

When I was a girl growing up on Winthrop Road in a "protected" village of wealth and privilege, I was allowed to wander on my own throughout our neighborhood as long as I remained within earshot of my mother's call. I can still hear her voice, ringing through the twilight, calling me home: "Jaaaaaaa-net. Jaaaaaa-net. Time to come ho-ome." But when I wandered too far afield and fell into the seduction plot, all homecomings were cancelled. I was one of "the girls who went away," beyond my mother's call. My baby and I were both exiled, she to another home forever; me to another "home" temporar-ily, until I was fit to return. With little deviation, we are socialized to follow the "master narrative" of the fallen woman and the illegitimate child, and although my daughter escaped the burden of shame and regret, I bore its indefatigable weight, waiting long and hard for her to find me and come home. When I unexpectedly found her instead, I feared she would close the door I cautiously approached and send me away, back into exile and loss; but she didn't. In a healing plot reversal of "the girls who went away," she invited me home. When I got to her door, she welcomed me in.

I live in my own village now. It's a disparate but inclusive arrangement founded on love and connections that will never again be severed. Its core is a melded, nuclear family that is complemented by a far-ranging, extended family, by nearby friends and friends far away, by fellow activists and fellow teachers, and by hundreds of committed students who have taught me as much as I have taught them. I write for all of them, but my book ends with a wish for unwed mothers everywhere: May you never know exile, may you rewrite the limiting scripts of family structure, may you successfully challenge debasing female stereotypes, may you defy outdated social codes, may you create new paradigms, and, most of all, may you always come home.

Notes

Introduction

1. Today rare copies of the first edition can be found for sale for up to $20,000.

2. In 1850, Hawthorne himself wrote out of a tumultuous period in America marked by the egregious Fugitive Slave Act, an example of the omnipresent reach of slavery even in Hawthorne's North. But Hawthorne himself was not a thoroughgoing progressive. Indeed, he was highly skeptical of abolitionists, likening them to "the terrorists of France . . . hell-bent on chaos" (qtd. in Bercovitch 353). As he wrote *The Scarlet Letter*, the first Women's Rights Convention was held at Seneca Falls, and the suffrage movement was beginning to foment, but Hawthorne's ambivalence about women who "stand up" to authority was made bitterly clear when he referred to ambitious women writers as a "damned mob of scribbling women." Even so, given the influence of women he admired such as Margaret Fuller, he created one of the most adamant female characters in American fiction to face down moral absolutism.

3. Although Hawthorne seems clearly under the influence of Romantics like Rousseau and Wordsworth, critics are divided. Darrel Abel maintains that Hester "typifies romantic individualism" (180), while Nina Baym insists that "almost nothing she does . . . can be labeled as an example of romantic individualism" (53).

4. In her recent novel *Hester*, Paula Reed tells the story of Hester's years away, years in which she takes off the scarlet *A* but is still ruled by it. In London, she is dragooned by Oliver Cromwell into using her psychic powers to identify conspirators, but when he sends them to the Tower to be tortured and hanged, she joins the traitors' cause to return Charles II to the throne. Pearl, a beautiful, unashamed free-thinker, refuses to repress her sexuality. When she becomes pregnant out of wedlock, Hester uses her friendship with the reinstated king to secure Pearl's marriage. Reed accounts for Hester's return to New England by having Hester decide that the only way to rid herself of her "terrible sight" (295) is to put back on the *A* and expiate her sins, which now include absence, abandonment, admission, arrogance, absorption, and ambivalence (291). As in

Hawthorne's romance, Hester takes up her needle and her good works. When young women seek her out for advice and commiseration, Reed's more defeated and less defiant Hester places the blame for their despair on patriarchy, telling them, "We have been taught too long and too well the lie that the gift of ourselves is poor and unworthy. We have come to believe it, and this lie taints every honest feeling, every true thing we do" (303). In this ultimately unsatisfying rendering, the rebellious Pearl is tamed and contained by the ideology Hester laments, and Hester lives out her days anticipating her reunion with Dimmesdale at "the gates of hell" (306).

5. Although Bloom's model is "intensely (even exclusively) male" and for some feminist critics "offensively sexist" (Gilbert and Gubar 47), the construct is useful for my purposes. As I examine the repetitions and revisions of the seduction plot, I follow Adrienne Rich's example of "seeing with fresh eyes, of entering . . . old [texts] from a new critical direction," always aware that literature affects "how we have been led to imagine ourselves, how our language has trapped as well as liberated us; how we can begin to see—and therefore live—afresh" (Rich 18).

6. In his theoretically significant book *Symbolism and American Literature*, Charles Feidelson maintains that the A, "accreted by generations who have lived with it and in it, is continuous in time" (9). I have taken Feidelson perhaps more seriously than he ever anticipated or intended.

7. The term "birthmother" is used in this work to describe women who surrender their children. The term is now in serious question among women who have surrendered a child or children, a portion of whom prefer "first mother" or just "mother." I have taken my cue from the international organization Concerned United Birthparents, which, highly aware of the controversy, uses "birthmother" in its publications.

Chapter 1

1. Historically, the assumption was that women should suppress, renounce, and deny their own sexual pleasures. Shari Thurer observes, "Ideologically speaking, women lost their sex drive in the nineteenth century . . . Sexual desire became the exclusive province of men and lower-class women" (213). When Queen Victoria advised her daughter on her wedding night to "Close [her] eyes and think of England," she was candidly affirming how women were expected to approach sexual intercourse for millennia.

2. Shakespeare's "Ophelia" has often been considered a prototype of the "fallen woman."

Chapter 2

1. Here I use "sentimental" not as pejorative (i.e., maudlin, irrational, and unrealistic) but as Ross defines it: "as a term . . . applied to texts that invoke or evoke powerful feelings from their readers: tears, joy, hope, sorrow" rather than the "subdued, negative,

bleak, cynical, grim, detached, and hopeless . . . features of the emotionally flat, depres-
sive (one might say almost pathologically disaffected landscape of the nonsentimental
writer, the realist or naturalist" (31).

2. I maintain that even in the Pennsylvania edition, Jennie has very little power inside the domestic sphere and no power outside it throughout the novel. Other feminist
critics, including Valerie Ross, Judith Kucharski, and Susan Albertine, disagree. For
example, Kucharski asserts that what ultimately distinguishes Jennie "is not her vulnerability but her strength . . . to survive, increasingly isolated, in a world so clearly not of
her own making" (18). Albertine observes, "The Pennsylvania edition allows Jennie to
appear much more powerful and thoughtful" (63).

3. Lingeman reads Jennie as "a male fantasy figure . . . all-loving, all-giving, all-
sacrificing"; Hussman reads her as "a wish-fulfillment stick figure of self-sacrifice" (49);
Oscar Cargill sees a "submissive woman created for masculine delight, without brains
and with conveniently few emotions . . . [she] is so much dough" (118); Charles Shapiro
finds her "all suffering, almost too fudgy in her passivity" (16).

4. Although I find Jennie's debasing and repetitive self-sacrifices signs of psychological ill health and self-loathing, Leonard Cassuto finds her "a perfectly integrated personality who can . . . consistently execute the balancing act between personal desire and
social stricture" (60). Miriam Gogol sees the portrayal of Jennie as an "artistic triumph,"
"psychologically accurate and realistically rendered" when considered in relation to the
dynamics of shame (143). And Carol Schwartz maintains that although Jennie "becomes socially marginal," she "retains a centered self" (18).

5. Several critics disagree with my bleak reading of the novel's conclusion. Ross argues, "Dreiser ends the novel in good dark cheer . . . Jennie [is] alive and well, watching
Lester fade into the world of indifference he helped create" (39). Kucharski asserts that
the adoption provides the conclusion "with an element of hope and faith with which it is
rarely credited"; Jennie has learned "how to survive the gradual disintegration of hope . . .
to emerge . . . with what life permits" (23, 21).

Chapter 3

1. In 1935, Zoe Akins wrote the Pulitzer Prize–winning adaption of The Old Maid.
After it received bad reviews, Wharton maintained it was "too delicate for our barbarous
press." In 1939, Warner Brother made a movie of The Old Maid based on the Akins
adaption with Bette Davis as Charlotte Lovell (Lee 595).

2. Lee sees both Charlotte and Delia as equally victims of their "age" (602), though I
argue that Charlotte's victimization is much more painfully consequential than Delia's.

3. Tintner reads the conclusion of The Old Maid not as Charlotte's tragedy but as
"two mothers [who] join in their love for Tina . . . Wharton has removed the mother
role from its biological determinants" (126). In so doing, Tintner maintains, Wharton is

suggesting that "natural families are not the families of our choice" and makes "plausible her own role as an adoptive mother, a role she played in regard to her friend's children late in her life" (125).

Chapter 4

1. For this analysis, I include the "Appendix," written fifteen years after the book was published. In an interview, Faulkner describes it as "the final effort to get the story told and off my mind, so that I myself could have some peace from it" ("Interview" 233).

2. The many contradictory voices of the text call into question what Jane Gallop refers to as "phallic illusions of authority" (20) and as Gwin suggests, call for feminist critique.

3. Deborah Clarke maintains that Caddy is "Faulkner's first major attempt to confront the relation between gender and art, between female sexuality and narrative authority" (20).

4. Although not all critics refer to Caddy's daughter as Miss Quentin, most do, including Deborah Clarke in *Robbing the Mother: Women in Faulkner*, and Donald Kartiganer, Howry Professor Emeritus of Faulkner Studies at the University of Mississippi, in *The Fragile Thread: The Meaning of Form in Faulkner's Novels*.

5. We later learn it is Jason who has left the gate open on purpose just so that Benjy will get out.

6. It can also be argued that Jason believes Miss Quentin was conceived incestuously and is the daughter of Caddy and Quentin. He remarks, "She's too much like both of them to doubt that" (164).

7. In 1915, sexologist Havelock Ellis observes, "it is notable that of recent years there has been a fashion for a red tie to be adopted by inverts as their badge (qtd. by Abate 294).

8. For example, he writes in the "Appendix" that Caddy "brought her infant daughter home and left the child and departed by the next train, to return no more" (210). However, Jason tells us of at least two incidents when she returns to Jefferson to catch a glimpse of Miss Quentin, and he implies there are others.

9. When Melissa Meek, the librarian, shows Jason the photograph, he initially replies, "It's Cad, all right," only to take it back seconds later after Melissa insists they must help her, responding "That Candace? . . . Don't make me laugh" (210).

10. Millgate finds Miss Quentin's "tragedy, simply because it is more directly presented . . . more moving" than Caddy's (98). Minter suggests, "In the stories of Caddy and Quentin II we observe the degradation of all that is beautiful" (351). Bleikasten finds Caddie to be "both the tragic victim of her family and the unwitting agent of its doom . . . a dream of beauty wasted and destroyed" (430) and Miss Quentin as "Caddy's debased copy" (422). Sally Page reads both Caddy and Miss Quentin as tragic, maintaining that Quentin and Mrs. Compson destroy Caddy's humanity "by scorning her grasp at life

and depriving her of a normal outlet for creativity, motherhood, love, and freedom[;] they kill the real Caddy and create a deadly serene lost woman" (65). In addition, Page maintains that "the tragedy of Caddy's life is repeated by her child" (Page 66).

Chapter 5

1. Angela Davis points out, "It would be a mistake to regard the institutionalized pattern of rape during slavery as an expression of white men's sexual urges . . . Rape was a weapon of domination, a weapon of repression, whose cover goal was to extinguish slave women's will to resist" (23).

2. According to Bracks, the lynching of Celie's father is "based on a real incident in Memphis in 1892, which clearly roots the characters with the social and political conditions of the time" (84–85).

3. Bracks notes that the isolation that went with the rural existence of black communities "bred a silence" that "allowed destructive behaviors within family units to go unchecked and unchallenged" (86), which is certainly the case with Celie's "Pa," whose moral laxity intrudes on every aspect of her life (85–86). Carolyn Williams suggests that the novel's epistolary form "is the most fundamental representation of a concern with women isolated from one another within the patriarchal network (qtd. in Wall 267 n. 35).

4. As hooks observes, "Homophobia does not exist in the novel. Celie's sexual desire for women and her sexual encounter with Shug is never a controversial issue even though it is the catalyst for her resistance to male domination, for her coming to power" ("Reading and Resistance" 285).

5. Shug's vision owes a lot to Emerson and his conviction that humankind and the natural word are parts of the Oversoul. She echoes his words in *Nature* (1836): "in the presence of nature a wild delight runs through the man, in spite of real sorrows." His most famous passage follows:

Standing on the bare ground—my head bathed by the blithe air and uplifted into infinite space—all mean egotism vanishes. I become a transparent eyeball. I am nothing; I see all; the currents of the Universal Being circulate through me; I am part or parcel of God. (6)

Wall suggests that Walker's pantheistic vision draws on disparate sources and rejects Gerald Early's characterization of it as "a fairly dim-witted pantheistic acknowledgement of the wonders of human potential that begins to sound quite suspiciously like a cross between the New Age movement and Dale Carnegie" (qtd. in Wall 268 n. 44).

6. Collins maintains that Celie writes herself free by writing to God: "The act of acquiring a voice through writing, of breaking silence with language, eventually moves her to the action of talking with others" (112).

7. Wall notes that the family is reconfigured with Celie and Nettie as the family's

progenitors. "Moreover, rather than remaining outside the circle of women, the re-deemed men (Albert, Harpo, Samuel) and the new man, Adam, join it. The 'family' that the end of the novel celebrates is a new configuration" (160).

8. Abbandonato argues that *The Color Purple* "is a conscious rewriting of canonical male texts," and we can trace its ancestry "all the way to *Clarissa*" (296).

9. Berlant defines *The Color Purple* as a "womanist" historical novel that "absorbs and transforms the traditional functions of patrifocal-realist mimesis" (218), while hooks compares the novel to revolutionary literature that has "as its central goal the education for critical consciousness, creating awareness of the forces that oppress and recognition of the way those forces might be transformed" ("Reading and Resistance" 292).

10. Harrison maintains that Walker's novel is revisionary in the evolution of the black pastoral; Walker "portrays actual change in the black rural community . . . a pastoral world that can be transformed from oppressive to triumphant" (103).

Chapter 6

1. I learned that my autobiographical response to the novel was not surprising when two years later I read Allison's memoir *Two or Three Things I Know for Sure* (1996), which in many ways is a companion piece to the novel. As I drew connections between Anney's experience and my own, Allison's memoir draws clear autobiographical connections between Bone's and Allison's abuse and self-formation by way of storytelling.

2. Matt Wray and Annalee Newitz define "white trash" as a "classist slur" and a "racial epithet that marks out certain whites as a breed part, a dysgenic race unto themselves" (2).

3. Allison herself attests to this intertwining modes of oppression in her own life: "The difficulty if that I can't ascribe everything that has been problematic about my life simply and easily to the patriarch, or to incest, or even to the invisible and much-denied class structure of our society" (*Skin* 15–16).

4. Shawn E. Miller maintains that the stamp is more about "Anney's wounded pride . . . than about any real consequences for Bone" (140) and that "the costs of illegitimacy have been negligible" (151). I, on the other hand, see the stamp as a symbolically consequential rendition of the damning *A*.

5. This ambiguity might have to do with Allison's commitment to avoid "pseudo-porn" in the novel. She comments, "There's no description of genitals; there's no description of the actual act of intercourse except from the perspective of this child who is being hurt terribly. For most of the book, you don't even know what the man is doing, and that's very deliberate. Because a lot of what has messed with my head when I read other books has been the enormous gratuitous detail" (Strong 9).

6. King notes that Bone is "at least seventeen when she tells a story called *Bastard Out of Carolina*" (136) by pointing out on that on the second page of the novel, Bone writes, "The first time I ever saw Uncle Travis sober was when I was seventeen" (2).

7. Horvitz maintains that the narrative "offers a unique possibility for healing," and observes: 'If fictional Raylene reconfigures trash into utensils, Allison transforms actual and remembered trauma into art" (239, 260).

Chapter 9

1. In the 1988 custody case, Mary Beth Whitehead, Baby M's biological mother, was hired by William Stern, Baby M's biological father, as a surrogate. After giving birth, she decided not to surrender the infant to Stern and his wife. After finding Whitehead less competent than the Sterns, the New Jersey Supreme Court denied Whitehead her custody.

Works Cited

Abate, Michelle Ann. "Reading Red: The Man with the (Gay) Red Tie in Faulkner's *The Sound and the Fury*." *Mississippi Quarterly* 54.3 (2001): 293–313. Print.

Abbandonato, Linda. "Rewriting the Heroine's Story in *The Color Purple*." *Alice Walker: Critical Perspectives Past and Present*. Ed. Henry Louis Gates Jr. and K. A. Appiah. New York: Amistad, 1993. 296–308. Print.

Abel, Darrel. *The Moral Picturesque: Studies in Hawthorne's Fiction*. West Lafayette, IN: Purdue UP, 1988. Print.

Abrahamson, Mark. *Out-of-Wedlock Births: The United States in Comparative Perspective*. Westport, CT: Praeger, 1998. Print.

Albertine, Susan. "Triangulating Desire in *Jennie Gerhardt*." *Dreiser* 63–74. Print.

Alexie, Sherman. Interview by Joshua B. Nelson. "'Humor Is My Green Card': A Conversation with Sherman Alexie." *World Literature Today* July–August 2010: 139–43. Print.

Alexie, Sherman. Interview by Dennis West and Joan M. West. "Sending Cinematic Smoke Signals: An Interview with Sherman Alexie." *Cineaste* 23.4 (1998): 28. Web. 1 July 2011.

Alexie, Sherman. *The Lone Ranger and Tonto Fistfight in Heaven*. New York: Grove, 1993. Print.

Allen, Paula Gunn. *The Sacred Hoop: Recovering the Feminine in American Indian Traditions*. Boston: Beacon, 1986. Print.

Allison, Dorothy. *Bastard out of Carolina*. New York: Plume, 2005. Print.

Allison, Dorothy. Interview by Lily Ng. *U.S. Literature after 1945—Authors*. N.d. Web. 5 July 2011.

Allison, Dorothy. Interview by Marilee Strong. "Talking Trash." *San Francisco Focus* 21 Jan. 2003. *Resources for Creative Writers*. Web. 31 May 2010.

Allison, Dorothy. *Skin: Talking about Sex, Class and Literature*. Ithaca: Firebrand, 1994. Print.

Applebee, Arthur N. *Literature in the Secondary School: Studies of Curriculum and Instruction in the United States*. Urbana: National Council of Teachers of English, 1993. Print.

Armstrong, Nancy and Leonard Tennenhouse. *The Ideology of Conduct: Essays on Literature and the History of Sexuality*. New York: Methuen, 1987. Print.

Barrineau, Nancy Warner. "'Housework Is Never Done': Domestic Labor in *Jennie Gerhardt*." Dreiser 127–35. Print.

Baym, Nina. *American Women Writers and the Work of History 1790–1860*. New Brunswick, NJ: Rutgers UP, 1995. Print.

Baym, Nina. *Feminism and American Literary History: Essays*. New Brunswick, NJ: Rutgers UP, 1992. Print.

Baym, Nina. "Melodramas of Beset Manhood: How Theories of American Fiction Exclude Women Authors." *American Quarterly* 33 (1981): 123–39. Print.

Baym, Nina. "The Significance of Plot in Hawthorne's Romances." *Ruined Eden of the Present: Hawthorne, Melville, and Poe*. Ed. G. R. Thompson and Virgil L. Lokke. West Lafayette, IN: Purdue UP, 1981. 49–70. Print.

Baym, Nina. *Woman's Fiction: A Guide to Novels by and about Women in America 1820–70*. 2nd ed. Urbana: U of Illinois P, 1993. Print.

Bell, Millicent. "Introduction: A Critical History." *The Cambridge Companion to Edith Wharton*. Ed. Millicent Bell. Cambridge, UK: Cambridge UP, 1995. 1–19. Print.

Bellafante, Ginia. "They Age So Quickly, at Least in Tree Hill." *New York Times* 29 Jan. 2008: B8. Print.

Bender, Bert. *Evolution and "The Sex Problem": American Narratives during the Eclipse of Darwinism*. Kent, OH: Kent State UP, 2004. Print.

Benstock, Shari. "*The Scarlet Letter* (A)doree, or The Female Body Embroidered." *The Scarlet Letter*. Hawthorne 288–303. Print.

Bercovitch, Sacvan. "Hawthorne's A-Morality of Compromise." *The Scarlet Letter*. Hawthorne 344–58. Print.

Berlant, Lauren. "Race, Gender, and Nation in *The Color Purple*." *Alice Walker: Critical Perspectives Past and Present*. Ed. Henry Louis Gates Jr. and K. A. Appiah. New York: Amistad, 1993. 211–38. Print.

Bevis, William. "Native American Novels: Homing In." *Recovering the Word: Essays on Native American Literature*. Ed. Brian Swann and Arnold Krupat. Berkeley: U of California P, 1987. 580–620. Print.

Bible, King James Version. Ed. Robert A. Kraft. *Electronic Text Center*. U of Virginia, n.d. Web. 22 Nov. 2008.

Bleikasten, Andre. "The Quest for Eurydice." Faulkner 412–30. Print.

Bloom, Harold. *The Anxiety of Influence: A Theory of Poetry*. 2nd ed. New York: Oxford UP, 1997. Print.

Boese, Alex. *Trial of Polly Baker, Museum of Hoaxes*. Hoaxipedia, 2008. Web. 1 March 2010.

Bouson, J. Brooks. "'You Nothing but Trash': White Trash Shame in Dorothy Allison's *Bastard Out of Carolina*." *Southern Literary Journal* 34.1 (2001): 101–23. Print.

Bowlby, Rachel. "'I Had Barbara: Women's Ties and Wharton's 'Roman Fever.'" *Differences* 17.5 (2006): 37–51. Print.

Boyle, T. Coraghessan. "The Love of My Life." *Making Literature Matter.* 3rd ed. Ed. John Schilb and John Clifford. Boston: Bedford / St. Martin's, 2006. 576–88. Print.

Bracks, Lean'tin L. *Writings on Black Women in the Diaspora: History, Language, and Identity.* New York: Garland, 1998. Print.

Brady, Mary Pat. "The Contrapuntal Geographies of *Woman Hollering Creek and Other Stories.*" *American Literature* 71.1 (1999): 117–52. Print.

Brennan, Stephen C. "The Sex Which Is One: Language and the Masculine Self in *Jennie Gerhardt.*" *Theodore Dreiser and American Culture: New Readings.* Ed. Yoshinobu Hakutani. Newark: U of Delaware P, 2000. 138–57. Print.

Brooks, Cleanth. *William Faulkner: The Yoknapatawpha Country.* Baton Rouge: Louisiana State UP, 1963. Print.

Brooks, Peter. *Reading for the Plot: Design and Intention in Narrative.* Cambridge: Harvard UP, 1992. Print.

Brown, Carrie. "Baby Love: A Young Mother Tries to Undo Some Bad Decisions." Rev. of *Girls in Trouble,* by Caroline Leavitt. *Washington Post.* 18 Jan. 2004. Web. 24 June 2011.

Brown, William Hill. *The Power of Sympathy.* Ed. Carla Mulford. New York: Penguin, 1996. Print.

Brownstein, Rachel M. *Becoming a Heroine: Reading about Women in Novels.* New York: Columbia UP, 1994. Print.

Budick, Emily Miller. "Hawthorne, Pearl, and the Primal Sin of Culture." *Journal of American Studies* 39 (2005): 167–85. Print.

Burns, Sarah. "Film Review: *Mother and Child.*" *CUB Communicator* Jan.–Feb. 2011. Print.

Burr, Ty. "Hip and Hysterical, 'Juno' Delivers." *Boston Globe* 14 Dec. 2007. Web. 24 Jan. 2008.

Cannon, Katie G. *Black Womanist Ethics.* Atlanta: Scholars Press, 1988. Print.

Cargill, Oscar. *Intellectual America: Ideas on the March.* New York: Cooper Square. 1969. Print.

Cassuto, Leonard. "Dreiser's Ideal of Balance." Dreiser 51–62. Print.

Cisneros, Sandra. *Woman Hollering Creek and Other Stories.* New York: Vintage, 1992. Print.

Cixous, Hélène. "The Laugh of the Medusa." *The Critical Tradition.* 3rd ed. Ed. David H. Richter. Bedford / St. Martin's, 2007. 1643–55. Print.

Clarke, Deborah. *Robbing the Mother: Women in Faulkner.* Jackson: U of Mississippi P, 1994. Print.

Cody, Diablo. *Juno: The Shooting Script.* New York: Newmarket Press, 2007. Print.

Cody, Diablo. "Reitman & Cody, Consorting with 'Juno.'" Interview by Terry Gross. *Fresh Air.* Natl. Public Radio. WHYY. Philadelphia. 6 Dec. 2007. Radio.

Cohen, Leah Hager. "Absent Mothers." Rev. of *Run,* by Ann Patchett. *New York Times.* 30 Sept. 2007. Web. 27 June 2011.

Collins, Patricia Hill. *Black Feminist Thought: Knowledge, Consciousness, and the Politics of Empowerment.* New York: Routledge, 1990. Print.

Daniels, Cindy Lou. "Hawthorne's Pearl: Woman-Child of the Future." *American Transcendental Quarterly* 19 (2005): 221–36. Print.

Davidson, Cathy N. "Introduction." *The Coquette.* Ed. Cathy Davidson. New York: Oxford UP, 1986. vii–xx. Print.

Davis, Angela Y. *Women, Race and Class.* New York: Random, 1981. Print.

Dean, Jill R. "'File It under "L" for Love Child'": Adoptive Policies and Practices in the Erdrich Tetralogy." *Imagining Adoption: Essays on Literature and Culture.* Ed. Marianne Novy. Ann Arbor: U of Michigan P, 2004. 231–40. Print.

DeNuccio, Jerome. "Slow Dancing with Skeletons: Sherman Alexie's *The Lone Ranger and Tonto Fistfight in Heaven.*" *Critique* 44.1 (2002): 86–97. Print.

Dermody, Dennis. "Juno." *Paper* 1 Dec. 2007. 14. Web. June 2008.

Dewey, Joseph. "A Time to Bolt: Suicide, Androgyny, and the Dislocation of the Self in Reynolds Price's *Kate Vaiden.*" *Mississippi Quarterly* 14.1 (Winter 1991). Web. 22 July 2012.

Diehl, Joanne Feit. "Re-reading *the Letter*: Hawthorne, the Fetish, and the (Family) Romance. *Hawthorne* 235–51. Print.

Douglas, Ann. "Introduction." *Charlotte Temple and Lucy Temple.* New York: Penguin, 1991. vii–xliii. Print.

Doyle, Jacqueline. "Haunting the Borderlands: La Llorona in Sandra Cisneros's *Woman Hollering Creek.*" *Frontiers: A Journal of Women Studies* 16.1 (1996): 53–70. Print.

Doyle, Laura. "'A' for Atlantic: The Colonizing Force of Hawthorne's *The Scarlet Letter.*" *American Literature* 79 (2007): 243–73. Print.

Dreiser, Theodore. *Jennie Gerhardt.* Ed. James L. W. West III. Philadelphia: U of Pennsylvania P, 1992. Print.

DuPlessis, Rachel Blau. *Writing beyond the Ending: Narrative Strategies of Twentieth Century Women Writers.* Bloomington: Indiana UP, 1985. Print.

Easy A. Dir. Will Gluck. Perf. Emma Stone, Amanda Bynes, Thomas Haden Church, Lisa Kudrow, Stanley Tucci, Patricia Clarkson. Sony, 2010. DVD.

Edwards, Jane. "The Lie behind the Question: Aren't Those Kids Better Off Adopted?" *Birth Mother, First Mother Forum.* N.p. 2 July 2013. Web. 24 July 2013.

Elias, Robert H. "Janus-Faced *Jennie.*" *Dreiser* 3–8. Print.

Emerson, Ralph Waldo. *Selected Writing of Emerson.* Ed. Donald McQuade. New York: Modern Library, 1981. Print.

"Emily Bronte: Publication of *Wuthering Heights* and Its Contemporary Critical Reception." Academic. Brooklyn. CUNY.edu/English (2011). Web. 23 May 2012.

Eng, David L. and David Kazanjian. *Loss: The Politics of Mourning.* Berkeley: U of California P, 2003. Print.

Erdrich, Louise. *Love Medicine: New and Expanded Version.* New York: Harper Perennial, 1993. Print.

Evelyn White, Hugh G., ed. "Hymn 2 to Demeter." Perseus Digital Library. Tufts, n.d. Web. 16 July 2013.

Faulkner, William. "Appendix Compson 1699–1945." *The Sound and the Fury*. Ed. Minter. 204–15. Print.

Faulkner, William. "Class Conferences at the University of Virginia." *The Sound and the Fury*. Ed. Minter. 234–37. Print.

Faulkner, William. Interview by Jean Stein vanden Heuvel. *The Sound and the Fury*. Ed. Minter. 232–34. Print.

Faulkner, William. "An Introduction for *The Sound and the Fury*." *The Sound and the Fury*. Ed. Minter. 225–32. Print.

Faulkner, William. *The Sound and the Fury*. An Authoritative Text, Backgrounds and Contexts, Criticism. Ed. David Minter. 2nd ed. New York: Norton, 1994. Print.

Feidelson, Charles Jr. *Symbolism and American Literature*. Chicago: U of Chicago P, 1953. Print.

Fessler, Ann. *The Girls Who Went Away: The Hidden History of Women Who Surrendered Children for Adoption in the Decades before Roe v. Wade*. New York: Penguin, 2006. Print.

Fetterly, Judith. *The Resisting Reader: A Feminist Approach to American Fiction*. Bloomington: Indiana UP, 1978. Print.

Fishbein, Leslie. "Prostitution, Morality, and Paradox: Moral Relativism in Edith Wharton's *Old New York: New Year's Day (The 'Seventies)*." *Studies in Short Fiction* 24.4 (1987): 399–406. Print.

Fiedler, Leslie A. *Love and Death in the American Novel*. Rev. ed. New York: Stein and Day, 1966. Print.

Flanagan, Caitlin. "Sex and the Teenage Girl." *New York Times*. 13 Jan. 2008: WK 13. Print.

Flavin, Louise. "Louise Erdrich's *Love Medicine*: Loving over Time and Distance." *Critique: Studies in Contemporary Fiction* 31.1 (1989). 55–64. Print.

Flynn, Carol Houlihan. "Defoe's Idea of Conduct: Ideological Fictions and Fictional Reality." Armstrong and Tennenhouse 73–95. Print.

Foster, Hanna Webster. *The Coquette*. Ed. Carla Mulford. New York: Penguin, 1996. Print.

Foucault, Michel. *The History of Sexuality: Volume 1: An Introduction*. Trans. Robert Hurley. New York: Vintage, 1980. Print.

Fox, Pamela. *Class Fictions: Shame and Resistance in the British Working-Class Novel, 1890–1945*. Durham: Duke UP, 1994. Print.

Freedman, Diane P. "Border Crossing as Method and Motif in Contemporary American Writing, or, How Freud Helped Me Case the Joint." *The Intimate Critique: Autobiographical Literary Criticism*. Ed. Diane P. Freedman, Olivia Frey, and Frances Murphy Zauhar. Durham: Duke UP, 1993. 13–22. Print.

French, Philip. Rev. of *Then She Found Me. Observer*. 21 Sept. 2008. Web. 12 June 2011.

Freud, Sigmund. "Mourning and Melancholia." Rpt. in *A General Selection from the*

Works of Sigmund Freud. Ed. John Rickman, MD. New York: Doubleday Anchor Books, 1957. 124–40. Print.

Galant, Debra. "In Person: The Parent Not Chosen." *New York Times.* 25 Apr. 2004. Web. 24 June 2011.

Gallop, Jane. *Reading Lacan.* Ithaca: Cornell UP, 1985. Print.

Gardner, John. *On Moral Fiction.* New York: Basic, 1978. Print.

Garlitz, Barbara. "Pearl: 1850–1955." *PMLA* 72.4 (1957): 689–99. Print.

Gilbert, Sandra M. and Susan Gubar. *The Madwoman in the Attic: The Woman Writer and the Nineteenth-Century Literary Imagination.* New Haven: Yale UP, 1979. Print

Gleiberman, Owen. Rev. of *Loggerheads.* 19 Oct. 2005. Web. 13 June 2011.

Gogol, Miriam. "Self-Sacrifice and Shame in *Jennie Gerhardt.*" Dresier 136–46. Print.

Gwin, Minrose C. *The Feminine and Faulkner: Reading (Beyond) Sexual Difference.* Knoxville: U of Tennessee P, 1990. Print.

Hall, Max. *Benjamin Franklin & Polly Baker: The History of a Literary Deception.* Chapel Hill: U of North Carolina P, 1960. Print.

Hansen, Elaine Tuttle. *Mother without Child: Contemporary Fiction and the Crisis of Motherhood.* Berkeley: U of California P, 1997. Print.

Hapke, Laura. "Dreiser and the Tradition of the American Working Girl Novel." *Dreiser Studies* 22 (Fall 1991): 2–19. Print.

Hardy, Thomas. *Tess of the D'Urbervilles.* New York: Oxford UP, 1983. Print.

Harrison, Elizabeth Jane. *Female Pastoral: Women Writers Re-visioning the American South.* Knoxville: U of Tennessee P, 1991. Print.

Harrison, Kathryn. "In Trouble." Rev. of *The Girls Who Went Away,* by Ann Fessler. *New York Times.* 11 June 2006. Web. 24 June 2011.

Hartin, Edith T. "Reading as a Woman: Reynolds Price and Creative Androgyny in *Kate Vaiden.*" *Southern Quarterly: A Journal of the Arts in the South* 29 (March 1991): 37–52. Print.

Hartl, John. "Fiction: The Suspense is Killing Me." Rev. of *Light on Snow,* by Anita Shreve. *New York Times Sunday Book Review* 19 Dec. 2004. *Nytimes.com.* Web. 22 June 2011.

Hawthorne, Nathaniel. *The Scarlet Letter.* Ed. Ross C. Murfin. Boston: Bedford Books of St. Martin's Press, 1991. Print.

Hedrick, Joan D. "Foreword." *The Pearl of Orr's Island.* By Harriet Beecher Stowe. Boston: Houghton Mifflin, 2001. Print.

Herman, Ellen. *Kinship by Design: A History of Adoption in the United States.* Chicago: U of Chicago P, 2008. Print.

Herman, Judith. *Trauma and Recovery.* New York: Basic, 1992. Print.

Hite, Molly. "Writing—and Reading—the Body: Female Sexuality and Recent Feminist Fiction." *Feminist Studies* 14 (Spring 1988): 121–42. Print.

Holden, Stephen. "An Adopted Gay Son Set Adrift Makes Spiritual Connections." Rev. of *Loggerheads. New York Times* 14 Oct. 2005. Web. 13 June 2011.

Holden, Stephen. "Being Naughty to Be Nice, as the Rumor Mill Awaits." Rev. of *Easy A*. *New York Times* 16 Sept. 2010. Web. 22 June 2011.

Holden, Stephen. "The Biological Clock Is Ticking, the Cause for Much Alarm." Rev. of *And Then She Found Me*. *New York Times* 25 Apr. 2008: B1, 16. Print.

Homans, Margaret. "'The Mother Who Isn't One': New Stories by Birthmothers." *Adoption & Culture* 2 (2009): 35–63. Print.

Honeycutt, Kirk. Rev. of *Juno*. *Hollywood Reporter*. 10 Sept. 2004. Web. 24 Jan. 2008.

hooks, bell. *Black Looks: Race and Representation*. Boston: South End P, 1992. Print.

hooks, bell. "Reading and Resistance: *The Color Purple*." *Alice Walker: Critical Perspectives Past and Present*. Ed. Henry Louis Gates, Jr. and K. A. Appiah. New York: Amistad, 1993. 284–95. Print.

Horvitz, Deborah. "'Sadism Demands a Story': Oedipus, Feminism, and Sexuality in Gayl Jones's *Corregidora* and Dorothy Allison's *Bastard Out of Carolina*." *Contemporary Literature* 39.2 (1998): 238–61. Print.

Houlihan, Patrick E. "'This Ain't Real Estate': A Bakhtinian Approach to *The Bingo Palace*." *Approaches to Teaching the Works of Louise Erdrich*. Ed. Greg Sarris, Connie A. Jacobs, and James R. Giles. New York: Modern Language Assoc.: 2004. 201–9. Print.

Hussman, Lawrence E. "Jennie One-Not: Dreiser's Error in Character Development." *Dreiser* 43–50. Print.

Irigaray, Luce. *This Sex Which Is Not One*. Trans. Catherine Porter. Ithaca: Cornell UP, 1985. Print.

Irving, Katrina. "'Writing It Down So That It Would be Real': Narrative Strategies in Dorothy Allison's *Bastard out of Carolina*." *College Literature*. 25.2 (1998): 94–107. Print.

Johnston, Patricia Irwin. Rev. of *Girls in Trouble*, by Caroline Leavitt. *Adoption Quarterly* 7.3 (2004): 95–96. Print.

Joyce, James. *Dubliners*. "A Painful Case." Ed. Margo Norris. New York: Norton, 2006. 89–98. Print.

Juno. Dir. Jason Reitman. Screenplay by Diablo Cody. Perf. Ellen Page, Michael Cera, Jennifer Garner, Jason Bateman, Allison Janney, J. K. Simmons. 20th Century Fox, 2007. Film.

"Juno." *Variety*. 8 Sept. 2007. Web. 24 Jan. 2008.

Kaplan, Alice. *French Lessons: A Memoir*. Chicago: U of Chicago P, 1993. Print.

King, Richard. "A Southern Renaissance." *Faulkner* 246–55. Print.

King, Vincent. "Hopeful Grief: The Prospect of a Postmodernist Feminism in Allison's *Bastard out of Carolina*." *Southern Literary Journal* 33.1 (2000): 122–40. Print.

Knight, Pamela. "Forms of Disembodiment: The Social Subject in *The Age of Innocence*." *Bell* 20–46. Print.

Knocked Up. Dir. Judd Apatow. Perf. Seth Rogen, Katherine Heigl, Paul Rudd, Leslie Mann. Universal Studios, 2007. DVD.

Kucharski, Judith. "*Jennie Gerhardt*: Naturalism Reconsidered." *Dreiser* 17–26. Print.

Kulik, Christopher. "Review: *Then She Found Me.*" *Cinema Verdict* 12 May 2008. Web. 12 June 2011.

Laslett, Peter, Karla Oosterveen, and Richard M. Smith, eds. *Bastardy and Its Comparative History.* Cambridge: Harvard UP, 1980. Print.

Leavitt, Caroline. "Dating the Birth Mother." *salon.com.* 29 Sept. 2000. Web. 26 June 2011.

Leavitt, Caroline. *Girls in Trouble.* New York: St. Martin's. 2004. Print.

Lee, Hermione. *Edith Wharton.* New York: Knopf, 2007. Print.

Lehrman, Karen. "She the People." *New Republic.* 38–41. TNR II, LLC, 1991. Web. 19 June 2011.

Lewis, R. W. B. *Edith Wharton: A Biography.* New York: Harper & Row, 1975. Print.

Lin, Ying-chiao. "The Necessary Disclosure: Confronting Childhood Abuse in Dorothy Allison's *Bastard out of Carolina.*" *Intergrams* 7.1–2 (2006). Web. 1 June 2010.

Lingeman, Richard. "The Biographical Significance of *Jennie Gerhardt.*" *Dreiser's Jennie Gerhardt: New Essays on the Restored Text.* Ed. James L. W. West III. Philadelphia: U of Pennsylvania P, 1995. 9–16. Print.

Loggerheads. Dir. Tim Kirkman. Perf. Tess Harper, Bonnie Hunt, Michael Kelly, Michael Learned, Kip Pardue, Chris Sarandon. Strand Releasing, 2005. DVD.

Louis, Margot K. *Persephone Rises, 1860–1927: Mythography, Gender, and the Creation of a New Spirituality.* Burlington: Ashgate, 2009. Print.

Low, Denise. Rev. of *The Lone Ranger and Tonto Fistfight in Heaven,* by Sherman Alexie. *American Indian Quarterly* 20.1 (1996): 123. Web. 1 July 2011.

Lydon, Michael. "Justice to Theodore Dreiser." *Atlantic* Aug. 1993: 98–101.

Matthews, John T. *The Play of Faulkner's Language.* Ithaca: Cornell UP, 1982.

Marx, Karl. "'Consciousness Derived from Material Conditions' from *The German Ideology.*" *The Critical Tradition: Classic Texts and Contemporary Trends.* Ed. David H. Richter. 3rd ed. Boston: Bedford / St. Martin's, 2007. 406–9. Print.

Maslin, Janet. "For Ex-Mayor's Family, Everything Is Political." Rev. of *Run,* by Ann Patchett. *New York Times* 20 Sept. 2007. Web. 27 June 2011.

McPherson, Hugo. *Hawthorne as Myth-Maker: A Study in Imagination.* Toronto: U of Toronto P, 1969.

Miller, Shawn E. "'An Aching Lust to Hurt Somebody Back': The Exile's Patrimony in *Bastard out of Carolina.*" *Southern Quarterly* 44.4 (2007): 139–54. Print.

Millgate, Michael. *The Achievement of William Faulkner.* New York: Random House, 1963.

Moore, Lorrie. *A Gate at the Stairs.* New York: Knopf, 2009. Print.

Morgenstern, Joe. "'Juno' Comes of Age with Unusual Charm." *Wall Street Journal* 5 Dec. 2007. Web. 24 Jan. 2008.

Morrison, Andrew. *Shame: The Underside of Narcissism.* Hillsdale, NJ: Analytic Press, 1989. Print.

Mother and Child. Dir. Rodrigo Garcia. Perf. Naomi Watts, Annette Bening, Kerry Washington, Jimmy Smits, Samuel L. Jackson. Sony, 2010. DVD.

Mulford, Carla. "Introduction." *The Power of Sympathy" and "The Coquette.* Ed. Carla Mulford. New York: Penguin, 1996. ix–li.

Murfin, Ross C. "Introduction: The Biographical and Historical Background." *Hawthorne* 3–19. Print.

Murfin, Ross C. "Introduction: The Critical Background." *Hawthorne* 205–22. Print.

Novy, Marianne, ed. *Imagining Adoption: Essays on Literature and Culture.* Ann Arbor: U of Michigan P, 2005. Print.

Novy, Marianne. *Reading Adoption: Family and Difference in Fiction and Drama.* Ann Arbor: U of Michigan P, 2007. Print.

Nussbaum, Felicity and Laura Brown. "Revising Critical Practices." *The New Eighteenth Century: Theory, Politics, English Literature.* Ed. Felicity Nussbaum and Laura Brown. New York: Methuen, 1987. 1–22.

Ovid. *Metamorphoses.* Trans. Charles Martin. New York: Norton, 2004. Print.

Patchett, Ann. *Run.* New York: HarperCollins, 2007. Print.

Pearce, Roy Harvey. *Hawthorne Centenary Essays.* Columbus: Ohio State UP, 1964. Print.

Pertman, Adam. *Adoption Nation.* New York: Basic, 2000. Print.

Petry, Alice Hall. "A Twist of Crimson Silk: Edith Wharton's 'Roman Fever.'" *Studies in Short Fiction* 24.2 (1987): 163–66. Print.

Pinker, Steven. "The Moral Instinct." *New York Times Magazine* 13 Jan. 2008: 32–37, 52–58. Print.

Price, Reynolds. *Kate Vaiden.* New York: Atheneum, 1986. Print.

Quindlen, Anna. *Blessings.* New York: Random House, 2003. Print.

Quindlen, Anna. "Let's Talk about Sex." *Newsweek* 153.11 (2009): 62. Print.

Quindlen, Anna. "Public Judgment Remains Frozen in the Baby M Case." *New York Times News Service.* 17 Apr. 1990. Web. 20 June 2011.

Reed, Paula. *Hester: The Missing Years of the Scarlett Letter.* New York: St. Martin's, 2010. Print.

Rich, Adrienne. "When We Dead Awaken: Writing as Re-vision." *College English* 34 (1972): 18. Print.

Riggio, Thomas P. "Dreiser's Song of Innocence and Experience: The Ur-Text of *Jennie Gerhardt. Dreiser Studies* 31.2 (2000): 22–38. Print.

Roberts, Diane. *Faulkner and Southern Womanhood.* Athens: U of Georgia P, 1994. Print.

Robinson, Cynthia Cole. "The Evolution of Alice Walker." *Women's Studies* 38 (2009): 293–311. Print.

Rorty, Richard. *Achieving Our Country: Leftist Thought in Twentieth-Century America.* Cambridge: Harvard University Press, 1998. Print.

Ross, Valerie. "Chill History and Rueful Sentiments in *Jennie Gerhardt." Dreiser* 26–42. Print.

Rowson, Susanna. *Charlotte Temple* and *Lucy Temple.* Ed. Ann Douglas. New York: Penguin, 1991. Print.

Sang-Hun, Choe. "An Adoptee Returns to South Korea, and Changes Follow." *New York Times* 29 June 2013. Web. 19 July 2013.

Sartre, Jean-Paul. "On *The Sound and the Fury*: Time in the Work of Faulkner." *Faulkner* 266–71. Print.

Saxey, Esther. "Lesbian Bastard Heroes: The Uses of Illegitimacy for Modern Lesbian Fiction and Identity." *Women: A Cultural Review* 16.1 (2005): 33–51. Print.

"*The Scarlet Letter* in Popular Culture." *Wikipedia.* 16 Jan. 2013. Web. 23 Jan. 2013.

Schiff, Sarah Eden. Rev. of *Class Definitions: On the Lives and Writings of Maxine Hong Kingston, Sandra Cisneros, and Dorothy Allison*, by Michelle M. Tokarczyk. *Biography* 32.3 (2009): 550–53. Print.

Schure, Edouard. *From Sphinx to Christ: An Occult History*. 1970. Whitefish, Montana: Kessinger, 1996. Print.

Schwartz, Carol A. "*Jenny Gerhardt*: Fairy Tale as Social Criticism." *American Literary Realism* 19 (1987): 16–29. Print.

Schwarzbaum, Lisa. "*Knocked Up*." *Entertainment Weekly.* 30 May 2007. Web. 11 June 2011.

Selina, Jamil S. "Wharton's 'Roman Fever.'" *Explicator* 65.2 (2007): 99–101. Print.

Scott, A. O. "Bye-Bye, Bong. Hello, Baby." Rev. of *Knocked Up*. *New York Times* 27 May 2007. Web. 11 June 2011.

Scott, A. O. "In a Melancholy Los Angeles, 'La Ronde' of Motherhood." Rev. of *Mother and Child*. *New York Times* 2 May 2010. Web. 13 June 2011.

Shapiro, Charles. *Theodore Dreiser: Our Bitter Patriot*. Carbondale: Southern Illinois UP, 1962. Print.

Shreve, Anita. "The Group, 12 Year Later." *New York Times Magazine*. 6 July 1986. *maryellenmark.com*. Web. 23 June 2011.

Shreve, Anita. *Light on Snow*. New York: Back Bay Books, 2004.

Sidney, Philip. "An Apology for Poetry." *The Critical Tradition*. Ed. David H. Richter. 3rd ed. Boston: Bedford / St. Martin's, 2007. 132–59.

Silberman, Robert. "Opening the Text: *Love Medicine* and the Return of the Native American Woman." *Narrative Chance: Postmodern Discourse on Native American Indian Literatures*. Ed. Gerald Vizenor. Albuquerque: U of Mexico Press, 1989. 101–20. Print.

Singley, Carol J. *Adopting America: Childhood, Kinship and National Identity in Literature*. New York: Oxford UP, 2011. Print.

Smith-Rosenberg, Carroll. "Domesticating 'Virtue': Coquettes and Revolutionaries in Young America." *Literature and the Body: Essays on Populations and Persons*. Ed. Elaine Scarry. Baltimore: Johns Hopkins UP, 1988. 160–84. Print.

Smothers, Ronald. "Guilty Plea by Mother, 20, in Prom Death." *New York Times* 21 Aug 1998. Web. 29 July 2012.

Solinger, Rickie. *Wake Up Little Susie: Single Pregnancy and Race before Roe v. Wade*. New York: Routledge, 1992. Print.

Spacks, Patricia Meyer. "Ev'ry Woman Is at Heart a Rake." *Eighteenth-Century Studies* 8.1 (1974): 27–46. Print.

Spines, Christine. "'Juno' Nation." *Entertainment Weekly* 8 Feb. 2008: 25–29.

Sprengnether, Madelon. *The Spectral Mother: Freud, Feminism, and Psychoanalysis*. Ithaca: Cornell UP, 1990. Print.

Stein, Joel. "The Shame Game." *Time* 4 Feb. 2013: 58. Print.

Stevens, Dana. "Superpregnant." *Slate*. 5 Dec. 2007. Web. 24 Jan. 2008.

Tan, Amy. *The Bonesetter's Daughter*. New York: Ballentine, 2001. Print.

Teichman, Jenny. *Illegitimacy: An Examination of Bastardy*. Ithaca: Cornell UP, 1982. Print.

Then She Found Me. Dir. Helen Hunt. Perf. Matthew Broderick, Colin Firth, Helen Hunt, Bette Midler. Thinkfilm, 2007. DVD.

Thomson, Rosemarie Garland. *Extraordinary Bodies: Figuring Physical Disability in American Culture and Literature*. New York: Columbia UP, 1997. Print.

Thurer, Shari L. *The Myths of Motherhood: How Culture Reinvents the Good Mother*. New York: Penguin, 1995. Print.

Tintner, Adeline R. *Edith Wharton in Context: Essays on Intertextuality*. Tuscaloosa: U of Alabama P, 1999. Print.

Todd, Janet. "Sensibility (1740–1800)." *The Literary Encyclopedia*. 1 Nov. 2005. Web.

Tomc, Sandra. "A Change of Art: Hester, Hawthorne, and the Service of Love." *Nineteenth-Century Literature* 56 (2002): 466–94. Print.

Torrance, Kelly Jane. "A Childhood Christmas Wistfully Remembered." Rev. of *Light on Snow*, by Anita Shreve. *Washington Times* 19 Dec. 2004. *Newspaper Source Plus*. Web. 23 June 2011.

Totten, Gary. "Dreiser and the Writing Market: New Letters on the Publication History of *Jennie Gerhardt*." *Dreiser Studies* 36.1 (2005): 28–48. Print.

Turner, Arlin. *Nathaniel Hawthorne: A Biography*. New York: Oxford UP, 1980. Print.

Updike, John. "A Boston Fable." Rev. of *Run*, by Ann Patchett. *New Yorker* 1 Oct. 2007. Web. 27 June 2011.

Vickery, Olga. "*The Sound and the Fury*: A Study in Perspective." Faulkner 278–89. Print.

Volk, Patricia. "books of the times; Caring for Shrubs and Something More." Rev. of *Blessings*, by Anna Quindlen. *New York Times* Oct. 2002: 7. Web. 19 June 2011.

Walker, Alice. *The Color Purple*. Orlando, FL: Harcourt, 1982. Print.

Walker, Alice. *In Search of Our Mothers' Gardens*. New York: Harcourt Brace Jovanovich, 1983. Print.

Wall, Cheryl A. *Worrying the Line: Black Women Writers, Lineage, and Literary Tradition*. Chapel Hill: U of North Carolina P, 2005. Print.

Walton, Laurel. "Handmaids No More." *United Church Observer* May 2012. Web. 3 May 2012.

Weinstein, Philip M. "'If I Could Say Mother': Construing the Unsayable about Faulknerian Maternity." Faulkner 430–42.

West, James L. W. III. "The Composition and Publication of *Jennie Gerhardt*." Dreiser, *Jennie Gerhardt* (1992) 419–95. Print.

West, James L. W. III. "Introduction." Dreiser, *Jennie Gerhardt* (1994) vii–xviii. Print.

Whaley, Annemarie Koning. "Business Is Business: Corporate America in the Restored *Jennie Gerhardt.*" *Dreiser Studies* 35.1 (2004): 24–37. Print.

Wharton, Edith. *A Backward Glance.* London: Constable, 1972. Print.

Wharton, Edith. *Old New York.* New York: Scribner. 1951. Print.

Wharton, Edith. *"Roman Fever" and Other Stories.* New York: Scribner, 1964. Print.

Wiegand, David. "Wisecracking Teen Gets Pregnant in 'Juno.'" *San Francisco Chronicle* 14 Dec. 2007. Web. 24 Jan. 2008.

Willard, Nancy. "Talking to Ghosts." Rev. of *The Bonesetter's Daughter,* by Amy Tan. *New York Times* 18 Feb. 2001. Web. 30 June 2011.

Williams, Delores S. "Black Women's Literature and the Task of Feminist Theology." *Immaculate and Powerful: The Female in Sacred Image and Social Reality.* Ed. Clarissa W. Atkinson, Constance H. Buchanan, and Margaret R. Miles. Boston: Beacon, 1985. 88–110. Print.

Williams, Raymond. *Marxism and Literature.* Oxford: Oxford UP, 1977. Print.

Wolff, Cynthia Griffin. "Introduction." *"Roman Fever" and Other Stories.* By Edith Wharton. New York: Scribner, 1964. ix–xx. Print.

Wollstonecraft, Mary. "From *A Vindication of the Rights of Woman.*" *The Critical Tradition.* Ed. David Richter. 3rd ed. Boston: Bedford / St. Martin's, 2007. 275–84. Print.

Wollstonecraft, Mary. *Mary: A Fiction.* Ed. Gina Luria. New York: Garland, 1974. Print.

Woolf, Virginia. *A Room of One's Own.* New York: Harcourt Brace. 1989.

Wray, Matt and Annalee Newitz. "Introduction." *White Trash: Race and Class in America.* Ed. Matt Wray and Annalee Newitz. New York: Routledge, 1997. 1–12. Print.

Wright, Richard. *Black Boy: A Record of Childhood and Youth.* New York: HarperCollins, 1993. Print.

Yardley, Jonathan. "An Accident Throws a Well-Connected Family into the Life of a Young Black Mother." Rev. of *Run,* by Ann Patchett. *Washington Post* 23 Sept. 2007. Web. 27 June 2011.

Index